From Small Talk to Microaggression

From Small Talk to Microaggression

A History of Scale

MICHAEL LEMPERT

The University of Chicago Press
Chicago and London

The University of Chicago Press, Chicago 60637
The University of Chicago Press, Ltd., London
© 2024 by The University of Chicago
Published 2024

33 32 31 30 29 28 27 26 25 24   1 2 3 4 5

ISBN-13: 978-0-226-83248-7 (cloth)
ISBN-13: 978-0-226-83250-0 (paper)
ISBN-13: 978-0-226-83249-4 (e-book)
DOI: https://doi.org/10.7208/chicago/9780226832494.001.0001

Library of Congress Cataloging-in-Publication Data

Names: Lempert, Michael, author.
Title: From small talk to microaggression : a history of scale / Michael Lempert.
Description: Chicago : The University of Chicago Press, 2024. | Includes bibliographical references and index.
Identifiers: LCCN 2024012453 | ISBN 9780226832487 (cloth) |
    ISBN 9780226832500 (paperback) | ISBN 9780226832494 (e-book)
Subjects: LCSH: Conversation analysis. | Scaling (Social sciences)
Classification: LCC P95.45.L468 2024 | DDC 302.34/6—dc23/eng/20240510
LC record available at https://lccn.loc.gov/2024012453

Contents

Preface

I am an interdisciplinary linguistic and cultural anthropologist who writes on social interaction. As a doctoral student, my interest in interaction was kindled by a minute of filmed face-to-face interaction that I studied for nearly four months. I pored over the transcript of talk I had prepared, which was dense with details, from spikes in loudness to pause lengths measured in microseconds. When my senses grew dull from replays, I was told to try muting the sound or watching in fast forward—which made those sixty seconds a strange choreography. Estrangement, I learned, was half the point of this "microethnography" seminar, expertly taught by Frederick Erickson at the University of Pennsylvania. Observing interaction with care required noticing what you ordinarily missed, and that meant a commitment to repeated scrutiny and experimentation with media playback.

Estrangement came somewhat easily in my case, because the clip featured two red-robed Tibetan Buddhist monks wrangling in speech and gesture over fine points of philosophy at a Buddhist center in Ithaca, New York. I had shot the video myself. I had switched into the social sciences from a humanities doctoral program in Buddhist studies. Transcripts of discursive interaction replaced seventeenth-century Tibetan texts but the substitution felt natural. "Fine-grained analysis" felt like another form of "close reading." And Buddhist debate seemed to demand video scrutiny because this form of argumentation was visually arresting.

Erickson would sometimes pause to comment on debates about scale that haunted the study of interaction and threatened his seminar's objectives—or at least its methods. How blinkered, a certain critic would say, that students should spend a whole semester on so little, when such data could hardly be representative of much and when urgent—"larger," as the rote scalar idiom goes—issues loomed. This hands-on course was designed to impart a certain empirical sensibility about the density, subtlety, and complexity of face-to-face interaction. Limiting students to a single minute had pedagogical motivation; it was propaedeutic—not something to emulate in real research. Still, he took to heart the criticism he shared, acknowledging that his own science had evolved over the years and was no longer comfortably, complacently "micro." He had coined "microethnography" long ago in the early 1970s, building especially upon American postwar traditions of research that used 16mm film to scrutinize interaction finely. His microethnography had also been torqued, improbably, by the civil rights movement. He trained his attention on interactions in schools, whose racial politics were notorious. With a small band of other educational researchers, he strained to pinpoint inequality and discrimination through close attention to transcripts of institutional interactions. For Erickson and many others like him, a mediatic, "microscopic" study of social interaction could expose power and domination at work within a key ideological apparatus in liberal capitalist democracies. The very idea that such fine-grained methods of knowing could be mobilized this way was somewhat contentious when he first proposed it, and deeply so when debates later erupted over what generally came to be called the "micro–macro problem."

Indeed, not long after Erickson first proposed microethnography, a friend and fellow traveler urged him to drop the prefix "micro" and rebrand; otherwise, his friend warned, Erikson would get tagged as myopic, just as he had been. Criticism like this, which came in many forms but always suggested a failing that was at once epistemological and ethical, turned on assumptions about the *scale* of this object called interaction and the limits of methods understood to be observationally micro.

It is this criticism and its legacy that inspired this book. As a topic, interaction does not belong to any one discipline but has been important in several, including sociology (notably, the traditions of conversation analysis [CA] and symbolic interactionism), anthropology (linguistic and cultural anthropology), and linguistics (interactional sociolinguistics, interactional linguistics)—traditions I know best. From Erickson and others, I inherited a defensiveness about this object and its micro-oriented methods. Indeed, my own home field of linguistic anthropology has in general become well practiced at justifying its topics and its use—never exclusive use but use nonetheless—of what most find to be comparatively "close," "fine-grained," "micro" registers of analysis.

For fields like linguistic anthropology, scale has been a defining and generative problematic, not the least because the field itself has often been distinguished from others based on its scalar commitments, whether imputed from without—fairly or not—or passionately claimed from within the fold. From within, for instance, it has been customary to say that we differ sharply from CA in sociology. Yes, we, too, may study conversation, we say, but *they* are transcript-fetishizing empiricists who don't "contextualize" expansively—socially, culturally, and historically—and instead try (in vain) to bracket this dense embeddedness to get at an unalloyed object. Our commitment to methodological "expansiveness" relative to rivals like CA has been about more than distinction, of course. It has led to generative, inspiring, thoughtful, illuminating scholarship. As a field, and as one of four subfields of anthropology, we also stand ready to respond to critics—including cultural anthropologists, our closest neighbors—who sometimes turn the same scalar argument we use on CA against us, as when they lump together traditions that study language and discourse and interaction and treat us as if we were all equally blinkered.

Even as the blustery micro–macro scale wars of decades past have largely subsided; even as many today, from critical geographers to flat ontologists, proclaim that the world doesn't come pre-scaled and remind us that *of course* scale is constructed; even as scholars in linguistic anthropology like myself have devoted energy to defying critics who find our object small and our methods myopic, this history of criticism has proved surprisingly hard to shake.

To better understand this history of scale, I decided that I should rewind and watch again, to take another, closer look. I decided to look at the ways scale surfaced in and around the social sciences of interaction in the United States, especially during the formative midcentury when these sciences first crystallized.

This is not a "history of interaction" in the round. It is a critical anthropological history that, like the subfield of linguistic anthropology which I know best, is sensitive to the complexities of language, communication, and, indeed, interaction. I recover what scholars themselves experienced as *problems of scale*—problems that were by turns practical, ethical, political, epistemological, and ontological—that have come to shadow their study of interaction.

Nor does this anthropological history stay within the lanes of the lineages of interaction analysis that now exist. Asked how he'd describe himself back in 1980, Erving Goffman was characteristically cautious. He remarked on the speciation of branded research traditions focused on interaction and was reluctant to locate himself in any one of them.[1] Over the last half century, many areas have claimed an important place for interaction, including "symbolic interactionism," "conversation analysis," "interactional sociolinguistics," "microethnography," and "linguistic anthropology," and while I make note of these distinctions from time to time, I am not primarily concerned with clarifying their genealogical relations let alone establishing how they might be assembled to offer a history of some superordinate object we may call interaction. Indeed, students of these schools may find themselves disappointed that this or that canonical scholar is not included or receives short shrift. As this is an anthropological history of interaction's *scale* and not a history of interaction tout court, I have chosen to foreground scholars—some familiar, others not—whose work offers opportunities to reflect on the troubles over scale that are the concern of this book.

The scholars I do foreground share certain things in common. Nearly all turned to recording and playback technologies, from repurposed wax-cylinder dictation machines to 16mm film to proprietary "interaction recorders." Although this is not a history of interaction, readers who seek such a history may find it helpful to see showcased here the long history of experimentation with medial technologies. But more important for this readership are the streams of research I discuss, which have been overlooked by discipline-internal histories of interaction. The ties between psychiatry—specifically talk therapy research—and interaction science examined in part 1 have been extremely important but largely forgotten. Neglected too have been feminist and educational interaction researchers from the '70s, discussed in part 3, who started to study power, domination, and politics before other scholars of interaction did.

Discipline-internal histories of interaction in general also often skip over the midcentury in an effort to canonize early American pragmatists such as George Herbert Mead and Charles Horton Cooley, yet it was in the midcentury that interaction science took off, which makes this period and its ferment important. It is customary among linguistic anthropologists to complain about the way interaction science walled off its object as if it were autonomous if not irreducible, as if interaction were a distinct "order" of reality—to use Goffman's famous term—with its own rules and regularities. I show how many midcentury scholars presumed something like this too, even if they didn't always assert it or elaborate on it much, as scholars came to do in the '70s and '80s when scale became an explicit problem. If we are interested in how interaction became constituted as a domain of its own, then we must look beyond canonical figures like Erving Goffman and recover others who had once overshadowed him but later disappeared from view.

Finally, as I emphasize, the problems of scale chronicled here are hardly limited to the study of interaction, even though this object is a particularly telling one to examine. Analogous problems of scale have erupted repeatedly—if variably—and in wildly different fields, from seventeenth-century optical microscopy to twentieth-century social sciences like economics, sociology, linguistics, and anthropology; and these problems have not gone away, in part because these troubles have helped define fields. *Scale* is a dimension of knowledge-making that concerns not just how finely or coarsely we observe objects as well as how these objects are understood to exist; it has also affected how different *fields* co-exist. We cannot drop scale any more than we can step away from ourselves, but we can at least begin to appreciate how important scale has been not just epistemologically and ontologically in knowledge-making, but also in terms of conditioning interdisciplinary interaction. As an aspect of the methodological dispositions that characterize fields, scale has been by turns a shibboleth of disciplinary distinction, an ethical and political quandary, and, quite often, a knot to tease apart—or try to cut out, if it proves too stubborn to undo.

1

Introduction

How Scale Broke the World

"I do not use 'microaggression' anymore," avows Ibram Kendi in *How to Be an Antiracist*. His influential 2019 book, which surged into public view during the mobilization against anti-Black racism that followed the brutal police murder of George Floyd in 2020, found fault with this familiar word. Black Harvard psychiatrist Chester Pierce had introduced it around 1970 to name the way white people subordinated Black people not just by "gross, dramatic, obvious" displays of violence but also and especially by less obvious but more frequent tactics involving interpersonal behavior. This was racism manifesting itself in "microscopic fashion." To the untrained eye and ear, microaggressions could be hard to notice, yet such "subtle blows . . . delivered incessantly" had effects of "unimaginable magnitude," for not only did they wear down an individual's psyche and body and cause harm—including suicide; societally, they also made institutional violence possible. Indeed, the "micro" of microaggression denoted behaviors that were "small" only in some senses but not others. Taken individually, microaggressions were "subtle" and relatively "minor" but they were anything but so when you considered their frequency and effects, which is why they mattered. Overt violence against Black bodies was all too obvious to him when he wrote, but Pierce noticed something more pernicious, something that could persist even as the most extreme forms of racism subside. "By itself a single . . . microaggression is relatively innocuous," yet "with [the] cumulative, never-ending accretion of microaggressions, the result is to render the victim defeated, demoralized and tyrannized." For his psychiatry, it was only through addressing the interpersonal that you could treat the pathology and public health crisis that was racism.[1]

Pierce's word only found its legs later, in the 1990s, when social psychologists rediscovered it and applied it widely to the world—so widely that it became a shibboleth of progressive talk and target of conservative ire. Anti-racist workshops of many kinds, on campuses and in workplaces, have come to teach how speech and interpersonal behavior can cause harm. Yet the name came to trouble scholars and activists like Kendi who argued that interpersonal racism matters but think "micro" suggests—or at least has come to suggest—something small if not trivial. "I detest its component parts— 'micro' and 'aggression,'" Kendi said, arguing that we drop the prefix micro and upgrade aggression to "abuse"—"racist abuse." "A persistent daily low hum of racist abuse is not minor," yet the prefix micro can seem to suggest this. The term "microaggression," Kendi has written, downplays the gravity of the offense, fails to call anti-Black racism what it is, fails to convey the urgency for remedial action. What we need, by contrast, is "zero-tolerance policies preventing and punishing these abusers."[2] Pierce himself had been more provocative, arguing that microaggressions make their perpetrators complicit with murder.[3]

Kendi's rebranding reveals his struggle to address the contested *scale* of interpersonal behavior, a term I will have much to say about shortly. It reveals his struggle to retain Pierce's position that interpersonal racism matters profoundly. This, despite the fact that within progressive circles many counter that the interpersonal doesn't matter as much as the institutional. One critique of "microaggression" is that the term misdirects, that it places undue focus on communication when it is "structural" or "institutional" racism that must be dismantled. Rather than being forced to choose between what appear as two scalar extremes, often alliteratively labeled the interpersonal and the institutional, many stress their complementarity and the risks of leaning too hard to one side. Take the sociologist of race, science, and technology, Ruha Benjamin. Her recent, public-facing book *Viral Justice: How We Grow the World We Want*, is a corrective against her home field of sociology's characteristic stress on the structural. While not abandoning structural change or the social movement activism exemplified by Black Lives Matter, she encourages the capacity for "microvision," the need to consider a "microscopic model of what it could look like to spread justice and joy in small but perceptible ways," so as to experiment at living moment to moment, situation to situation.[4]

I will soon ask that we take one step back from such vexing scalar antinomies for a moment in order to understand how they resemble questions that people have had about the scale of interaction for a very long time. Indeed, when Pierce first introduced microaggression more than a half century ago, many radical feminists were also arguing that daily communication mattered intensely, that seemingly "small" aspects of talk, from terms of address to speech interruptions to nonverbal behaviors like unwanted touches, kept women down in daily life. And it was daily life—not just, say, gender equity under the law—that needed transformation. Others within the women's movement countered that the System, be it institutionalized gender discrimination or capitalism or both, mattered more.

And so the debate raged, echoing many, many antecedents. Consider a charge leveled at early English Quakers. This seventeenth-century movement had sought to reform speech and social interaction in a granular way. To cultivate indifference toward worldly status, they famously tried to avoid paying deference to other humans through honorific uses of second-person pronouns and through eschewing elevating titles and salutations and physical gestures of respect. Richard Bauman reminds us of a cutting rejoinder from William Penn aimed at all those who say Quakers "strain at small things." "First, nothing is small, which God makes matter of conscience to do, or leave undone." Second, since non-Quakers beat Quakers and imprison them for the way they interact, then surely such outsized reactions reveal just how significant these "small" things are.[5]

Rejoinders like these call to mind countless debates, inside and outside the academy, that turn on questions about the scale of social interaction. Talk among a clutch of people may feel instinctively "small-scale" in many ways, so if conversation is felt to have, for example, a racial or gender "micropolitics," we may well wonder how this politics relates to a politics elsewhere. We may wonder not only about whether and to what extent fleeting speech and behavior matters in social life, but also how to assess interaction *in general*, how to weigh its importance relative to other facets or domains of social experience.

In *A History of Scale*, I focus on this kind of puzzlement, not because I want to settle what interaction's true scale is, but because I want to insist that we study how people themselves struggle with questions of scale. To do this we will need to stop treating the interpersonal as a self-evident object and domain of its own, endowed with an intrinsic scale. I focus in particular on the sciences of social interaction in America which for some seventy-five years have been by turns fascinated and frustrated by the diminutive scale of their object of knowledge, and which have often had to justify why they look at so little so closely.

So closely, because what else befits a small object than fine-grained analysis? At its broadest, I look at the trouble that can come from trying to look at a thing closely, "microscopically." This is a book about the unexpected effects of microscopy, as well as its allure. Not literal microscopy, involving, say, light or fluorescence or electron microscopes, but microscopy as a trope for how to know. The microscopy that concerns me belongs again to one family of sciences, the social sciences of interaction which, in America, first spread in the mid-twentieth century. As the heirs to these traditions will tell you, to know face-to-face interaction properly—which is to say, microscopically—you do not hover over one instrument but chain together several. Recording and playback technologies preserve and permit review of the sounds and images of humans talking. Faithful transcripts make legible not just what people say but exactly how they say it and sometimes also what they do with their bodies. Transcripts, in turn, allow you to conduct the fine-grained analysis necessary to know what happens when people interact. While some insist on returning to the richness of source media through repeated playback, for many others a transcript is what you analyze and is akin to a light microscope's glass slide with specimen mounted on it.

Transcripts assume many guises, from easily read records to dense texts that try to preserve *how* people speak and bristle with marks and diacritics legible to specialists. (While "transcript" is now the common term, suggesting conversion from sound to paper, the older "typescript" spotlighted the typewriter that made them.) At first many of these transcripts recycled conventions from play-scripts and novels, which tended to use standard English orthography and break up conversation into neatly delineated speaking "turns." To heighten the naturalism, interaction researchers tried to restore to these texts the messiness of real talk by adding details such as interruptions, pauses, and dysfluencies like false starts (figure 1). Linguists marshaled their international phonetic alphabet to reveal the actual sounds of speech, and some even added signs for phenomena such as intonation and voice quality (figure 2). A few brave inscribers tried to show what conversationalists did with their bodies (figure 3). They used sound film to make the body visible and synchronize

```
(5.09) NB II:2:17-18
 1  Emm:        [Wanna c'm] do:wn 'av [a bah:ta] lu:nch w]ith me?=
 2  Nan:                             [°It's js] (      )°]
 3  Emm:        =Ah gut s'm beer'n stu:ff,
 4              (0.3)
 5  Nan: ->     ↑Wul yer ril sweet hon: uh:m
 6              (.)
 7  Emm:        [Or d'y]ou'av] sup'n [else °(        )°
 8  Nan:        [L e t-] I : ] hu.    [n:No: I haf to: uh call
 9              Roul's mother, I told'er I:'d call'er this morning
10              I [gotta letter]'from'er en .hhhhhh A:nd uhm
11  Emm:          [°(Uh huh.)° ]
12              (1.0)
```

FIGURE 1. Typical CA transcript whose conventions were first developed by Gail Jefferson. The transcript features nonstandard orthography intended to approximate the sounds of speech and special conventions to mark details such as speech overlap, pause lengths, and shifts in loudness. Emanuel A. Schegloff, *Sequence Organization in Interaction: A Primer in Conversation Analysis* (Cambridge, UK: Cambridge University Press, 2007), 65.

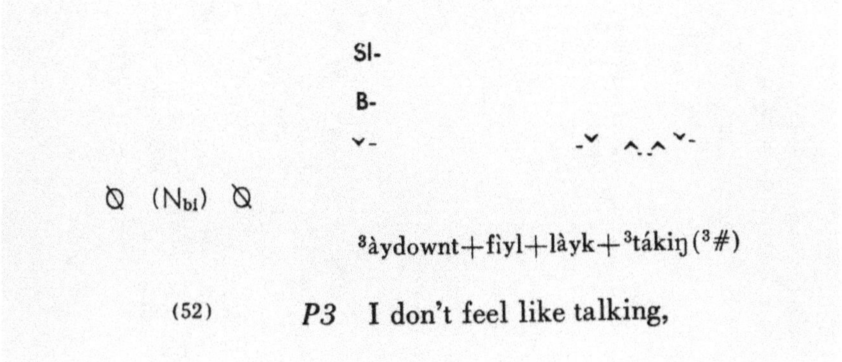

SI-

B-

˅-   -˅ ˄.˄ ˅-

◌̸ (N$_{bi}$) ◌̸

^{3}àydownt+fîyl+làyk+^{3}tákiŋ (^{3}#)

(52)   *P3* I don't feel like talking,

FIGURE 2. A fine-grained transcript based on a sound recording that paired standard English orthography with highly detailed phonemic and paralinguistic transcription. Robert Everett Pittenger, Charles F. Hockett, and John J. Danehy, *The First Five Minutes: A Sample of Microscopic Interview Analysis* (Ithaca, NY: Martineau, 1960), 23.

its shapes and movements with the flow of co-occurring speech (which was no trivial feat in the absence of nonlinear digital video playback; if you weren't careful, frame-by-frame analysis could wreck acetate film).

These scholars of interaction imagined what they did as a kind of "mediatic microscopy," a kind of close, granular viewing and hearing analogous in some way to the literal microscopes of the natural and biological sciences. Regardless of which recording and playback technologies they used, how they converted source media into the secondary media of paper transcripts and what importance these transcripts held, and, of course, how they went about analyzing these mediatic artifacts, most scholars of interaction—with some notable exceptions—have felt, and still feel, that mechanical recording is a must. No matter how powerful your memory or how well you observe, without media as capture and playback technologies, you cannot keep pace with interaction and retain its details. Interaction is too fast and fleeting, too rich and too subtle.

This mediatic science displaces a lot. Forget the tacit knowledge and savvy that comes from years of intensive socialization into life with other humans, socialization that allows you to make rapid (and usually accurate) inferences about what people mean. Forget the rules of thumb gleaned from everyday strategizing about interaction—not to mention the interpersonal dos and don'ts dispensed by cultural institutions of various kinds. As the empirical sciences of interaction came to insist, without recording-based "microanalysis," as it is sometimes known, this object of knowledge will remain as elusive as respiration. We know we breathe, but reflection alone can't tell us how or why.

I will have quite a bit to say about what inspired this turn toward mediatic microscopy, but for now consider the sheer reach of the metaphor. That

SUBJECT B

PHONETICS

		11040	41	42	43	44	45	46	47	48	49	50	51	52	53
FRAME NUMBERS (1/48 SECOND)															
HEAD		U		(D,L) sli	R,D,QR			D,R sli	D,R,QL sli		D,R			R,D	R,DV sli
EYES		I,2 D V sli							I,2 UV sli						
BROWS															
MOUTH	UPPER LIP	F,D sli / L—C sli		B V sli / V sli / —C—	B sli / —C		—C Vsli / —C	Vsli / —C	C	(F,UI sli / —C	F,U sli / —C			F,U sli / —C	D,F sli / —C
	LOWER LIP	U,B		B sli	B,U		B,UV sli / U	B,UV sli U	U		U,F sli			U,F sli	U,F
TRUNK		B,S sli		B sli	Tr sli			B sli	Tr		L,B sli			F,Tr sli	R
RIGHT SHOULDER		F		F,S	F,RO sli			RO	RO					F,RO sli	F,RO
RIGHT ELBOW		F		F,S			F,S	F						F,S	(F,S) sli
RIGHT WRIST		LCK		E sli	LCK					F sli				LCK	LCK
RIGHT FINGERS	FIRST	(B,C)E		8,F / C,E	(B,C)E			(B,C)E sli		(B,C)E sli				(B,C)E sli	(B,C)E sli
	SECOND	C,F sli		(B,C)F	(B,C)F		(B,C)F	(B,C)F		(B,C)F				(B,C)F	Æ sli
	THIRD	(B,C)F sli		(B,C)F	(B,C)F sli		(B,C)F fst	(B,C)F		(B,C)F				LCK	
	FOURTH	(B,C)F sli		(B,C)F	(B,C)F sli		(B,C)F fst	(B,C)F		(B,C)F				LCK	
RIGHT THUMB		Æ		(B,C)F / Æ	(B,C)F									LCK	

FIGURE 3. Portion of an exceptionally fine-grained, film-based transcript that tracked body movement as a speaker utters "I." W. S. Condon and W. D. Ogston, "Sound Film Analysis of Normal and Pathological Behavior Patterns," *Journal of Nervous and Mental Disease* 143, no. 4 (1966): 340.

microscopy and *micro-* are bigger than any instrument is evident in the lexi-con. Words like microscope—a neologism that dates to 1625—once denoted a narrow class of instrument but quickly inspired extensions like microscopic eye and microscopic vision for exceptional human sight, and microscopic intellect for a subtle, penetrating mind.[6] Poetry could be figuratively micro-scopic; art, also. In the nineteenth century, *micro-* named sciences featuring microscopes, such as microcrystallography and micromineralogy, but "mi-cro" would later baptize new areas of study, such as microeconomics, micro-sociology, and microhistory, which did not require that practitioners peer into optical magnifiers. If we leave aside the now infrequent use of *micro-* as a strict reference to the microscope and consider instead the broader discursive life of *micro-* (often meaning just small in size or extent), we can see that this prefix has attached itself to all manner of things: units like microhm, cat-egories like microbe, instruments like micrometer, consumer appliances and electronics from microwave to microcomputer, and, indeed, the racialized vio-lence of microaggression.[7]

   In this book, I trace how social scientists repurposed recording tech-nologies to pry into the recesses of human social interaction.[8] As a study of metaphoric rather than literal microscopy, this book reminds us of the kalei-doscopic variety of microscopic sciences, with their different conditions of possibility, forms of technoscientific mediation, practical and epistemological labor, stakes and stakeholders, politics, ethics, and aesthetics. But this book is not solely about interaction and the microscopy used to know it but especially about a thing that would entwine, support, and constrict both: *scale*.

What Does Scale Mean?

The question cannot be answered, not immediately, as it is precisely what must be asked afresh. This book builds on an earlier, edited volume in which my contributors and I collectively experimented at studying scale in social life. This required that we try to bracket our scalar metalanguage to open ourselves to scale as a dimension of sociocultural practice.[9] We argued there for a "pragmatics of scale" that sets aside our passionate arguments (what does scale really mean? How many scales are there and how do they relate?) in favor of examining the practices, techniques, and projects by which actors scale their worlds.

   This requires patience, at the very least, with the word scale's polysemy. Like any term that gets used a lot, scale means many things. In technical reg-isters of scientific practice, scale can mean a quantitative or qualitative rating instrument, like a familiar five-point Likert scale that asks you to rank how much you agree or disagree. In cartography scale usually means the Euclidean geometric notion of uniform scaling, the idea that you can preserve an object's identity—its proportionality—when you enlarge or reduce it. In microeconomics, "economies of scale" refers to an inverse correlation between quantitative output and total cost, where some goods can be produced cheaply only when production increases. A sense of scale familiar from social theory has to do with mereological "part-whole" relations, as with individuals imagined to function as "contributory" parts of collectivities, or localities nested or encompassed somehow *within* the compass of a nation-state or world-system.[10] One reason not to purify scale and settle upon one definition is that distinct senses sometimes get combined in practice in ways that we should not miss.[11]

In adopting an ethnographic stance on scale here, I will not define up-front and control the concept too tightly, because that would bleach out a notion that is rarely pure for its users, and it is the users I care about. Scale will serve as an anthropological caption for and approximation of an orientation and reality that sociohistorical agents themselves embrace, if sometimes only fitfully, unevenly, and aspirationally. My concern here is with scale as it manifests itself in and around scientific practice, but only seldom do the scholars I discuss stop and theorize scale let alone worry about terminological consistency. When prompted to talk about their methods, they may speak variously of "close," "fine-grained," "microscopic" analysis. When they reflect on the reality of what they study, they may say that they scrutinize "face-to-face" or "small-scale" encounters, which they contrast with larger units of human togetherness. Most often the actors I consider do not talk about scale so much as enact it quietly in their techniques, such as through the way they transcribe talk from recordings and strain to preserve ephemeral details that are usually lost.

But there is one basic distinction that is useful to make up-front in order to grasp many of the troubles of scale that fields have experienced, and that is a distinction between *epistemological scale* and *ontological scale*. Many in science studies would want to reject a distinction between epistemology and ontology, but we need to restore it for ethnographic purposes. Scale in its epistemological sense typically has to do with observation, as when interactionists aspire to scrutinize a few minutes of human encounter in ways they take to be close, thick, fine, granular, microscopic, and so on. Yet scale is also frequently used in an ontological sense, to refer not to how we observe or analyze but to how these observed or analyzed objects themselves exist. In a valiant effort to untangle the knot of scale in his field of human geography, Nathan Sayre makes a distinction between "observational scale" and "operational scale," where the former is scale in its aforementioned "epistemological moment," the latter in its "ontological moment." Sayre separates these "moments" analytically in order to have us appreciate how and with what effects they come together in practice. He cares especially about the way the two can reinforce and naturalize each other such that they seem to fuse.

Sayre is right to steer our attention toward the intimate relation of epistemological and ontological scale, which is far more common and consequential than we realize. Familiar words like microorganism, for instance, can denote an organism *revealed* by a microscope as well as an organism that is *itself* micro, in the sense of being very small. As label or prefix, "micro" is often ambiguous in denoting epistemological and ontological scale, such that when people feel pressed to gloss it, they often find themselves sliding between the two. It is not that I wish to hold these two senses apart analytically in a bid to solve our troubles with scale. I separate these senses only to make us alive to their interplay. Again and again, I will highlight the productive back and forth between these two dimensions of scale. We will see how micro and cognate terms denote at once, or by turns, a fine-grained register of observation and a relatively small object, level, or order of social reality. We will see at other times how scholars become aware of what they take to be a troubling conflation of epistemological and ontological scale and work to disentangle and purify the two, as if to remind their peers—and especially their critics—that *of course* they know observational scale is just a matter of perspective, that the world itself is not carved up by scale.

There is much to appreciate about observational scale itself, apart from its entanglement with scalar ontology. Sayre also offers a definition of observational scale drawn from ecology that has analogs in other fields. Observational scale involves two parameters, *grain* and *extent*.[12] Grain here means units of measurement whereas extent means spatial and temporal reach. Consider a meter stick, he says, "whose grain is a millimeter, extent is a meter, and which can be used to measure the length of all sorts of different things."[13] The distinction between grain and extent shows up in many fields, even as it is understood and treated differently. As I note again and again in these pages, the two are almost always taken to be inversely correlated. If you want to cover a lot, spatially or temporally, most feel that you can't do so finely, just as fine-grained analysis requires a concession: that you look at less. (This may get its matter-of-factness from the way humans get maximal visual acuity by fixing an object in their narrow line of sight.)[14] Big data enthusiasts boast that they have the computational power to overcome this and do fine-grained and extensive analysis simultaneously, thereby unseating this conventional methodological wisdom; their ambitions notwithstanding, most think you must sacrifice extent for grain to look closely.

Sayre's discussion of observational scale is elegant, though in privileging measurement, it cannot accommodate the variety of scalar epistemologies we encounter ethnographically and historically. Different fields have different investments in epistemological scale and have elaborated and debated it variously. And while I follow his lead in examining the epistemological and ontological dimensions of scale—as an ethnographic distinction—we must recognize that this does not exhaust scale as discourse and practice.

We need only remember the resonant contrast between "thick" and "thin" description, which Clifford Geertz adapted from the philosopher Gilbert Ryle and made famous in his push for an interpretive anthropology. Thick description was what ethnographers provided, when they showed how humans imbued social life with meaning, revealing semiotically distinct kinds of winks where their scientistic peers could only see "objectively" indistinguishable blinks, as Ryle's analogy went. Thick and thin were not directly about observational scale but quickly got linked to it, as Geertz capped off his discussion of thick description with a bold declaration of its final characteristic: "it is microscopic." I will not reprise here all the memorable clarifications and qualifications that followed, like, "the anthropologist characteristically approaches . . . broader interpretations and more abstract analyses from the direction of exceedingly extended acquaintances with extremely small matters"; "anthropologists don't study villages (tribes, towns, neighborhoods . . .); they study *in* villages"; they "confront . . . the same grand realities" and move "from local truths to general visions" without the frantic "size-up-and-solve" strategies of other social sciences.[15] Let us only remember how thick description became a sensorial trope for a scaled register of disciplinary knowing. Whether visual or haptic, the thick-thin contrast conjured a *sense* or *feeling* of epistemological scale—what contemporary linguistic anthropologists would understand as *qualia* ("sensory experiences of abstract qualities such as heat, texture, color, sound, stink, hardness, and so on," as Lily Chumley writes).[16] Thickness and thinness chained together associations that stretched beyond epistemology—and beyond observational scale—and thus had implications for scholarly being as much as knowing. Not unlike the multimodality of lifestyle commodification, where dress, bodily comportment, hair style, and so on, get so tightly bundled that, in tugging on one, you pull up the rest by implication, so, too, have scalar distinctions often become forms of distinction that involve a whole characterology (what *kind* of scholar, with what attributes, with what politics, would choose to go thick or thin, close or distant, micro or macro?). Although I devote my energies to understanding the epistemological and ontological life of scale, at times I follow scale beyond itself. I note, for instance, how the "small" scale of the interpersonal could be gendered and binarized as "soft," or how a supremely focused, doggedly "microscopic" gaze could instead be gender-coded male; how scrutiny of the small could be politically subversive for the way it promised to expose and end domination in everyday life, or how it could be a symptom of a slow, patient (read: complicit) liberalism. To study scale ethnographically is to go beyond it.

But how should we do this? Bruno Latour once advised that we should not "settle scale in advance," because scale is artifice, "the actor's own achievement."[17] In social theory, he complained that "we tend to think of scale— macro, meso, micro—as a well-ordered *zoom*." "Zooms," "panoramas," "the local"—these are *effects*, and we need to appreciate what they do and how they are enacted. But the problem with exploding the analytics of scale at the same time that we call for its study is that we usually stop at demolition. Indeed, until recently, few studies made scale-making an explicit focus, with some notable exceptions.[18]

Ethnographically, studying scale-making requires reflexivity, for as Gabrielle Hecht reminds us, scale is "both a category of analysis *and* a category of practice."[19] This reflexivity does not just require the usual anthropological bracketing of readymade distinctions so that we don't impose them on what we study. It must also include a serious investigation into how we—within and across our respective fields—scale our objects of knowledge.

This does not mean that scholars of interaction invented interaction's diminutive scale, as we might say in an older, constructivist idiom. People hardly need a science to tell them that interaction is comparatively small, because they are primed to discover this scalar truism through the way they habitually interact. As the ethologists of human interaction like to observe, when we talk face-to-face, we tend to stand close. In open spaces, we congregate in clusters, in what Erving Goffman called "eye-to-eye ecological huddles,"[20] so as to monitor each other's communications with ease. Greetings and leave-taking expressions bound off conversations in time, opening and closing them, as if these were discrete and finite. Words can sometimes reinforce this. Apart from whatever else the metonymic expression "face-to-face" may suggest, it confirms scalar intuitions. It suggests a physical immediacy of human copresence and contact that we tend to contrast with spatially and temporally distributed and highly mediated kinds of human connectivity, be it digitally mediated or what not. This *scalar ontology* of interaction, this version of conversational reality as a compact, neatly perimeterized event, with channels dug by interactants themselves, is not the only one available, however.[21] By contrast, conversationalists themselves sometimes become acutely aware of the porosity of their little huddles and the extraordinary reach of their talk. (As when speakers adjust what they say due to onlookers and over-hearers or due to worries about what someone might later share with some-one else; or when they consider all the dramatic reports, stories, and reenact-ments of events that happened earlier and elsewhere, which get invoked in a here and now but do not belong to it.[22])

Even as it is no accident that interaction should be drawn and redrawn as "small," interaction has no intrinsic scale—no one version of itself, no single scalar ontology. And as we will later see, even when interaction gets config-ured and enacted and elaborated on as small, this smallness rarely means or does the same thing; and, crucially, it is never as small as it purports to be.

Although interaction's scalar ontology and multiplicity has rarely been explored as such, quite a few have recognized that what we call social inter-action is socially and historically variable. Some media historians and histo-rians of communication have stressed the impact of media technologies on interaction—including on the very idea of it. John Durham Peters argued that it was experiences and troubles with new media technologies, from pho-tograph to phonograph, radio to telegraph, that helped redefine the "face-to-face," much as the emergence of "mass media" reconfigured its diminutive counterpart, "the interpersonal." As Peters emphasizes—and I emphatically agree—we cannot treat the face-to-face as "an already constituted zone of hu-man activity." But in these pages the medial technologies I want to spotlight are those that scholars of interaction themselves tried to exploit epistemologi-cally in order to know social interaction better. I do this because these medial practices and techniques helped fashion interaction into a scaled object.[23]

Another, simpler way of putting this is that microscopy has never been pure method but instead has helped produce its object and define its proper-ties, including its ontological scale. It is customary in science studies to argue that methods make objects, but this constitutive process isn't always easy or automatic; it can be slower, messier, more complicated and more interesting when looked at carefully. Again, as Sayre has correctly stressed, scale is by turns epistemological *and* ontological, and it is the drama and fallout of this interplay that I spotlight in these pages.

As some scholars who studied interaction experimented with microscopy, they (and quite a few of their detractors) watched as their object seemed to shrink more than ever before. They became convinced that interaction *itself* was micro in the sense of being spatially and temporally small and terribly subtle. And as interaction became complexly, densely small, as small as the methods needed to see it, new challenges and threats arose, as we shall see.

To appreciate this generative interplay between epistemological and onto-logical scale, with all its practical, conceptual, disciplinary, ethical and even political fallout, let us slow down, as it were, and separate scale's epistemo-logical and ontological moments. Where better to begin than by restoring some discomfort with that too familiar expression "microscopic world," a trope that had become unremarkable by at least the late eighteenth century? Writing about early microcinematography in cell biology, Hannah Landecker reminds us how banal the expression "microscopic world" now seems, even if it is never a small feat to enworld the micro, such as by coming to see and act on "a spatially distinct location residing inside bodies."[24]

Let us page back to microscopy in a literal sense, back to a light micro-scope and an *urtext* of early microscopy, to a moment when speaking of a microscopic world could be surprising, and sometimes troubling.

The Vanishing Point and the Problem of the Paracosm

When English natural philosopher Robert Hooke invited readers of his in-fluential book *Micrographia* (1665) to see what he saw through his single-lens microscope, he began with a deceptively simple object: the "point of a sharp small needle" in which "the naked eye cannot distinguish any parts."

This point was nowhere to be found. What you see under magnification is not a conical shape tapering off sharply but rather a "broad, blunt, and very irregular end," its surface coarsened by a "multitude of holes and scratches and ruggednesses."

Take a graphical point, if you prefer, like the one that stops this sentence. A text's orthographic period sits gracefully circular and uniform on the page. Enlarged, it grows ragged, ugly. Nothing can smooth out these imperfections, Hooke adds, because the surface of paper is itself hopelessly scarred and pit-ted. Shifting his geometric attention from point to line, Hooke disconcerts readers further by reporting on what he could not see at his razor's edge. "I could not find that any part of it had any thing of sharpness in it." And as he scans things around him, like the fine weave of fabrics—linen, silk, taffeta—his refrain? That their beauty is only surface deep, "For the Productions of art are such rude mis-shapen things, that when view'd with a Microscope, is little else observable, but their deformity."

To be sure, natural points—hairs, thorns, bristles, the minuscule claws of insects—are finer than the finest manufactured needles, much as the organic weave of plants surpasses the best fabrics. Magnification humbles all human artistry, revealing its coarseness compared to nature's and encouraging read-ers (as early microscopists liked to do) to savor divine design in the smallest of things.[25] Hooke crows about the ingenious architecture of the fly's foot, the flea's "polish'd suit of sable armour," the "very fine crusted or shell'd" mite. At times *Micrographia* reads as a bestiary of the subvisible. A tour of God's tiniest creatures, it imparts moral lessons, the main of which is that the world below is no less perfect than the world above—and must be, after all, for it is the *same* world God created.

But was it the same? Historian Catherine Wilson suggested that Hooke seemed genuinely surprised by how dramatically different things looked under the lens. He expected to discover the equivalent of an alphabet or grammar that could explain surface complexity. He thought "magnification would result in simplification," yet the opposite seemed true.[26] Hooke's surprise has become something of a cliched plot twist in microscopic discovery narratives. In a searching essay on scale and complexity, Marilyn Strathern was at pains to remind readers that no matter what observational scale you adopt—whether you bore down into reality microscopically or zoom out to some bird's-eye view—complexity always awaits, like a fractal that reiterates its intricate pattern at every level, at every scale.[27] As for the early light microscope, if the instrument wasn't to blame for the complexity it unleashed—and some did charge that the microscope was so prone to distortion that it couldn't be trusted—then one had to explain the fact that "the rudiments of Nature are very unlike the grosser appearances."

This dissonance could suggest that the lens really did improve upon the human eye, serving as a prosthesis with which to see nature's subtleties—a familiar argument in favor of the instrument. It could also affirm the epistemological power of observation—a tenet of the fledgling Royal Society's then contentious empiricism. But the sheer extent of this roughness did something else, too. It invited you to think that the objects under scrutiny were not a motley collection of minute bodies but denizens of one sweeping subvisible world, as Wilson aptly captioned it.[28]

After all, the rough texture of objects showed up a lot and was not limited to things made and modified by the human hand. Pristine flakes of ice forming on water were "curiously quill'd, furrow'd, or grain'd." Although he lacked a microscope powerful enough to see the finest natural hairs, Hooke now expected them to be blemished with little "hills, and dales, and pores."[29] By dwelling so often and so long on irregularity and roughness, Hooke left readers with the sense of a dominant sensorial impression, of roughness. We can think of this again in terms of *qualia*. Observational scale is abstract but can be experienced, as if synesthetically, resulting in sensuous encounters with the things under observation. The fact that these scalar qualia of roughness recurred so often had implications for ontological scale. It could invite you to think that an aesthetically unified domain was under observation, a microscopic *world* whose existence Hooke sometimes spoke of using the seductive trope of early empire: a "new world," a "terra incognita."[30]

Microscopy, then, was no ordinary method, but a method that could disclose a world, and by name at least, microscopic worlds credited their eponymous instruments. Landecker, for instance, details how film-based techniques such as time-lapse helped temporalize the microworld in cellular biology, such that one could come to inspect and know the "very slow" and not only the spatially small.[31] In an altogether different context and trained on sound, Eitan Wilf's ethnography of jazz pedagogy describes how educators and students use a machine playfully called the Amazing Slow Downer to analyze, savor, and emulate a composer's solos. The sociotechnical mediation in microscopy varies enormously—to say nothing of the projects, institutions, aspirations, and interests that all this observational scaling serves; here, I only wish to note the trouble that so often accompanies a microworld's autonomy, regardless of how and why that autonomy comes about. For once the micro begins to get enworlded, it becomes that much more urgent to reconcile its existence with *this* world.[32]

Again, take roughness. A decade before Hooke's book, Walter Charleton, who dabbled in microscopy but meditated hard on its philosophical significance, weighed the implications of the idea that "no body can be so exactly smooth and polite," not even "the best cut diamonds" or "the finest crystal."[33] So much for Aristotle, Charleton reasoned, who must have been duped by his eyes when he argued that the qualities of bodies were spread evenly and uniformly across their surfaces, like a cloth stretched taut.

The texture of microscopic objects could in this way disturb the surface world. More disruptive still were the subvisible world's most infamous inhabitants, the microorganisms. In a storied discovery from 1674, Dutch microscopist Antoni van Leeuwenhoek peered into a drop of lake water and found it teeming with "little animals," or animalcules, that looked a thousand times smaller than anything he had ever seen.[34] Here was a paradigmatic "world within a world," which piqued the imagination. It could be humbling theologically to discover an ocean-full of God's creatures in a single droplet. "So much beauty is found concentrated in so small a space," Malebranche wrote.[35] It could also be disquieting. So plentiful were these animalcula that they could even undermine confidence in solid bodies. Leibniz, who was very impressed with microscopy and with the discovery of microorganisms, wrote that "many bodies that appear solid are nothing but a mass of these imperceptible animals." "Perhaps the block of marble itself," he mused, "is only a mass of an infinite number of living bodies like a lake full of fish."[36] This vast subvisible world could nurture a corrosive doubt about who, or what, was actually in control. If animalcula roiled beneath bodies, then what big agents might these little ones displace? What if this swarm of subvisible life were the "real" cause of things?[37]

✳

I offer these fragments from early, literal microscopy to remind us that a world does not automatically come from close viewing and that when it does, this enworlding of the micro can be troubling. In the spirit of the trope, let me now resolve microscopy more finely, to see if we can tease apart the entwined threads of microscopic knowing and being, epistemological from ontological scale, as people sometimes feel compelled to do.

When it came to early light microscopes, not everyone trusted the eyes, let alone artificially enhanced vision, but to be provoked philosophically or theologically by what you saw, you had at least to entertain the microscope's basic epistemic conceit: look closely at something—in this case, with technological prosthesis—and you should be able to see it, and by extension know it, better. (I will not belabor the familiar ocularcentrism that takes the visual as the paradigmatic way to know the world.) By "it" we assume that we are still looking at the same object and merely increasing optical power.

Yet is this sharper thing truly "the same" thing? Ordinarily, we do not doubt that it is. The observed qualities may have shifted (from smooth to rough, for example), yet we do not then think that the object has changed let alone that we have somehow strayed into another reality. Instead, the thing remains part of one singular, *continuous world*.

But sometimes the object may grow so alien that we begin to wonder whether more than an order of magnification has changed. If the object looks or behaves oddly enough, we may wonder whether it operates by its "own" rules and lives in its own world—a world that may even require a special body of knowledge if not a science of its own. That is, if the otherness of the object under a literal or tropic microscope gaze becomes sufficiently disturbing, to us or to those others looking over our shoulder, this may get us to worry about how this object exists. In extreme cases, we may even suspect that there are different ontologically scaled worlds where things behave differently, which can prompt us to think about how exactly these scales hang together, as we assume they must. Too much unexpected complexity, for instance, and the object may no longer even fit in a microcosm—a world nestled "within" or "under" our macroscopic world, either epitomizing or recapitulating it or else revealing its elementary forms. The microcosm may break off into a paracosm, a world apart from our own. And even if we grant neighborly coexistence to this exiled microworld, we cannot ignore for long the question of its relatedness—its kinship—for without this tie, the whole world may fall apart. Let us call this *the problem of the paracosm.*

We should pause and remember the theorization this can unleash. In many social sciences, this problem has been treated, at base, as a problem of inclusion, of (re)connecting part and whole. When social science *micro*-analysts of many stripes have narrowed their gaze on a practice, a discourse, a narrative, a ritual, a technique, a formation, a category, or an interaction, they have tended to think that continuity with the proverbial wider world is ensured by the fact that they have been looking at a "piece" of it, even if they are not quite sure what this continuity involves. Microscopy, that is, has often involved an assumption of mereological decomposition, as if one has broken things down from whole to part.[38] When the threat of the paracosm looms and they feel pressed to explain how their little part relates—and, by implication, why it deserved scrutiny in the first place—their answers have been many. This is no surprise, as part-whole relations are many. As analytical philosophers of mereology would remind us, the word "part" and cognate terms paper over such multiplicity. A part, for instance, may refer to something that is *substantively* continuous with the whole, like a "piece" or "portion" of ice whose composition is the same throughout. It can also be used to refer to something that is substantively continuous yet *functionally* separate from its whole, as with the leg of a solid wood table; and so on.[39] To be sure, many imaginative social theorists have tried to dispense with part-whole relations, in favor of, say, flat or rhizomic ones, and I do not mean to dismiss the differences within this intricate theorizing by suggesting that everything boils down to a matter of mereology. I only wish to flag the ferment, and trouble, that the problem of the paracosm has caused. And these are just the intellectual troubles, because as we will see these issues frequently stray far into the political, the ethical, the practical, and much else.

I want to remember the caustic and even world-sundering power of microscopy. I want to stress not only the making of microscopic worlds but especially the complications and threats that enworlding the micro can pose to "our" world.[40]

Small things and their scrutiny haven't been the only sources of scalar trouble, of course, but quite often they have caused ontological scales to come apart, and in the humanities and social sciences, this has left fields pondering such antinomies as the interpersonal and the institutional, and indeed, micro and macro. The most spectacular and famous case of the paracosmic occurred in twentieth-century quantum physics, but scale has also birthed and broken worlds in social science disciplines as diverse as sociology, economics, and anthropology. In these pages, I do not revisit the many ways in which disciplines like my own have been vexed by big things, things that seem to push the envelope of established time depths, that spur us to consider "deep time" or the *longue durée*; nor do I reconsider all the struggles to make sense of dizzyingly vast systems and structures—from world systems to *dispositifs*—whose outer limits and far-flung organization have felt hard to grasp epistemologically.[41] Perhaps predictably, in the social sciences we have devoted a lot of time reflecting on large matters; less frequently do we appreciate how small things and their analysis have vexed us to a comparable degree. Many of us have in fact come to worry about how the world hangs together as a result of the small, but what lessons for the present hide in these many crises of scale? In *A History of Scale*, I use the story of interaction's troubling scale to encourage reflection on the way small things and their microscopy in the social sciences can spark concerns about how objects, and their disciplines, relate.

How Interaction Became Small and Not Small at All

The chapters that follow trace how, why, and with what effects interaction science became microscopic and came to talk about and treat its object as small. In the United States, this object I call "interaction" has gone by several other names, notably "social interaction" and "face-to-face interaction" as well as "interpersonal relations" and "small groups." Interaction science took off in the years after the Second World War and flourished during the early Cold War. Like other sciences of the time, these were self-consciously interdisciplinary sciences that imagined interaction as a boundary object that belonged to no field in particular, whereas nowadays interaction is broken up and scattered across fields, only some of which regularly interact. These fields include sociology, linguistics, anthropology, communication studies, social psychology, and computer science. Applied domains such as education studies, clinical psychology, and industrial-organizational psychology, have also all had serious investments in the sciences of interaction, even if they have not always agreed on what to call their object or even recognized that they were up to something similar.[42]

Before midcentury, interaction did not have a widely known science of its own, nor was it yet a passionately microscopic pursuit, so how and why did some of its influential midcentury enthusiasts come to adopt this observational and analytical sensibility? The story that follows has historical shape and pace, beginning slowly and haltingly in the late 1920s and early '30s, then accelerating in the 1950s and '60s, then erupting in the '70s as scale acquired a contentious and explicit politics. By looking across and tracing relations among a number of interaction scientists, I offer not one but three distinct yet historically overlapping accounts of how and why interaction became small, which are presented in parts 1 through 3. These are not the only stories that can be told about the scaling of interaction from this time, but they are revealing ones when it comes to the interest and trouble scale has caused.

Part 1, "Fine-Grained Analysis," is about the talk of talk therapy and the effort to record and analyze it. It examines how psychiatry and the sciences of language and communication came together around experimentation with recording technologies in a bid to understand the way therapeutic discourse worked—and how they inadvertently ended up scaling social interaction along the way. The story begins in the late 1920s and early '30s, a time when interaction did not yet exist as a well-known object of knowledge that deserved a science of its own. In the late '20s, in a corner of the social sciences, a couple social scientists wanted to get records of psychoanalysis sessions in order to understand psychoanalysis better. They proposed using mechanical recording technologies like wax-cylinder dictation machines to capture the speech exchanged between analyst and analysand. They would get "objective" records—especially paper transcripts—of the talking cure.

Observationally and analytically, this kind of research was not at first microscopic in its approach to talk, but it soon became so. Researchers began to pore over the source media and their transcripts in pursuit of something more than what they understood as the "verbatim," something we may call *the communicative unconscious*. They began to chase down the subtle, fugitive tells of talk—or what can be compared to what is usually called, in semiotic terms, *indexical* signs, signs that, like a symptom or a pointed finger, "indicate" or "pick out" contiguous features of context. And yet as they got indexically microscopic in their search for the traces of the communicative unconscious, they often felt disoriented, perplexed, and, more often than not, overwhelmed. In response to the frustrations caused by this form of mediatic microscopy, some decided to look at less data (a matter of extent) even more closely (a matter of grain). A version of the grain-extent inverse took hold.

They were not just shrinking observational scale when they did this. They were also beginning to treat interaction itself—ontologically—as an intrinsically small reality that now *demanded* such microscopic scrutiny. Interaction became both small and microscopically knowable through a historical shift in semiotic ideology, or assumptions about how signs work, that we may caption as *indexicalization* (or, more technically, dicentization). This was a shift, again, that involved a slow coalescing of psychoanalysis, the sciences of language and communication, and recording and playback technologies. In effect, part 1 chronicles how the generative conflation of observational and ontological scale happened over time, and how it created all sorts of troubles. These troubles aside, research on talk therapy spread by the post–World War II period, and this stream of microscopic research at the psychiatry–communication interface helped also spread convictions about what talk-in-interaction in general was and how best to know it. A certain scalar ontology came into view. Human discursive interaction itself was imagined to be saturated with subtle indexical signs, so much so that many felt you needed technologies and techniques of close reading to catch these chatterings of the communicative unconscious, these tells of talk.

Part 2, "Small Groups," starts later, in the years after World War II. It traces out a second and distinct configuration of knowledge practices that incited another scaling of interaction as small. This story of interaction's small scale has to do not with psychiatry but rather with the imperatives of postwar and early–Cold War social science. I focus on "small-group" interaction science, as it was often called, which embraced an explicit discourse of scale as it tried to enact a commitment to scientism and social engineering that the rebooted postwar "behavioral sciences"—as the Ford Foundation's influential rebranding of the social sciences read—felt obliged to take seriously.

"Small" in small-group science was a curiously bold word. Far from suggesting something limited or trivial, small evoked a potent, focused, rigorous science, a science that preferred the laboratory and emulated the natural sciences. It was confidently technocratic, too, as small also suggested a science whose object, unlike big groups, was manageable, something you could control and improve.

By imputing smallness to interaction, these scholars engaged in some serious misdirection. If their label seemed to shrink interaction spatially and temporally in some respects, other things they said and did stretched interaction's surface and folded it in and around other things, which ended up making interaction anything *but* small.

There is a lesson here for us. In this second story of scale, as in all such stories, scalar labels only tell half the story, as they usually conceal interscalar assumptions and arguments about the relationship between ontological scales. Small is always implicitly tethered to its relational complement, which sits on the other end of the cline and often needs to be drawn out from the shadows. But more than this, when "small" and "micro" get discursively spotlighted by their scholars, these terms usually conceal interscalar arguments that, in the case of small things, "expand" and thereby unsettle their self-styled limits—as if to surprise us and teach us about the true reach and true importance of these little objects and close ways of apprehending them. Again, for Pierce, racial microaggressions were small in *one* sense (comparatively subtle) but *not* in others (frequency of occurrence, magnitude of effects), which is why they mattered. The same for second-wave feminists who criticized seemingly small conversational behaviors, such as speech "interruption" by men, arguing that these behaviors—however seemingly minor and fleeting—were complicit in reproducing something as totalizing and durable as "male supremacy"; interruption in principle isn't limited to *any* one kind of setting but could occur any time men and women talked together. Again, small in some respects, decidedly not small in others. This imbalanced, *asymmetrical interscalarity* reveals how self-consciously scalar projects such as these involved more than only a stark, simultaneous foregrounding (of the small, micro, close, etc.) and backgrounding (of the contrastive but complementary large, macro, distant, etc.); they also involved interplay among the two scalar halves that seemed designed to transform what the former meant and did, that is, to rescale performatively the self-declared smallness or microscopic orientation into something strangely, unexpectedly vast: a whole world hiding in plain sight, for instance; a deep if not universal truth about the human condition revealed through a microanalytic gaze; a potential unleashed by "splitting the social atom."[43]

Indeed, for the postwar small-group analysts, interaction itself, this self-consciously "small" thing to know, was declared to be *always* and *everywhere*. Weren't humans interacting all the time, whenever they were physically copresent, wherever they were—at home, in public, at work, at school? And didn't these people often suffer from interpersonal troubles that they only half understood? That is, despite the diminutive size imputed to this object, a size they often talked about literally as a matter of fewer countable bodies compared to big groups, these researchers stressed how these little groupings of humans were nevertheless happening all the time and in every corner of the social world, which is what made their small-group science so very relevant. Just as interaction was everywhere, so everywhere interaction scientists stood ready to be useful, to leverage their expert knowledge to make small groups—and by extension the social world itself, as a whole—better. Part 2 shows how interaction got fashioned in this way into a small but potent technology—a liberal technology—that could be used in a seemingly infinite variety of contexts. If the trajectory in part 1 can be captioned as indexicalization, the trajectory in part 2 may be captioned as *interactionalization*.[44] Interaction became an interscalar technology to better the social world, a few people at a time.

Parts 1 and 2 reveal how different streams of research on interaction shrank their object, albeit for different reasons, in different ways, based on different techniques. Each stream faced practical, epistemological, and sometimes ontological challenges, but for neither was scale politically troublesome, at least not until the late '60s and early '70s. Part 3, "Micropolitics," turns to this politicization of scale. For many young sociologists, for instance, small-group science came to feel conservative and incompatible with social justice movements. Its scientism alone—which could include stealth observations made behind a one-way mirror—felt epistemologically distanced and politically retrograde. The question of how ontological scales related hadn't worried postwar small-group researchers much, but this new politicization made them concerned with it and forced them to confront the problem of the paracosm. Most of the small-group practitioners were never forced to spell out how exactly interaction related to its proverbial wider world, and so they made little effort to link so-called micro and macro, as scholars would strain to do a few decades later. There was an implicit interscalar mereology to their sciences, to be sure, but this was never something they felt obligated to draw out. And because they didn't draw this out, this left them vulnerable to later critics who now wondered what they really had to offer this wider world, a world roiling with injustice, violence, protest, and division. How did small groups connect to big ones and to the macrosocial? And was the microscopic observation they sometimes adopted necessary, or did it cause them to become distracted by excessive detail? Pressure began to build to clarify questions of interscalar kinship, which usually meant clarifying mereological, part-whole relations, and also to clarify why microscopy was a must. Scale was fast becoming a problem.

At the same time that an older small-group science became suspect for those in the political vanguard, small was getting reinvented yet again. New "microsociologies" and "microethnographies" arose, and a social justice movement—the women's liberation movement—became invested in a very different kind of "small group," this being another, early name for second-wave feminism's key institution, the "consciousness-raising group." In part 3, I examine the interplay of second-wave feminism and the sciences of communication through which interaction became both a site of everyday gender politics and an object of empirical research on male supremacy. I illustrate this with an exploration of how researchers studied unwanted touches and speech interruptions as techniques that reproduced patriarchy in everyday life. To adapt Carol Hanisch's second-wave adage, I trace how the *interpersonal* became political. In a final chapter, I show how a similar politicization of the small was going on for researchers inspired by the civil rights movement, for "microsociologists" and "microethnographers" who in the 1970s used fine-grained analyses of video recordings to try to pinpoint and address discrimination—often anti-Black racism—in schools. Although these new scholars of the small argued that interaction had a micropolitics that made their microanalysis important if not urgent, to critics the dynamics they uncovered appeared as tempests in transcripts.

And this criticism put the interactionists on their heels. It led most of them to defend themselves. Some rushed to theorize interscalar relations in order to establish why what they studied mattered and why their gaze had needed to be microscopic; others tried—usually in vain—to ditch scalar distinctions like micro and macro, which usually didn't serve them well anyway. This contestation in the '70s evolved notoriously into the all-out scale wars of the 1980s, which featured essays, articles, and books that promised to adjudicate the truth of how micro and macro related. These debates roiled fields such as sociology, which had had a serious commitment to the study of objects like small groups, social interaction, and conversation. They also affected contestation over what made fields and subfields similar and different.

The legacy of these debates for the study of social interaction is hard to overstate. Nobody who studies interaction today in fields like sociology and anthropology can do so without feeling the effects of this contestation, because, as I argue in the conclusion, these debates were generative, both in terms of scholarship and in terms of how fields and subfields came to distinguish themselves. Scale hasn't just been important in defining objects of knowledge. It has also been important in defining how fields devoted to these objects relate, based on which was expansive and which blinkered, for instance, which loose and which focused and rigorous. This is why scale ultimately is about us—about our own relations and interactions—and why, as Hecht advises, we need to engage scale reflexively.

✶

It is admittedly difficult to do this, as we do not recognize the extent to which scale lives on in the distinctions and techniques we use. Throughout this book it should be plain that all-too-familiar scalar words and expressions, such as "small," "close," "fine-grained," and "microscopic"—and of course all those contrasting terms on the other end of the scalar spectrum—cannot be treated as self-evident. Each is as complexly and variably resonant as any discourse that gets used a lot and so must be studied carefully. In each case we must ask what scalar distinctions mean and do, just as we must ask how and with what effects scale gets configured and enacted through practices and techniques.

Several times, not just once, microscopy helped ontologize its object, at times making interaction into a microworld of a certain kind. As interaction science became normatively microscopic in terms of observation, interaction as an object began to shrink. And once it became unquestionably subtle and small, this object of knowledge began to screech with feedback effects by demanding microscopy *because* of its diminutive nature. Once a microscopic object existed "out there," autonomous, in need of a microscopic gaze, new disciplinary and interdisciplinary stances became possible. If you wanted, you could stick a flag in the firmament of interaction and make the old federalist argument that it was a separate, irreducible reality that demanded a separate, irreducible science; because if interaction is its own reality that can't be explained by appeal to others (psychology, sociology, linguistics, etc.), then "it" must need a science of its own. You could feel morally committed to (or put off by) this object with more conviction than when microscopic observation was mere method.

While I train my attention on interaction, readers will find folded into these stories of interaction's changing scale and its accompanying troubles subplots of many kinds, including Cold War–era technophilia; anxieties about fascism, racism, and sexism; technocratic aspirations and machinations. There were plenty of practical and material hardships right from the start, too. It was hard to run recorders continuously and engineer a recording environment that didn't intrude on the interaction too much. This story of how interaction science went microscopic is riddled with complicating actions of many kinds: machines and media that didn't work or worked too well—producing acoustic and visual data too rich to parse; paralyzingly obsessive efforts to capture and analyze *everything*, to chase down ever finer details on less and less data; publications delayed, or dropped, due to the labor and cost that this research demanded; and the crush of critics and unsympathetic funding agencies who threatened to stop these little sciences in their tracks.

Though the book's climax centers on social-scientific contestation over the small, interaction's diminutive scale hasn't always been a problem and has never been for the devoted few. Small can be enthralling, electric, tantalizingly concrete: an aperture through which to glimpse the nuance and concentrated richness of human life as "actually lived"; a hands-on way to take the pulse of everyday life or point your finger at hidden suffering or resistance or the sub rosa exercise of power—as Pierce wanted us to see with his notion of microaggression. In redirecting our gaze back toward people, we stop trying to explain the world by appealing to gauzy metaphysical abstractions like society, culture, ideology, structure, Discourse. If you want to know exactly when, where, and how social life happens, what could be better than the spatially and temporally "situated" (a word some practitioners of this science like to use) dynamics of human encounter and exchange?

And speaking of *how*, in scrutinizing human interaction so finely, many of its enthusiasts appreciate if not rhapsodize about process: they watch as identities crystallize and splinter; actions as they unfold, twist, and turn; groups as they form, and fall apart.[45] Want to catch the fleeting nuances of gender performance or see how the threads of intersectionality twist and braid? Or detect, in the qualities of the voice or carriage of the body, the dramaturgy of class? The whole human world can become a slow-motion morality play that celebrates the truth, and virtue, of chronic contingency and human interdependence. Nothing is so stable that it can't be undone, because, to bend the words of Mikhail Bakhtin, every action is only half ours. Like Leibniz's musings on the solidity of marble as an illusion produced by a dense swarm of animalcula, so anti-realist interactional microscopists can liquefy the hypostasized solids of "self," "society," "culture," and "Discourse," dissolving them into a fog of particulate actions afloat *between* humans. Interaction can be awfully corrosive, indeed.

Yet "small" still stings. No matter how confident the devoted interactionists may seem, small today remains a term of derision. Synonymous with trivial and tedious, small indicts research that lacks significance. Ask a sociologist today whether the recording, fine-grained transcription, and microanalysis of human conversation—as done in the sociological tradition of conversation analysis (CA)—is a good way to get at, say, racial injustice, and most will instinctively snap, no; to cite one of the many moralizing scalar adages, you'd miss the proverbial forest for the trees. The charge of "small" fingers morally suspect studies that miss, or ignore, the big picture.[46] Here again we hear echoes of those critics from the early history of the microscope who charged that studying tiny things was for the profligate. A waste, a moral failing, because bigger and more important game loomed. (Notice here and elsewhere the cliched correlation between scale and value. This, despite the occasional maverick who inverts the correlation in protest, as the economist Schumacher did in his 1973 bestseller, *Small Is Beautiful*, or as second-wave feminists did when they declared the personal as political.) It was also in the seventeenth century that a young, snarky empirical science launched that canard about the metaphysical folly of scholastics who debated how many angels could dance on the head of a pin.[47] With microscopy, it isn't only observers like Hooke who can't see the point.

Small as such may still be negatively freighted, but of late "the interpersonal" has been experiencing something of a resurgence, both as an important if contested micropolitical site—on several social justice fronts—and as a topic of renewed scholarly attention. And, yet again, this object has been shadowed by questions of scale. In efforts to address anti-Black racism in social life, for instance, some wonder whether harmful speech and interactional behavior—which would be considered microaggressions in Pierce's sense—should be considered just as pernicious and as urgent to address as, say, institutionalized racist policies; or how the kind of harm that manifests itself in social life, between copresent humans, should be understood—causally and otherwise—in relation to such seemingly sweeping formations as racial capitalism and the carceral state.

Or take anti-racist pedagogies promoted on many US campuses, which have concentrated intently on the interpersonal. Many have drawn inspiration from Tema Okun's widely circulated paper on "white supremacy culture," first drafted in 1999 and revised since. As Okun recounts, her paper was triggered by interpersonal events. "On the night I wrote the first draft, I arrived back to my apartment in a frustrated lather about a meeting I had just attended, a meeting where many of the characteristics named in the article kept showing up." In her paper she tried to extract from the patterns of behavior she experienced certain white supremacist values that this behavior expressed—and reproduced—usually without people's awareness. These captioned values included "perfectionism," "sense of urgency," "defensiveness," "paternalism," and "objectivity." One was "fear of open conflict," which included "equating the raising of difficult issues with being impolite, rude, or out of line; punishing people either overtly or subtly for speaking out about their truth and/or experience."[48] She would later reissue her list with cautions about how it should, and shouldn't, be used, while also defending it against charges of various kinds, from within and from without. This contestation aside, what is striking is the way this intervention forged a link between concrete, experienceable interpersonal behavior and an abstract, totalizing formation called white supremacy culture—not unlike the way certain feminists a half century earlier had forged links between interpersonal life—unwanted touches, address terms, and speech interruption—and male supremacy. This new ferment around the politics of the interpersonal has also given new urgency to scholars of speech and interaction, much as it did when second-wave feminist researchers began to look empirically for patriarchy through close, microscopic studies of talk and conversation.[49]

Again, I do not seek to resolve these issues, but rather to have us understand with more care the recurring issues and tensions of scale they involve. One way to appreciate this is by tracing out different versions of interaction, by chronicling the varied lives interaction has lived as a small-but-not-so-small thing to know in psychiatry (part 1), in postwar social science (part 2), and in the scholarly discovery of "micropolitics" during the ferment of the late '60s and '70s (part 3).

Although I narrate the scaling of only one object of knowledge in the chapters that follow, interaction's fate has been entangled in the careers of the many objects defined in relation to it, often at its own expense. Again, scalar distinctions are relational, such that scaling one object can implicate and even help mutually constitute others. I hope this book encourages a turn toward scalar projects at work within and across our disciplines, not only because scale deserves a place on a list that includes such staple problematics as objectivity, representation, and mediation, studied in fields such as the history of science and science and technology studies; but also because such a turn may allow us to see more clearly how the scales of our knowable world have been settled for us in advance. It is in this sense that I intend this critical history of interaction as a parable for the present.

PART I

Fine-Grained Analysis

Discourse may be treated as one long "slip of the tongue."
THEODORE SCHWARTZ (1962)

FIGURE 4. John Dollard recording a psychoanalytic interview, as if to store, retrieve, and "amplify" through playback the "small voice of the unconscious." Image from Mark Arthur May Papers, 1891–1977 (MS 1447), Yale University. Series V: Photographs, undated—box 16, folder 2. Quote from Fredrick C. Redlich, John Dollard, and Richard Newman, "High Fidelity Recordings of Psychotherapeutic Interviews," *American Journal of Psychiatry* 107, no. 1 (1950): 42.

The first of our three stories of scale concerns the talk of talk therapy. It begins in the late 1920s with the desire to get something deceptively simple: a record of therapeutic talk—at the very least, a paper transcript—made from a sound recording.

But record psychoanalysis? The idea alarmed purists. No less than Freud himself had cautioned against any kind of recording, by hand or by machine. And yet by midcentury research on the talk of talk therapy became common—and recording commonsense. In 1960, psychologist David Shakow argued that you *had* to record talk therapy mechanically if you hoped to understand it, because of the nature of its communication.

> In this situation the faint and minute, the fleeting and momentary, the devious and abeyant are often the primary data. Indeed, it is because data of this evanescent kind play such an extremely important role in making possible the understanding of what is going on that the peculiar recording approach I have advocated becomes unavoidable.[1]

Or as the cliché goes—and this was something many researchers took seriously—it isn't what you say but *how* you say it. If you could discover all the ways speech betrays interiority—the telltale or indexical qualities of communication—you could understand how patients truly felt, what their complexes were, what they meant. Freud seemed confident that he could catch the tells of his analysands without mediatic prosthesis, but midcentury researchers like Shakow felt they needed help. No matter how gifted or well trained, humans were "limited in how much they can grasp, in how much they can remember of what they do grasp, and in how much and how well they can report even the slight amount they have grasped and remembered."[2] They needed mechanical recorders.

In part 1, I trace the making of a few of these mediatic microscopes, with their practical challenges and piecemeal development; their flashes of insight into discursive interaction amid frustration and even failure; the way they could open up a vast world—even as this enworlding caused troubles of its own. I consider how all of this came to nurture intuitions about what interaction in general was, and how it helped *scale* this object of discursive knowledge as small, both epistemologically and ontologically. When this story started, again, interaction did not exist as something that deserved a science of its own; nor did it require a microscopic eye and ear. We will see how this stream of research, which brought psychiatry, the sciences of language and communication, and media technologies into articulation, end up scaling this object in ways that proved exciting and troubling.

2

The Chattering Unconscious and the Tells of Talk

Mediatic Reception and Recall

Why record talk mechanically, when you can absorb speech using the disciplined human capacity for reception, which is surely more sensitive than any machine?[1]

Indeed, Freud put his faith in human storage and retrieval, including in his own. He boasted that he "still possessed the gift of a phonographic memory" as late as 1917, at the ripe age of 61. As a schoolboy, he could snap and summon pages of text and remember lectures after hearing them just once, or so he wrote. James Strachey, who knew Freud's writings intimately, disagreed, sniping privately that Freud's confidence in his memory was "delusional" and that he "constantly contradict[ed] himself over detail of fact." Strachey, who edited the voluminous standard edition of Freud's writings, had a forensic sensibility and an archive of paper memory—texts and correspondence and records. What matters here is not Freud's true capacity but the direction of his confidence in human reception and recall.[2] Freud championed the human capacity to record, unaided even by small tools like pen and paper, let alone machines like the literal phonograph he invoked.

Recording would get in the way of receptivity. In his advice to the psychoanalyst, Freud famously explained how the analyst should let attention float freely and avoid note-taking, "for as soon as anyone deliberately concentrates his attention to a certain degree, he begins to select from the material before him."[3] He imagined exceptions, like the need to jot down significant dates or dream imagery. He briefly entertained but dismissed the desire to collect "verbatim records" to assess psychoanalysis scientifically. Records wouldn't be enough. "Exhaustive verbatim reports of the proceedings during the hours of analysis would certainly be of no help at all,"[4] and the therapeutic cost would be high. The analyst couldn't pay attention while recording copiously

what was said, and a third-party observer would disrupt the intimate relationship between analyst and analysand that enabled transference—the acting out of psychopathology that may manifest itself as resistances toward free
association. How could you expect associations to flow freely when some-
body else listens in? Practically and clinically, recording should be avoided
and receptivity cultivated.

Receptivity to *what*? Ultimately, Freud argued, what the analyst receives is
not actually a stream of overt communication—palpable verbal and nonverbal
signs that can be perceived, stored, and recalled, as with normal feats of memory. Mechanical recording can capture only materially manifest signs, whether
acoustic or visual. What the analyst receives is ethereal. The transmissions of
the unconscious, like the unconscious itself, are not empirically observable
and hence not mechanically recordable. No machine could ever capture these
signs—which also meant that no machine could verify whether the analyst had
captured them; this, to the consternation of social scientists who complained
that psychoanalysis had poor records and little epistemic accountability.

Surely, they countered, getting *some* records—records of talk at least—
however limited they may ultimately be, made sense. Why not create paper
transcripts of talk that would show what was *actually* said behind closed
doors, transcripts that could be reviewed repeatedly and by more than one
party and in this way serve as "objective" records for weighing psychoanalytic
claims about its effectiveness?

Indeed, this was the motivation of a handful of social scientists in the late
1920s and early 1930s who turned to recording technologies to study psychoanalysis. Efforts in the States to record the sounds of psychoanalysis began
with wax-cylinder dictation machines, whose cylinders were then played back,
transcribed on paper "verbatim," and then shaved down for reuse. The ratio-
nale for recording mechanically changed over time as researchers began to
draw out certain affordances of their machines and began to search for certain
kinds of signs that they at first had neglected. Their relationship to recording
technologies—why they felt they needed them, how they tried to exploit them
epistemologically—was, as one might expect, as plastic as any human interpersonal relationship that evolved over time. It shifted in various ways, yet I want
to spotlight a trajectory of change that reveals one way in which interaction
became small and its observation fine grained and "microscopic."

Let us call this trajectory *indexicalization*. I want to use indexicality somewhat loosely to accommodate historical specificity in semiotic ideology—
group-relative stances on what signs exist and how to know them[5]—but the
notion is the familiar one of semiotician Charles Sanders Peirce. Indexicals
are signs that relate to their objects by existential contiguity, like smoke that

points to fire, a weathervane indicating the wind that blows it, the pronoun "I" that points back to the speaker who utters it. Take a pointing gesture. An extended index finger is a convention that indicates—indexes—a thing, telling you how to "find" it in the world. In speech, likewise, you can treat the perceived qualities of *how* something is spoken—loudness, pausing, pacing, voice quality, and much else—as if these qualities indexed something, quietly steering you *toward* something significant that, with training, you might notice. Something like an indexical sensibility became very pronounced in research on therapeutic talk. As interpersonal psychiatrist Harry Stack Sullivan wrote, "much attention may profitably be paid to the telltale aspects of intonation, rate of speech, difficulty in enunciation, and so on and so forth," for "it is by alertness to the importance of these many things as *signs or indicators of meaning, rather than by preoccupation only with the words spoken*, that the psychiatric interview becomes practical" (emphasis mine).[6]

Over time, researchers transcribed and analyzed therapeutic talk differently in their hunt for what they understood to be indexical signals, and they did this while trying to exploit the indexical affordances of recording and playback technologies. This tilt in semiotic ideology toward indexicality affected not just how these scientists transcribed and analyzed talk but also what they wanted out of recording technologies. This turn did not happen at once. Nor should it be taken to imply that these humans were in control, that they "used" these technologies as they saw fit, as epistemological prosthesis. To steer our attention toward the practices whereby indexicality *became* desired and evident to social actors, let us instead speak of this more processually as *indexicalization*. (Stricter Peircean usage would invite us to call this *dicentization*, as Christopher Ball discusses, because this does not concern indexical signs qua signs but rather their interpretive treatment *as* indexicals.)[7]

I tell this story of media indexicalization, because indexicalization in epistemological scale helped make interaction ontologically small. The denser and subtler the recordings of talk were taken to be in terms of their hidden indexicality, the less you had to analyze—and, indeed, the less they felt you *could* analyze—which nurtured the impression that interaction had to be grasped at a particular scale. When humans interact, they emit little fleeting signals, lots of them, some terribly subtle. Indexicalization lured the analyst into seeking out seemingly ever finer qualities of human communication in search for what exactly did the pointing. Which were the relevant indexical signals? Could you put your finger on the sign itself, as if it were some discrete, neatly observable thing? And when they couldn't find the indexical or settle definitively on what it pointed to, these intrepid indexicalists could choose to look "closer," as it were, by resolving the grain of observation into finer units. Perhaps they just needed to look at less data more finely. A few minutes of talk, a few seconds, even, might suffice.

Indexicalization had hidden costs and unintended effects that illustrate how knowing indexicality was anything but easy. By turns alluring and maddening, indexicalization nurtured the hope that you could put one's finger on the nerve of interpersonal life. But no matter how detailed the transcripts were, it never seemed enough, and a similar dissatisfaction infected the source media. Even the kaleidoscopic sensory experiences of sound film could seem impoverished, for the more indexicality you craved, the closer you edged toward the interpersonal real for which no media was a substitute.

As the desire for indexicality began to build, it affected what people wanted out of recorders and hence altered their evolving relationship to these medial technologies, as we will see. Indeed, at stake throughout was the question whether and to what degree human and nonhuman recorders were similar, who needed whom, and how the two might connect.

Freud himself seemed to acknowledge the parallel between human and nonhuman recorders and tension between the two. Although he placed faith in human recording, he did sometimes use technological tropes to conjure a sense of what good human-to-human receptivity was like. The analyst "must turn his own unconscious like a receptive organ towards the transmitting unconscious of the patient," he wrote, and then, using a trope of telephony and sound transduction, he advised—

> [the analyst] must adjust himself to the patient as a telephone receiver is adjusted to the transmitting microphone. Just as the receiver converts back into sound waves the electric oscillations in the telephone line which were set up by sound waves, so the doctor's unconscious is able, from the derivatives of the unconscious which are communicated to him, to reconstruct that unconscious, which has determined the patient's free associations.[8]

We could treat passages like this as suggesting that Freud was more indebted to the telephonic than he knew, that this communicative unconscious was based on a vast infrastructure of poles, wires, and a physics of transduction.[9] Still, we should not dismiss Freud's stated confidence in human receptivity, even as his trope acknowledged competing technologies of information transfer and storage that may well threaten to demote or even replace the humans. His was a fresh analogy and not yet a doubled analogy, as some might wish to call it. Writing about stem cell research, for instance, Sarah Franklin wants to be alive to the bidirectional flow of tropes. She is interested in the likenesses between two otherwise dissimilar things—and their associated domains—in biosociality. Writing of the "analogic return," she flags "the way analogies [can] 'travel back' to change their objects." In biosociality, "the direction of analogical flow—from nature to culture—is reversed, so it flows backwards"; that is, unlike the simple " 'borrowing' of analogies in one direction ('just like nature')" we also recognize "their ability to 'travel back' ('just like technology')."[10]

Something like a doubled analogy did eventually form: mechanical recorders became the apotheosis of the receptive human analyst that Freud had envisioned, such that these recorders could now help analysts improve their own indexical receptivity. This analogic return, which was based on a likeness between psychoanalyst and interaction analyst, human recorder and mechanical recorder, each with a semiotic capacity for indexicality—did take shape, but it took some time to develop and was contested along the way. Some midcentury mechanical recording enthusiasts did come to take tropes like Freud's very seriously, suggesting an analogic return of sorts. But at first there was no widespread confidence in mechanical recording when it came to talk. It wasn't obvious that mechanical recorders could help analysts understand discourse any better than they could without them. Over time, some stuck to Freud's conviction that humans were the most gifted and sensitive of listeners; others sided with the machines, arguing that they could pick up signals of the unconscious better than any human could; still others posited a parity between the two and envisioned a happy epistemic partnership. I take note of these competing configurations of the human–technology interface in the pages that follow, but what I want to highlight, again, is an overall trajectory of indexicalization, as it was this trajectory, this shift in semiotic ideology, that made microscopic apprehension seem necessary and made discursive interaction itself into something that was intrinsically, ontologically small.

Indexicalized Media and Mechanical Objectivity

Again, why bother to record the talking cure? Let us reconsider this question as we return to a time before interaction was a widely known object of knowledge, and before it was a small-scale reality that demanded microscopic methods.

The inception of recording begins on a familiar note, with a desire by some social scientists to get "objective" records of behavior. This, at minimum, meant getting paper transcripts of what people said in a psychoanalysis session. It did *not* begin with a desire for indexicality in communication, nor even with the confidence that machines are any better at getting objective records of talk than humans equipped only with pen and paper.

In their magisterial history of objectivity, Lorraine Daston and Peter Galison chronicled how "mechanical objectivity" burst onto the scene in the midnineteenth century.[11] Their expression named a family resemblance among epistemological practices in diverse sciences, all seized by distrust of human subjectivity. While it had once been a virtue for the scientist to rely on his discerning, disciplined faculties, suspicions deepened about his mediating mind and will. In response, many wanted to reduce or eliminate this human element. "Mechanical" didn't necessarily mean machines—standardized procedure and protocol could suffice—but machines epitomized this turn from and against the subjective. This ethic of human noninterference coincided with efforts to register the real more directly and faithfully—or, as we might say, indexically. "Camera obscura tracings, photographs, and the inscriptions of self-registering instruments were all, at one time or another, *touted as nature's own utterances*" (emphasis mine).[12] Elsewhere in *Objectivity*, we hear this refrain that the mechanical suppression of subjectivity occurred alongside efforts to let nature express itself. Mechanical objectivity and mechanical inscription were two sides of the same proverbial coin.

Yet we have not always looked carefully at the inscriptional side of mechanical objectivity.[13] It is perhaps no surprise that our interest in objectivity should come at the expense of the inscriptional methods exploited in its name, because these methods were meant to bypass the humans in order to let nature speak. By spotlighting inscriptional mediation here, I want to draw out the semiotic ideologies that accompanied it, ideologies that came to prize the indexical.

It is well known that nineteenth-century mechanical objectivity was accompanied by the proliferation of "mechanical forms of writing or image making, generally with little or no intervention of the human hand."[14] This enthusiasm for inscription is evident onomastically by the spate of instrument names formed from -*graph*. Even as the graphical method iconically "represent[ed] scientific phenomena or data, by lines and points in a coordinate system,"[15] these machines got their epistemic backing from their point-by-point indexical correspondence with nature. It was indexicality that ensured that *nature* was talking.

There is a real affinity between mechanical objectivity and indexical inscription, but we should not imagine that the two always and easily go hand in hand. And yet that's what expressions like "indexical media" suggest. Used by some in media and film studies, this expression epitomizes the tendency to think that media like the photograph and film bear an intrinsic non-arbitrary relationship to the real by virtue of an indexical link that is understood narrowly as causal. Take forms of photography in which photosensitive paper is said to register faithfully—indexically—the impresses of light, for instance. Leaving aside the issue of the iconicity that is entwined with indexically here, the simple point is that light is assumed to make its mark: done. As Kris Paulsen and others have argued, this idea of indexical media has been used as a signpost in a dubious plotline of media death under digitization. For once untethered from the objects to which these media were once causally hitched, such media, the story goes, are dematerialized and subject to unfettered editing and recontextualization.[16] The problem is that "indexical media" presupposes what we need to explain: How do media come to be understood and treated *as* indexical? How, and with what effects, do such indexicalized media become objects of epistemological longing? And, most importantly for us, what effects did indexicalization have on the scale of its object, on its scalar ontology?[17]

In what follows, I show how indexical media came about. I narrate the slow, laborious, and fraught manner in which the indexical affordances of sound-recording technology became a focus of epistemological interest. We are accustomed to debates about the continuity and discontinuity of different, successive media (e.g., in transitions from radio to film), but here I focus on (dis)continuity in relation to "the same" media form as it evolves in relationship to those who hope to use it—and, in this case, use it indexically. In this respect, I build on histories that demonstrate, though seldom in these terms, that the indexicality of media technologies cannot be taken for granted.

Consider, for example, the fitful career of media indexicality in Edison's early phonograph. Some sense of indexicality always accompanied discourses of "fidelity," but these discourses were neither stable nor intuitive. Fidelity required that you first ontologically distinguish playback sounds from sources to demonstrate that the two were even linked.[18] As Emily Thompson suggests, fidelity never meant one thing because Edison's phonograph wasn't imagined to do one thing. One sense of fidelity did trumpet the phonograph's power to preserve traces of the acoustic real, a capacity we may call *indexical fidelity*; here the medial role of the recorder is downplayed—it is immediatized—as one is invited to hear playback as the vivid if not auratic presence of a spatio-temporally distinct sonic source.[19] When Edison later decided to market the phonograph for business,[20] fidelity veered toward what Thompson calls "audibility and intelligibility," where indexicality took a back seat to "the retrievable truth of the message."[21] When the Edison company again shifted marketing toward music playback, indexical fidelity returned as the "quality of tone" that created "the illusion of real presence."[22] Indexicality flitted in and out of fidelity as it followed the machine's fortunes. It wasn't always there.

Or take the inception of gramophone recordings in colonial South India, as described by Amanda Weidman. Gramophone promoters did not expect that people would immediately recognize the indexical fidelity of recordings. They would need a demonstration. Some of the earliest recordings in Madras featured Tamil mimicry artists who conjured with voice alone naturalistic scenes of urban life: trains whistling by; noisy horse-cart drivers; the chirps of birds and prattle of city denizens. You would learn to recognize the machine's indexical fidelity through comparison with an already familiar kind of *human* recorder.[23]

In studies inspired by Walter Benjamin's influential writings on the "optical unconscious," a notion he had used to consider the way new visual media seemed to expand the perceptual envelope, we often learn that media manipulation during playback is key to drawing out indexical affordances.[24] Wilf's ethnography of jazz pedagogy, for instance, details how instructors slow down playback of exemplary recordings so as to heighten the aural sensitivity of students and grant them access to an "acoustic unconscious,"[25] and a recent historical essay on Ray Birdwhistell's film-based science of embodied communication similarly spotlights media manipulation, especially frame-by-frame analysis.[26] The indexical of "indexical media" seems to need human labor.

I underline human labor here, again, not to reinstate a story of humans using media as epistemological prosthesis. This is not usefully told as a story of who was in control, the humans or the medial technologies with which they interfaced. It is rather that I want to avoid arguments that too quickly decenter humans by ceding causal agency to medial technologies, by crediting or blaming *them* for pushing humans around—and thereby deliver the moral lesson that human autonomy is illusion and hubris. As important as this decentering has been and arguably still is, we should not allow it to become a rote exercise in "causal accounting, as the figuring (out) of agency," as Paul Kockelman puts it. If we assume we know in advance who-did-what-to-whom, we will not bother to explore the interface, the entanglement, and evolving relationship of human and medial technology, as I want to do here.[27]

All of which is to say, simply, that indexicalization did not come about when people turned on recorders. Indexicalization happened *after* the strictures of mechanical objectivity were imposed and after recording had begun.[28] Indexical media formed instead through an emerging relationship, from the sense that human and machine, psychoanalyst and mechanical recorder, had a similar capacity for receptivity.[29]

Objective Transcripts: By Hand or by Machine?

In 1929 New York City and in Chicago, two researchers working independently began experimenting with sound-recording technologies that didn't require human observers. The two men—Earl F. Zinn under the auspices of the Social Science Research Council (SSRC), and Harold D. Lasswell of the University of Chicago's political science department—abandoned human stenographers and note-takers and repurposed wax-cylinder dictation machines that had been marketed for business. They wanted "objective," "verbatim" paper transcripts. Psychoanalysis had been scientifically suspect for some time, so getting transcripts was one way to begin to settle the matter, and because Zinn and Lasswell were sympathetic with the talking cure, they were, in effect, helping scientize psychoanalysis by recording it.

When Zinn and Lasswell first wanted to study psychoanalysis objectively, it was not obvious that they should even bother with mechanical recording. Their decision to use mechanical recording was not based on the assumption that it was inherently more objective than, say, human stenography, but rather because, as Freud had argued, a human observer would disrupt the intimacy of analysis.

To be sure, cinematography, with its superior visual opportunities for "objective" observation, had already attracted many sciences, including psychology and psychiatry. High-speed cinematography could slow the blur of motor disorders to reveal patterns, just as frame-by-frame analysis showed stages of pathology invisible to the naked eye. Yet the same enthusiasm did not extend to sound-recording technologies, which remained relatively unexploited by social scientists in the 1920s.[30] The visual may have once been an adjunct to sound, for "what we now call cinema was also once perceived as an 'enhanced phonography' or a 'phonography with added visuals,'"[31] but early twentieth-century psychology's use of media, for instance, was methodologically ocularcentric. This, despite the fact that there had been good examples of scientific sound analysis from the late nineteenth century,[32] and despite the fact that no less than Edison himself had envisioned his phonograph's utility for science when he cast about for its potential uses:

> The most skillful observers, listeners, and realistic novelists, or even stenographers, cannot reproduce a conversation exactly as it occurred. The account they give is more or less generalized. But the phonograph receives, and then transmits to our ears again, every least thing that was said—exactly as it was said—with the faultless fidelity of an instantaneous photograph. We shall now for the first time know what conversation really is; just as we have learned, only within a few years, through the instantaneous photograph, what attitudes are taken by the horse in motion.[33]

Like the storied chronophotography of Muybridge, whose studies of horse locomotion revealed what evaded the naked eye, so discursive interaction—"conversation"—might one day be analyzed. Edison touted his machine's indexical fidelity as he likened the phonographic to the photographic.[34]

Despite Edison's early pitch, it was only after the Second World War that social scientists began in a sustained way to exploit recordings in order to study what they took to be the indexical dimensions of human communication. Before Zinn and Lasswell, psychological studies occasionally used recorders like the Ediphone and Dictaphone dictation machines, but discourse was not the focus. In anthropology, some promoted sound recording, but this was mostly for salvage ethnography. The idea was to preserve and curate dying languages and cultures rather than produce recordings and transcripts that would allow you to study discourse itself.[35]

Even when they first decided to record mechanically, Lasswell and Zinn cared little about indexical fidelity. They originally wanted a verbatim transcript that preserved the literal, denotational, what-is-said of discourse—what many called "the content." They were fine with standard English orthography and didn't worry how its conventions might omit things. Of course they cared about *what* people said, because psychoanalysis turned on verbal signs such as free associations. For objective transcripts of "content," though, you didn't need machines. Stenography by hand was equally objective. It is telling that although Adolf Meyer promoted copious recordkeeping in psychiatric hospitals, which included "verbatim" records of his patients' spontaneous discourse rather than only paraphrases and summaries,[36] he felt, as others did, that note-taking and stenography were objective enough.[37] When Zinn began to enjoy success with dictation machines in 1930, he wrote to Meyer and argued that stenography was inferior to mechanical recording. That he had to argue this reveals the general view that you could get objective transcripts in many ways. You didn't need a machine.

As Miyako Inoue reminds us, "verbatim" names a language ideology whose motivations, practices, and effects need scrutiny.[38] Usually verbatim transcripts means a record faithful to form—minimally and prototypically, the words and expressions someone uses—in contrast to third-person perspective reporting, paraphrase, and analysis.[39]

So why turn to machines, if verbatim content is all you seek? Again, the problem was practical and clinical. How could the analyst record when he was expected to remain receptive? He couldn't stop and write, and notes written afterward would be selective due to limitations of memory. Nor could you recruit a note-taker because of a pernicious observer effect. It was to bypass this observer effect while meeting the demand for mechanical objectivity that Zinn and Lasswell decided to record.

Earl F. Zinn's Wax-Cylinder Psychoanalysis

In 1929, after seven years as executive secretary of the National Research Council's (NRC) Committee for Research on Sex Problems, Earl Zinn had a new job. He became director of the New York–based Committee for the Study of Personality, a SSRC subcommittee housed under the Committee on the Family. A private donor had asked the NRC to explore the "objective recording of psychoanalytic data," as the SSRC wrote in its annual report, adding that this was a "difficult field as yet virgin to rigorously controlled scientific exploration."[40]

The original request did not call for psychoanalysis to be recorded, only for it to be used. In December 1928, philanthropist George Coe Graves pledged $20,000 a year for three years, provided that the SSRC conduct research on "problems concerned with the interaction of personalities within the family," and, crucially, that "the psychoanalytic technique [be] one of the methods employed." Graves's request came from conversations with Zinn, and Zinn surely had had a hand in shaping what this request meant. Back in 1925 and 1926, while surveying research in Europe on behalf of the Committee on Sex, Zinn had interviewed psychologists and psychoanalysts. In a letter to Robert Yerkes, Zinn had complained that the analysts seemed unconcerned about the "scientific validity of their data" and he even proposed to convene a conference session on the "problem of research methods."[41] When Zinn reported his findings for the NRC, he added that "the Secretary is strongly of the opinion that an experimental examination of the [psychoanalytic] method is feasible, and that it would prove fruitful."[42]

The SSRC decided to proceed cautiously. Zinn's study would be exploratory.[43] As Zinn reported, "the logical first step in such an evaluation would be to collect as accurately and completely as possible the basic data of psychoanalysis, which are verbal productions of both patient and analyst during the course of an analysis."[44] He would "test and perfect the method of mechanical recording and . . . experiment with the technique of conducting analyses under these conditions."[45] In part to insulate itself from any legal fallout, the SSRC had Zinn's group go it alone and incorporate itself, whence came the "Committee for the Study of Personality, Inc."[46] Its experimental period would last up to 18 months and begin by October 1, 1929. Zinn would be its director.

Zinn requested a laboratory in New York City. He would enlist accredited analysts and hire three secretaries to transcribe discourse.[47] Aware of the sensitivity of recording, Zinn called for "tactful direction and supervision,"[48] which meant, minimally, that the analysts would secure consent for recording from their patients and that the three secretaries Zinn hired to transcribe discourse would serve as "confidential clerks." Zinn projected that "complete reports on at least four and possibly six analyses could be obtained in the time indicated by the donor, namely one year to eighteen months."[49] This proved too ambitious, as recording itself was difficult. Partnering with Alexander Graham Bell's Dictaphone Company, Zinn began trial recordings in January 1930 and by spring announced success in recording "accurately." Accuracy meant a faithful transcript of content. Although one needed to keep the hidden microphone within four feet of speakers, Zinn wrote to Adolf Meyers that he could now "record clearly ordinary conversation" and even capture speech that fell to a whisper. It was not that Zinn wanted to record how speech could sometimes fall to a whisper or spike in loudness. The *manner* of speech—including such prosodics—wasn't his aim. The *what* of speech, not the *how*, was what mattered.

Although recording machines replaced human recorders such as notetakers and stenographers, Zinn had to make these machines disappear. Dictation machines were not unobserved observers, not unless they were made so. Even when out of sight and connected by wire, they hummed and whirred. Zinn placed his out of sight in an adjoining room. He used a condenser microphone and four-stage amplifier, and his customized dictation machine featured a double mandrel for continuous recording.[50] A visible microphone and apparatus might remind speakers and hearers of third-party observers who might later listen in. Any sign of the recording apparatus could unsettle the subject, and perhaps also the analyst. The mike must not become a mechanical metonym for the human ear, lest the analysand—and analyst—feel "observed." The imagined chain of replay, a chain in principle infinite in length, could leave subjects so self-conscious that the interaction would become stilted, unnatural. It took discipline to speak comfortably before a microphone. (A 1930s advertisement for the Speak-O-Phone recorders preyed on this anxiety in businessmen. "It is no more necessary to become self-conscious when facing a microphone than when speaking through a telephone," the ad assured. Practice with the Speak-O-Phone and acquire the "knack of being natural.")[51] When efforts to record talk therapy expanded in the 1940s and 1950s, experts shared tips and reports on how best to make recording inconspicuous (see chapter 7). Zinn was able to assure Meyers that he was "successful in arranging things so that our consultation room differs in appearance not at all from the ordinary doctor's office."[52] He had engineered what he hoped was a naturalistic recording environment.

Zinn's secretaries used dedicated playback ("transcribing") machines to prepare the transcripts. As the wax cylinders had to be shaved for reuse, Zinn had them transcribed promptly and retained no permanent sound records. Once he achieved recording "accuracy"—again, in a non-indexicalized sense—Zinn turned to "quantity production" by trying to record the course of analysis for a few patients.[53]

The Chattering Body: Somatic Indexicality in
Lasswell's Exhaustive Recordings

News of Zinn's recordings reached the University of Chicago, where, as Zinn and the SSRC knew back in 1929, researchers had been up to something similar. Chicago had its own personality committee, a self-consciously interdisciplinary lot that in 1929 was readying itself for a move into the new social sciences building. As Zinn began his work in late autumn 1929, Lasswell, a psychoanalytically inclined political scientist, was gearing up for a wildly ambitious, interdisciplinary recording initiative. It would take place in room 334, the "laboratory for personality studies," which was "equipped with an exceptional range of technical instruments, designed to permit an effective record of a prolonged interview"—as Lasswell's project was known.[54] Lasswell's plans resembled Zinn's in certain basic respects. Both sought "objective" records featuring a verbatim transcript. But Lasswell wanted more. Ideally, he wanted everything, for speech was part of a vast array of facts to be collected and correlated. As he complained about the state of psychoanalytic recordkeeping, he itemized what comprehensive documentation would include.[55]

> You would want these documents to show every word which passed between the interviewer and the subject for the whole period. You would want these documents to include supplementary notes by the analyst who would report upon the physical movements of the subject during each hour. You would want at least some of these documents to present the results of accurate measuring devices which showed how some of the bodily changes actually varied throughout the interviews (the galvanic reflex, the couch movements, respiration, blood pressure, and various other phenomena can be recorded with great precision).[56]

Lasswell knew this would be laborious, so, like Zinn, he would limit himself. He narrowed his observational extent. He would "study certain selected individuals as intensively as possible by all known methods for the sake of obtaining exhaustive records." "We can cooperate in our research unit by trying all our tricks on a certain number of common subjects," wrote Lasswell to Edward Sapir.[57] As for transcription, he would do this by "invisible stenographer, or a mechanical recording device."[58] Note that he was not yet committed to mechanical recording. He assumed you could get verbatim transcripts in other ways. What he insisted on was objectivity without human observers. He cared about collecting words and said nothing about qualities of utterance and their symptomological significance.

In listing what else he wanted besides words, Lasswell was not frugal, and here was where he felt indexicality lurked, not in speech so much as in the body. He wanted the "psychoanalyst's notes on the daily interview" and the "subject's notes on the daily interview." He wanted "specimens of the subject's handwriting"—a topic Lasswell researched with University of Chicago freshmen. He'd need a "physical and psychometrical examination record," and, of course, he'd need outcome data.[59] In his best, clinical, agentless passive voice, Lasswell even proposed, "the rigidity or the flouncing of the subject on the couch should be recorded."[60]

In a Festschrift, a friend and former student poked at Lasswell's early "infatuation with objectivity," adding that this led him to use "cannons to kill flies."[61] Lasswell's empiricism may be compared with the fervent "life history" data collectors in Chicago sociology. Thomas and Znaniecki's *The Polish Peasant*—a voluminous, data-heavy study of Polish migrants in Chicago—saw the very city of Chicago as bristling with facts, which demanded field-based observation.[62] Personality was similarly a wellspring of facts.

The cannon Lasswell constructed during the 1929–1930 academic year required help from colleagues, especially the physiologists. Lasswell, who had spent six months training under the eclectic Elton Mayo at Harvard in 1926–1927, shared the latter's enthusiasm for somatic indicators of psychological states that could be measured quantitatively. In this somatic semiotics, one sought evidence of otherwise gauzy, abstract claims about mind—claims that behaviorists dismissed as unscientific—by pinpointing embodied indexes of interiority such as galvanic skin response, blood pressure, heart rate, and respiration. Ideally, these measures would all be "synchronized on the same strip of moving bromide paper film."[63]

Lasswell would get to the bottom of analysis, which for him meant getting to the body. In *Psychopathology and Politics* (1930), he recited the aphorism of the physician, from whom "no mortal can hide his secret," for "he whose lips are silent chatters with his fingertips and betrays himself through all his pores."[64] Or as Freud had put it, "He that has eyes to see and ears to hear may convince himself that no mortal can keep a secret. If his lips are silent, he chatters with his fingertips; betrayal oozes out of him at every pore."[65] As Lasswell would later argue, somatic measures reveal what speech "means," clinically speaking. "The subject who listlessly says 'Of course I hate my father' is not by this act becoming aware of hitherto repressed hatred, nor is he showing that he has necessarily achieved insight into his father hatreds"; these words are but "avowals" that must be traced to physiological states.[66] Physiological indicators formed a matrix of privileged indexicals to which all other signs, including speech, should be traced back. His research epitomized what Rebecca Lemov has called a "subjective turn" in the social sciences in which one tried to access the mind through the aperture of the body.[67] Speech was not thought to have its own indexicality; only later did he extend this sensibility to discourse, as we shall see.

Lasswell's first trial took place in spring 1930. Whereas Zinn engineered a naturalistic recording environment, Lasswell was content to remove only the human observers. His room resembled a lab, save for a couch on which the subject could recline. Lasswell sat behind a desk. Before free association began, psychologist and physician Richard Jenkins conducted a physical examination and physical anthropologist Wilton Krogman took anthropometrical measurements. As for the "verbatim record of each interview," this was recorded mechanically with a "condenser microphone . . . to pick up the sound in the interviewing room," sound "amplified and the recording done by special cutting heads on ordinary Dictaphone rolls." Lasswell didn't bother hiding the microphone. For physiological measures, Lasswell enlisted the help of psychophysiologist Nathan Shock and benefited from technical assistance from Chester William Darrow and lie detector specialist Leonard Keeler. Lasswell himself would jot down "movements of the subject," and, to synchronize these, "a time marker [would be] . . . used to make a signal on the moving film and in the acoustic machinery."[68] In his utopian lab, disciplines and data would mix and meld. His project was lauded as a paragon of cross-disciplinary inquiry (and, not inconsequentially, just the kind of project the Laura Spelman Rockefeller Memorial Fund was eager to fund[69]).

Progress was slow, however. Five years passed before Lasswell's research surfaced in print. In a 1935 article, Lasswell finally responded to those "inclined to criticize psychoanalysis for the subjectivity of the reported data." Here was a "rigorous" approach that offered "more precise recording and reporting."[70] For Lasswell's subjects rigor meant physical restraint and intrusive monitoring.

A microphone was put on a shelf by the couch; a pneumatic cuff was attached above the left ankle and maintained under constant pressure; the left hand of the subject was fitted in a special glove-like apparatus where contact was maintained on the palm and back of the hand. A pneumograph was attached to the subject's chest. Blood pressure readings were taken just after the apparatus was attached to the subject and before the beginning of the interview, and again at the close of the interview before the instruments were detached from the subject. The interviewer recorded all observable movements during the interview according to a prearranged set of symbols. Movements of the springs of the couch were originally taken but were abandoned as nondifferentiating. The continuous verbatim record was obtained by means of wax cylinders on two Dictaphones which were alternated by an assistant in an adjoining instrument room. The needles were mounted on a specially designed cutting head fitted for electrical recording (the subjects were aware of the presence of the microphone).[71]

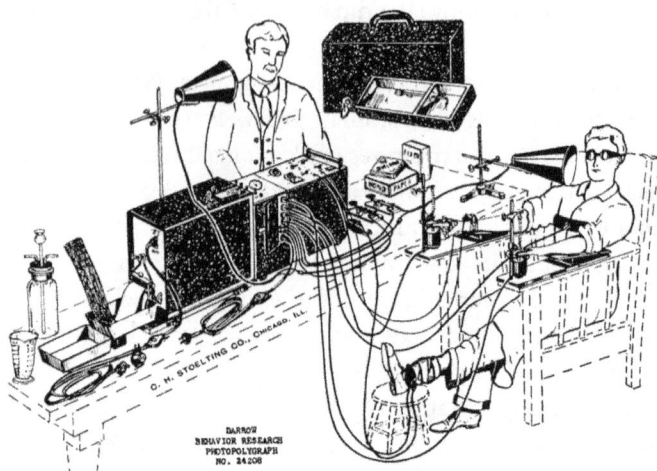

424 N. Homan Ave.

(Details on Application)

C. H. STOELTING CO.
Manufacturers · Publishers · Importers · Exporters
PSYCHOLOGICAL AND PHYSIOLOGICAL
APPARATUS AND SUPPLIES

Chicago, Ill., U.S.A.

Darrow Behavior Research Photopolygraph

FIGURE 5. To spy subjectivity through the analysand's body, Lasswell drew inspiration from Darrow's intrusive psychophysiological recorder. "Darrow Behavior Research Photopolygraph (Back Matter)," *American Journal of Psychology* 47, no. 3 (1935): i.

The scene must have resembled that of the portable photopolygraph (figure 5) developed by Darrow—a pioneer in psychophysiology who had helped Lasswell and who spent most of his career at the Institute for Juvenile Research in the department of psychiatry at the University of Illinois' College of Medicine in Chicago. Despite the intrusive setup, Lasswell now cooly played the part of psychoanalyst. Though he had not trained in psychoanalysis as Zinn would later do, Lasswell got some practice doing talk therapy under Mayo.

> The general procedure closely resembled the orthodox psychoanalytic interview. The subject reclined on a couch, the interviewer sat behind and out of sight of the subject. The subject was instructed to say without reservation everything that crossed his mind. The interviewer seldom intervened.[72]

Lasswell never got his exhaustive account. For one, it wasn't easy to record speech clearly and continuously—even without the challenges of engineering a naturalistic setting. A year after starting, Chicago's personality committee complained that its "present sound-recording apparatus [was] proving unreliable." Noting Zinn's success in "the only other verbatim recording experiment," the committee proposed another $1,500 to get the equipment Zinn had been using.[73]

In early 1932, the SSRC began pressuring Lasswell to make progress and publish. "Have the records [been] synchronized as far as possible? Are the records as complete as possible?" the SSRC probed. They complained that there "appear to be no psychiatric records nor autobiographical and case records" and advised that Lasswell should "spend time on the analysis and editing in full of one case which would be examined by a larger committee."[74] In spring 1933, Lasswell asked for more money, arguing that his results seemed to "warrant the preparation of a book which will reprint illustrative interviews which are carefully edited and show how changes in verbal reference are connected with physical changes."[75] The next year he promised a "brief manuscript."[76] Growing impatient, the SSRC voted that Lasswell "wind up the present phase of the study and to prepare material for publication."[77] The "book" Lasswell envisioned in 1933 shrank to a "brief manuscript" in 1934 and then fragmented into articles. As with his research, Lasswell had to settle for less.

Incipient Indexicalization in Zinn's Trove of Transcripts

Zinn published nothing from his early trials and didn't need to, though he shared advice on sound recording. In fall 1931 Zinn, who only had a master's degree, sailed to Europe to train for a year at the Berlin Psychoanalytic Institute, where he worked closely with Hanns Sachs and brought his transcripts to share with the Berlin group.[78] When he returned, misfortune struck. Zinn's donor Graves died suddenly on a boat set for the South Seas.

Zinn tried to access the moneys left by Grave, and after some legal wrangling, he got about half. But in the end, he left New York in 1933 for a two-year research stint at Worcester State Hospital in Massachusetts. Not only did he propose recording an entire course of psychoanalysis—a goal that had apparently eluded him; he also aimed at a "thorough-going testing of the psychoanalytic hypothesis."[79] Now trained in psychoanalysis, Zinn would be the analyst. During his stay, Zinn served as house analyst and logged many hours with David Shakow, who was director of research.[80]

Zinn focused on a single schizophrenic patient, a man in his early twenties who lived in a locked ward at the hospital and had to be escorted to and from Zinn's office.[81] His analysis lasted from autumn 1933 to early summer 1936. When Zinn left Worcester for Yale's Institute of Human Relations (IHR) in late 1935, he had the patient transferred to Yale's facilities. At Worcester, Zinn had kept the recording a secret, disclosing it to the patient only upon his arrival at Yale.

Zinn participated in the IHR's Monday seminars and sometimes shared his material with colleagues, but, to his frustration, he never managed to publish an analysis of his transcripts. In 1939, he let them go. Typists prepared four copies of his six-volume set of some 3,000 pages, titled, somewhat misleadingly, *A Psychoanalytic Study of a Schizophrenic*. This wasn't a study but a

November 19, 1933

No. 1

A. Would you let me get through here? We haven't got much space,
we're pretty crowded. Do you want to sit up here?
P. All right.
A. Do you smoke?
P. Yes sir, I do. Thank you.
A. So do I. (Short pause) Well, I've been trying for some time
to arrange to see you. I'm interested in your problem and I should
like to see whether I can help you. (This sentence is not clear.)
I expect to be here for some time and I would like to try to help
you if you think we can work together. (Medium pause)
P. Well, I don't know, I think we can. I haven't any problems
especially now. I guess I'm just down here, that's all. (Short
pause) I get--I get all--I don't know, I'm straight and then I'm
crooked and then I'm straight again and everything else.
A. How do you feel this morning?
P. Well, I'm just out, that's all. I don't know. I'm all right.
A. Well, I can arrange for you to come here every day and when you
feel like working, we can do some work. If there should be times
when you don't feel like working, why you just tell me and I'll wait
till you do.
P. All right.
A. And I think we may learn something that will help you.
P. Well - - - I haven't any--I don't know - - I haven't any particular problem. I just sort of - - you're treating me just as though
- well, as though I had a problem down here. I haven't got any at
all. There's nothing that matters to me especially because I---I'm
just with them, that's all. I'm trying to be with them. (Medium
pause)

FIGURE 6. Partial and asymmetrical indexicalization in Zinn's psychoanalytic transcript. Earl F. Zinn, *A Psychoanalytic Study of a Schizophrenic* (New Haven, CT: Institute of Human Relations, Yale University, 1939), p. 1.

trove of transcripts spanning 424 sessions. Save for a few that he summarized because of technical troubles, Zinn supplied the world with data. "These volumes contain only the raw data of this study," he wrote, for "I have purposely refrained from intruding my views, except insofar as they are inherent in my role as analyst."[82] The last volume included "extra-analytic material": diaries of the mother and patient, a "baby book" with excerpts "containing references to his activities, health, 'cute sayings,' etc.," and a summary of the hospital record.[83]

As artifacts, transcripts are unavoidably selective and betray how one conceptualizes discourse and interaction.[84] In Zinn's case his transcripts resembled a typical playscript format that chunked speech into speaking turns with line breaks for turn boundaries. Speakers were indicated most often by role categories, "A" for analyst, "P" for patient. Proper names were changed or redacted. Standard orthography was used, as Zinn wasn't trained to follow the linguists and use a phonetics alphabet.

That Zinn's transcripts reveal a degree of indexicalization is evident by the details he included. To observe transference and all the resistances that crop up, he transcribed behavior that did not contribute to denotational text.

Unusual behavior, such as laughter, weeping, shouting, etc., have been indicated parenthetically in the text where they occurred, as well as breaks in the flow of associations. These latter have been indicated as "pause," "medium pause," "long pause."[85]

Zinn also flagged major embodied behaviors and events: the lighting of cigarettes, the opening or closing of doors, noise from the hall. As for conventions, he was not consistent, perhaps because different secretaries did the work; perhaps also because he had to recycle his wax cylinders and couldn't retranscribe recordings for consistency. It wasn't clear, for example, how he evaluated pause lengths (judgment of transcriber, the result of measurement, some combination thereof?), and the conventions themselves sometimes varied. Some transcripts were improbably free of pauses, suggesting that someone forgot to transcribe them. In listing his transcription conventions, Zinn neglected to mention that he had also transcribed variation in speech delivery such as false starts, cut-off speech, and repetitions (e.g., "It's about—about—it's called"[86]). Speech overlap, interpreted as "interruptions," was usually indicated parenthetically. Even the contemplative response cry "hmm" occasionally appeared.

Zinn may have watched for countertransference, but his own stream of communication seemed suspiciously fluid; pauses were seldom marked and never in a context that might reveal something psychological about him. False starts, repetitions, and dysfluencies were also indicated for the patient but rarely for the analyst and, again, never in a way that invited symptomological readings. Aside from this transcriptional asymmetry, Zinn did try to preserve some symptomological details. It is unclear what his transcripts from 1930 looked like, but his comments at the time suggest that indexicality was, at the very least, not a priority. The SSRC had also insisted that he only explore the feasibility of recording and transcription and not assess psychoanalysis. Yet Zinn's six-volume set that began mid-decade and appeared at the decade's close suggests a measure of indexicalization. His transcript preserved some indexical traces, even if there is little evidence that he actually analyzed these microscopically.

That Zinn began to draw out the indexical potential of mechanical recording is evident when, at the end, he expressed regret about everything he missed. "Complete objectification of the psychoanalytic procedure should include visual and auditory data in addition to verbal content. These constitute no small part of the total impression."[87] Zinn knew that there were traces of interiority that he had failed to capture and transcribe. Zinn also had a hard time making their indexicality analytically legible, a problem compounded, no doubt, by the sheer volume of his collection. Time and again he expressed frustration at not having published an analysis. Other scholars—notably Carl Rogers, who stumbled upon Zinn's work rather late—borrowed his volumes, two sets of which sat on shelves at Yale. In his preface, Zinn made a final promise to publish, but that never happened, and by the mid-'40s, Zinn left Yale, and the academy.

Discourse Indexicality in Lasswell's Late Trials

Lasswell, too, stumbled upon indexicality in discourse only late into his project. In a 1935 article entitled "Verbal References and Physiological Changes During the Psychoanalytic Interview,"[88] Lasswell summarized tentative correlations between speech and body that suggested a more indexical orientation toward conversation. Slowed speech rate, for instance, was associated with increased psychophysiological tension (as measured through heart rate and galvanic skin response), an association that offered a window onto psychoanalytic process. Speech rate—a prosodic quality of speech—had become indexicalized. But it was in a 1938 methodological essay, after his research was over, that Lasswell's indexical sensibility spread. He now used his psychoanalytic studies to propose methods for coding discourse that could be extended to "interpersonal relationships" generally.[89]

> The study of interpersonal relationships is held back by the absence of satisfactory categories for the description and comparison of symbols. Although the present discussion is conducted with reference to the psychoanalytic interview situation, the categories which are proposed are often directly transferable to many other symbolic situations in society.[90]

Lasswell's essay suggested a new if limited interest in the indexicalities of discourse. He had chased correlations between speech and body and had privileged the body, yet now he seemed to recognize that speech had its own indexical signs. Of interest were participant deictics like *I* and *you*, whose denotational meaning derives from the context of utterance. In contemporary parlance, deictic expressions are referential indexicals, but Lasswell seemed to realize that these could also have *non*-referential indexical relevance, too ("nonreferential," much as a perceived accent can index demographic facts about a speaker irrespective of what that speaker is talking about).[91] If a patient, for example, starts pointing to the immediate, here-and-now therapy event using deictics and referring "directly" to the analyst, this may be clinically relevant. The transcripts required for this type of discourse analysis would not need to be terribly detailed, because indexicality was not pervasive and not also to be found in, say, the qualities of the human voice or in the way speakers may pause, speed up and slow down, raise or lower their voice, and so on. Lasswell never treated the transcript as an indexically *saturated* text, which would have required him to transcribe and pore over less discourse with more care.

✶

There was little recording-based talk therapy research in the 1930s and a lot of it beginning in the years after the Second World War, when American interest in psychoanalysis peaked.[92] By midcentury, many researchers recorded and analyzed talk therapies, be it classical psychoanalysis or Rogerian client-centered psychotherapy. The newly founded National Institute of Mental Health (NIMH) funded much of this research, with some venturing from sound recording to sound film.[93] It was during this ferment that some came to search intensively for indexicals using recordings. The indexicalization that began during Zinn and Lasswell's recording efforts flourished in the mid to late 1950s—again, in recording-based research on talk therapy, as we will see next.

Lasswell and Zinn weren't the only ones after indexicality, to be sure, and Lasswell especially owed much to two other men in his circle, Edward Sapir and Harry Stack Sullivan. Each had hoped to study indexicality with mechanical recordings of talk, but unlike Lasswell, they didn't get very far. For Sapir, who cared about talk rather than specifically talk therapy, the interest in indexicality was largely aspirational.[94] When Lasswell began his project, he did so in conversation with Sapir, who had famously helped draw psychiatry into the domain of the social sciences in the mid-1920s, and this included the science of linguistics in which he specialized.

Indeed, it was this coming together of psychiatry and communication science that arguably facilitated the idea of what we may call *the communicative unconscious*. Speech betrays facts about speakers. Freud had newly theorized this truism, yet might it be that linguistics could lend a hand? Could linguistic analysis—using recording machines, especially—help one understand the truth of this truism, perhaps more precisely and objectively than what the psychoanalyst could offer?

In midcentury America, when scholars sought indexicality in psychiatric recordings, quite a few came to credit Sapir for having started it all, specifically through his 1927 essay, "Speech as a Personality Trait." (Unsurprisingly, for those on the clinical side of research, it was Freud's writings on telltale speech that mattered more.) "Speech is intuitively interpreted by normal human beings as an index of personal expression," the abstract of Sapir's essay began. Could a linguist figure out *how* these judgments were actually reached, and what the exact vocal triggers were? "We can go over the entire speech situation without being able to put our finger on the precise spot in the speech complex that leads to our making this or that personality judgment." And the voice, Sapir added, is obviously not the only source of "unconscious symbolisms." "If you wrinkle your brow, that is a symbol of a certain attitude," and "if you act expansively by stretching out your arms, that is a symbol of a changed attitude to your immediate environment."[95]

Here was the communicative unconscious. Although Sapir did not make this argument in this essay, he soon came to feel that you needed recording technologies to get at the indexicalities of speech. In 1929, just as Lasswell was busy planning his recording initiative, Sapir had been eager to try his hand at recording too, and for reasons that were even more self-consciously indexical than Lasswell's initial efforts.

> We are hoping, at the University of Chicago, in the setup which Dr. Lasswell referred to this morning, to install a device for the exact recording of speech, which can then be studied at leisure in order that we may work out some of the more obvious traits of personality which are revealed in speech. [...] As a matter of fact, we react to speech keenly in ordinary life. It is perfectly obvious that our judgments of people and of situations are, to a large extent, due to such phenomena as tone of voice, chronic hesitation in speech, and all the rest of the voice and speech characters, only these impressions are never formulated in so many words. Indeed our vocabulary for peculiarities of voice and for ways of handling speech is strangely limited. One of the things we should like to do is develop such a vocabulary on the basis of almost microscopic study of actual speech records. As I say, I have no results at all; I have everything to learn.[96]

An "almost microscopic study" of speech records. Sapir, by 1930, was particularly eager to get his hands on a Speak-O-Phone brand recorder, which inscribed sound onto aluminum disks. With recording and playback, he hoped to undertake a "study of personality aspects of the human voice."[97]

Lasswell was also in close orbit with the psychiatrist Harry Stack Sullivan, architect of an influential "interpersonal" psychiatry, which argued, against Freudian drive theory, that interactions with others shaped personality. Before Sapir left Chicago for Yale, he and Lasswell had tried to get their mutual friend Sullivan an appointment at the University of Chicago. Sapir's interest in the communicative unconscious, and the idea that you could capture it with the help of recording technologies, was not simply shared by Sullivan. Sullivan had already been exploring this possibility before he met Sapir.

Sullivan worked at the Sheppard and Enoch Pratt psychiatric clinic in Baltimore from 1923 to 1930, and by 1926, after he had become director of

clinical research, he led efforts to type up doctor–patient interactions, to create "verbatim" records through stenography.[98] In 1925, before he met Sapir,
Sullivan envisioned that phonographic recordings could help him transcribe
talk more accurately. Recordings could help pinpoint variation in the voice
("tonal qualities," "register," "sharpness of enunciation") that indexed affect.[99]
Sullivan liked to stress that a clinician had to pay careful attention to what
people actually said in a psychiatric interview, in order to figure out what they
were truly experiencing.

In their efforts to get their friend Sullivan to the University of Chicago,
Sapir and Lasswell had Sullivan submit a proposal for what he'd do there.
Sullivan outlined a recording initiative bolder than even Lasswell's. More
machines would be deployed. He'd pull out all the stops. Besides an "apparatus for recording extensive interviews verbatim" and all the instruments for
physiological recording, as Lasswell used, Sullivan went further by proposing
"photographic (including stereographic and cinematographic) equipment."[100]

Sullivan's appointment fell through; Lasswell left Chicago in the 1930s;
Sapir's hope to exploit the Speak-O-Phone never materialized and he left
Chicago for Yale. For Lasswell, as for Zinn, indexicalization came—but came
late and the momentum flagged. The aspiration to get at the communicative
unconscious through mechanical recording had been seeded, but a mediatic
indexical science of communication did not materialize until the period after
the Second World War, by which time the memory of Zinn's and Lasswell's
recording efforts had largely faded.

The First Five Minutes

It had not been easy to record. When Harold Lasswell, Harry Stack Sullivan, and Edward Sapir envisioned using recorders to help them undertake an "almost microscopic," as Sapir put it, study of the communicative unconscious, they did not anticipate that it would take so long or that this goal would ultimately elude them.

Still, they could at least imagine the discoveries they'd make. In his introduction to interpersonal psychiatry published in 1938, Sullivan conjured the scene well. Here was how he'd catch the communicative unconscious. Imagine, Sullivan proposes, a hypothetical married couple, Mr. and Mrs. A. It should be possible to use mechanical, microscopic prosthesis to notice every little way the two react. Of course we cannot trust what the couple says *about* their relations, Sullivan cautions. When asked what he thinks of their relationship, Mr. A insists that his wife is "uniformly amiable to him." He is wrong. His own reactions tell a different story. He "tells more than he knows."[1]

The hypothetical story Sullivan unspools is mundane. It starts with a verbal slight from wife to husband. As if replaying the interactional scene in slow motion with high-speech cinematography, Sullivan invites readers to observe along with him, to see exactly how Mr. A reacts to her words. "He glanced *sharply* at her and looked away *very swiftly*. The postural tensions in some parts of his face—if not, indeed, in other of his skeletal muscles changed *suddenly*, and then changed again, more *slowly*" (emphasis mine).

Sullivan probes deeper—into Mr. A's body. Imagine now that this same man had been given barium milk, so that we can see the "tone of the muscles in his alimentary canal by aid of the fluoroscope at the time that Mrs. A disturbs him." Sullivan pinpoints Mr. A's interpersonal tension as corresponding gastrointestinal tension. Here the pace of Sullivan's observational writing

slows to a crawl, as he draws out and granularizes description: "We have noticed that the shadows cast by the barium in the fluid that fills his stomach
and small intestines is of a certain character. The insult comes. We observe,
from change in the shape and position of the shadow, that the tone of his
stomach walls is changing. His pylorus is becoming much more tense, may
actually develop a spasm. The lumen or internal diameter of the small intestines is diminishing; their muscular walls are now more tense." The clinical
observations continue in this way for several lines more, after which Sullivan
turns, at last, to the tells of talk:

> Now if also in our apparatus for augmenting our observational abilities, we
> had included a device for phonographically recording the speech and adventi-
> tious vocal phenomena produced by Mr. A, we would have found interesting
> data in the field of this peculiarly expressive behavior. Here, too, there would
> appear a series of phenomena, beginning, perhaps, with an abrupt subvocal
> change in the flow of the breath. There might appear a rudimentary sort of
> a gasp. A rapid inhalation may be coincident with the shift in postural ten-
> sion that we observed in the skeletal muscles. There may then have been a
> respiratory pause. When Mr. A speaks, we find that his voice has changed
> its characteristics considerably, and we may secure, in the record of his first
> sentence, phonographic evidence of a continuing shift of the vocal apparatus,
> first towards an "angry voice" and then to one somewhat expressive of a state
> of weary resignation. In brief, with refinements of observational technique
> applied to the performances of Mr. A as an organism, we find that we can no
> longer doubt that he experienced, even if he did not perceive, the personal
> significance of Mrs. A's hostile remark.

For Sullivan in the 1930s, this was all still a thought experiment. The search
for indexicality started slowly in the '30s, but this tilt in semiotic ideology toward indexicalization became pronounced in the 1950s and '60s, a time when
research on talk therapy and on interaction took off. Some ventured deep
into the indexical wilds of interpersonal life, much as Sullivan, Lasswell, and
Sapir had hoped. There were now spectacularly indexicalized studies of face-
to-face talk that involved experimentation with recording technologies, none
more striking than *The First Five Minutes: A Sample of Microscopic Interview
Analysis.*

Indexical Saturation

The First Five Minutes epitomized the extremes to which indexicalization
could lead.[2] The book had its origins in an influential collaboration. Coauthor
and linguist Charles Hockett had participated in an interdisciplinary sound

film initiative that began in 1955 at the Center for Advanced Study in the
Behavioral Sciences (CASBS) in Palo Alto and concluded, somewhat disap-
pointingly, in 1968.[3] The "Natural History of an Interview" (NHI), as it came
to be called, had gathered linguists Norman McQuown and Charles Hockett,
as well as psychoanalysts, psychiatrists, and anthropologists to collaborate on
what at first was intended to be a "fine-grained analysis" of a short filmed psychotherapeutic interaction. Neo-Freudian psychiatrist Frieda Fromm-Reichmann
started the collaboration. Not coincidentally, she had worked closely in Maryland with her colleague Harry Stack Sullivan, who, again, had argued for the
interpersonal in psychiatry and who was an indexicalist when it came to the
speech of a patient. The subtle tells of talk-in-interaction would lead you to an
understanding of a patient's true condition, and recording technologies could
help the analyst catch, store, and retrieve these. *The First Five Minutes*, which
benefited from support from the recently formed National Institute for Mental Health, shared much with the CASBS initiative, except that it examined
less data and used sound rather than sound film.[4]

As its title proclaimed, *The First Five Minutes* limited itself to just five
minutes of psychotherapeutic interaction. It offered a self-consciously microscopic approach to interaction that treated the transcript as *indexically
saturated*, where anything—any transcribable sign—could be a candidate
for indexical interpretation.[5] While conceding that even this transcript was
incomplete—it only covered speech—this was, the coauthors wrote, "our best
attempt to represent all those audible items that ordinary English spelling
omits: the pronunciation of the successive words, the intonation, the location and duration of pauses, hems and haws, sighs, gasps, coughs and throat-
clearings, and such variables as rate of speech, register, volume, and tone-
quality" (figure 7).[6]

As coauthor Robert Pittenger, a psychiatrist, emphasized after the book
was published, they had needed to represent "minute variations in intonation,
volume and so on," because through these variations "we communicate feelings which are often subtle, of great range, but of which very frequently we
who speak them, and others who take them in, are quite unaware."[7] Mechanical recording was no longer just a means to ensure non-intrusive mechanical
objectivity. Analysis was now unimaginable without machines, for how else
could you be faithful to the indexical plenitude of life? Psychiatrist Henry
Brosin, who interacted with Hockett through the CASBS–NHI collaboration,
would look back upon works like Freud's *Psychopathology of Everyday Life*
(1901) and read it as a call to study all that people unintentionally "give off"
and not just what they intentionally "give," to use Erving Goffman's distinction.[8] This was an indexicalized view of communication in which every tic,

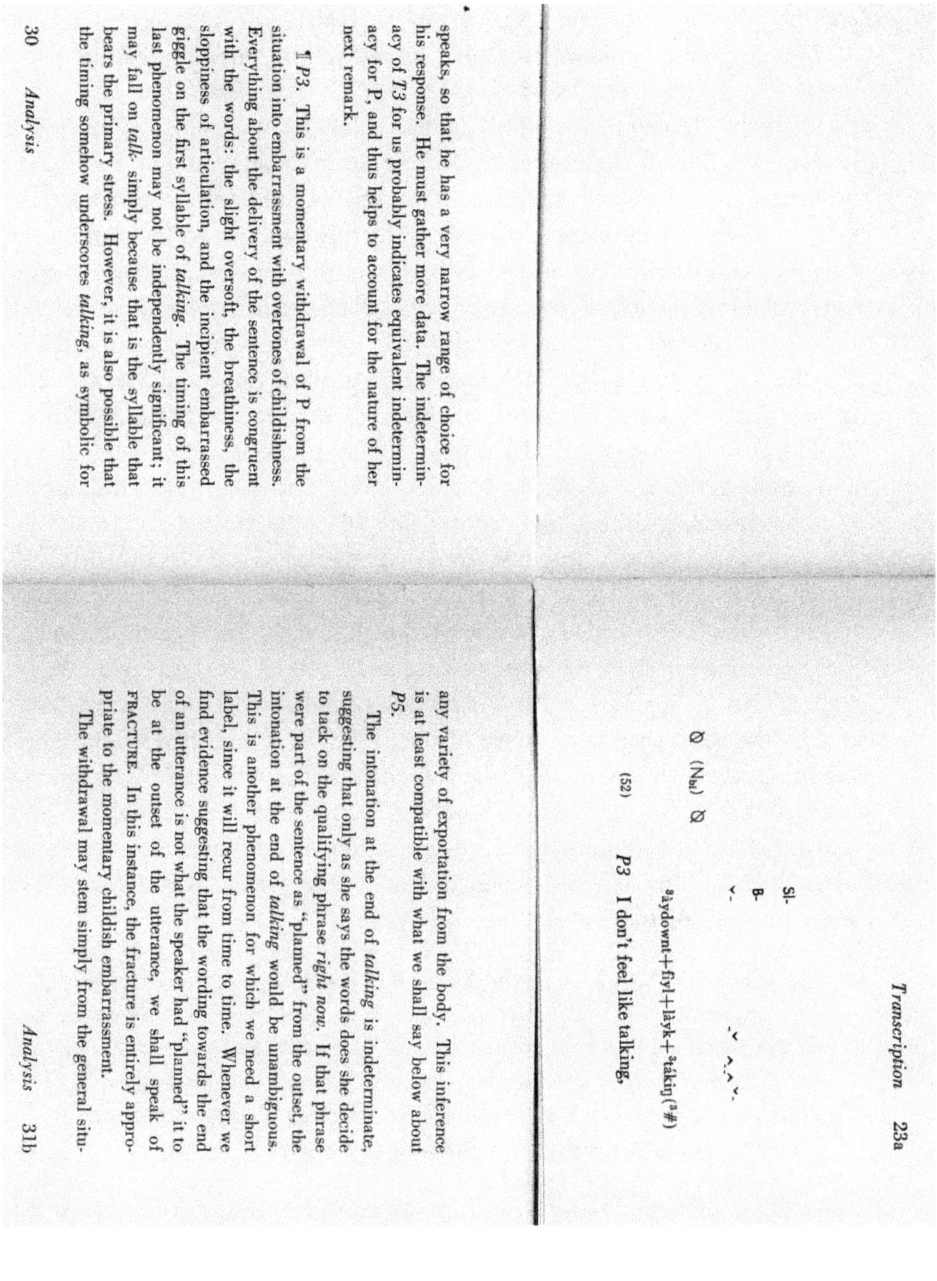

SI-
8-
ˇ-   ˇ ^.^ˇ.

Ø (Nʷ) Ø ^{3}aydown+fiyl+läyk+²tákiŋ(^{3}#)

(52)   P3   I don't feel like talking.

speaks, so that he has a very narrow range of choice for his response. He must gather more data. The indeterminacy of T3 for us probably indicates equivalent indeterminacy for P, and thus helps to account for the nature of her next remark.

¶ P3. This is a momentary withdrawal of P from the situation into embarrassment with overtones of childishness. Everything about the delivery of the sentence is congruent with the words: the slight oversoft, the breathiness, the sloppiness of articulation, and the incipient embarrassed giggle on the first syllable of *talking*. The timing of this last phenomenon may not be independently significant; it may fall on *talk-* simply because that is the syllable that bears the primary stress. However, it is also possible that the timing somehow underscores *talking*, as symbolic for

any variety of exportation from the body. This inference is at least compatible with what we shall say below about P5.

The intonation at the end of *talking* is indeterminate, suggesting that only as she says the words does she decide to tack on the qualifying phrase *right now*. If that phrase were part of the sentence as "planned" from the outset, the intonation at the end of *talking* would be unambiguous. This is another phenomenon for which we need a short label, since it will recur from time to time. Whenever we find evidence suggesting that the wording towards the end of an utterance is not what the speaker had "planned" it to be at the outset of the utterance, we shall speak of FRACTURE. In this instance, the fracture is entirely appropriate to the momentary childish embarrassment.

The withdrawal may stem simply from the general situ-

FIGURE 7. Indexical saturation in *The First Five Minutes* (1960), p. 168. Transcript features phonemic and paralinguistic detail and a "Dutch door" design that separates observation from analysis.

every aborted sentence, every interruption demanded inspection. The result was a lopsided book that treated snippets of speech to copious exegesis. One reviewer raised an eyebrow at a four second pause unpacked with a 40-word commentary for the patient and 45 for the therapist.[9]

Indexicalization and microscopic analysis were entwined. Zinn had wanted "quantity" to see the whole arc of analysis for an individual. Lasswell, too, had chased quantity. After all, he had called his study that of the "prolonged" psychoanalytic interview. Quantity didn't matter in *The First Five Minutes*. Rather than compare reams of transcripts, this book sampled a small swatch whose threads were magnified. Militantly naturalistic, the coauthors defended this diminution of data in part by railing against the "overweening drive for quick nomothetic results of high statistical reliability, whatever the cost in relevance."[10] They protested the processing of human subjects in "batches." They pointedly shrank interaction to show what could be learned from a narrow band of life. When interaction was indexically saturated, you could learn a lot from a little. Here was an inverse correlation between grain and extent: the more indexically saturated interaction was, the less discourse you could examine. Interaction could shrink till it asymptotically approached a singularity: a proverbial grain of sand that revealed, hopefully, a world.

This diminution of data collection was surely also a practical concession to the demands of the mediatic microscope. It was hard to look this closely. The challenges recall those faced by Zinn and Lasswell, who expressed frustration with their progress. Zinn expressed trepidation when he wrote that this is "the best sense I can make of this welter of complexity."[11] Before he began, Lasswell confessed that "the bulk of a verbatim report of an hour's conversation per day over several months is almost overwhelming" but insisted that just as historians are "accustomed to plow through whole libraries of pages about Napoleon or Bismarck," so he would persevere.[12] Lasswell also sensed something more unsettling.

> The phenomena which are discernible at any cross section of the personality are inexhaustible. If the observer tries to enumerate all the body movements, all the electronic gyrations, all the *nuances* of social adjustment which are thinkable in such a cross section, he is likely to become lost in aimless classification. Such an observer is quite likely to prove unable to discover hypotheses about the connections between one variable and another.[13]

Recalling ethnomethodologist and interactionist Harold Garfinkel, we may speak of Lasswell's fear as the haunt of the *plenum*, the inexhaustible "fullness" of reality imagined to loom at the edge of the empiricist's categories and methods.[14] Like the "great, blooming, buzzing confusion" of concrete experience that William James imputed to infants,[15] Lasswell feared an elemental state of near infinite complexity that his empiricism had to hold at bay. As a safeguard, he'd set up a perimeter. After all, how could something bounded in time and space—an interview in a lab, bookended with a beginning and end, inscribed on wax cylinders and other instruments—become unmanageable? The spatiotemporal containment he engineered and the moat of colleagues he gathered around him to study "the same" thing fostered the expectation that he should be able to contain the threat of the plenum. Even so, he recognized the need for disciplined if not blinkered observation. As Lasswell proposed finally in 1938, the best discipline was to go thin, to develop highly schematic coding systems to test hypotheses and avoid getting lost in the blooming, buzzing fullness of interpersonal reality.

In *The First Five Minutes*, the tactic for handling the plenum was to shrink interaction much, much more. Indexical saturation ran so deep that five minutes of interaction would suffice and could, in fact, still overwhelm you. "One fears and avoids direct encounter with human behavior, in all its incredible complexity, as one would shun a Gorgon's glance," the coauthors wrote.[16]

> It is true that the more directly and intently we examine the behavior of single human beings, the more complexity we see. A single glimpse in sharp focus can make the investigator stand aghast, if not petrified; he may decide, for the sake of his own ego, not to look again. But if he can persevere, in due time he discovers that the complexity, no matter how incredible, is not random but *patterned*. The members of any single human community share literally thousands of behavioral conventions which are as dominant as our rule of keeping to the right [on the road], but which are much more subtle than that because they are learned, acted, responded to, and taught almost entirely out of awareness.[17]

Like the indexicalized transcript and the recorder that helped produce it, here was an indexically saturated take on interaction. Too fast and subtle to be grasped in real time, interaction could only be known after the fact, with recordings. This technosemiotics differed from that of projective tests (e.g., Rorschach, Thematic Apperception), which also promised access to an unconscious, as it were. As Rebecca Lemov details, projective tests, which were enormously popular in midcentury American social sciences, could slice through exteriors like an X-ray to reveal "what the individual does not want to tell . . . and what he himself does not know."[18] For projective tests to grant access to interiors, you elicited behavior using an experimental stimulus. You would get a subject to find form in an amorphous inkblot, for instance. By contrast, the multimodal semiotics of interaction epitomized by *The First*

Five Minutes assumed that the unconscious was *immanent* in communication. It was waiting to be transcribed. It needed no cause to show itself.

Methodologically, one practical problem with this microanalysis was that less really was more. The more indexically saturated the transcript, the more meticulously you had to transcribe. These five minutes took Hockett somewhere between 25 and 35 hours.[19] Norman McQuown, another linguist from the NHI project, once spelled out how painstaking transcription and analysis can be. "About 120 hours were required to transcribe phonetically the first half-hour of the interview," he reported, and another "20 hours to retranscribe a fifth of this material and analyze it functionally."[20]

Even with so little, *The First Five Minutes* coauthors never seemed to touch bottom interpretively, as suggested by their searching, painstaking exegesis.

> *P3.* This is a momentary withdrawal of P from the situation into embarrassment with overtones of childishness. Everything about the delivery of the sentence is congruent with the words: the slight oversoft, the breathiness, the sloppiness of articulation, and the incipient embarrassed giggle on the first syllable of *talking*. The timing of this last phenomenon may not be independently significant; it may fall on *talk* simply because that is the syllable that bears the primary stress. However, it is also possible that the timing somehow underscores *talking*, as symbolic for any variety of exportation from the body. [. . .]. The intonation at the end of *talking* is indeterminate, suggesting that only as she says the words does she decide to tack on the qualifying phrase *right now.* [. . .] In part she may be saying, "I haven't said much yet, really; that is, because I am not in the mood to say much, since I don't know you nor how you will respond."[21]

It took nearly three pages of analysis to dissect the patient's line, "I don't feel like talking," and the conclusions were cautious. The authors were at pains to show their work, forensically separating out and citing the specific qualities of talk that had triggered their inferences. How dense and ruminative this close reading was.

It is perhaps not surprising that the authors should want to be exhaustive—to discuss every transcribed detail, rather than prioritize a few telltale signs that might have mattered more than others in terms of their clinical significance. Anything, after all, can potentially reveal *something* about a speaker, so what is—and, crucially, what *isn't*—indexical? And even if you suspected *that* a sign was indexically relevant, this alone wasn't terribly informative; it was often no mean hermeneutic feat to show what an index "really" pointed to. Peirce was acutely aware of this problem, arguing that indexicals are inherently under-determined—as was psychoanalytic hermeneutics. A 1938 essay on silence, for instance, reminded analysts that silence could not

THE FIRST FIVE MINUTES

be assumed to be a sign of resistance. It could index an "acting out of the silent behavior of the analyst" at one moment, an "expression of anal obstinacy and anal aggression" at another.[22]

Reducing transcription to five minutes of interaction was an understandable response to indexical saturation. Less transcription should make microscopy manageable, even if it could never dispel the sense that more indexicality lurked. And if you couldn't put your finger on the communicative unconscious, perhaps you needed to look *more* finely. An analogous cycle of frustration and intensified microscopy appears in Eitan Wilf's study of jazz pedagogy. When students slowed playback of a master's difficult passage, this ironically increased acoustic complexity and made it more challenging to imitate; this frequently incited closer listening in a dynamic of "asymptotic approximation" in which they could never quite reach the source.[23] Here, it was perhaps more common to complain not about insufficient transcriptional granularity but insufficient indexical fidelity. Richer recordings were needed. "The fullest sort of observational procedure" would be "a film with not only a soundtrack but also an olfactory track, a taste track, and a touch track. There can be no question but that human beings communicate via all these sensory modalities."[24]

Apart from the generative tensions of this microanalytic methodology, we should observe how indexicality created a bundle of needs: analysts "need" mechanical recording for accuracy understood in terms of indexical fidelity; they "need" to convert that recording into an indexically faithful transcript in order to make that indexicality epistemological available—something they can know; they then "need" fine-grained, microscopic analysis to retrieve the indexicality from the transcribed text. And for such methods to succeed, they must listen to *less*—a move motivated by indexical saturation and by the need to contain the threat of the plenum. Discursive interaction became scaled as a small thing that required microscopic scrutiny.

Indexicalization in this way affected many things. It was never exclusively about media inscription. It encompassed the technics of recording and playback, conventions for transcribing discourse onto paper, styles of close analysis. It even suggested what kind of creature the human analyst was; in this case, a being endowed with the capacity (if limited) to sense, store, and retrieve the indexical signals of other humans. When it came to mechanical recorders, the indexically saturated transcript paralleled a new appreciation for what recording technology could do. It approximated and drew out affordances of the technologies used to produce it, namely, their capacity for indexical fidelity. This fidelity was one sense of accuracy,[25] an accuracy that had rarely been exploited in social-scientific sound recordings and never for knowledge about discursive interaction. What is more, indexicalization was never only about knowing. It also affected scalar ontology, for under strong indexicalization, discursive interaction *itself* was now a thing teeming with tacit little signs.

Psychiatry and the Science of Interaction

Research on talk therapies using recording technologies had started slowly in the 1930s, yet this type of research accelerated after the Second World War, when the sciences of social interaction also began to coalesce. Wax-cylinder dictation machines gave way to diverse recording technologies, including sound recording on disc and magnetic tape, and, especially in the '60s, synchronized 16mm sound film. In the 1950s, Shakow sat on the faculty at the University of Illinois College of Medicine, and then became chief of the Laboratory of Psychology at the National Institute of Mental Health (NIMH). But back when he was director of psychology research at Worcester State Hospital in the 1930s, he was fascinated by visiting researcher Earl Zinn and his sound recordings of psychoanalytic sessions.[26] For years, Shakow patiently gathered information about recording technologies. The Speak-O-Phone, which cut sound records on aluminum—a machine Sapir had hoped to get. The Gray Audograph, which recorded on paper-thin Flexograph plastic discs and had been used by the military. The Bell and Howell 16mm Filmosound Recording Projector—synchronized sound film being for many the gold standard.

The midcentury indexicalization epitomized by *The First Five Minutes* can be found in many sciences of the face-to-face and not just those focused on the talk of talk therapy. To be sure, only some midcentury interactionists argued for microscopic methods and had such a feverishly indexicalized view of recording and transcription, but increasingly, interactionists of many persuasions came to think that mechanical recording and transcript-based analysis were indispensable.

This indexicalized approach to interaction had come about through a close dialogue and division of labor between psychiatry and the communication sciences. By midcentury, a number of influential communication scientists claimed, in effect, to have objectified the unconscious as something you could study and know. The communicative unconscious consisted of all those tacit verbal and nonverbal signs that operated behind people's backs.[27] Knowing these signs required capturing details about speech that hadn't been studied well before, such as volume and voice quality, details that were being consolidated under a new branch of postwar linguistic science that George Trager dubbed *paralanguage*. The body, that great matrix of indexicality, was added too as nonverbal behavior—or *kinesics*, as Ray Birdwhistell called it—complemented paralinguistics.[28] Trager and Birdwhistell were part of a network of linguists, anthropologists, and psychiatrists who together produced a multimodal semiotics of communication that required recording technologies.

In general, the study of interaction has owed much to psychiatry and to the study of talk therapies. We may recall that two influential midcentury interactionists, sociologists Erving Goffman and Harold Garfinkel, did important early research in mental health institutions.[29] Emanuel Schegloff, who drew from both men and from Gail Jefferson as he helped charter what would be called conversation analysis (CA), put the matter plainly later in his career. You couldn't just say you wanted to study "ordinary" social interaction and expect to get funded. Studying interaction in therapy and with those diagnosed with psychopathologies could justify this research. Into the early '70s, interaction science's indebtedness to psychiatry continued as interactionists like the late Charles Goodwin, for instance, turned to study interaction in group therapy; group therapy foregrounded interaction among participants even more sharply than the one-on-one therapist-client dyad, making interaction a significant topic of research. Echoing Schegloff, Goodwin once remarked that "therapeutic settings, presumably characterized by pathology in need of a remedy, constituted one of the few places where the analysis of human interaction was socially supported."[30]

Most relevant for the stream of microanalysis discussed here, featuring *The First Five Minutes*, is the network of psychiatrists and social scientists that participated in NHI. Stretching well beyond CASBS and lasting until the late '60s, NHI influenced generations of interaction researchers through such microanalysts as Albert Scheflen and Ray Birdwhistell at the Eastern Pennsylvania Psychiatric Institute (EPPI) and Henry Brosin, William Condon, and others at the Western Psychiatric Institute and Clinic. Though he could hardly be categorized as an indexicalist, on the West Coast there was the spirited polymath Gregory Bateson—anthropologist, cybernetician, and much else—who had already tried his hand at analyzing the role of communication in psychotherapy during a collaboration with psychiatrist Jurgen Ruesch a few years before NHI began, and whose Palo Alto group used film to explore schizophrenia as a communicative pathology.[31] More than most, Bateson demonstrated how you could learn broader lessons about human interaction from empirical studies in psychiatry. Much as Schegloff and Goodwin conceded, as Bateson put it pragmatically later in his life, "it was from psychiatry that we got our money."[32]

Even among those who did not work directly at the interface between psychiatry and communication science, a turn toward indexicality can be sensed. In the 1960s new forms of research on language in context were fast emerging that were often set under the banner of "sociolinguistics." Not everyone was dedicated to understanding "social interaction" per se, yet many were committed both to recording and indexicality. John J. Gumperz (1922–2013) was committed to all three. Based in the department of anthropology at Berkeley, he had evolved from a scholar of dialect variation and multilingualism to a recording enthusiast who maintained a trove of tapes and recording equipment in his office. He famously came to study all the subtle ways in which conversationalists broadcast their sense of what's going on—their definition of the situation—as the interaction unfolds in real time. Gumperz's recording-based conversational analysis would often later be called "interactional sociolinguistics."[33]

*

As for psychiatry and the sciences of communication, they had come together over their shared interest in recording technologies. When it came to the growing desire *to know* the communicative unconscious, it wasn't the recorders that had sparked it all. It was not their indexical fidelity and receptivity that lit the way, but rather the observant human psychoanalyst, trained as he was to be the most sensitive of indexical receivers. Yet as the relationship of psychiatry and the communication sciences thickened, human and nonhuman recorders became comparable in their indexical receptivity—as did the figures of psychoanalyst and fine-grained interaction analyst. They began to resemble each other, and bleed into each other. You could wrangle about who was more and less receptive, who came first, who guided whom. Even so, likened through their dialogue, these figures, these dueling analysts, were imagined to be comparably skilled in their sensitivity to indexical signs.[34] People imagined then—as they continue to—that interaction researchers and talk therapy clinicians share a preternatural semiotic receptivity. They can read people. They can notice signs that others miss. One requires recording machines to do this noticing; the other, at least in principle, does not.

In his memorial for the psychoanalyst Frieda Fromm-Reichmann, who is credited with spearheading the NHI collaboration, anthropologist and fellow participant Gregory Bateson wrote of her indexical receptivity, her "extraordinary sensitivity to the overtones and nuances of human behavior," even though "she felt insufficiently conscious of the actual nonverbal cues from which she arrived at her conclusions."[35] Echoing an aim of NHI, Bateson suggested that the careful study of verbal and nonverbal cues, with the help of machines, could make explicit her virtuosic, indexical sensitivity. Shortly before the collaboration began, Fromm-Reichmann had conducted her own exploratory study on intuition at Chestnut Lodge Sanitarium. Using recording and transcription, she had hoped to pinpoint empirically her communicative sources of clinical inference. In convening NHI in 1955, she turned to communication scientists for help.

The interaction microanalysts and their partners in psychiatry did have their differences and disagreements, of course. Those in the clinical camp ultimately cared more about clinical practice, whereas the communication scientists cared more about language and communication in general. For instance, Bernard Covner, a student of Carl Rogers at Ohio State, argued back in the 1940s that talk therapy research would help improve "the counseling interview," an important discursive practice in social work, psychology, and psychiatry. In a series of four articles on the importance and challenges of phonographic recordings, Covner stressed the benefits of seeing "what actually takes place behind the closed doors of the interviewing room." You could use these data to identify "the type of approach which works best in certain situations; the proper time for ending an interview; the causes for an interview getting out of hand; and countless others."[36] By comparing recording-based transcripts to the typical interview reports prepared only from memory and notes, you could also come to appreciate how badly researchers needed mechanical recording. The "interview report was a poor substitute for the typewritten transcription or 'typescript' of the phonographic recording," Covner concluded, a conclusion he reached by coding and quantifying major and minor "substitutions," "amplifications," and "omissions" introduced by the inaccurate human recorder and preserved by the mechanical one.[37] As for therapy, what about consistency, too? Whatever form of therapy you professed to practice, it remained to be seen whether you were actually adhering to its methods and principles. Was the Rogerian, for example, truly nondirective in practice? If not, if therapists varied in what they did despite what they professed, how could the clinical world even begin to adjudicate among better and worse methods? Snyder, another student of Rogers from Ohio State, addressed this problem alongside the most pressing question of all: Which methods actually *worked*? (A dutiful Rogerian, his answer was that nondirective methods worked best.)[38] Research on what worked and didn't, and on all the attendant hows and whens of therapeutic process, benefited from national support after the passage of the 1946 National Mental Health Act and the emergence of the NIMH,[39] which channeled federal dollars to projects on psychotherapy, including recording initiatives like the "Linguistic–Kinesic Analysis of Schizophrenia," which led to *The First Five Minutes*.[40]

In this way research on talk therapy would benefit clinical practice. But the communication scholars involved in talk therapy research hoped to do a lot more than just this. Yes, therapeutic interaction was distinctive—a special kind of social interaction—but *The First Five Minutes* promised that it would teach its readers about more than only one kind of institutionalized interaction. The book would teach us something about dyadic forms of interaction generally. Larger truths were to be found in these pages.

Indeed, in a way, this research didn't ultimately seem to be about therapy at all. It was about interaction in the round. For the linguists and psychiatrists who collaborated to analyze talk therapy, they promised to contribute at once to the science of communication and to therapeutics. These researchers studied therapeutic scenes and often based themselves in psychiatric research centers, yet they saw themselves doing basic science. They thought that they were learning about communication and interaction in general, even as they promised to contribute to psychiatry along the way. In fact, wasn't there something exemplary about therapeutic talk? Two individuals, their attentions locked, their voices and bodies exchanging subtle and evanescent signs. Wasn't this what face-to-face communication prototypically was? Might the talk of talk therapy offer a window onto discursive life generally? A science of interaction lurked in the science of talk therapy, particularly for those like Bateson and Hockett, who studied communication and language for a living.

This cross-disciplinary partnership was productive, as many midcentury scholars of the face-to-face came to owe a serious debt to psychiatry and to research on talk therapies in particular.[41] Ironically—given Freud's own resistance to recording—talk therapy became arguably the most important form of human interaction to be recorded by scientists of interaction in midcentury America. By the 1950s, the "talk" of talk therapy had become a familiar object of study while becoming, strangely, an instance of something else. Therapy became a token of a type, face-to-face "interaction," as it was often called, which many midcentury social scientists came to think was its own reality that merited a science. As research on interaction expanded in the years after the Second World War, therapeutic interaction enjoyed a privileged place. Therapeutic talk had been demoted in one sense: it was now only *one* type of interaction among many. Yet in another sense it had been elevated. Therapeutic talk seemed an exemplar of interaction in general. And so, works like *The First Five Minutes* would serve dual purposes, illuminating talk therapy specifically and discursive interaction in general. Yet what *was* this book's contribution, really? What knowledge did it impart about interaction in the round, let alone therapy in particular?

The First Five Minutes was not for the impatient. It seemed in no rush to deliver predictions or advice. Not until very late in the book did it hand over such knowledge. Instead, the book's format was intensely immersive. It recruited readers to the role of naturalists who were to lose themselves in a pro-verbial forest of transcription covering nearly 70 percent of the book's pages. Had the authors posted up-front informational takeaways, this would have allowed readers to cheat—to skip the transcripts. What a slow, tortuous route this must have seemed from the standpoint of the technocratic imperatives of much postwar behavioral science, which, as we shall later see, aspired to policy relevance if not full-blown social engineering.

It was not that *The First Five Minutes* offered some walk at Walden. It boasted "findings" and "practical applications," as its two parting chapters be-latedly declared. Yet these were short and anticlimactic, because, if you read the book linearly, you had to trudge through dense transcripts and tolerate epistemological uncertainty along the way.

Consider the lean "findings" chapter. Listed here were nine abstract prop-ositions about human interaction. In fact, these were "findings" only in the limited sense that the authors claimed not to have assumed these in advance but only came to appreciate them as the project unfolded. These nine were true not only of these five minutes or of the therapeutic encounter as such, but of human interaction generically. Take "Immanent Reference," the first proposition: interlocutors in conversation "*are always communicating about themselves, about one another, and about the immediate context of the com-munication*" (emphasis in original).[42] A footnote credited Bateson's concept of metacommunication, for which this definition was something of a para-phrase. The authors were arguably equally indebted to such psychoanalytic principles as transference and countertransference, which taught one that psychopathology would play out indirectly in face-to-face interaction. In-deed, the authors freely admitted that the nine weren't really even *theirs* but had been culled from literature. They had then consolidated truths and, at best, had simply illustrated them in this book.

Consider, too, the disappointing "practical applications" chapter, which barely reached five pages. Here was a list of things the clinician ought to listen for. Take note of ambiguous deictic expressions and unusual places of stress in a patient's speech. Listen for speech dysfluencies and subtle-but-telling de-viations from modal styles of talk. Beware of false starts and cut-off speech, for instance, which reflect "abandoned directions of statement." Note "vari-ations in degree of smoothness of delivery," "blends" (a.k.a. Freudian slips of the tongue), and "pauses, sighs, gasps." Listen for "variations of volume, register, tempo and voice quality," a prosodic super-category comprising six moves that were captioned colorfully, as if they had been drawn from an eti-quette manual: the "hot potato," for instance, is the tactic through which the "speaker realizes that what he is saying at the moment is frightening, and so tries to get it over fast"; the "getaway" exploits speech rate as well, because the "speaker realizes unpleasant or threatening connotations of something already said, and talks fast in order to put as much metaphorical ground as possible between himself and the distasteful topic"; and acceleration is used for yet a different end in the "road hog," where the "speaker thinks he detects an impending interruption, and speeds up . . . in order to forestall it."

As the list of recommended things to listen for grew, the implication seemed to be that what the clinician really needed was some training in linguistics. The reader should *become a* microanalyst of speech, to a degree. Indeed, this is what Pittenger would say after this collaboration. Therapists ought to learn a little linguistics, much as he had done. They didn't need to become a linguist "any more than a concertgoer needs to be a conservatory graduate," an analogy upon which he expanded.

> An untrained individual may be delighted by and responsive to music before "knowing anything" about it other than to hear it as a flow of familiar impressions. But with even a little training on a musical instrument, or about the "structure" of music, an individual can discriminate various elements and listen to aspects of music he had overlooked before. His experience is enriched; his perceptions broadened.[43]

It wasn't that the clinicians lacked a sense of what to listen for; if anything, it was *their* intuitions about what to observe that had guided the microanalysts in the first place (even if the linguists weren't always ready to give them credit). This "collaboration" of *The First Five Minutes*, if it can even be called that, was thus asymmetrical; it privileged communication science—linguistics and paralinguistics. These sciences were mobilized to make clinical sensitivity sharper and tacit knowledge explicit. With the help of machines, the microanalysts would teach the clinicians to pinpoint and recognize what they had entrusted to imperfect intuition and inference.

> What concerns us . . . is precisely the nature of the behavior on which the inferences are based, what other inferences could be made, and the conditions under which the inferences are valid. We want to know about these things partly as a matter of basic scientific interest and partly because such knowledge is obviously crucial in training new therapists. Yet these are matters on which most participants, be they patients or therapists, novices, or experts, can offer only the sketchiest information.[44]

While *The First Five Minutes* may have delivered little actionable knowledge, it thus offered a program of training, a pedagogy of noticing: fine-grained analysis.

Consider this pedagogy in relation to the architecture of the book. *The First Five Minutes* featured an unusual "Dutch door" design in which the upper half was cut and separated from the lower, allowing each equal half to swing open independently; the top, flush with space, presented the transcript of talk, while the bottom was cramped with the analysis (figure 7). This meant readers could, and should, experience interaction separately from analysis. This design, coupled with the original sound recordings that were supplied to clinical professionals along with the book, was immersive and pedagogical. Observation could "educate the senses" profoundly.[45] By the midcentury, many talk therapy recording enthusiasts would argue that exposure to sound and sound film was valuable for clinical training, especially since training continued to be hamstrung by the inability to observe dyadic therapy directly—again, because of a presumed observer effect.[46] One 1950 essay argued for the vicarious experience of indexicality: "In the teaching of psychotherapy . . . it is important that every inflection of the voice, every whisper, yawn, sigh, slight and almost imperceptible dropping or raising of the voice be recorded with lifelike quality."[47] Another essay touted the benefits of listening repeatedly to five-minute-long segments, for by "tuning in to the subtleties of interaction" the clinician can cultivate "empathic capacity."[48]

Just watching and listening repeatedly wasn't enough. Indeed, epistemologically, the indexically saturated transcripts were better than the primary recordings. *The First Five Minutes* would teach people to notice details much as a linguist would, details that casual listeners—and untrained clinicians—would likely miss. Once you mastered the transcription conventions and could read the text with some fluency, you could learn to "hear" what was transcribed in the source media. Clinicians were invited to practice fine-grained noticing through playback of the accompanying sound recording. Such an indexically saturated transcript resolved semiotic density. In interaction, there were too many signs packed in together. A granular transcript pried them apart and thinned them out. It promised to *parse* this signage; instead of the rush of simultaneous signs that overwhelmed the senses, the fine-grained transcript offered a way to "read" discourse linearly and sequentially, as if it were a text. It promised to domesticate the plenum, separating layers of semiotic lamination to reveal a finite number of isolable indexical signs.

However impractical this may have been, this pedagogy of audition encouraged you to listen to the sound recording and follow along with the transcript to train the ear. This multimodal playback, where fine-grained transcript reading could accompany sound playback, seemed designed to improve observational acuity. Here was what the book was really for. By acting, in effect, like the fine-grained analyst, the clinician could in this way cultivate the capacity for indexical receptivity. Recording-based analysis was not only an epistemological prosthesis but a pedagogy *for* the clinical sensorium. Once you could read this transcript fluently, you could go back and hear it all in the recording at normal playback speed. The ultimate aim of bringing this fine-grained analytic sensibility *back* to the original recording was to develop a capacity that you could bring *forward* to future interactions of any kind; you could become in this way a more indexically receptive human. This pedagogy would help ensure that clinicians noticed symptoms and made accurate diagnostic inferences.

We may again recall Freud's technological metaphor for human receptivity: The analyst "must adjust himself to the patient as a telephone receiver is adjusted to the transmitting microphone."[49] Recording enthusiasts literalized Freud's trope, in a way. Those with one or both feet on the talk-therapeutic side of the cross-disciplinary dialogue continued to pay deference to the humans. Humans were still the best at picking up indexical signs. Yet the talk therapists conceded the importance of recording-based audition and analysis. "Many researchers do not have Freud's sensitivity to hidden facts in mental life," one essay acknowledged. "Such people can understand only when the small voice of the unconscious is, so to say, amplified."[50] Those on the communication science side were less sanguine about the unaided sensorium and believed instead that full receptivity of the unconscious was only possible with machines. They used technologically mediated observation to try to make the fine-grained social science analyst into a maximally sensitive "receiver"—the apotheosis of the psychoanalyst. Here was the analogic return in full force.

In a sense, the midcentury technosemiotic analysis of discursive interaction had struggled to materialize the receptivity prescribed by Freud. Stated in reverse, the clinical virtue of indexical receptivity insinuated itself into research on the talk of talk therapy, creating the fine-grained analyst in the psychoanalyst's image. This virtue of receptivity, along with paired notions like the communicative unconscious, offered a sense of how to *know* interpersonal relations in general. It was as if these two analysts—the psychoanalytic and the fine grained—were themselves face-to-face, and sometimes it was unclear who was analyzing whom.

Marveling at the hybridity, or, worse, trying to tease out which parts belong to which field in an effort to establish provenance and chronicle disciplinary interaction, is not my point. Instead, I have detailed how this amalgam called interaction, with its changing dependencies on recording machines, came about through an historically fitful and fraught desire for indexicality. This shift toward indexicality was facilitated but not inspired by mechanical objectivity. Medial machines and transcripts were not originally designed to allow nature—here the nature of human interaction—to speak directly. Only slowly, painstakingly, through the lure of an immanent communicative unconscious and the possibility of capturing its traces by a combination of human and nonhuman faculties, did "indexical media" come about. This shift in semiotic ideology had scalar effects. It unwittingly scaled interaction and the methods for knowing it, leaving practitioners with a firm sense about and feel for what human interaction was and what it took to know it well.

4

The First Five Seconds

Such elusive objects, the chattering body and the tells of talk. The communicative unconscious lured recording enthusiasts of the talking cure into thinking they could catch, store, recover, and identify indexical signs, but this was anything but easy. As this chase ensued, the search for indexicality itself did much to shrink observational scale. It inspired "microscopic" approaches in terms of grain and extent. It also did much to shrink interaction itself as an object imagined to have an intrinsic, ontological scale. Indexicalization created challenges, which had thus far been largely practical and epistemological. Feeling overwhelmed by too much data or by the richness of a sample, for instance. Not knowing how to transcribe it all, let alone analyze it. Never quite knowing *where* the significant indexicals hid and worrying that more indexicality lurked. Unsure where the indexicals led, *what* they pointed to. And when frustration set in—as it invariably did—a familiar sunk-cost response was not to give up but to redouble efforts and look at less even more closely. But a graver problem loomed, and it would not be solved by more mediatic microscopy. This was the problem of the paracosm, a problem born from scalar enworlding itself. If interaction was starting to seem like an autonomous microworld that demanded a microscopic gaze, then how was the subvisible and subaural world connected to what you could ordinarily see and hear? What was its ontological interscalarity? And if interaction wasn't connected, or only loosely, then, some could ask, why did this small science matter?

*

Three years after *The First Five Minutes* was published, coauthor Robert Pittenger seemed a little defensive. He published an essay reminding the world why his book mattered. Pitched to his colleagues in psychiatry, he addressed the question of his book's "significance for mental health." And that meant defending the book's microscopic orientation.

Why, again, had he and his coauthors limited themselves to five minutes? Because they had pursued "the most minute audible particles of a given interview, by putting them under the microscope, as it were, so that an otherwise all but invisible weave of human interchange can be made visible." "From the point of view of microscopic study," Pittenger added, "five minutes [was] a very large sample," that in fact "a few seconds" would have been "more common."[1]

Some critics in psychiatry complained that the book was myopic, its grain excessively fine. Why hadn't the authors tried harder to find diagnostic cues and pathological signs?[2] What was the psychiatric payoff of this demanding observational scale, really? Where was the parallel to literal, non-metaphoric microscopy in medicine, where "viewing a tiny block of tissue from the liver under a microscope may save a patient's life"?

The First Five Minutes did anticipate and entertain criticism of its observational scale. In the last section of its "Findings" chapter, "Forest and Trees: The Dangers of Microscopy," the coauthors reflected, if only briefly, on the hazards of their method. Although "magnification for closer-grained and repeated examination is justified," they conceded that "this justification in no way obviates the danger of distortion through changes of scale."[3]

Which dangers? Not every five-minute segment mattered to the same degree. "Equally brief events are sometimes of crucial importance, sometimes only marginal." And because they didn't situate their five minutes with respect to a larger event or structure of social life, it was true, they conceded, that the "lengthy concentration of attention on the one event can easily blow up its significance far out of proportion." More unsettling still was their recognition that the properties of objects can seem to change as you change observational scale.[4]

> There are important properties of things and events that are not invariant under change of scale. An elephant's legs have a much higher ratio of cross section to volume than do an insect's, since the weight of muscle increases as the cube of a linear dimension, the strength only as the square—an ant the size of an elephant could not even stand, let alone walk. . . . A cube one inch on an edge has a surface-to-volume ratio of 6 to 1; if it is cut into eight cubes one-half inch on an edge the total surface-to-volume ratio becomes 12 to 1 though the total volume is unchanged. The plot of an excellent short story can yield an execrable novel, and vice versa.[5]

Even as they nodded at the strange experience of interscalar dissonance, as it were, they volunteered nothing more—nothing about how this might matter for social interaction or even for the five minutes they had just transcribed and analyzed. Nor did they worry about the way such dissonance could corrode connections between small and everyday worlds to the point that the former might drift off as a paracosm. They felt no urgency to explain the kinship between the micro- and surface world, because no matter how small interaction was—and no matter how fine grained the methods of its scrutiny—scale was not yet a widespread problem.

As interaction became scaled as a microworld requiring intensive microanalysis in the 1950s and 1960s, the problems began to build. By the 1970s it became possible to have strong and often moralizing opinions about the scales of social life and about those who specialized in them. It became possible to entertain serious doubt about the kinship between micro and macro and to demand an account from the microscopists that spelled out how the two were connected, if, indeed, they were connected at all. Yet back in the early and mid-1960s at least, tropic microscopy was not too troubling.

Among some researchers on interaction, in fact, you could sense a quiet race toward increased granularity. Looking more finely usually involved changing up the media. Above all, there was the tantalizing potential of sound film whose indexical plenitude was felt to far exceed media that only captured the acoustic signal and which could be analyzed, ideally, "frame by frame"; some proposed drilling down on the sound of sound film with instruments like the cathode-ray oscilloscope, which opened up the possibility of a practically fathomless micro observational scale.

✶

Although microscopy and mechanical recording technologies increasingly went hand in hand, not everyone chased indexicality, or chased it in the same way. In Berkeley's doctoral program in sociology, for instance, Emanuel Schegloff defended a dissertation in 1967 whose title trumpeted its diminutive scale as loudly as Hockett, Pittenger, and Danehy's book. It even upped the ante: *The First Five Seconds: The Order of Conversational Opening*.[6] Yet the indexicality here was rather different, as it didn't mean all those traces and ties *between* conversation on the one hand and features of a distinct "context" (intrapsychic, interpersonal, or what not) on the other. With Harvey Sacks and Gail Jefferson, Schegloff would become one of the chief architects of an influential interaction science that would eventually call itself "conversation analysis" (CA). What transpires in a matter of seconds—something as seemingly trivial as a conversational opening—was important; it mattered because it occurred at the beginning of an interaction and was more intricate than people realized. Intricacy here meant the density of normative rules that governed what you felt you should do first and what you felt you should do second, in response to others' talk. Though Schegloff did not conceive his project in terms of indexicality, his effort, in a way, was to examine only co-textual, co-indexical relationships *among* conversational moves, how moves, that is, pointed to and implicated each other. The indexicality he hoped to investigate was in this way strictly internal to "conversation," as if conversation were an autonomous object with its own virtual grammar that could predict the surface traffic of conversational inter-action.

What Schegloff hoped to avoid, in fact, was the indexical saturation that *The First Five Minutes* chose to explore, even as Schegloff also chose to study face-to-face interaction by way of technologically mediated interaction—in his case, a corpus of some 500 telephone calls recorded during a research stint at the Disaster Research Center at the Ohio State University. Using a Soundscriber recorder, the center had routinely and automatically recorded incoming and outgoing calls to and from its Complaint Desk.

In his dissertation Schegloff entertained a telling doubt about his data that revealed how he tried to limit indexical saturation. He wrote that some might complain that phone calls were not as rich as face-to-face talk and therefore *not* a good way to get at face-to-face interaction. In terms of richness this was true, in a way, but phone calls had an advantage precisely for this reason, he argued. The telephone isolated speech and eliminated the body, which was the source of dense "expressive" (indexical) signaling. An "intrinsic property of visual media" is that "a variety of messages, and relationships between them, can be transmitted simultaneously, and a corresponding property of acoustic media (at least insofar as talk is concerned) [is] that material must be primarily transmitted not synchronously, but serially." The problem with the visual was that it was flooded with indexical signals that pointed this way and that, thereby overwhelming the analyst.

> He may be able to see, at once, the kind of ecological environment another is in, his location in it, his dress, deportment, postural configuration, bodily tonus, the rapidity of gesture, ethnically relevant facial configurations, racial characteristics, etc. . . . None of these resources is determinatively available in advance for telephone interactants, and, moreover, such information must, as we shall see, typically be developed sequentially, over the course of the early portion of the interaction. . . .[7]

Schegloff didn't seek indexical ties between voice and context, either. He did not treat the human voice as an indexical faculty—in sharp contrast to *The First Five Minutes* (and to Sapir, who had proposed that the human voice could be seen as a wellspring of indexicality). To be sure, Schegloff cared deeply about recording and transcription. Reflecting on the development of CA's approach, Schegloff acknowledged that CA had "needed recording technologies to flourish," and that "without it, it would never have arisen."[8] Fidelity in transcription mattered acutely, for "even good transcribers under the best of conditions . . . cannot produce transcripts of maximum fidelity on the first, try," and so he "undertook to review and correct the transcripts" which amounted to "roughly 200 hours" worth of data; yet this fidelity was not indexical fidelity. His transcripts were not the indexically saturated texts of *The First Five Minutes*.[9] And although his dissertation did also focus unapologetically on a "small" part of conversational talk—openings—he drew on a large corpus of data through which he hoped to generalize, suggesting that this was no "natural history" either.

There were other mediatic microscopists of the face-to-face who used recording technologies but did not chase indexicality at all. Robert Freed Bales, for instance, a key figure in the influential "small-group" analysis movement of the post–World War II period, as we will see shortly, embraced the trope of microscopy to stress how granular he was, and he even engineered a special machine, the "interaction recorder," to help record the flow of communicative action in what he felt was exquisite detail—but not the detail of indexical traces. And then there was Erving Goffman, Schegloff's ostensible mentor at Berkeley. (Tension existed between the men, and Goffman later became a public antagonist of CA before his death.) Goffman—who Pierre Bourdieu remembered as "discoverer of the infinitely small"[10]—had studiously rejected the scientism and technophilia of small-group researchers like Bales, and, for different reasons, he rejected Schegloff's vision for CA. Goffman's distinctive way of writing and analyzing social interaction was often seen as microscopic in grain and extent, and while he could chase indexicality at times, he refused to do so by means of special machines, tape recorders, and transcripts.[11]

The mediatic indexicalization of interaction that I have traced was most evident among the network of researchers who operated in the psychiatry–communication–science interface. It was this network that had so markedly indexicalized the science of the face to face and for whom five seconds was, as Pittenger wrote, a common sample size.

In 1967, for instance, the same year Schegloff's dissertation was published, William Condon, affiliated with the Western Psychiatric Institute and Clinic at the University of Pittsburgh's medical school, published an article whose featured analysis covered about five and half seconds of interaction. Like Schegloff's worries about the visual plenum, Condon recognized the challenge of simultaneity, which made sound film seem overwhelming. It is true, he began, in an essay coauthored with William Ogston, that "confronta-

tion with a sound motion picture of human behavior overwhelms the observer with a rapidly flowing and shifting scene of sound and motion," leaving
you with "no clear boundary points dividing the flow of events into discrete
segments." With what units and through what methods could you parse this
flow? Could the *simultaneity* of signaling, from different sources—verbal and
nonverbal—be grasped epistemologically? "What does the lowering of the
voice, 'while' the eyes widen, 'while' the brows raise, 'while' an arm and fingers move, 'while' the head lowers, 'while' a leg and foot shift, 'while' the face
flushes, have to do with what was said or left unsaid?"[12]

Such intensive noticing, which tried to synchronize simultaneous audio-
visual indexicalities, was much more demanding than what *The First Five
Minutes* had attempted, for that book had only worked with sound. Condon began by an "intensive viewing of a film of a psychotherapeutic interview," which "literally involved hundreds of hours of viewing the film over
and over." Eventually he and Ogston engaged in frame-by-frame analysis using a Bell and Howell time-motion analyzer. This hand-cranked machine,
threaded with 16mm film, was none other than "the familiar slow-motion
projector used by football coaches to analyze films of games."[13]

The interaction researchers at Pittsburgh made up one important node in
the psychiatry–communication network of multimodal microscopists whose
research was tied to the Natural History of an Interview (NHI) collaboration. At the Western Psychiatric Institute and Clinic it was Henry Brosin who
oversaw the research and who had been part of NHI at the Center for Advanced Study in the Behavioral Sciences (CASBS). The CASBS collaboration
lost some members and gained others as it fanned out to include new sites—
university departments, medical schools, and psychiatric institutes.

In the early 1960s, researchers in the communication–psychiatry interface
maintained great enthusiasm for the fine grain of their research, yet when
caught off guard, they confessed that they weren't sure how microscopic they
should get or even what this microscopy might ultimately yield.

In the research division of Philadelphia's Eastern Pennsylvania Psychiatric
Institute (EPPI), which was hitched to Temple University's medical school,
two principals—psychiatrist Albert Scheflen (1921–1980) and anthropologist Ray L. Birdwhistell (1918–1994)—directed research on interaction. Birdwhistell's postwar science of embodied communication called "kinesics" had
teamed film-based microanalysis with American structuralist linguistics.[14]
He joined the NHI collaboration in 1956 and joined EPPI in 1959 as senior research scientist, a position he held for a decade.

In 1964 Birdwhistell held a small conference at Temple to discuss mechanical recording technologies for "linguistic and kinesic context analysis."

F I G U R E 8. Behavioral film viewing at the Western Psychiatric Institute and Clinic, Pittsburgh, Pennsylvania, 1963. Reproduced with permission from Special Collections, Falk Library of the Health Sciences, University of Pittsburgh. Front row, from left: E. Joseph Charny, Otto O. von Mering, Henry W. Brosin, William S. Condon, Kai T. Erickson, Edith Fleming. Back, from left: Felix F. Loeb, Jack A. Wolford, Robert L. Vosburg, William E. Mooney, Herbert E. Thomas, Michael Kehoe. Photo by M. Stuart, 1963.

Among the participants were members of the Pittsburgh group, as well as the University of Chicago linguist Norman McQuown, a key member of the original NHI collaboration. "Dr. McQuown and I were talking just a few moments ago," Birdwhistell shared in his opening remarks. "And we had the feeling that we'd like to regard this as the end of a staircase of the development of this approach." Yet "we're not quite certain that we're not walking on a mobius ring."

Indeed, what progress had they made, where were they headed? When Harvey Sarles, one of the "anthropological linguists" from Pittsburgh, spoke, it seemed some progress had been made. Sarles belonged to an industrious team that took pride in microscopic deep dives. His group had been trying "to get as fine grained as possible."

As you get into speech, any of you who have actually worked with interactional speech—the recording of this stuff very accurately, even by a secretary, gets more and more difficult if you want to start talking about pauses and exactly what goes on. It's not what happens—it's not what a secretary types up on a typescript. . . . My view of my job in doing this is to get as—to get completely accurate, and I think we're a long way from this.

Sarles's team analyzed film not just in the "slow motion" of 48 frames per second but even 64 frames per second.[15] They analyzed the sound of sound film on B rolls using a sound reader that allowed you to hear speech from the last frame. "On any film," Sarles declared, "we can get about as fine grained as you want on phonetic changes."

That sounded like progress, but McQuown chipped in. "I just want to interject two more quotes about what 'we think' in your last remark, because we don't know yet how fine grained we have to go." True, Sarles admits. "This is unknown." He adds that this "is one of our kicks—to become as fine grained as possible," and "we think it's paying off." His group had been experimenting with their most ambitious instrument yet: the cathode-ray oscilloscope, which allows you to "get complete accuracy in the time domain," and although his team is not yet working at this scale, the oscilloscope allows you to descend "down to a nanosecond."

"Complete accuracy" had its challenges, and costs. At EPPI in Philadelphia, Birdwhistell and Scheflen relied on their resident research filmmaker, Jacques Van Vlack, whom Birdwhistell had met and cultivated during his last job at SUNY Buffalo. At Birdwhistell's conference Van Vlack explained the equipment they used at EPPI. He spoke on lighting and microphones and the differences between a dramatic Hollywood film and a "behavioral film" designed for research purposes.[16] He demonstrated two projectors. One was an old hand-cranked one; the other, a sophisticated—and expensive—automatic slow-motion projector.

At EPPI they mostly used the old hand-cranked unit. It was easier. Its downside was the irritating, distorting flicker that infected the image during frame-by-frame analysis. In contrast stood the impressive PerceptoScope. It had been used with 70mm film to analyze rockets when they blow up, Van Vlack explained. The PerceptoScope was finicky. It "wrecks film" and "it will wreck film probably in the next day or two" during the conference. Rocket scientists don't care about orientation, either; the image might be sideways or upside down, so at EPPI they had to jury-rig "a device consisting of eight prisms that sets [the image] right." The real advantage, Van Vlack stressed, was that when one does descend down to one frame a second—each frame being one-twenty-fourth of a second in real time—"each individual frame is frozen in the same position as the preceding one, so you can see the differences between one frame and the next." You could see changes frame to frame with unparalleled accuracy, and with no flicker. Birdwhistell added a

complaint about the noise of this machine and the fatigue of analysis generally. The PerceptoScope was loud. You could put a box over it and operate
it remotely, from behind, but "most of us can only work a few minutes on a
film anyway."

Ray L. Birdwhistell and the Enworlding of the Kinesic Micro

Mediatic microscopy was laborious, expensive, and exhausting. Even its proponents recognized why people might question the time and cost, especially
as it offered no quick, practical payoffs and so was not for the impatient social
engineer. As the '60s wore on, these patient, industrious microanalysts of the
face-to-face would feel increased pressure to justify their rigor and their patience. Yet even within this circle, concerns festered about where their science
was headed. Maybe they were stuck on a mobius strip.

To see how these issues began to eat at the science of the face-to-face from
within, let us trace these concerns as they began to build in the scholarly
career of one of our protagonists, a passionately microscopic scientist of the
NHI group, Ray Birdwhistell, who dared work with the rich, dense visual
channel that Schegloff, perhaps sensibly, avoided. As Martha Davis writes,
Birdwhistell transformed the film projector into a mediatic "microscope," a
class of instrument he had apparently been committed too for a very long
time.[17] He became a major figure in the study of embodied communication,
or what he termed "kinesics." We will see how late in his career, Birdwhistell
began to suffer from his enworlding of the micro. His "analyses," Brenda Farnell writes, "tended to dissolve into microanalytical minutia from which he
seemed unable to emerge," and he himself seemed aware of this.[18] Birdwhistell
began to want to reconnect the subvisible world of bodily communication
with a vast "context" that had always seemed just beyond his grasp. Birdwhistell, that is, faced the problem of the paracosm, the question of how ontological scales fit together, and what their interscalar kinship truly was.

Birdwhistell was not a linguist like Hockett and McQuown but an anthropologist. His kinesics crystallized only after he received his PhD in anthropology from the University of Chicago in 1951. Though his dissertation
had nothing to do with body motion, he had been turning toward the topic,
with encouragement from Margaret Mead and Gregory Bateson, whom
he had met in the 1940s and whose photoethnography *Balinese Character*
detailed visually and textually how forms of bodily practice and comportment were socially learned.[19] With an invitation from E. T. Hall, Birdwhistell
joined the Foreign Service Institute (FSI) in DC in 1952, and during his six-

month stint, he participated in a seminar with linguists George Trager and Henry Lee Smith that resulted in his landmark essay, and charter, "Introduction to Kinesics" (1952). Hall's "proxemics," Trager's "paralinguistics," Birdwhistell's "kinesics"—these were postwar sciences of communication baptized at FSI that extended communication beyond language while drawing inspiration from linguistic structuralism. After a decade at EPPI, he made his last move in 1969 to the University of Pennsylvania's Annenberg School for Communication.

Birdwhistell's Penn years were curious. His 1970 book, *Kinesics and Context*, published with encouragement from his new colleague Erving Goffman, consisted almost entirely of previously published essays, but he did not research or publish any new material on kinesics. In the classroom, in place of formal syllabi, he expected students to make their way through his writings, and he taught classic ethnographic monographs—by Evans-Pritchard and Radcliffe-Brown, among others—alongside his own science of body motion. But it was not his special science of kinesics that he tried to impart. Instead, he is said to have turned to broader issues of methodology.[20] It is fitting that the title of his oeuvre juxtaposed "kinesics" and "context," because context was a preoccupation. During this time, Birdwhistell became attracted to the expansive holism of the ethnographic imagination and even tried his hand at the literary registers on which ethnography could draw for its descriptive, immersive, and evocative power. At Penn, he cautioned against filming and prohibited the recording of his own lectures. He insisted that his students not be in a rush to film and analyze human behavior too finely. They should postpone microanalysis until they grasped the fullness of context, and this fullness meant appreciating how multiplex—how integrative—a setting really was. Finding fullness was apparently hard work, for Birdwhistell continued to delay imparting his methods of kinesics. Only a couple students at Penn tried their hand at a science that he did not explicitly teach.

Whatever else this reveals, it suggests Birdwhistell's struggle to reconcile his kinesic science with the anthropologist's integrative if not holistic sensibility, a sensibility he may have had from the start but desired with urgency late in his career. The reasons for this desire are not internal to his scholarship and biography, of course, but rather have to do with much else, not the least the then-emerging critiques of time-intensive, naturalistic—and thus expensive—micro-analytical research like his, which came to a head when Paul Ekman countered Birdwhistell's program with a competing psychologistic approach to nonverbal behavior that was neatly experimental, that addressed concerns about small sample sizes and generalization, and that

pursued universals rather than reveling in cultural variation, as the anthropologists were accused of doing.[21]

✳

Birdwhistell first introduced "kinesics" in the early '50s. This meant the study
of the embodied dimensions of social interaction—or, more precisely, "communicative body motion." Defined positively and by analogy with *linguistics*,
this science assumed, as Adam Kendon and Stuart Sigman summarize, that
"human body motion is culturally patterned and . . . can be analyzed using
the same mode of approach that is used in analyzing the structure of spoken
language."[22] "The same" can be misleading, because as Kendon and Sigman
also stress, Birdwhistell expressed only measured enthusiasm toward linguistic structuralism.

Despite his deepening investment in the analogy to linguistic structure, it
was still only an analogy, and his science was really a mix of things.[23] Cybernetic ideas inflected his thinking, no doubt through his close conversations
with Bateson and participation in the Macy conferences, and his visual methods, which involved slow-motion playback and frame-by-frame analysis of
film, obviously had no provenance in disciplinary linguistics.[24] Birdwhistell's
science was no structuralist calque, even if it sounded like one.

His kinesics was also *not* merely a science of gesture, though he found that
notion to be a useful foil. "Gesture" was a misleading colloquialism. It was, at
best, a "shorthand notation" that directed attention to the "highly noticeable
'peaks' of body motion," as Kendon and Sigman put it. At worst, it lured one
into committing a metonymic fallacy that conflated part for whole. When
Birdwhistell used the term gesture—and he liked to handle the term critically,
sometimes enclosing it in scare quotes—he did not limit it to hand and fore-
arm communication like a "salute" or "wave" but included facial gestures like
a "smile" or "wink," and embodied behaviors like a "bow." All were gestures.[25]

Although he drew away from the familiar notion of gesture, he credited
the notion with helping him develop kinesics. It was his own frustrated attempts to "isolate" gestures, he reflected, that helped him see that "kinesic
structure [was] parallel to language structure." Gestures were "astonishingly
like words," he wrote, and supplied an anecdote to illustrate his discovery.[26]

> During World War II, I became at first bemused, and later intrigued, by the
> repertoire of meanings which could be drawn upon by an experienced United
> States Army private and transmitted in accompaniment to a hand salute. [. . .]
> By shifts in stance, facial expression, the velocity or duration of the movement
> of salutation, and even in the selection of inappropriate contexts for the act,

the soldier could dignify, ridicule, demean, seduce, insult, or promote the re-
cipient of the salute.[27]

The caption "hand salute" spotlights the hand, which is, indeed, visually sa-
lient, yet Birdwhistell is at pains to shine a light on the work of secondary
articulators, including stance and facial musculature. He wants us to appreciate the delicate and deliberate manner in which the varied use of such (co-)
articulators could alter the salute's illocutionary force—what the salute is understood to "do" as a form of social action. A dense mesh of embodied signs
surrounded and shaped the meaning of the hands. "Those aspects of body
motion which are commonly called gestures turn out to be like stem forms in
language," he wrote, which "require suffixual, prefixual, infixual, or transfixual
behavior to be attached to them to determine their function in the interaction
process." Gestures had no isolable pragmatic meaning. They did not "stand
alone as behavioral isolates." It was naive to seek a "glossary of gestures."[28]

In terms of transcription, he covered no less than eight regions of the
body, literally from head to toe, and he had a particularly delicate annotation system for the hands and fingers. He offered notation for different bodily
articulators, but the hands, for example, were not to be studied separately
from the head, for Birdwhistell usually treated these as if they belonged to a
"kinesthetic-visual" channel. He hypothesized—and his research confirmed
his suspicions—that these articulators worked "together," that the kinesthetic-
visual was a single, cohesive channel of semiotic activity.[29] Bodily communication had a measure of autonomy. By virtue of its autonomous channel and
its internal cohesion, body motion had its "own" structure, as it were, and so
he at first kept linguistics and kinesics similar but separate. Working strictly
on silent film or on the silent projection of sound film, Birdwhistell tried to
identify structured body movement independently of speech.[30]

In the mid-1950s, linguistics and kinesics converged at last in a collaborative "multichannel" study of filmed human interaction. In 1956 Birdwhistell
joined the NHI. He was recruited to produce a kinesic transcription, which
was to be done "as independently as possible" on "silently projected film." Only
after the linguists had supplied their faithful phonetic transcription would the
group then stitch the two channels back together to inspect their relations.

The Social in or above the Kinesic?

How much of social and cultural life could you see in and through these dense
transcripts of synchronized language and body motion? The NHI collaboration
made it possible to speak confidently of an integrated "linguistic–paralinguistic–

kinesic method," an awkward amalgam that the NHI group rebranded in the early '60s as "context analysis" (cf. content analysis). Birdwhistell liked the new name,[31] and although the label could make it seem as if context were settled, as if it were coextensive with rather than exterior to the communication they studied, this didn't make the "problem" of context go away.

In the opening pages of *Kinesics and Context*, Birdwhistell acknowledged the problem. He acknowledged the distance between kinesics and what social scientists expected of a truly social science of embodied communication. In deference to Goffman, who pursued the normative underpinnings of face-to-face interaction—and did so humanistically, without the heavy prosthesis of recording technologies—Birdwhistell repeated "Goffman's challenge to linguistic–kinesic investigators," which was "to recognize the hiatus which exists between linguistic–kinesic units and those necessary to investigate the social situations he has isolated."[32]

"Hiatus" was putting it mildly, and its existence was not news to Birdwhistell. When he first envisioned his kinesics, Birdwhistell had asserted that embodied communication had its own structure, much like language (la langue) as envisioned by Ferdinand de Saussure, and it was this structure that kinesics would have to first figure out. Yet this was not all kinesics was. In his charter for kinesics back in 1952, he had already envisioned three areas of study: pre-kinesics, micro-kinesics, and social kinesics. As with Saussure's purified *la langue*, which was autonomous in the sense that it could be abstracted from its context and studied in isolation, and which was meant to serve as a firm foundation for linguistics, so kinesics per se would not address the *social* significance of communicative body motion. For this Birdwhistell added a supplemental science, "social kinesics," which he left largely programmatic.[33] As he put it in 1955, social kinesics "is concerned with . . . [kinesic] morphological constructs as they relate to the communicational aspects of social interaction," and "its data are systematic body movements *in their social context*" (emphasis mine).[34] That he had to carve out such a thing at all suggested that there would be no beeline route from body motion to the social.

If the social aspects of body motion couldn't be known through kinesics proper, what else did you need? Did kinesics shade into or link up to social kinesics at a certain point? How high, as it were, could the analyst ascend in terms of the constituency of behavioral organization?[35] Was it possible to build up from kinesic structure and eventually arrive at the structure of social life and organization?

The answer to the last question seemed to be no. Kinesic constituency remained hierarchically shallow. Kinemes (minimal meaningful units of body movement akin to the "phoneme") combined to form kinemorphs, which in turn could form "complex kinemorphs"—analogous to words; these, in turn, could combine to form the "complex kinemorphic constructions," which "have many of the same properties of the spoken syntactic sentence."[36] Not unlike the way linguists like Zelig Harris came to press beyond the limits of the sentence to a larger expanse that he called "discourse," so Birdwhistell in his work edged upward and outward, but he didn't get terribly far.

Compare with linguist Kenneth Pike's wild structuralist synthesis from the mid-1950s, which offered an Icarian extreme that Birdwhistell did not pursue.[37] For Pike linguistic structure was no mere analogy. Verbal and nonverbal behavior were equally "behavior," and behavior, Pike argued, was structured hierarchically through and through.[38] It was all "wheels within wheels." With extended examples of a church sermon and football game, Pike made it seem as if you could mereologically decompose behavioral events into their parts and reveal their neatly nested levels of organization, as if they had all been generated by one big, underlying cultural grammar. Wholes could be reduced to the articulatory movements of speech—and one could dive deeper still, beyond where the linguist was prepared to go, perhaps to a "molecular" level. One could move effortlessly up or down the structure, for it was all just a matter of epistemological focus, of perspective.[39]

Birdwhistell was deferential toward Pike but made it clear that he "object[ed] to any attempt to subsume all social behavior under a linguistic, kinesic rubric."[40] Unlike Pike he did not shift his focus from part to whole, or scale behavior rung by rung till one could see panoramically—everything at once. At least for much of the '60s Birdwhistell's kinesics remained a comfortably microscopic science, a science tethered to its object of body motion and not worried—or so it seemed—with the sweeping influence of culture and society that Birdwhistell-the-anthropologist knew well but whose relevance for kinesics he did not feel the urge to clarify or demonstrate.

A Highway Scene in Five Seconds

Birdwhistell's charter from 1952 said kinesics wanted to understand the human body in its "cultural context," but it wasn't at all clear how his science would do this. Despite his insistence that "no kine, act, or action carries social meaning in and of itself," that "social meaning appears in a *total context*" (emphasis mine), his modest illustrations of social kinesics in three early scenes—in a bus, at a home, and on a street corner—offered little guidance. The scenes were transcribed but left unanalyzed. None had been informed by any serious fieldwork, nor did they seem to demand it. Instead, Birdwhistell relied on some observation and quite a bit of introspection.[41]

To be sure, Birdwhistell enticed his publics time and again, in his writings and in his behavioral films, with the idea that kinesics would reveal a sociocultural world hiding in plain sight, a world that, following E. T. Hall, he could call "microculture."[42] His public-facing film, *Microcultural Incidents in Ten Zoos*, based on a 1966 illustrated lecture, hopped across zoos in cities such as London, Paris, and Tokyo, comparing family interaction near and sometimes with nonhuman animals.[43] As for scholarship, in a presentation on the kinesics of child development at the second Macy conference in 1955, for instance, Birdwhistell reported on a study-in-progress in which he claimed he could already see how children's bodies were undergoing enculturation. A female infant, for example, "by the age of 15 months had learned portions of the dia-kinesic system of the Southern upper-middle-class female," in the sense that "she had already incorporated the anterior roll of the pelvis and the intrafemoral contact stance which contrasts sharply with the spread-legged and posteriorly rolled pelvis of the 22-month-old boy filmed with her."[44] Here kinesics seemed poised to validate and extend the vision of multimodal socialization that Bateson and Mead had opened up in their famous photograph-rich *Balinese Character*. In essays from the early 1960s, Birdwhistell touched on sociological topics such as gender displays and classed styles of bodily practice, yet these remained self-consciously tentative discussions. There were no accompanying fine-grained kinesic transcriptions let alone a clear discussion of how these sociocultural dimensions of kinesics should be theorized.[45]

In his scholarship, Birdwhistell went the furthest in trying to close the gap between kinesics and context in his most systematic statement on kinesics, a chapter called "Body Motion" published in *Kinesics in Context*.[46] As the chapter had been written for NHI, which had come to see its output as a training manual,[47] Birdwhistell's statement led with an empirical hook: a short, simple example—a "highway scene" that consisted of five seconds of film in which actions were exchanged but no words. He introduced the scene with a capsule description in narrative form.

> Just west of Albuquerque on Highway 66 two soldiers stood astride their duffle bags thumbing a ride. A large car sped by them and the driver jerked his head back, signifying refusal. The two soldiers wheeled and one Italian-saluted him while the other thumbed his nose after the retreating car.[48]

A spare story: one that any untrained observer could relay. Yet Birdwhistell then slows things down, as it were, retelling the same story several times to show you what you missed. First, he retells the narrative by means of a fine-grained transcription of the men's linearly unfolding bodily movements, articulator by articulator (figure 9). He then puts this transcription back into

Soldier No. 1:

				Car passes								
Head	H > 1°	.	.	.	.	.	.	.	.	.	.	Hffbbz .
Forehead-brows	Hfb-b	.	.	.	.	.	.	.	.	.	.	.
Eyes	$\dfrac{\text{oo}}{\text{driver}}$	.	.	.	.	.	.	.	.	.	$\equiv$oo$\equiv$ / car	.
Nose	Mz	.	.	.	.	.	.	.	.	.	oMo	.
Cheeks		.	.	.	.	.	.	.	.	.	.	.
Mouth	L-L	.	.	.	.	.	.	.	.	.	tl-l.	.
Chin		.	.	.	.	.	.	.	.	.	.	.
Neck		.	.	.	.	.	.	.	.	.	.	.
Shoulders	$11 \geqq 1°$	.	.	.	.	.	.	.	.	//	.	.
Trunk	TpTp	.	.	.	.	.	.	.	.	. Txpivot	.	.
Hips		.	.	.	.	.	.	.	.	.	.	.
Right arm	RAN|RA2:45$\leq$$\geq$3:45n	.	N	N	.	$\vee$	$\vee$	$\vee$	$\vee$	RAN(4 $\leq$ 5)n	RA25n .	.
Hand and fingers	R/1?4P	.	.	.	.	.	.	.	.	R/14-p	.	.
Left arm	LAn-15'3u\[A:TA] .	.	.	.	.	.	.	.	.	LAn 3n .	.	.
Hand and fingers	L/1c2C3C4C5C belt	.	.	.	.	.	.	.	.	L/14c(on R. biceps)	.	.
Right leg	Y45Y .	.	.	.	.	.	.	.	.	RY $\leq$ 3°(Y45 + 30"Y).	.	.
Foot	.	.	.	.	.	.	.	.	.	.	.	.
Left leg	Y45Y .	.	.	.	.	.	.	.	.	(Y45 + 30'Y) .	.	.
Foot	.	.	.	.	.	.	.	.	.	Ly5 $\geq$ Ly3°	.	.

FIGURE 9. Fine-grained transcription (partial) of bodily articulators in the "Highway Scene." Ray L. Birdwhistell, 1970, Kinesics and Context: Essays on Body Motion Communication, p. 270.

prose. He "translates" it, as he put it, converting his dense notation into a clinical, etic account of interpersonal behavior. His initial pragmatic summary of the driver had been that he had "jerked his head back, signifying refusal." When Birdwhistell expands this, it becomes a methodical account of body parts in motion—slow motion.[49]

> The driver of the car focused momentarily on the boys, raised both brows, flared his nostrils, lifted his upper lip, revealed his upper teeth, and with his head cocked, moved it in a posterior-anterior inverted nod which in its backward aspect had about twice the velocity of the movement which returned the head and face to the midline and, thus, to driving focus.[50]

Birdwhistell's redescription is more observationally fine grained; still, where are the social dimensions of behavior? Only in his last telling do we discover it. Each iteration "tell[s] the same story," albeit "with varying degrees of fullness." Here is a glimpse of the social in that final fullness:

> We postulate the arm and thumb as an "appeal for a ride," the spread-legged stance modified by the thumb-in-belt as "male defiant," and the whole as an act conveying a "defiant appeal for specific assistance." This complex of behavior is consistent with the role of these late adolescents, in uniform, who are avoiding "begging." These young soldiers are in no position to play the role of the college boy who "thumbs" a ride but whose college sticker and clothes belie the ingratiating stance and head cock plus smile with which he modifies his petition.

What he has created expositionally is a zoom, for he moves the reader's gaze in and out with respect to "the same" scene, as if he were shifting observational scale.[51] The fullest, final interaction is also the most socially rich. "In the time it takes an auto to pass a fixed point at 70 miles an hour, a communicational transaction has taken place, . . . a social group is established, a social ritual is performed, and, presumably, the lives of three human beings are somehow affected." Birdwhistell has us stand in awe at the fact that five seconds of interpersonal life, without words, can reveal a "microcosm"—as he put it—rife with tensions of gender and class and the tooth and claw of ethological ritual.

By disclosing aspects of social life that were not evident on first telling, Birdwhistell argued, in effect, that his mediatic science of body motion would deepen understanding of social life. "The ritual of 'thumbing a ride' is familiar in American culture," he writes, "yet a closer analysis of this special incident is illustrative of the hidden complexity of such scenes."[52] Achieving the unproblematic immanence of this hidden social complexity "in" embodied communication was hard work—the detailed transcription alone suggested that. As for method, to see the social, he says that one must undertake "cross-context analysis," looking at "the same" (in this case) gesture (thumbing a ride) in different settings.[53] There is no evidence that he actually did this here (and perhaps he felt that there was no need for cross-context analysis insofar as he was a member of "the same" culture); yet the basic claim was that you could know the social better through kinesic analysis—and not everyone believed this, or believed that the labor of such intense scrutiny was worth it. Birdwhistell was in effect implicitly countering a view that saw such feverishly fine-grained analysis as gratuitous, as if it offered only a high-resolution image of a scene whose outlines you could already easily see.[54]

Soaking: A Pedagogy of Mediatic Immersion

If in his statement on kinesics written for NHI, Birdwhistell tried to narrow the gap between kinesics and context, he let the gap widen at the University of Pennsylvania, if only as a paradox and provocation for others to grasp how the divide is ultimately illusory. One of Birdwhistell's most memorable courses from his Penn years was a methodology seminar that had students study a living room. The project consumed the whole semester, and eventually two, becoming known as the "living room courses."[55] The task was deceptively straightforward. Gain access to a living room and produce "as complete a description of the room as is possible." The rules were few. To estrange oneself from this familiar category of dwelling space in order to understand it better—a time-honored tactic in anthropological epistemology—students were not to pick a familiar room or room of someone they already knew. The other restriction was surprising: no mechanical recording instruments. No cameras and no tape recorders—a condition that made his science of kinesics impossible. You could talk to and interview people, of course. You could take copious field notes and create written inventories of objects. You could even measure and map things by hand if you wished.

How his pedagogy had changed. In a 1963 essay devoted to the "the use of audiovisual teaching aids" in anthropology, Birdwhistell had pathologized the "machinaphobic" instructor who feared mediatic prosthesis. Arguing that students would learn best if they experimented firsthand with photography and film, he shared the results of an exercise he used—an exercise that was, in fact, an earlier incarnation of his living room course from Penn, except that this earlier version included visual recording. Having selected a home, students at that time were encouraged to "select a room within the dwelling upon which to concentrate," to map the space by hand, to build a scale model rich with details, if possible, and to use a wide-angle lens to "take at least two photos of the room from standard angles."[56] Birdwhistell lauded their experimentation:

> Many students have simply constructed cameras, and with a little support some quickly learn how to make use of them. One of my students, for instance, took pictures at the eye level of each family member in his favorite sitting position. Another, quickly learned the trick of "hiding behind his camera" and took pictures at regular intervals which were tied in with a tape recording of family interaction. Still another urged various family members to pose in the room, in an endeavor to see whether he could find out anything about each family member's own photographic self-image.[57]

At Penn, by contrast, Birdwhistell subtracted the one thing that he and most interactionists had insisted upon: mechanical recording technologies. Without recording technologies, how could one grasp the delicate and dense structure and mercurial dynamics of communication, much of which escaped attention? Birdwhistell did qualify his enthusiasm for film—"the camera cannot substitute for the trained eye," he wrote early on—and cautioned scientists about epistemologically naive uses of mechanical recording.[58] Yet he never doubted that his science needed recording and playback technologies. By the '70s, sound and even video recording was becoming affordable, and, in the case of sound, de rigueur, yet Birdwhistell now discouraged it.

How curiously blinkered his exercise was. *Only* the living room. Birdwhistell had fashioned a pedagogy designed to teach what context really was. Students were to see that the room wasn't the inert environment they imagined. As his students recounted, they were to "approach a living room not as a 'thing,' but (as Birdwhistell phrase[d] it) '*behavior* which is in a sense 'slowed down.'" (Note the tropic extension of a temporalizing microscopy to "unmediated" techniques of noticing.)[59] And as behavior, they should see that it was, in broad terms, structured—riddled with unspoken rules and regularities. Deeper still was the lesson that the family living room wasn't just a space of human traffic and convergence. It was also a sociocultural nexus where socioeconomic class reared its head; where normativities of gender and intergenerational kinship surfaced; where little routines took root and got knotted up. The living room—an allegory for *any* behavioral event—was akin to what Marcel Mauss had once called a total social fact.

A committed comparativist of so-called primitive societies, Mauss had theorized their state of tight societal integration with this expression, which he adapted from Durkheim's notion of a social fact. Mauss introduced it in 1925 to describe forms of gift exchange like the Northwest American potlatch. Gift exchange was a *nexus* in which "all kinds of institutions are given expression at one and the same time." Marveling at the confluence and copresence of seemingly disparate aspects of social life, Mauss saw in the gift "an enormous complex of facts" in which "everything intermingles." In "total social phenomena," he explained, "all kinds of institutions are given expression at one and the same time—religious, juridical, and moral, which relate to both politics and the family."[60] At least for this category of sociocultural behavior—prestation—he found it futile to parcel out the world into neatly circumscribed islands of social life—religion, law, morality, politics, etc.; as if these were autonomous domains over which equally autonomous disciplines enjoyed jurisdiction. Tug on one thing—the gift—and the whole world reverberates.

The family room was like a total social fact. Its spatial boundedness was deceptive, by design. It posed as a metaphoric, spatialized "context"—a literal enclosure, a box—but it wasn't. It was naive to think you could exhaust its fullness, though the exercise seemed to demand students to do so. The task of supplying "as complete a description as possible" was bait. When Birdwhistell waxed philosophical, he seemed to enjoy the dizzying feeling that came when you suspended yourself between the seemingly irreconcilable antinomies of "pattern" and "part," "context" and "event" and refused to offer a theory to reconcile these.[61] He did not try to link, for example, micro and macro, as many students of language-in-use strained to do in the 1980s and '90s. He did not supply solutions to the problematics of context and scale.

In a published interview with Birdwhistell in the mid-1970s, fellow microanalyst Ray McDermott pressed him on his ideas about context. McDermott set up the question sympathetically, "We cannot decide beforehand what counts as a significant piece of communication without knowledge of the context of that piece." To this most would nod quickly in agreement, especially the anthropologists; yet Birdwhistell, a relentless antireductionist, seemed unwilling to constrain context. Context, Birdwhistell stressed, was "not an environment," "not a surround," that could be studied independently of the action transpiring "within" it. The trope of enclosure was wrong, for context was immanent in, not independent of, communicative behavior.[62]

The Ethnographic Sublime

Birdwhistell never abandoned the linguistic analogy on which he founded his science, but the expansion of his interest in parakinesics, which stretched the contextual envelope of kinesics, and his pedagogy of immersion in a boundless context late in his career, can be read as symptoms of Birdwhistell's mounting frustration with kinesics, a science he never formally disavowed but from which he quietly retreated.[63] Birdwhistell and Goffman, whose careers intersected at Penn, seemed to be heading in opposite directions with respect to language. Goffman's trajectory suggested a linguistic turn, helped along by his new colleagues Dell Hymes and William Labov, whereas Birdwhistell seemed to be pulling away from linguistics and its foundational role in his science of embodied communication.[64]

Pedagogically, Birdwhistell's turn from kinesics was not subtle, as Sigman himself, a student of Birdwhistell's, recounted. "From the very beginning I found Birdwhistell's teachings curious, indeed confusing. He spoke about kinesics only obliquely and instead spent most of his time talking about the nature of description, etic and emic formulations of behavior, and the proper 'location' of context."[65] His attitude was transmitted to his students, who organized a reading and discussion group tellingly under the banner of "ethnography"—not kinesics.

Birdwhistell's evolving stance on kinesics is evident not only in what he did and did not teach, or in what he had to say about context, but also in his closeted attraction to the ethnographer's holistic craft. In a 1977 edited book in honor of Gregory Bateson, Birdwhistell offered a chapter titled, "Some discussion of ethnography, theory, and method." This was an unusual essay, not the least stylistically.[66] A long section, modestly titled, "Bits from an Ethnographer's Journal," shared first-person observations of a beach and dock on Philadelphia's Schuylkill River from 1966 and 1968. Birdwhistell added footnotes in the early 1970s, which he preserved in this essay. From the margins Birdwhistell posed questions, commented on, and sometimes sniped at his past self. In introducing this ethnographic journal, he wrote that for five years he had been "attempting to study the social, the interactional, the communicational behavior of a variety of American fathers and children." This was to be comparative. He had hoped to discover intercultural differences in father-child relations, along the lines of Polish American, Italian American, Jewish American, and old Main Line American. Note the integrative ambitions that ranged across levels of analysis, one of which is segregated out as "the social."

The journal opens atmospherically:

> It is a midafternoon tide. As the sea withdraws the sandpipers scamper, feeding on the little things and, maintaining toe-depth, advance and retreat at the wave edge. A child approaches. The sandpipers themselves become a wave, slip airborne down the beach near the gulls, who posture, pose, and threaten with one another. Locked in gull talk, they pay no apparent attention either to the sandpipers who dance at the waves' edge or to the garbage-feeders who rise and fall with the swell just beyond the surf break.[67]

Birdwhistell quickly turns to the humans.

> From my window the beach seems populated by groups and by isolated peo-
> ple. Some appear alone, rooted in the sand. Others, as I telescope my percep-
> tions, turn slowly on invisible spits, basted, brushed, and picked at by their
> companions. These periodically dip their hot bodies in the surf or make a
> brief exhibitory promenade up the beach and back. In contrast are those who
> spend the sun time in the water, who return to touch base before dashing back
> into the sea.

Birdwhistell issues page after page of florid, metaphor-rich prose penned in
an evocative literary register. Birdwhistell the ethnographer replaces Birdwhistell the kinesic microanalyst, as if seized by the disciplinary return of the
repressed.

As his journal winds on, observation gives way to searching, first-person
meditations on theory and methodology—and, indeed, on *context*. With
Bateson as his imagined interlocutor, Birdwhistell meditated on context in
a way that reveals much about his dissatisfaction with the linguistic analogy. Much as Bateson savored the aesthetic of the paradox, so Birdwhistell
wrote that the apparent opposition of "pattern" and "particle" came down to
a matter of perspective. "While particle provides the possibility of immediate variation, pattern precedes particles." Aligning with Bateson, he went on
to say that "we agree that pattern, looked at through time or in structured
lamination of the here-now, is itself, *from another view*, a particle that gains its
operative stability and resilience through its own position as aspect of over-
pattern" (emphasis mine).[68]

His was a restless holism. As soon as you alighted upon one pattern, you
had to move on, shift perspective, and see that that pattern is also at once a
particle in a superordinate pattern, ad infinitum. This dialectic didn't resolve
itself, nor could you step away from it. This was not Dilthey's hermeneutic circle in which anthropological interpretivists like Clifford Geertz hap-
pily ran, yet it seemed equally endless and inescapable. Nor were the shifts
in perspective that Birdwhistell speaks of like Pike's discussions about shifts
in focus. Pike argued you could illuminate any part of a structure comfortably from afar. He neatly stacked up the linguistic and extralinguistic world
with la langue–like hierarchized constituency, so that you could ascend and
descend a single, structuralized world with ease. Birdwhistell's universe was
disconcertingly bigger, wilder. Consider, from 1962, a similarly unsettling reflection: "The exciting thing about such an assembled, multilevel description
of the communicational process is that it becomes immediately clear that it
is just as easy (and unrewarding) to describe the lexical material as modifiers

of the remainder of the behavior as it is to define the remainder of the communicational behavior as modifying the lexical."[69] Birdwhistell, unlike Pike,
offered no sure footing, no way to scale structure. You could not get "above"
or "outside" behavioral structure to apprehend it as a totality. You could not
know it in its plenitude.

Birdwhistell's weakened confidence in a truly structuralist kinesics, his
retreat from recording technologies and microanalysis, his pedagogy of immersion in context and attraction to ethnography, are instructive. The trajectory of trouble stemmed in no small part from kinesics' baptismal moment,
when Birdwhistell autonomized kinesic structure by treating it as if it were
a separate system distinct from its "social" dimensions; indeed, this disconnect came to concern him, for as he also knew well from the very beginning,
kinesics was interesting precisely because sociological phenomena such as
gender, class and region played out through all manner of embodied signs.
The problem became one of reconnecting this autonomous and mediatically
scaled kinesic structure with the sociocultural world.

The divide between kinesics and the social was not simply the result of
an over-extended linguistic–structuralist analogy, however. It was a gap reproduced if not widened by Birdwhistell's own sensibilities about viewing.
"Birdwhistell could spend months studying a few seconds of film," Martha
Davis notes, and this intense granularity in observational scale helped create
the conditions for his concern about how best to grasp the fuller context of his
microscopic science.[70] Birdwhistell insisted that one first view the film many
times at normal playback speed before beginning analysis.[71] A dozen times is
what he recommended as early as the '50s. Only after repeated viewing, what
members of the NHI team sometimes called "soaking," should one then slow
things down and start dissection.[72] Whatever else this method did—mediatic
playback is itself an ethnographic object of great importance—it surely intensified the sense of a disconnect between the impressions of communicative
action formed under conditions of global viewing and the fragmented impressions that occur from piecemeal microanalytic scrutiny, because under the
proverbial microscope, wholes are nowhere to be found.[73] For Birdwhistell,
and, indeed, for most recording-based microanalysts, repeated playback and
fine-grained analysis unveiled new forms of complexity, which heightened
rather than mitigated dissonance between part and whole.[74]

Dwelling: The Infinite Scalarity of Communicative Life

To an audience of anthropologists in 1970, at their annual conference, Birdwhistell spoke passionately of the way human communication involved as-

tonishingly dense "laminations" of structure that can be peeled apart analytically but were, in fact, intercalated in ways we scarcely understand. In a
demonstration using the old NHI clip, he noted how a seemingly tiny stretch
of communication involved some 145 distinct "layers" of structure that needed
to be accounted for. Clocks may deceive us into thinking that time in communication flows as a "single stream," but "I think of it as a laminate of events as
small as three thousandths of a second and as large as six generations." "We're
living in the multiple laminates, the relationship of which makes it possible
for social structure to work."[75]

Multiplex lamination, note, was *not* hierarchical constituency. Birdwhistell
never spelled out what this implied about the structuralism that birthed his
science, but it is hard not to see it as a cutting commentary on what it could
not deliver. Perhaps behaviors were not as hierarchically structured as he had
first imagined; perhaps they did not stack up so neatly or so high. Perhaps the
structuralist analogy was misleading.[76] His own doubts were helped along by
critics, notably rival scientist of the nonverbal Paul Ekman, who back in the
'60s had faulted Birdwhistell for thinking embodied communication was too
much like language.[77]

The 1970 conference event was a double session on the theme of "film as
data for culture studies." It stretched over two mornings and featured many of
the usual suspects, notably Margaret Mead and Norman McQuown and was
anchored by Birdwhistell himself. When Alan Lomax opened the session on
the first day, he spoke like Hooke of a subvisible frontier: "Ray Birdwhistell
and his collaborators have learned enough to turn us all on visually, as you
will discover this morning when they take you into the unfamiliar world of
microanalysis of visible behavior. They have found realm upon realm of orderly, learned behavior below the level of the visible everyday." The speaker
line up was organized in terms of observational scale. The sessions moved
from the most micro-observational studies on up, beginning, as expected,
with William Condon who announced that he would be descending "into
the very microworld of fractions of a second on film," and proceeded to show
off footage of the exquisitely fine-grained dance of interactional coordination
and synchrony.

In his own session Birdwhistell told his audience that he had worked on
and would describe segments "slightly larger than [what] we just saw from
Mr. Condon." This would entail a "much larger, longer here-now ethnographic present" than Condon's, and although this added up to a mere fifteen
seconds of clock time, it was a "*huge* period of time." To appreciate the density
and complexity of human behavior, the student must be "willing to live in
that kind of time." Yet one must not confuse microscopic observation, and

its demand to inhabit the micro and see things from this scale, with reality itself. Epistemological and ontological scale had clearly gotten conflated, and Birdwhistell would disentangle the two. What one observes may well seem like a distinct level of reality that is isolated if not paracosmic, but ultimately it is not. For "anyone who decides to work in this kind of field," Birdwhistell counseled, it is crucial that he have "the capacity to live in an order of time and not think in terms of it being long or short."

> If there's anything that I want to say to you, if you take films anywhere, *don't worry about the quantity*. There is plenty in any piece, if you know how to live in that piece and look at it. But you've got to live in that piece without becoming a Lilliputian or another without believing you're a giant.

So much for critics who would find Birdwhistell's object too small in extent and only tenuously tied to the surface world. Birdwhistell argued that the interaction scientist, like the anthropologist doing fieldwork, must be willing to take up residence in an observational scale of experience while recognizing that this is ultimately not a "level" that is as separate as it may seem. Just as the anthropologist aspires toward an "ethnographic presence" in the field, so here one must learn to dwell—serially, not simultaneously—in distinct "here-nows," which may be "as short as the milliseconds which Professor Condon took you through into . . . the multi-hours that we think about in a kinship system." Interaction is neither paracosm nor microcosm, because the very idea of a nested world of smaller and larger, micro and macro, is wrong. "If you listened here over these last two days you've heard one of us say that the other person works—'well, he works in the macro, I work in the micro, but . . . that's really because we worked with clocks.'" Social time, by contrast is a "fantastic multiple laminate" that exists "outside of the observer's time," which means that "the length of a time of a [linguistic] phone or the length of a time of an eye blink, or the length of a time of a kinship system are relative."

Epistemologically, then, observational scales are real and constraining. The capacity to observe is limited but the world is not; the world is not made up of separate levels parallel to observational scales and the horizons they seem to open up and foreclose. Birdwhistell advises that you can and should live and dwell "in" the timescales of mediatic microscopy for a while. We can think of this in terms of the experience of observational scale, as observational scales can be inhabitable.[78] Still, later in his career at least, Birdwhistell suggests that we must always remember that this is an epistemological state, not a state of the world. In reality, any scrutinized piece of social life is *infinitely* embedded—"multiply laminated"—from above and below; which means that even the finest microscopy can never touch bottom.

We may again remember Leibniz and his indebtedness to the microscope. His idea of infinite worlds within worlds—mundi in mundis in infinitum— was one that, as Christiane Frey wrote, "endlessly miniaturizes the micro-scopically observable cosmos in a mise en abyme. Every piece of nature can be comprehended as a garden full of plants and a pond full of fish. But every twig of the plant, every member of the animal, every drop of his juices is in turn such a garden and such a pond." Look as closely as you want, then. Divide up matter as finely as you wish. You will not find elementary units that support everything from below. For Leibniz, Frey reminded us, these "limits of seeing are not also limits of nature,"[79] which suggests that although we can never apprehend the infinite state of nature, we can speculate metaphysically about it. So, too, did Birdwhistell defer to the future the possibility of ever knowing the true state of communication in its multiplicity and fullness; as a plenum, this state of communicative reality exceeds the limitations of observational scale. Such a stance ensured that no scale is too small to matter, that they all somehow intersect and make up communication as it truly, fully, really is.

When Birdwhistell spoke of needing to live in the micro, this was not simply a way to emphasize that mediatic microscopy requires patience and takes a long time. It was also advice for living. "For me as a humanist," he said, "it's very exciting to think that though I may have only about 35 years to live, I have millions of microseconds to live, and that the shape and the size and the feelings of those things are something that can be experienced, and experienced on purpose. If I sound sentimental, it is because I am sentimental."

This hopefulness, the way it invited you into close, rapturous observation wherever and whenever you happened to be, the way it assured you not to worry about exactly how it was all connected, is reminiscent in a certain way of the interscalar bliss that overcame the protagonist at the climax of the 1957 film *The Incredible Shrinking Man*, which was based on the book by Richard Matheson. After accidental exposure to a cocktail of radioactive mist and insecticide, breadwinner Scott Carey is alarmed to discover himself shrinking at a rate of one-seventh of an inch per day. In a kind of tale of white suburban male emasculation, he comes to lash out at as wife, flirts and almost has an affair, suffers humiliation after humiliation, including having to live in a doll house. Yet after a harrowing battle with his own cat that leaves him alone, trapped in the basement, he rediscovers a primal masculinity by hunting for food, by vanquishing a spider, and by later escaping the literal and figurative confinement that is his own home. Existentially, though, fear of annihilation consumes him as he continues to shrink, only to discover that in the end the "infinite and the infinitesimal" meet, that for "God there is no zero." He finds peace.

✻

If Birdwhistell could sometimes imagine a comparable serenity for the analyst, was this not just too comfortable, too isolationist? Would kinesics and sciences like it yield practical knowledge only after many years, and refuse to do something *now* to curb a world roiling with interpersonal trouble and suffering? Having postponed social kinesics so very, very long, Birdwhistell's science of meaningful movement raised questions about what kind of knowledge it could or would deliver.

For critics, a similar complacency had seemed to infect *The First Five Minutes*, which buried its takeaways and insisted that you educate your senses. If observational acuity was the real pedagogical mission of *The First Five Minutes*, it made for an impractical science, a science with no actionable knowledge: no recommendations on how to improve therapeutic interaction or interaction in the round. In a very different context, Anna Tsing speaks of ethnographic arts of noticing that do not aspire to generalize as a science.[80] An analogous observational sensibility can be felt here, where the plenum of interpersonal reality became something to approach and experience deliberately—yet purportedly free from external pressures that seek knowledge for purposes of social control. At best, *The First Five Minutes* could make clinicians into more semiotically sensitive and mindful creatures, but it could not, or would not, give instructions on how to manage other people.

As with Birdwhistell, that book had stayed silent about the many recognized ills of interactional life that people cared about: inefficiency, maladjustment, misunderstanding, prejudice, domination, and authoritarianism. It did not even sort out the effective from the ineffective among different and competing talking cures as other recording projects—notably those by Carl Rogers and his students—endeavored to do.

Aside from its pedagogical justification, the immersive, experiential design of *The First Five Minutes* did have a scientific defense, and it was a defense Birdwhistell supported. Its methodological sensibility was defended as *natural history*. Indeed, this is no surprise, as this project owed much to the eponymous NHI collaboration that had included Hockett from the start and later incorporated Birdwhistell.[81] As Bateson wrote in his first draft of the NHI's introduction, "our primary data are the multitudinous details of vocal and bodily action recorded on this film." "We call this 'natural history,'" he explained, "because a minimum of theory guided the collection of data." The "data themselves are sufficiently uncorrupted by theory so that the six authors, each with particular theoretical bias and interest, could simultaneously approach this mass of detail."[82]

"None of us believes in any sort of history (including case history) for its own sake," wrote the authors of *The First Five Minutes*. If they veered too far toward description, this was only to counter "the danger of being so anxious to achieve generalizations that one glosses over fine details which, given time and patience, might well yield deeper and more significant generalizations."[83]

In the clinical psychology world, recording enthusiasts like David Shakow agreed and had spoken elegantly about this very issue. A veteran of Worcester State Hospital, where he stayed from 1928 to 1942, Shakow had directed research in psychology for years and had become a leading voice in what would break off from psychiatry and become the distinct field of "clinical psychology." He had been an analysand of Zinn's in Worcester in the 1930s and inspired by Zinn's recording efforts. Back in the late 1940s, well before NHI, Shakow defended natural history. In an annual roundtable on "the objective evaluation of psychotherapy," Shakow complained that "the patient, naturalistic phase, which biology has found so important before going on to its experimental phase, has in its essentials been skipped in psychotherapy, just as it has in psychology."[84] In defending naturalistic observation over experimental research design, he was firing back a rejoinder in a much larger debate in the social sciences (in social psychology, for instance, this debate resolved itself decisively in favor of the "experimental"—in a specific sense— after the Second World War).[85]

What was at stake here was never only questions of epistemology and methodology, for these competing ways of knowing also had practical, disciplinary, and political implications. And one thing that critics alleged of natural history was that it wasn't good at effecting change. You could train people to observe well, to notice what others missed, yet it was hard to imagine a less fitting methodology for social change. With such slow and largely inductive methods, how would interactionists improve the world at anything other than a glacial pace? How would they steer social life through their expertise? That their work was objective and scientific was plain, if not ostentatiously on display; but what and who was this research really *for*? As we will see next, most postwar interaction scientists who worked outside of this small but influential network of psychiatrists and communication scientists wanted to deliver knowledge that would change the world. They aspired to be technoscientific and technocratic social engineers, and they, too, shrank interaction as intensely as those who chased the communicative unconscious, but they did so for very different reasons. These other postwar sciences of interaction—small group analysts, as they often called themselves—from the start promised to step into the fray. They did not chase the communicative unconscious, yet they, too, often fashioned themselves as "microscopic" observers of social interaction, and they would try to make themselves more useful to their patrons and to the world.

PART II

Small Groups

FIGURE 10. Observing interactional problem-solving behind a one-way mirror in Robert Freed Bales's special room. Reproduced with permission from Harvard University Archives.

There is another story to be told about interaction's scale, about how and why it shrank in midcentury America and seemed to require a microscopic gaze. This story does not involve psychiatry and the desire to chase down the indexicality of the communicative unconscious, yet it is equally the story of medial technologies and the emergence of discursive interaction as a distinctive and scaled thing to know.

Interaction had no widely known science of its own until the years after the Second World War. Of course, "social interaction"—even when it wasn't called exactly that, and even when this expression evoked something more abstract and expansive than face-to-face interaction between two or more humans—had mattered long before this.[1] In America, it had mattered intensely among early pragmatists like Charles Horton Cooley, John Dewey, and George Herbert Mead.[2] Yet none of these men had tried to fashion interaction into an autonomous, irreducible object and agitate for a science dedicated to its study—as happened in midcentury. While the *scale* of this postwar object—its presumed smallness and its concomitant need for a microscopic gaze, a gaze made possible with mechanical recording and playback technologies—crystallized when these new sciences of interaction arose in the years after the Second World War, it is true that interaction had been treated as small by social scientists many times before.

Cooley's sociology, for instance, had scaled interaction richly. Cooley took special interest in "small, face-to-face groups"—especially those that made up what he memorably called "primary groups." Primary groups, notably "the family, the play-group of children, and the neighborhood or community group of elders," were "characterized by intimate, face-to-face association and cooperation." Their intimacy (which didn't necessarily imply harmonious relations) was a function not only of size and proximity—how "small" these groups were in terms of countable humans and how "close"-ly they resided—but rather of an inverse correlation between spatial and temporal scale. Primary groups were small on the first count but large on the second, for Cooley stressed that these were *durable* groups, not ones that rapidly appeared and disappeared.[3] In this self-consciously scalar take on interaction, we find a familiar *asymmetrical interscalarity* in which the small was not truly small and needed to be recognized for its unappreciated reach. That was how scale could surprise you.

As object, Cooley did envision the primary group—at least in part—as a miniature world. He conceded that primary groups were microcosmic *to some extent*—the "German family and the German school bear somewhat distinctly the print of German militarism," for instance—but he insisted that these interactions also had universal properties that made them partly free of cultural and societal specificity and diversity. Primary groups, that is, enjoyed a measure of autonomy. Note that even as Cooley carved out a foundational form of interaction that differed from the rest of social life, he did not call for a science to study primary group interaction on its own. Nor did he think this object required a special microscopic gaze. If anything, observationally speaking, the "primary" of primary groups meant that these groups had empirical immediacy. They were easier to know compared to larger, more diffuse forms of social organization.[4]

When interaction again became self-consciously small after World War II, this was part of a different and far more ambitious effort to carve out interaction as its own object of knowledge. In our first story, we saw how small could mean mediatic indexicality and the search for the chattering communicative unconscious, but as a resonant discourse in postwar social science, small could also suggest something very different, as we will soon see.

In fact, smallness became essential to this new object's identity. It helped baptize it as a novel thing to study and know. "Small-group" analysis, as this nascent science of interaction was often called, became a postwar boom industry, complete with its own recording technologies. The word small was plastered onto this object in a way that it never was among those who worked in the psychiatry–communication–science interface.[5] And small was a curiously bold word. Far from suggesting something limited or trivial, "small" evoked a potent, focused, rigorous science, a science that preferred the laboratory and fashioned itself after the natural sciences. It was confidently technocratic, too, as small also suggested a science whose object was manageable, something you could control and transform. As something small—but, again, not truly small at all—interaction could in this way become a technology that would transform the world. Rather than indexicalization, which was the ideological thru line of our first story, let us speak instead of *interactionalization*, the transformation of this new object into a method of its own, something that promised to fix the whole world, one interaction at a time.

5

Rigorously, Manageably Small

The "small" that helped baptize small-group science in postwar America came without apology or disclaimer. It was no term of derision. Small didn't finger research with limited significance. Nor was it a concession about the limits of what you could know. On the contrary, small amplified the science's importance and broadcast its rigor. Unlike all those big groups that the social scientists struggled to predict, small groups of humans—which ranged "from two to something around twenty"—looked tractable.[1] Their diminutive size made them more amenable to the researcher's control; prototypically they "fit" in a lab and would bend to experimental protocol. Circumscribed, controlled, small groups could thereby receive the full force of epistemic scrutiny, scrutiny that was often fine grained if not microscopic in observational scale; for what else do you do with little objects, except to break them down and see what makes them tick?[2] In this way, as we will see, small groups allowed you to be *rigorous*. As we will also see, small groups offered unprecedented opportunities for social engineering, for a small group was also *manageable*.

Disarming by name, small-group analysis had big ambitions. Often laboratory-based, technophilic, and technocratic, this research was imperious in what it claimed it could know and help control. It could figure out and fix any species of interaction, from chess matches to marital disputes, in any place, from cockpits to classrooms.

Small-group analysis thrived as it embraced the twin virtues of scientism and social engineering that social science patronage demanded. These demands came not only from the federal funding agencies of the immediate post–World War II and early–Cold War period—the newly reorganized Department of Defense or the National Science Foundation, for instance—but also of the private foundations. To be serviceable under the usual technocratic division of labor, such "soft" social scientists who embraced social engineering, who offered knowledge about an imperfect social world so as to improve its operations from the top down, were to remain objective in the sense of politically disinterested;[3] they must not stray into ideological, value-driven, activist research, especially if those values veered too far left—too close to the wrong side of the polarized, moralized, geopolitical divide. The Ford Foundation's influential postwar "behavioral sciences program" was a telling piece of branding in this respect. As others have stressed, the word "behavior" conjured the behaviorists' austere mechanical objectivity, as if to declare that there shall be no more speculative science. It also sought to calm the nerves of conservative patrons for whom the "social" in social science could sound too much like "social reform" (read: New Deal) and was, after all, only a suffix away from socialism.[4] Small groups seemed safe to study, because a clutch of humans surely wasn't the tinderbox of big groups with their ideologies and politics.

A field's autonomy had often been predicated on its object's autonomy. Founding a field by sticking a flag in an object and declaring it independent—as if it had essential properties that couldn't be explained by any existing science—was a familiar baptismal gesture found in many disciplinary charters. Recall, for example, the irreducibility of "the social" in Durkheim's sociology, or Ferdinand de Saussure's efforts to establish linguistics by walling off a pristine core of language (la langue) from encroaching fields like psychology, history, and sociology.

Here interaction was strangely unmoored. It was to be an object *without* a field, because another familiar demand made on the postwar social sciences was that of interdisciplinarity. Interdisciplinarity implied, among other things, a "discipline-blind and task-oriented culture of inquiry," and there was no faster "means to policy relevance."[5] What better thing to study than an object whose name meant relations *between* agents? Here was a boundary object—interaction—that was suspended across fields and made its home in none; that invited the very collaboration expected of the rebooted behavioral sciences. And once these disparate fields joined hands to know this object, the object returned the favor. Interaction could function reflexively. It could reflect back upon the scholarly agents gathered around it, affirming that they too were interacting well, just as they should.

All of which is to say that small-group science's embrace of scale was inseparable from the imperatives of postwar and early–Cold War social science. Inseparable from, not reducible to. Although I adopt here a conventional form of interscalar argument, where I interpret aspects of a focal object (interaction) by appeal to a contextual (sociohistorical) "surround," I do not suggest, to put it crudely, that context "did" it, that interaction got made and scaled this way as a function of some encompassing and determinative Cold War apparatus (*dispositif*), for instance. My argument is more limited. I only wish to explain the allure of the discourses and techniques of scale that accompanied some of these midcentury sciences of interaction and that help explain their family resemblance. Accounting for this allure requires that we follow interdiscursive traces and appreciate how the trope of mediatic, "microscopic" observation, along with the claim that this object interaction is intrinsically, ontologically "small"—resonated with other projects that these scholars took seriously, or at least felt pressure to take seriously.

Nor do I mean to suggest that small-group science was all that cohesive. Not everyone walked in lockstep. As a new big tent interdisciplinary enterprise, small-group researchers could certainly try to look inclusive. They could sweep everyone into their fold and try to ignore their differences (even when members disagreed or disputed that they were even members). Notably, research on talk therapy, which began in the interwar period and took off after the Second World War, was sometimes marshaled under the banner of small-group research, but it was hardly the same. It had a less technocratic outlook as well as a searching, hermeneutic sensibility, as we saw in our first story of scale. It could care about "meaning" in interaction in the way that a psychoanalyst did. More naturalistic than experimental, it allowed its researchers to wander into the wilds of interpersonal life and seek out indexical traces that the practical small-group engineers experienced as noise.

Despite the disputes that could erupt among the postwar sciences of the face-to-face, most came to share a few basic assumptions: that interaction was its own reality that needed science and special methods to know; that compared to other objects in the social-scientific universe, interaction was small-scale in its spatial and temporal dimensions; and that, as a small thing, interaction demanded an appropriate observational scale, which usually meant fine-grained, if not "microscopic," methods of some kind.

Recorders Dedicated to Interaction

The more passionate you were about microscopy, the more likely you insisted on mechanical recording. A few talk therapy researchers had started to experiment with commercially available sound-recording and playback technologies in the early 1930s, as we saw, and this type of research expanded after the war. But during the 1940s, just before enthusiasm for small-group research began to surge, interaction also got its "own" machines—customized recording technologies for the study of interaction—which testified to the growing importance and independence of this new object of knowledge.

As we will see in the next chapter, Harvard in the 1940s was home to two such "interaction recorders," machines designed to help some humans understand, and predict and control, how other humans interacted. Comparing the two machines, and the men who promoted and used them, offers a vantagepoint on the way these medial technologies made interaction a scaled object to know and control.

One interaction recorder belonged to sociologist Robert Freed Bales (1916–2004)—an enterprising methodologist and star student of Talcott Parsons who, in 1946, was invited to join and later direct Harvard's new Laboratory of Social Relations.[6] Housed in Emerson Hall, outfitted with rooms for psychological experiments, a sound-proof room with one-way mirrors, a statistical computation room with IBM equipment, and a machine shop—the shop that built Bales's recorder—the lab served as the research and training wing of the new interdisciplinary Department of Social Relations that melded sociology, social anthropology, social psychology, and clinical psychology.[7] His interaction recorder mechanically dispensed paper at a fixed rate. A trained transcriber would observe interaction in real time behind a one-way mirror and classify each interactional move as it occurred, in the order it occurred, using a system Bales developed.

The other interaction recorder belonged to Eliot Dismore Chapple (1909–2000), an anthropologist by training and student of W. Lloyd Warner. Chapple enjoyed an affiliation with Harvard's business school for a spell but lost his position, and after a one-year stint in anthropology and four years at the medical school, he left Harvard in 1945. Chapple had broken dramatically from Warner in the mid-1930s, and from his field, and did not end up holding a tenured academic job.[8] When anthropologists remember Chapple, it is usually for his role as architect of and agitator for an "applied anthropology" that returned attention homeward. Chapple created and edited the first journal of applied anthropology and joined forces with no less than Margaret Mead whom he had befriended in Washington during wartime service on the Committee for National Morale. More relevant to remember here is Chapple's screeching methodological U-turn in the 1930s when he dropped the qualitative for the quantitative, messy interpretation for steely measurement.

Anthropology would be reborn as a natural science of human relations, where human relations meant observable *interactions* among two or more individuals that could, and should, be measured. For this he also needed an interaction recorder, and his would also dispense paper at a fixed rate. While his machine evolved considerably over the years, at base it required that observers watch humans carefully and press a button whenever people communicated and release it whenever they paused. You didn't code what people communicated but simply marked the onsets and offsets, yet from this alone you could learn much about interaction.

Harvard's "social relations" wasn't quite "human relations," certainly not as Chapple understood human relations, yet Chapple and Bales were not so different. Bales, too, saw interaction as a matrix of social life. Bales, too, had committed himself to scientism, with its methodological rigor and fits of technophilia, just as he also accepted the value of social engineering. There was tension between the two men and their machines, at least from Chapple's side, but in the immediate postwar period, Bales and Chapple were not public rivals any more than their interaction recorders were, even if their machines did each come to brandish the determiner "the," as if each were alone and unique.

Differences and tensions aside, both machines shared a basic conceit. Mechanical sound or sound film recorders were indiscriminate in what they captured, yet these recorders were styled as *dedicated* tools.[9] As Rebecca Lemov reflects, the Cold War would become "a methodological boom time in which experts turned a fine-tuned, hyperfocused eye on their dedicated tools, the 'special instruments,' 'special procedures,' and 'special rooms' of the social sciences."[10] It was not the fact that they had built a dedicated recorder that was unusual but rather the thing to which their recorders had been dedicated—interaction, which was not yet widely recognized as an independent thing to know.

Although influential for a spell, both recorders fell into disuse. Chapple pressed on with his machine into the early '70s even as few followed him. When Bales's method called Interaction Process Analysis (IPA) morphed into a revised system in the late '60s and early '70s called SYMLOG, his recorder became superfluous. Mainstream sound recorders and sound film, which were flexible and pledged no loyalty to any source, supplanted Chapple's and Bales's dedicated recorders. By the 1970s, portable tape recording became the media technology of choice for social scientists of all persuasions, including most interactionists.

When it came to studying behavior, the turn away from human recorders toward mechanical recording had been happening in many quarters. As we saw in our first story, it wasn't obvious initially that you even needed mechanical recording technologies to understand the "talk" of talk therapy. Only slowly did talk-therapy researchers become entranced by mechanical fidelity—indexical fidelity in particular—and came to think that it was indispensable. After the end of the Second World War, mechanical recording technologies were becoming attractive for many social scientists. As Lemov writes, some anthropologists at the time, as well as the Chicago-trained life history sociologists, became drawn to the power of recorders with big and small footprints, as research budgets and recording situations allowed. Lemov notes how Dorothy Eggan and Elizabeth Colson, for instance, had once imagined themselves in the "stenographic-ethnographic" role of "recorder," yet by the mid-1950s recording now implied recording machines.[11] Human recorders had lost their clout.[12]

Even though these two interaction recorders crested and then fell during the midcentury, they are instructive to remember. They offer a window onto the interaction sciences at a moment when interest was beginning to build and interaction's existence was beginning to thicken and take form. By turns similar and different, at times quiet rivals, these machines give us a technosemiotic vantagepoint onto the early life of interaction as it began to coalesce as an intrinsically small object that was best known microscopically. As I juxtapose these two men and their machines over the next two chapters, a third small-group scientist, Kurt Lewin, will make an important cameo.[13] Lewin and his students used interaction science to promote democracy in interpersonal life—thereby demonstrating the tremendous social engineering potential of interaction science. Before we turn to the recorders of Bales and Chapple over the next two chapters, let us trace in broad terms what they shared and how they epitomized a then nascent small-group science that made smallness so central to its identity.

Shrinking Interaction

What was this "small" of small-group science, both as discourse and as scalar effect of the technics of recording? "Small" was a scalar shorthand. As discourse, it formed a compact argument about interaction that combined observational and ontological scales. By definition, again, the "small" of small group distinguished it from the big groups that the social scientists usually studied—classes or ethnic groups or polities, for instance. Just how small was small was sometimes a live question, and while Bales knew there was more to small groups than size, he committed himself to a range that stretched "from two to something around twenty."[14] This suggested that small groups didn't differ from large ones in kind but *extent*, a quantitative parameter whose unit was the individual human body. Groups were aggregations of countable bodies. Smaller groups had fewer, bigger ones more. (In effect, Bales adopted the operational definition that a group was small if it fit in his special room and could be subjected to his microscopic methods.)

If extent—measured in countable bodies—implied that this object was a relatively small thing, it also triggered that old concession of observational scale: the grain-extent inverse. If you wanted to look at something finely, you couldn't look at a lot; which, by force of habit, made the converse true—that if you weren't looking at a lot, you must be looking closely. Since interaction was declared to be small in extent, it invited observational microscopy by implication, which is precisely what people like Bales and Chapple felt they offered. The "small" of small groups helped shrink interaction while motivating its fine-grained, microscopic study.

Interaction Immediatized

Bales's small-group science was self-consciously scalar, yet this scaling was not just an artifact of what he said about his subject matter and his methods. It was the technics of his recorder and its laboratory conditions that shrank interaction more than any resonant discourse about scale ever could. In fact, both Chapple and Bales and their machines were most uncannily alike in how they walled off interaction, purified it of "context," and shrank it into a spatially and temporally bounded event while making it intensely present as a small but concentrated burst of human activity; and how they exploited the mechanical flow of paper to resolve this burst of activity, to break down its density microscopically, as if with high-speed cinematography, so that they could discern how the face-to-face worked.

The most striking similarity between the two recorders is that they both exploited the flow of paper to record interactional change over time. Chapple's operators tapped keys to graph ink on moving paper; Bales's penned codes by hand on a stream of 18-inch-wide ribbon that scrolled slowly by a ticker through his machine at a rate of 3 inches per minute. As Bales conceded, his machine was, in essence, an elaborate paper dispenser: a "case containing a driving mechanism for a wide paper tape upon which scores can be written."[15] To record interaction as it unfolded in time, in paper time, Chapple and Bales treated interaction as if it were *immanently recordable,* as if everything you needed to know about the face-to-face was deictically right *there*; as if interaction were no less, and no more, than the event of mechanical recording itself. There would be no need for you to collect additional evidence. No triangulation using interviews conducted before or after the fact, for instance; no demographic information gathered about the participants; and no observations to see how people behaved in other settings. This risked muddling things up and obscuring interaction itself.[16]

This immanence of recording gave interaction a vivid presence and immediacy—effects heightened by the way interaction had been spatiotemporally bounded off. The recording event was walled off literally when interactions were recorded, as they usually were, in special built environments:

a lab or special room or office, for instance; and the temporal boundaries—the beginnings and endings—were shored up with greeting and leave-taking protocol, and much else. There was no doubt about when the interaction began and ended, where it transpired, who was involved. And as for *who*, both Chapple and Bales black-boxed individuals. The human interactants were individuals without histories, backgrounds, intentions, or states of mind. There was no interiority to plumb. No sociological habitus to grasp or cultural assumptions to tease out. All the messy contextual entanglements of human interpersonal life had been cut away, which left only pure *interaction*.

How presumptuous these recording regimes were, as they dismissed all those established fields that already had methods for understanding humans. They claimed, in effect, that nobody yet knew how humans interacted, because nobody had bothered to record them properly.

Immanent recordability may be seen as an extension of a general and widespread experimentalist sensibility that had been adapted from the natural sciences and was fast becoming hegemonic after the Second World War.[17] As Kurt Danziger has traced in the history of social psychology, for instance, "the social" became narrowed in the 1920s to make it amenable to a certain conception of rigorous, lab-based experimental science. Floyd Allport notoriously reduced the social to the sheer physical copresence of individuals and disputed the existence of groups qua groups, which you couldn't observe scientifically. As Danziger draws out, this meant, in particular, limiting social psychology to the study of effects that were "local, proximal, short term, and decomposable." *Local*, in the sense that effects were "observed in a particular time and place" (in the lab and for the duration of an experiment, and no longer); *proximal*, in the sense that you measured the "immediate presence of some effective agent, known as a 'stimulus'"; *short term* in the sense that the effects studied were those that didn't last but rather were limited to the duration of the experiment; (and *decomposable* meant you could resolve complex effects into simplex ones, in order to trace out cause and effect with delicacy).[18] Local, proximal, short term—these were closely related scalar effects of a laboratory sensibility and regime that produced "the social" as a small but scintillating thing to know. Something like this scalar performativity was also at work with Chapple and Bales, as we will see.

For now, by way of introduction, let us only appreciate how striking this interactional immediacy was. Among the many theorists of social and interpersonal life who preceded Chapple and Bales, it was not unusual to note how far-reaching human interaction could be, for unlike the brute ethological encounters between physically copresent animals about which Darwin had written, humans routinely interact with agents who are not strictly speaking *there* and cannot be directly observed. By this we can think not only of incorporeal agents such as spirits and gods and the dead, but also of innumerable others who may loom in the background as potential overhearers, as when speakers delicately adjust what they say based on who they think may hear them later. Here we may also remember something more abstract, George Herbert Mead's notion of a "generalized other," which referred not to a biological human but to the personological equivalent of Freud's superego—sociological norms incarnate. Mead suggested that humans learn to perspective shift. They learn to see themselves through the eyes of this normative other, which is real but immaterial. Its existence can be inferred but not observed. This generalized other is a virtual interlocutor—not an empirically manifest animal you can see or touch. And yet this generalized other serves as a constant conversational companion without whom the social self would not develop.

Max Weber, too, had suggested that meaningful interaction in social life involved anticipating how others will or would react, for in any social relationship, "the action of each takes account of that of the others and is oriented in these terms."[19] For Weber these others could be separated in space and time; they didn't need to be physically copresent. Interpersonal psychiatrist Harry Stack Sullivan put the matter dramatically. Even when "only two people are actually in the room, the number of more-or-less imaginary people that get themselves involved in this two-group is sometimes really hair-raising. Yes, it's a two group, but two or three times in the course of an hour, to be conservative, whole new sets of these imaginary others are also present in the field."[20] All of which is to say that diminutive scaling of interaction that was so vivid in Chapple and Bales was a performative effect of their recording science, not its precondition. A new small version of interaction was in the making.

Interaction Recorders

What kind of microscopy did this small science of interaction require—interaction that was localized and immediatized as if it were limited in spatiotemporal scale? If there was one thing that made Bales and Chapple so very similar, it was the fact that their microscopy was temporalizing. Both tracked time—*linear, unfolding time*—by having human operators make marks on paper that flowed mechanically and continuously at a uniform rate.

Getting at the temporality of an epistemic object through moving strips of paper was familiar from many medical and scientific devices; breaking down complex phenomena by resolving their *density* had been done before, too. Time-and-motion studies in industry, as well as psychological research on child development, often resolved density with the help of visual media like film, for instance.[1] Nor was it novel, strictly speaking, to want to chart interactional change over time. Lasswell, after all, had tried to look across lots of therapeutic events in his "prolonged interview" research, as did Zinn with his marathon effort to transcribe the whole course of treatment. However, neither man had tried to scrutinize change over time in a *single* discursive event, as Chapple and Bales wanted to do. They wanted to break down interaction itself to see what occurred within it.

Breaking down a single event like this suggested a version of the face-to-face as discrete and circumscribed. Again, this was not the only version of interaction available. It is true that the ethologically minded interaction scientists would soon point out how human face-to-face interaction always involved spatial and temporal boundary making. Yet this was the result of human communicative labor. Humans had evolved to do this boundary-making instinctively, by forming little huddles, for instance, or jutting out elbows to keep nonparticipants away. The sense that interaction is a bounded event may be nurtured daily through semiotic routines and habits, yet other versions of interaction stressed porosity rather than boundedness, and these too were no less founded on human habit. As those who promoted and cultivated the "art of conversation" knew all too well, for instance, humans routinely make subtle interdiscursive reference to other events and absent people when they talk. In a way, what Chapple and Bales and others like them did was to exaggerate familiar interactional boundary-making practices. They deepened interaction's rootedness this way, which was something lab-based experimental science had also primed them to do. They gave interaction a clean perimeter and beginning and end, which meant that all that was left was for the observer to resolve the event minutely to see what happens in its time course.

Why did they need machines to track change over time? Because interaction, as an object, was *dense*: there was too much going on, too much for the unaided human observer to store and retrieve.

For Chapple, to resolve the density of interaction, you needed to get past language. You needed to ignore what people said. As we will see, Chapple insisted that the observer measure only the stops and starts of a conversation. But because there were so many onsets and offsets in the time course of a single interaction, you needed a recorder to help you keep pace and generate a faithful paper record.

For Bales, the truth of interaction was not obscured by language per se. As he saw it, you simply needed to look beneath language to see what pragmatic moves people were doing at any point in time—expressing "solidarity," for instance, or exhibiting "tension release." It wasn't that hard to notice these. Bales framed his methods as "microscopic," a trope he used to praise the granular way his operators observed. The basic unit—action—was "the smallest discriminable segment of verbal or nonverbal behavior to which the observer . . . can assign a classification under conditions of continuous serial scoring."[2] As granular as this may have been, it didn't require that you pore over recordings or transcripts to identify these segments. With some training, any observer could recognize underlying actions in real time. It wasn't that interaction went by too quickly to see it well without the aid of machines. It was not like Muybridge's chronophotographic study of horse locomotion in which the unaided human senses couldn't see whether the legs touched the ground. Any careful observer could recognize what was going on moment by moment in interaction. They didn't need epistemic prosthesis. The problem was rather an issue of the density of actions per unit time. In a "leisurely adult interaction in groups of six or seven," Bales estimated that the scorer will face 10 to 15 acts per minute. Without a recorder, Bales felt, it would be difficult to keep pace with this density of action and store facts on paper for later inspection and analysis.

As scoring interaction had to be done in real time, Bales's scorers did not have time to think about what these discrete moments added up to. Mereologically, they had one task, to watch as small, particulate actions march by. Later they would have time to see how these actions added up and what patterns they formed. But for now they were to produce a good pragmatic transcript.

Again, for both men, interaction was *dense*, which is why a recorder was useful. The psychoanalytically oriented recording enthusiasts also thought interaction was dense, as we saw, but for them it was also *subtle* and *deep*. Interaction was the scene of the communicative unconscious, where humans emitted subtle indexical signs that escaped their awareness and were hard for observers to catch. These were fleeting, evanescent signals, so there was no promise they'd occur again. And even if you found them, you'd need to figure out what they pointed to. Coding interaction in real time—by classifying actions or by marking onsets and offsets—would never reveal the indexical depth and saturation of communication.

Clocking Interaction

Chapple's interaction science was elegant in its brute simplicity. To know interaction, you had to measure it, and measurement required that you ignore *what* humans communicate and chart only *when* they start and stop.

Chapple introduced his minimalist science and its recorder as the 1930s drew to a close, first through an article, then a full-length book. *Measuring Human Relations* (1940), written with the help of collaborator Conrad Arensberg, was, as the bold title suggested, methodological, and pointedly so. In effect, the book indicted his former teacher, Lloyd Warner. He tagged as unscientific Warner's intensive, sprawling, multiyear study of a New England city, Newburyport, Massachusetts. At Harvard in the early 1930s Warner had adapted anthropological methods for use at home, in America. He made Chapple, his first student to earn a doctorate, a core member of his research team. Despite the data collection, coding, and analysis that Chapple was entrusted to oversee, and that yielded some "ten thousand pages" of evidence—the stuff from which the five-volume "The Yankee City" was published—it was all folly, Chapple came to charge. Warner had tried to be exhaustive. This stemmed from a descriptivist fallacy. "The ethnographic tradition," Chapple complained, "assumes that everything in a society should be described."[3] Chapple had helped Warner's team vacuum up evidence with the naive optimism that "if only enough different methods and techniques are brought to bear on a problem, something is bound to turn up."[4] Now Chapple realized that this was all terribly misguided.

A basic stumbling block had been language itself. "What we were try-ing to do was to get at the observable facts of human relations through the interpretation of the language of our informants."[5] His team had relied "just on words, symbols, statements," which no hermeneutics or content analysis could crack. Chapple's suspicion of linguistic mediation could rival in pitch that of the seventeenth-century empiricists—like Locke for whom natural hu-man language, with its "cheat and abuse of words," needed reform lest it slow the march of science.[6] Chapple's complaints echoed many contemporaries, notably behaviorists and logical empiricists, who had little patience for what couldn't be observed or verified. According to the operationalist sensibility that Chapple came to embrace at Harvard, meaningful concepts were only those that could be defined in a way that made their referents measurable.[7] Hence a dictate: "In scientific discourse," Chapple declared, "all words must have precise operational meaning." And so he bestowed operational meaning upon interaction.

Interaction became a parsimonious thing. It no longer resembled the florid centuries-old object known as conversation, which had been thick with intention, and little games and contests of status and character that required skill—an art—to navigate. (Think of Stendhal's *The Charterhouse of Parma* or Castiglioni's *The Book of the Courtier*.)[8] Nor was interaction a microworld dense with invisible rules or norms that needed magnification.

Chapple's interaction hid in plain sight. It involved two or more human animals and their observable communicative actions as they unfolded in lin-earized, measurable time. "Individuals are considered to be in interaction if the action of one individual is followed by the action of another individual," and by action was meant a "manifest (hence observable) phenomenon" that "may be made up of words, gestures, in general, of overt muscular activities."[9]

As Chapple saw it, you should ignore meaning, which was all just gossa-mer anyway, not something you could grasp, let alone measure. Aren't these communications, at base, concrete, observable *actions*? And if they are, why try to ferret out the intentions and emotions behind them—"we shall leave to others the inquiry into the feelings or general states of consciousness of our subjects"—not because these don't exist but because they cannot be mea-sured?[10] Unlike Bales, who wanted to classify what people did, there was no need to sort out what kinds of actions people were engaged in—"no distinc-tion is made among kinds of actions"—because, as Chapple suggested, action was simply the result of underlying muscular activation that caused a per-ceivable *change* in an organism. All that was left was to chronicle this change. Here was the reason you should track the observable starts and stops of com-munication. If an organism changes, you can assume that one or more quanta of action have occurred and carefully note *when* the change happened. "A *unit of action*," then, "is that period of activity recorded from the initial change in muscular state until a second change brings the activity to an end."[11] Every unit of action in this way had its duration. Chapple pried apart interaction. He made inter-action a neatly hyphenated temporal affair between *actions*.[12]

Just as he emptied communicative actions of content, he did the same with individuals. In the social psychology of the 1920s, Floyd Allport notoriously called out what he called "the fallacy of the group." Groups were fictions; only individuals could be observed and were legitimate objects of study.[13] Chapple black-boxed humans and treated them as mere terminals for the back and forth of particulate action. Stripped of historical, psychological, and socio-logical accretions, they became a bare, dyadic "A" and "B." There were no roles for these individuals to inhabit, such as "speaker" and "hearer," which carried normative expectations about how to behave. There was no sociology here. With actions and actors so thoroughly refined, Chapple set out to measure the sequence and duration of actions between individuals, from which he would calculate much else, too.

The Biography of a Recorder

You could try to measure interaction by hand, with a stopwatch and paper, using logbooks gridded out to record who communicated to whom and for how long, which is what Chapple at first did. "Using a watch and record sheet, we observed the flow of events between people in situations ranging from as-sembly lines to salespersons with customers."[14] He could measure the duration of contact in minutes, the time between contacts, who initiated contact, and so on. But it was "extremely laborious," he found, and not very accurate. For efficiency and accuracy, he would need a machine.[15] As Seth Watter describes, Chapple's had a long and slow gestation.[16] In a real sense, it wasn't one machine but several—and some iterations were not even strictly speaking his;[17] the re-corder's biographical continuity, from conception to birth to maturity, was an effect of narrative emplotment, with some patent law to make it stick.

Over the course of Chapple's own writings, the way he described his re-corder changed, and here we can make out a kind of serialized bildungsro-man for his machine. It came in installments. The official moral biography of his recorder had a simple arc, that of steady growth or "evolution" as he liked to call it. A closer reading reveals ups and downs, trials and a hard-won transformation of character into a truly dedicated, fully scientific, confidently technocratic instrument—which reflected, in a way, Chapple's own occupa-tional challenges as he evolved from untenured academic to social engineer.

When his recorder made its official debut in print in 1939, Chapple seemed a little embarrassed by its rudimentary state. He conceded that it was a "simple device" that had been "improvised," in the sense that it had been cobbled together from existing things. He had incorporated an "*old* noiseless typewriter" (emphasis mine) to which he affixed other found objects, such as "a roll of adding-machine paper." To mark the start of communication, the operator pressed a key, the button bearing the letter A for interactant A, B for B, on adding-machine paper that was jury-rigged to flow upward and continuously at a uniform rate of 15 inches per minute.[18] The paper was not perforated, not sectioned off or unitized; after all, you didn't know in advance what the gross temporal dimensions of the interaction would be until the event was over. You'd measure the length of the paper inscription and convert length into duration. Here was a timeline: linear temporality materialized with mechanized paper.

Though still a "crude recording apparatus," Chapple assured readers that it was fast developing into "an accurate instrument," and develop it did. By 1939 his "recording typewriter," as he called it, had evolved: "a more accurate instrument was built." Or as he put it again in 1939, "a recording device was constructed."[19] As Watter describes, the agentless passive was something of a sleight of hand, as it invited you to think Chapple had invented it. In fact, Chapple was indebted to an event recorder called a Marsto-Graph.[20] When you pressed a key it inked a line, and when you released it, it stopped—leaving gaps between lines that could elegantly represent silences, Chapple realized. Marston had promoted this recorder for industry studies in the style of time-and-motion, and Chapple adapted it (or, more likely, he had it adapted by the company that built the Marsto-Graph) by adding a second key so that he could track two interactants, A and B. It was now a dedicated recorder for the study of dyadic human interaction.

This iteration improved upon Chapple's first model. It was now much more than the sum of its recycled parts. By turns an "apparatus," "instrument," and "device," his machine could now do what it was really designed for. It was really a "*recording* device," a "*recording* apparatus." Not until the patent filed in 1942 did his machine mature enough to earn the agentive nominalizer *-er*. By this point it had grown far beyond the Marsto-Graph, because it now featured moving pens that traced automatically computed curves. It now had a serial number and a bold new name: "Interaction Recorder."

Yet only a year after Chapple filed his first patent, this interaction recorder traded in its name for a new one that redefined it. It was no longer a recorder but a *chronograph*, "The Interaction Chronograph." It hadn't changed substantively since the patent filing to warrant the rebranding. And the new word

FIGURE 11. Early iteration of Chapple's improvised interaction recorder. Jacob E. Finesinger, Stanley Cobb, Eliot D. Chapple, and Mary A. B. Brazier, *An Investigation of Prediction of Success in Naval Flight Training* (Washington, DC: Civil Aeronautics Administration, 1948), 22.

had, in fact, already made a cameo in Chapple's description of the device in 1941, which mentioned, albeit adjectivally and in passing, that this was really a "chronographic device." Now the word was promoted to a proper name that became the machine's public identity, and it stuck.[21]

Why the change? The shift from "recorder" to "chronograph" was not cosmetic, nor was it done on a whim. The rebaptism reflected its owner's occupational precarity. In 1940 Chapple had to leave his post at Harvard's School of Business Administration. After a fellowship year in anthropology, he migrated to the medical school in 1941 where he would teach and research among the physicians. His position was only half-time and wasn't likely to become anything more than that, so he left in 1945.[22] Before he left he incorporated as the E. D. Chapple Company, Inc. Unsure of his academic prospects, his plan would be to consult independently and sell his interaction chronograph as a tool for rationalizing and improving interaction in all domains of institutional life—medical, industrial, military, and corporate.

The new name reflected the growing technocratic aspirations of both Chapple and his machine. First, it amped up the scientism. In terms of register, *-graph* was a well-worn suffix familiar from the rise of the so-called graphical method in the nineteenth century, a time when many scientists became worried about the subjectivity of observation and turned toward machines that could inscribe nature "directly," and thereby overcome limited and fallible human faculties.[23] *Chronograph*, a term familiar from the second half of the nineteenth century, had been used to dub a number of time-measuring instruments, scientific, military, industrial, and commercial. One "chronograph" from Chapple's time had been developed by the army to measure the velocity of bullets, and in 1946 it was used to see just how fast Cleveland's Bobby Feller, a.k.a. Bullet Bob, could pitch a fastball.

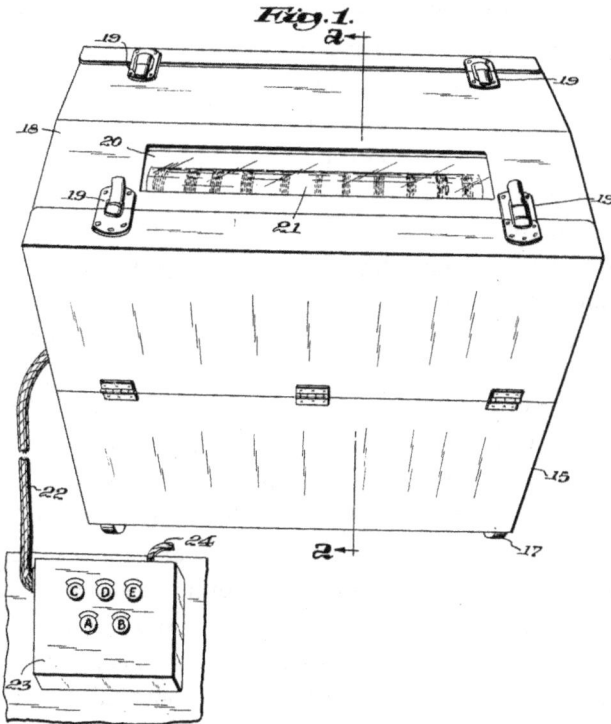

Sept. 9, 1952   E. D. CHAPPLE   2,609,618
                        INTERACTION RECORDER

Filed Nov. 27, 1948   16 Sheets—Sheet 1

Fig.1.

Inventor:
Eliot D. Chapple
by Brown, Critchlow, Flick
his Attorneys.

FIGURE 12. Patent illustration of Chapple's evolved interaction recorder, 1952 (filed in 1948).

Second, "the interaction chronograph" stressed something new about what this machine did. Although Chapple had only flirted with the word chronograph before 1943, and although his patent filing didn't embrace this name, his filing did emphasize something that he hadn't emphasized before.

> The present invention aims to devise an instrument or machine which can be operated by the physician, observer, or examiner, to indicate, trace, or plot, as the examination or interview progresses, quantitatively those factors in which he is particularly interested, and which will present these results in such visual form that the person conducting the experiment can readily estimate by inspection the general character of the result and can quickly determine the mathematical values, if that is necessary.

With some fanfare he announced that his machine could share its results in *visual form*. It was not a recorder, then, not if that meant a machine that stored up information that could then be retrieved. It continuously plotted slopes on a coordinate system by means of automatic pens. The operator still just had to press keys but now the machine did the rest. It visualized interaction, and this visualization was meant to enhance legibility for non-experts. You could "readily" understand the results and even "quickly" determine the exact values, he emphasized.

Chapple's machine had been reborn. It was now a diagnostic imaging technology. Unlike, say, the X-ray or sonograph or microscope, whose noisy images required training to read, his visuals would be accessible. They would be as clear and ergonomic as medical instruments that monitored heart rate, blood pressure or temperature. Indeed, it is no accident that *the physician* should appear as first on his list of beneficiaries in his patent. Before he left Harvard in 1945, Chapple was at the medical school and found himself collaborating with physicians and psychiatrists. The doctors wanted "graphical representation," he realized.[24] The public rebranding of his machine as the interaction chronograph thus marked its refashioning into a technocratic instrument whose ease of operation and ergonomic visuals would enhance its marketability. Its burnished technoscientific veneer also removed any trace of ideological interest, bolstering its status as a value-neutral instrument that would offer up knowledge for *others* to use. It condensed the virtues of scientism and social engineering.

*

In 1946, a year after Chapple left Harvard without a tenure-track job, Bales landed a plumb position in Harvard's new Laboratory of Social Relations, directed by Chicago-trained sociologist and statistician Sam Stouffer. Bales

earned tenure quickly—an unusual feat—and followed Stouffer as director. Here was Bales, perched in a well-funded lab, who was advancing his
own equally ambitious interaction science featuring his own "interaction
recorder"—not long after Chapple had tried to do pretty much the same.
Bales's influential methods book, *Interaction Process Analysis* (1950) made
little reference to Chapple's work, and the reference he did make was brief
and somewhat critical. It isn't hard to imagine why Chapple might have har-
bored some animus toward Bales's enterprise, even though scholarly animus
apparently came easily to Chapple. (He was "hard-nosed" and "abrasive" and
reported by many to be something of an intellectual *infant terrible*.[25]) Chan-
neling how Chapple must have felt, one friend and former colleague dismissed Bales as a "copy-cat who tried to do something afterward which does
not even come close" to Chapple's work. Bales, he charged, "took this basic
idea" of Chapple's and enjoyed "enormous academic acceptance," whereas no
one—no academics, anyway—"paid a goddam bit of attention" to Chapple.[26]
In 1950, when Bales's textbook came out, Chapple egged on a colleague to
write a critical review of that "beautiful blue book called *Interaction Process
Analysis* by one Robert Freed Bales" for the journal Chapple founded, *Human
Organization* (previously *Applied Anthropology*), adding that he couldn't do it
himself for obvious reasons.[27]

The parallel between the men and their machines ran deeper than either
would have cared to admit, and not because of imitation or independent invention. Both paralleled each other because their fledgling sciences of the
face-to-face epitomized changes that had been sweeping over the social sciences and that had intensified in the postwar period. Beneath their similarities, both superficial and deep, were also real differences—differences that remind us that even though interaction could be treated similarly—as an object
that existed independently, that needed mechanical recording to know, that
was intrinsically small and demanded microscopy—it was a family of objects,
complete with some sibling rivalry.

Consider some of the small but telling differences. Both Chapple and
Bales located their science of interaction within a superordinate science of *relations*, human relations for Chapple, social relations for Bales. (A natural fit,
for what was interaction if not *relations* in their most concrete and elementary
form?) Social relations, human relations, interpersonal relations—these were
kindred terms. These X-relation fields each had their own boundary objects
that were designed to incite new forms of scholarly activity and collaboration. "Relations" was reflexive, in the sense that the social sciences who studied them were expected to *relate* to each other more intently, to renew their
commitment, in a word, to interdisciplinarity. They would avoid disciplinary

entrenchment and embody a virtue that Jamie Cohen-Coe has captioned as "open-mindedness."[28] When torqued by "social," "human," or "interpersonal," the X-relation sciences could signal different commitments and epistemic concerns, of course, and they privileged some fields at the expense of others. At Harvard, social relations was more sociology and social psychology than anthropology, for instance, while interpersonal relations put psychiatry front and center. Yet each embraced interdisciplinarity.

Interdisciplinarity usually ran from the ecumenical (share, talk, debate) to the integrative (collaborate, reconcile, synthesize), but it was never supposed to undermine anyone's autonomy. Chapple's, by contrast, was supradisciplinary rather than interdisciplinary, as he had melted down fields, leaving a highly refined natural science of man. By contrast, Harvard's Laboratory of Social Relations where Bales worked embodied the interdisciplinarity that most social scientists and their patrons adopted. They would be ecumenical and collaborative. They would ensure that disciplines that had been hermetically sealed off in the past would work together, keeping up the recent wartime collaborative spirit.[29]

In respect of their scientism, though, Bales and the Laboratory of Social Relations matched Chapple. Rigorous and experimental, the lab's researchers would observe, explain, test, and, most importantly, "predict human behavior much as physics had explained and predicted atomic behavior." Like the natural sciences, the lab would remain simultaneously value-neutral and socially relevant. Like the Manhattan Project, its scientists would, as Talcott Parsons put it, try their best at "splitting the social atom."[30] Bales, like Chapple, was also a methods enthusiast. Published a decade after Chapple's *Measuring Human Relations*, Bales's *Interaction Process Analysis*, was, as the subtitle read, "a method for the study of small groups."

Both men wanted to record interaction on paper, though they had different investments in their proprietary recorders. Bales's interaction recorder was supposed to be in the service of his method, Interaction Process Analysis (IPA), and it was this proprietary method that mattered most. Chapple's recorder, by contrast, had its method baked in, which made the machine indispensable. You had to buy it. Bales was never as personally invested in his recorder as Chapple, who had monetized his machine with the hope of making a living. (In 1948, Bales published an essay that introduced his recorder to the world while freely sharing details on how to build one. He never filed for a patent).[31] Bales claimed that his recorder was just for convenience—though a great convenience, it would seem, given the spotlight he shined on it. "The absolute minimum necessity," he insisted, "is a single trained observer with some way of recording scores."[32]

Inferring Interaction

Chapple had his operators clock communication, pressing buttons whenever people started and stopped. There was no meaning to grasp or actions to watch for and identify. Bales's operators were to be content blind in a different sense. They were to ignore the propositional content of language. They should not listen for language per se but rather for the underlying *communicative action* that language helped express and effectuate. That is, Bales's machine coded the pragmatic value of utterances in the sequential order in which they occurred. You had to recognize what people did in and through speech, such as "gives suggestion," "gives opinion," "disagrees," "shows antagonism."

Mercifully for his coders, the number of things that humans did in interaction was not terribly many. At one point, Bales had coded for as many as 87 distinct actions, but by the time of his textbook in 1950, through trial and error—and a powerful alchemy that Bales could never quite disclose—he had reduced the universe of possible communicative actions to twelve—an even dozen. There were twelve and only twelve types of action that a trained observer had to code (figure 13).[33]

Coding actions this way implied that actions were monofunctional (they did one and only one thing) and came conveniently one at a time.[34] (On multifunctionality, compare with the idea that a signal, verbal or nonverbal, could do several things at once and function at multiple levels, as interactionists Gregory Bateson and Ray Birdwhistell would stress.) Bales's monofunctionalism was tailored well to the affordances and limitations of his recorder, for how else could actions be easily transcribed on a piece of paper that scrolled through a machine at a uniform rate? In Chapple's science, unlike Bales's, interaction time was chronometric; it required quantitative measurements of utterance boundaries using standard units like seconds. Bales, by contrast, did not measure interactional time in standard units and then use that as a superordinate grid for plotting the communicative actions of various durations that occur "in" it—in time. For Bales it was instead the *procession* of actions itself, the way they came one after the other, sequentially, that made up interaction's small-scale temporality.

Bales's dozen was no unordered list.[35] Synoptically, he diagrammed their internal affinities with numbers, lower and capital letters, arrows, boxes, captions, and a key, creating a cohesive universe of Ptolemaic elegance. Problem-solving loomed large, for if you divided by two, the 12 fell into six pairs of actions, each addressing a different "problem." There were problems of "communication," "evaluation," "control," "decision," "tension reduction," and "reintegration." How troublesome face-to-face life seemed. And Bales brought

Chart 1. The system of categories used in observation and their major relations.

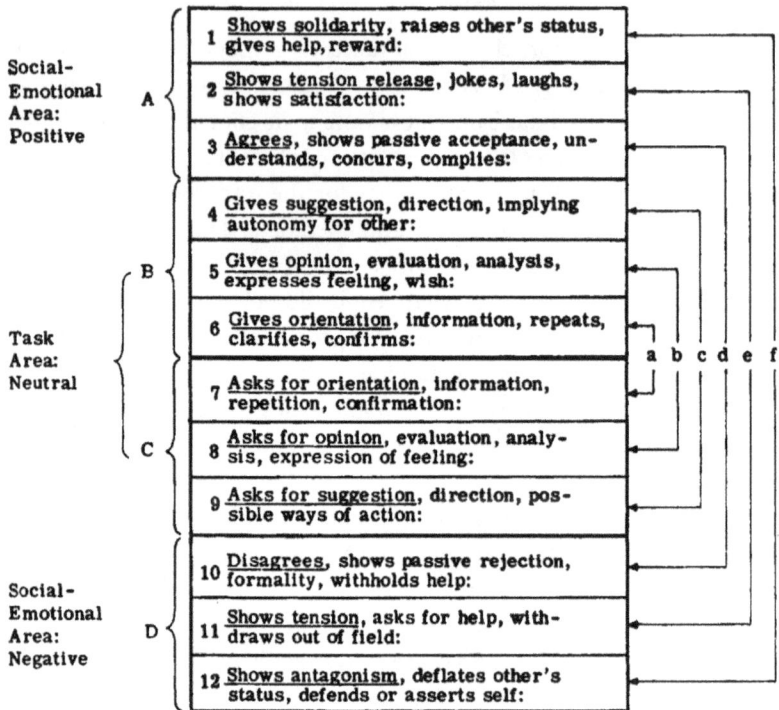

Social- Emotional Area: Positive	A	1 **Shows solidarity**, raises other's status, gives help, reward:
		2 **Shows tension release**, jokes, laughs, shows satisfaction:
		3 **Agrees**, shows passive acceptance, understands, concurs, complies:
Task Area: Neutral	B	4 **Gives suggestion**, direction, implying autonomy for other:
		5 **Gives opinion**, evaluation, analysis, expresses feeling, wish:
		6 **Gives orientation**, information, repeats, clarifies, confirms:
	C	7 **Asks for orientation**, information, repetition, confirmation:
		8 **Asks for opinion**, evaluation, analysis, expression of feeling:
		9 **Asks for suggestion**, direction, possible ways of action:
Social- Emotional Area: Negative	D	10 **Disagrees**, shows passive rejection, formality, withholds help:
		11 **Shows tension**, asks for help, withdraws out of field:
		12 **Shows antagonism**, deflates other's status, defends or asserts self:

a b c d e f

KEY:

a Problems of Communication
b Problems of Evaluation
c Problems of Control
d Problems of Decision
e Problems of Tension Reduction
f Problems of Reintegration

A Positive Reactions
B Attempted Answers
C Questions
D Negative Reactions

FIGURE 13. Robert Freed Bales's pragmatic categories for scoring interaction, 1950. Bales, *Interaction Process Analysis*, p. 9.

on the trouble. He liked to prompt subjects with problem-solving tasks, such as by having them play out competitive games like chess—and then see how they got along. There were more urgent Cold War games, military ones, to which these little games alluded. In a stint for RAND in the early 1950s, he puzzled over problems in air-defense communication, such as how people decide between friendly and enemy fighters.

*

How could the operators of his recorder claim to get at what people do? Bales's machine, unlike Chapple's, trusted the human capacity to interpret human action. Indeed, both machines relied extensively on human labor, but they treated this labor differently. Neither was truly the capture technology that they could sometimes purport to be. Though Chapple's chronograph was computational, and Bales's was designed to make it easy to transfer scores to IBM punch cards and then compute away, both were at base coding instruments—akin, in a way, to transcription machines like the older and widely deployed stenograph and stenotype machines. One coded for temporal utterance boundaries, the other for the underlying pragmatic value of utterances. (Bales made an analogy with stenography as well as with typing and telegraphy.) Enthusiasts for machines like these were usually eager to show off their mechanical objectivity, exaggerating their independence from humans. Both Bales and Chapple needed human labor for their recorders to record. Chapple's machine—begrudgingly, it seemed—did still need the humans—disciplined, mechanized humans—to press buttons. These humans shouldn't observe and track what humans say to each other, because they'd get distracted—like unwitting anthropologists—by the morass of meaning. Like the repurposed typewriter from which his chronograph had evolved, Chapple needed the skilled human hand even if he didn't think this labor was all that skilled.

Indeed, Chapple made it sound like his operators had it easy. All they had to do was depress a key whenever someone begins, whenever a person "talks, nods, smiles, or gestures" and release that key when that person stops and falls silent. Yet this labor was surely not so easy.[36] It required concentration and the capacity for a kind of self-imposed sensory deprivation. She—and as Seth Watter comments, the operator was, not surprisingly, gender coded and prototypically female—had to blinker herself. Chapple's operator had to dam up impressions that rushed to mind and concentrate only on timing.

By contrast, Bales's operators had to knife through superficial impressions to get to the gist. They must not let themselves get caught up in discourse by trying to "follow the threads of the argument." The best scorers "remember very little about the meeting as a whole." They fall into something of an observational trance. They acquire "an ability to inhibit all but the present context of acts, and to avoid jamming incoming stimuli with internal reflections."[37] Coding each act, one by one, just as they occur, the operator makes real-time inferences of pragmatic meaning quickly, accurately, and indefatigably. Bales celebrated this close, granular method as "microscopic" and spoke of these surveyors of the minute as highly skilled.[38]

In fact, so tricky and taxing was this interpretive labor that Bales devoted a chapter to the supervisory work of "training observers."

> How does the observer go about his job? He has the Interaction Recorder in front of him, and on it is the list of categories into which he classifies every item of behavior he can observe and interpret. The classification which he makes is clearly and unequivocally a matter of interpretation; that is, it involves the imputation of meaning, the "reading in" of content, the inference that the behavior has function(s), either by intent or by effect. Strenuous efforts are made to clarify the bases upon which these inferences are made, to cancel out the effects of value judgments from the observer's own particular point of view, to standardize the process of inference, and to determine whether the operation is reliable.[39]

Crudely, if two or more observers could agree on what was happening, then the coding was likely reliable. Bales devoted pages to the problem of intercoder reliability, which would mitigate the risks of relying on interpretation. As it turned out, the process of getting observers to agree wasn't so easy. It required training, and some hiring and firing. (Here one begins to sense a gendering of Bales's labor pool: the allusions to typists and stenographers, the praise for docility and shuttered senses—for shutting out noise and not thinking too much—could presuppose a mechanized, feminized observer-subject).[40] Bales didn't simply defend *inference*, which he did to the hilt; he touted his inferential coding system as superior to the methods of the vulgar positivists epitomized by one man whom he named, Eliot Dismore Chapple.

Here Bales flashed his Weberian commitments (as refracted through Talcott Parsons), whose sociology turned on an "interpretative understanding of social action"—the storied Verstehen sensibility. Yet how could you be sure you were getting the actor's point of view behind this one-way mirror? Bales blended Weber with George Herbert Mead (the American pragmatist whom Herbert Blumer was enshrining as a canonical figure in the history of interaction science.[41])

> The observer attempts to take the "role of the generalized other" with regard to the actor at any given moment. That is, the observer tries to think of himself as a generalized group member, or, insofar as he can, as the specific other to whom the actor is talking, or toward whom the actor's behavior is directed, or by whom the actor's behavior is perceived. The observer then endeavors to classify the act of the actor according to its instrumental or expressive significance to that other group member. In other words, the observer attempts to

put himself in the shoes of the person the actor is acting toward and then asks himself: "If this fellow (the actor) were acting toward me (a group member) in this way, what would his act mean to me? That is, what is he trying to do, either for himself or for us jointly (i.e., what is the instrumental significance of his act) or what does his act reveal to me about him or his present emotional or psychological state (i.e., what is the expressive significance of his act)?"[42]

You could adopt the stance of the generalized other easily, because, after all, you *belonged*. Observer and subject were not so very different, not in language nor in culture. Whether or not this would satisfy the anthropologists, Bales's IPA did present itself as an interpretive science that got at the native's point of view.

As an interpretive science, if a deliberately thin one, Bales seemed ontologically conflicted, however. There was a problem. If interaction really was a system with a life of its own, as Bales often wanted to argue, then why did he insist that his scorers track the behavior of *individuals* so fastidiously? Indeed, when he waxed philosophical about the way groups were more than the sum of their proverbial parts, it undermined a basic observational unit of his: the individual human animal. Interaction as observed—as inferred and scored on paper—required that you account for each and every action. Every action had its provenance. Every action had its source, as if it originated from someone in particular and was always a reaction or address to copresent others. Observationally, what concerned you was the traffic of *who-did-what-to-whom*. This may have been operationally convenient if not necessary, but this linear and unidirectional flow of action—a veritable postal or football model of communication in which sender sends message to receiver—was not the version of communication that Bales wanted to endorse philosophically. Indeed, when Bales charted change over time for groups rather than individuals, when he examined how actions fluctuated over phases of a whole event, spiking here, dipping there, forming distinctive contours—that is, when he studied interaction as a global dynamic system—he dropped the crude billiard-ball sociology of interindividual action that his coding system presupposed.

A Coalition of Parts: The Small Group Lives

In his most heady philosophical moments, Bales denied that individuals existed. His coding system had let individuals enjoy the fiction that they were sovereigns of their own actions, yet now he deposed them.

The actor is not coextensive with the biological individual we observe. It is thus impossible to locate in any exact physical sense the author of the acts we observe. The author or actor involved in any present act is, for conceptual purposes, only a point of reference adopted for the analysis of that particular act. If the observer demands a more concrete way of looking at the problem, he may think of the author of a given act as that part of the person, or that coalition of parts, which for the moment is in command and is managing the motor apparatus.[43]

There are no individual authors of action, only a "coalition of parts." In such moments Bales could sound a bit like John Dewey when Dewey reveled in processual wholeness and railed against the behaviorist's atomistic mechanics of stimulus and response; and he could sound a bit like the cyberneticians who modeled systems rather than the workings of so many little parts. Whichever holism or holisms he indexed, the point was that interaction science, then, wasn't the study of skin-bound mechanized beings. Just as advertised, it was *process*—"interaction process analysis." This processual dissolution of the individual had its limits. It was hardly the intimate, rapturous *I–Thou* relation described by the Jewish existentialist philosopher Martin Buber, for instance. In Buber's liberative dialogism, ego can experience alter with such reverent attention and presence that the two seem to merge. Nor did Bales's redistribution of agency rival Gregory Bateson's cybernetic and ecological sensibility which broke down boundaries not just between humans but between humans and the world. Minimally, for Bales, acts were simply wrested from the hands of individuals and redistributed to the small group and nothing more, a group that now existed on its own.

Bales competing ontologies of interaction—one in which discrete individuals acted on each other, the other in which the group had a life of its own—can look incompatible when held up to each other and compared, as I have done here, but they needed each other and enjoyed a productive antagonism. This uneasy coalition of ontologies antagonized into existence the very thing that Bales hoped to know. After all, you could not know interactional life—the life of group dynamics—directly, through observation. You could break things down microscopically when you watched and listened to others. You could observe and record actions minutely and granularly in the order they occurred, but you could not make out what patterns the actions formed. And we may remember that he asked his observers to restrain themselves from following the threads of discourse and from attending to things in anything other than piecemeal fashion. As the dynamics of interaction were too dense to unpack in real time, you first had to record it and track it on paper to see it. It was mediatic recording that made knowledge of interaction possible.

Interaction as a Liberal Technology

A small group was a *manageable* group. Its scale did not only mean that it would yield to scientistic rigor. Small also suggested a measure of docility. Face-to-face interaction could be controlled.

Compare the manageable plasticity of the small group with the notoriously volatile *crowd*, an object theorized famously by Gustave Le Bon in the late nineteenth century. "Under certain given circumstances . . . an agglomeration of men presents new characteristics very different from those of the individuals composing it." A crowd had a life of its own. Like a small group, it had properties that existed independently of its parts and therefore couldn't be explained by appeal to individual psychology. Yet the similarities end here. For Le Bon, what forms in a crowd, be it as small as a half-dozen or as large as hundreds or even thousands, is a "collective mind," a "mental unity," a "single being." Crowds, unlike small groups, are not made up of interacting individuals; rather, they behave as if they were one big individual. In crowds the unconscious reigns and spreads like fire. "No longer conscious" of one's acts, the individual becomes entranced and hyper suggestible, as if under hypnosis, such that he acts with "irresistible impetuosity." A monstrously illiberal figure, the crowd lures humans into surrendering their autonomy and capacity for reason. (Le Bon likens the illiberal crowd to familiar Others, including so-called primitives: The individual who gives in to a crowd devolves into a "savage"; the "workman" who throws himself into collective action is seduced into thinking that every employer is out to exploit him.[1])

A small group was not so irrational or illiberal, even from the perspective of small-group scientists who, as we shall see, worried a lot about the creep of fascism into interpersonal life. After all, Bales's clutches of humans, whom he surveilled indoors—in contrast to the prototypically boisterous outdoor crowds—were busy thinking and dutifully trying to solve problems. True, for Bales, small groups still did behave in irrational and inefficient ways. They could get derailed by poor leadership or squabbling factions, and social science ought to know how those dynamics happen, how cohesion can be improved and efficiency boosted. But on the whole, small groups were earnest, industrious, and civil. Hard at work, liberal in spirit. They didn't sacrifice individuality for some rapturous supraindividual state of collective agency. Individuals held onto who they were when they talked. They remained *accountable* for what they said and did to others—as evidenced by the fact that the analyst could write down and track an individual's acts over time. No wonder that the science of small groups, unlike that of the crowd, was a lot more sanguine about the prospects for control.

*

In a stock-taking exercise, a theme issue of the *American Sociological Review* from 1954 gathered more than a dozen papers that together made "the case for the study of small groups."[2] How *practical* this new form of study was, editor Fred Strodtbeck crowed. Whatever small-group analysis meant—and it certainly wasn't unified in theory or method—it was clear that it would be good for social engineering and hence good for postwar social science patronage. "A bomber costs several million dollars, and may conceivably be lost by failures in the interpersonal relations of the crew."[3] And really, what aspect of social life *didn't* involve interaction and hence didn't stand to benefit from scientific involvement if not oversight? Another early, enthusiastic reviewer of small-group research recited its track record of stimulating change: "hostile attitudes lost," "alcoholics have been cured," "neurotic disabilities alleviated," "emotionally disturbed children helped," "productivity raised," "roles and status changed," "frustration reduced most successfully," "and disabilities accepted."[4] More than a few hoped knowledge of group dynamics would help stem authoritarianism and grow democracy.

Interaction Profiling

For Eliot Chapple, psychiatry had been his chronograph's first real proving ground. His 1942 patent had illustrated his machine's utility by citing the case of physician and patient, a case that came from his own research at Massachusetts General Hospital. In a paper coauthored with a Harvard psychiatrist, Chapple demonstrated correlations between psychopathology and interaction patterns. Timing, Chapple argued, could tell you a lot about individuals, and Chapple became interested in what it could reveal about one of his two interacting individuals, the interviewee, who, in this case, already had a psychiatric diagnosis.[5] It should be possible to use this interaction recorder to see pathology in how someone interacts.

Chapple's operational definition of interaction had allowed for four logical possibilities: A talks or acts while B is silent; B talks or acts while A is silent; "both talk or act at the same time"; both A and B remain silent.[6] These were meant to be culture-free descriptions. "Silence" was a purely operational definition that had nothing to do with its colloquial cognate (which, of course, was rich with meaning and value).

The operator pressed keys to code these four. When Chapple developed his patentable recorder in the early 1940s, his machine could automatically plot a series of curves based on their measurements. Illustrating with the case of a physician and patient, he described how the first curve showed the patient's "activity"; the second curve showed his "interruptions" of the physician; the third curve indicated the physician's interruptions of the patient; and the fourth showed "initiative"—whether the patient persisted in communicating even when the physician interrupted him and whether he "initiated" action when both fell silent.[7]

Action; silence; failure to respond; interruption; initiative; adjustment. These were resonant words. A whole characterology lurked under their surface. The chronograph could, in this way, map interaction patterns onto "personality and temperament"—the durable if not "invariant" properties of individuals.[8] Using computations based on clocking onsets and offsets of communication, the chronograph could locate individual humans in a universe of moralized cultural figures. Many of these figures seemed familiar. You could find analogs to the "chatterer" and "the bore," for instance—brutish conversationalists portrayed, and proscribed, by the doyen of etiquette, Emily Post. Chapple disavowed any such characterology, but it was hard to miss it, and, tellingly, the terms he used changed slightly over time and seemed responsive to his target audiences and markets.[9] As he developed his recorder for industry in the 1940s, for instance, "initiative" and "adjustment" became resonant words for attributes that his recorder could reveal and that management was anxious to measure.

As for industry, Chapple's patent mentioned personnel screening as a major thing his chronograph could do, and he soon got the chance to demonstrate its predictive power through a contract with a thriving Boston department store, the Gilchrist Company. Chapple focused on sales personnel.[10]

In the leadup to the Gilchrist study, Chapple had been busy developing a way to standardize and control, in experimental fashion, how the interviewer dealt with the interviewee. He standardized the interviewer's behavior, so that

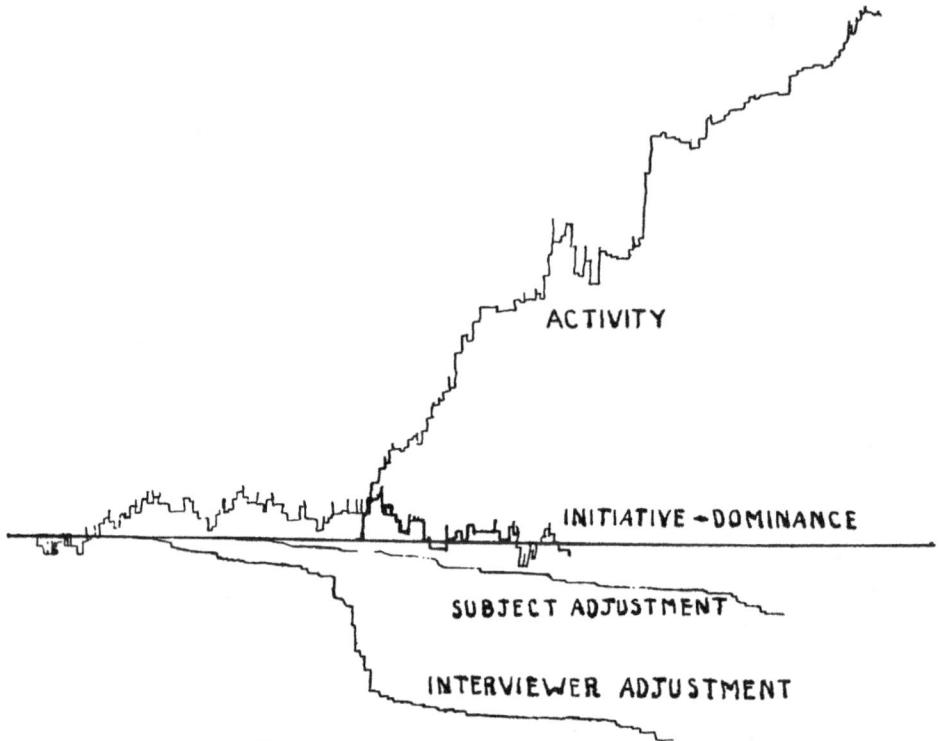

CHART I. Interaction Chronograph Sample Record.

FIGURE 14. Interactional profiling in industry. Chapple's "Interaction Chronograph" as a diagnostic imaging technology. Eliot D. Chapple and Donald Gordon Jr., "An Evaluation of Department Store Salespeople by the Interaction Chronograph," *Journal of Marketing* 12, no. 2 (1947): 175.

he would have a baseline against which to see how interviewees varied. This experimentalization of the interview meant that the interaction chronograph focused even more intently on one member of the dyad. It did not help you know interaction in the round. As a diagnostic imaging technology, and as a screening device, it revealed truths only about the interviewee.

Chapple's standardized interview was defined less by the kinds of questions asked and more by how the interviewer behaved. For a fixed period of time, the interviewer had to interrupt the interviewee repeatedly, for instance; or fall silent for uncomfortably long stretches of time.[11] You would then watch and see how the interactant reacted—did they talk quickly during a silence, did they persist when they were interrupted?—and from these reactions you could glimpse who the interviewee really was.

At Gilchrist, this screening was done on site, as naturalistically as possible. Interviewers were recruited from the ranks of personnel. The chronograph was "partially concealed by a screen or bookcase," while the "observer [was] seated at a desk beside it." The interviewer wouldn't mention the machine, and the machine wasn't in the subject's field of vision. Once the interview got underway the interviewee would never notice it.[12]

Chapple suspected that different sales environments required different interaction styles. Selling furniture demanded a slow, patient, low-involvement style, whereas those who peddled fast-moving goods behind a counter in women's hosiery and cosmetics were in a "high-transaction" environment and needed to be interpersonally intrepid if not aggressive. He didn't think you could learn styles that weren't already ingrained. He offered no remedial training, because interaction rate, for instance—the ratio of action to inaction—was invariant. It was biologically basic to who you are.

The Gilchrist study came on the heels of a trade book Chapple had co-authored with the assistant dean of Harvard's business school. *How to Supervise People in Industry* (1946) was, as the subtitle read, "a guide for supervisors on how to understand people and control their behavior." This nontechnical book didn't mention or explicitly recommend his own science and proprietary machine, but it expressed Chapple's views about the invariability of humans:

> Every person has a characteristic way of acting with other people. He may be talkative or taciturn, aggressive or timid. In different situations and with different people his behavior may seem to vary to a considerable degree. Nevertheless, it remains fixed within fairly definite limits, and what a person will do can be predicted with comparative ease and accuracy.[13]

In this human resource analytics *ante litteram*, Chapple's aim was to find out how individuals differed so that management could select and place people rationally and objectively. Chapple compared interaction rates with data on sales performance and on one's place in the company hierarchy, for instance, to show that his machine had great power to predict sales performance. The chronograph "made it possible to measure the person's activity or drive, his tempo of acting, his initiative, dominance, and capacity to adjust to others, as these characteristics actually occur and not as they might be inferred from what is said in the interview or from answers on a written test."[14]

In *Nation's Business* from 1947, a colorfully titled piece, "Your Personality Sits for a Photo," broadcast Chapple's claims about his machine's ease of use, objectivity, and power to access personality. "These measurements, in the form of a simple graph, can be read by anyone, with no special gifts or learning or intuition required. And since people, for profound biological reasons, tend to behave pretty much like themselves at all times, a single observation by the interaction chronograph yields a reliable picture of what a person is really like." In coverage in *Popular Science*, under the title, "Machine Probes Your Personality," the author mused, if cheekily, about the interaction chronograph's future markets: selection of a winning baseball team manager, perhaps, or a president, or a mate?[15]

The Gilchrist study helped earn the interaction chronograph a place within a busy field of somatic and psychologistic tests for screening people in industry. Chapple distinguished his by stressing the way it yoked mechanical objectivity (minimal human interference) with technocratic ergonomics (an interface that was easy to use and whose results were easy to interpret). Its "objectivity," he wrote, "stems from the fact that it is based solely on observations of actual behavior of individuals—not guesses or predictions of how they will act; that it examines a definite measurable factor (time), just as is done in physics, chemistry, and the other 'exact sciences'; and that it yields a record which can be read by anyone, erudite or untutored, intuitive or obtuse."[16] A record legible to all would also be an indisputable record that would eliminate questions about who gets hired and who belongs where.

By 1948, the Chapple Company had offices in Boston and New York, and its machine had grown. It was bigger and boasted a sophisticated computer that merited an updated patent filing. The latest iteration eliminated the visual ergonomics of slopes—it now output rows of numbers—but the numbers were printed immediately and at a brisker pace.[17] In the 1940s Chapple had ventured into other kinds of personnel screening. He interviewed and profiled cadets for a study commissioned by the Squantum Naval Air Base in Quincy, Massachusetts, the aim of which was to predict success in flight training.[18] But psychiatry became Chapple's enduring focus, as he eventually took up residence at Rockland State Hospital in New York in 1959 and remained there till the early 1970s.

Interaction as a Democratic Technology

Chapple's recorder sorted out humans in domains like medicine and industry. When expertly managed, interaction could also be a technology of its own, a way to change the world. Here is the epitome of a trajectory we can call *interactionalization*, where interaction emerges as an independent, agentive force in its own right rather than only something to be known and controlled. Of the many tantalizing applications had Bales surveyed in his 1950 textbook, one resonated widely. Bales illustrated how you could "profile" how group leaders behave in a "democratic-directive role," to see what actions they did as well as how group members responded.[19] Scholars of small groups had already concretized democracy before this, treating it as an observable kind of interpersonal relations defined especially by a distinctive leadership style. If you could pinpoint what made democratic interaction democratic, you could nurture it in the world, just as you could identify and quell its obverse, authoritarianism. This wasn't the more familiar psychologization of these contrastive, moralized styles of governance and subjectivity, which saw these styles as internal states that made a human individual more or less susceptible to fascist propaganda and practices. Exteriorized, taken out of the head, democracy and authoritarianism became qualities of small-group life.

Stacked up against Adorno's monumental *The Authoritarian Personality*, which came out the same year as *Interaction Process Analysis*, Bales's contribution looked paltry. His was a modest offering and programmatic gesture in what was then a swift current of research on authoritarianism and democracy. Bales was overshadowed especially by the "group dynamics" research of Kurt Lewin (1890–1947) and his students, whose experiments on leadership styles had attracted attention.[20] Lewin became a major figure in small-group science and founded The Research Center for Group Dynamics at the Massachusetts Institute of Technology in 1945. Much like the Department and Laboratory of Social Relations established a year later, Lewin's interdisciplinary center located group dynamics at the intersection of psychology, sociology, and cultural anthropology.[21]

Nowhere was the practical if not emancipatory power of interaction analysis—and interactionalization—more on display than in the influential work of this German Jewish émigré and social psychologist. So confident was Lewin about the relevance of his science and impatient about the pace of social change that he alarmed some of his peers with what he came to dub "action research," which addressed discrimination and rushed to defend and extend democratic lifeways. "The main methodological interest," Lewin wrote when he introduced his MIT center to the world, would be "the development of group experiments and particularly change experiments."[22] He cited FDR, who in 1936 had praised the valiant social scientists who, like engineers, "bring under proper control the forces of modern society." How fitting that MIT should host his center, for "engineering in a progressive spirit" was precisely what he would offer.[23] Like Chapple and Bales and small-group researchers generally, Lewin's saw their relevance everywhere, because interaction was everywhere. In labor relations, for instance, Lewin's group undertook industrial consulting for the Harwood Manufacturing Corporation in rural Virginia, beginning in 1939 and stretching into the '40s. The Lewinians tried to heal race relations and curb antisemitism.[24]

Some found Lewin's group too zealous about its progressive virtues. A 1953 commentator praised Lewin and his students but added that the "proselytizing of a faith in democratic leadership is not the scientific aim of small-group study." A dispassionate science of small-group interaction should only "delimit the conditions—social, cultural, psychological, and situational—under which this empirical relationship holds."[25]

Matthew Hull describes Lewin's science as a democratic technology of speech. Following Latour, technology doesn't name a thing with definable properties but rather an orientation and aspiration that, Hull explains, "guides efforts to demarcate and isolate some sociomaterial process or entity from its myriad connections, especially with humans, in order to make it transferable and usable across different social boundaries."[26] Technologizing means that you try to cut away figure from ground and hold the two apart to such an extent that you can imagine a discrete technology—tool, machine, method, etc.—that humans instrumentally "use," that can be "applied," that can have "effects." Technologization, processually conceived, is gradient. When it comes to such demarcation and autonomization, we can speak of degrees, which is useful to emphasize here as few interaction scientists enjoyed the confidence of the Lewinians when it came to what they thought they could "do" with face-to-face life. Hull outlines Lewin's science of interpersonal democracy in relation to wartime and postwar America and then traces how this was translated and ported over to South Asia in the decolonizing years after the Second World War, such as through Ford Foundation-funded efforts to bring "democratic group life" to Delhi. Here let us return to a few highlights that illustrate how Lewin's technology first developed.

Lewin's first leap toward a democratic technology of interaction began in the 1930s. While a professor of child psychology at the Iowa Child Welfare Research Station, he worked closely with students Ronald Lippitt and later Ralph White to develop experiments that led to a preliminary publication in 1938 and then an often-cited 1939 article, "Patterns of Aggressive Behavior in Experimentally Created 'Social Climates,'" which studied clubs of 10-year-old boys and tested the effects on their behavior of three different leadership styles: "authoritarian," "democratic," and "laissez-faire."[27]

An imaginative social psychologist who read widely, Lewin borrowed from Gestalt theory and topological geometry to model "tension" in social relations and its resolution. It was Lippitt who had been curious about leadership among groups of boys and wondered if you could experimentally compare autocratic and democratic styles. With Lewin's help and various trials, they made this into an experiment—albeit experiment in a sense that didn't survive very long after postwar psychology's narrowing of what counted as experimentation.[28] Lewin didn't try to make the experimental situation naturalistic. The point wasn't to see how people reacted under ordinary circumstances recreated in the lab. The experimental situation was, rather, an ideal-typical model with exaggerated features meant to facilitate hypothesis testing. (Lewin took his cues here from the philosopher of science Ernst Cassirer).[29] He engineered social climates so that they would be maximally distinct and contrastive. "On the whole, everything was kept constant except the group atmosphere," to see what difference this atmosphere made. The democratic leader gave options, for instance, and made "all policies a matter of group discussion," and he allowed the boys to work with whomever they wished. To see what transpired, they'd record behavior by gathering all kinds of evidence.[30] Two women did the stenographic transcription, for instance, recording the conversation they heard, and every minute on the minute, a buzzer rang, which spurred the group observers to spring into action to see what dynamics were now in play. Lewin himself raced around the outside of the make-shift wall of blankets that enclosed this experimental theater and stood on a step ladder to peer through the fabric and film the interaction discreetly with a handheld movie camera.[31]

The questions animating this research burned with relevance. Which group climate incited "rebellion against authority, persecution of a scapegoat, apathetic submissiveness to authoritarian domination, or attack upon an outgroup?" And, was there something quietly, dangerously seductive about authoritarianism? Was it true, for instance, that democratic life might be more "pleasant" but authoritarian life more "efficient"?[32] It was impossible to miss the allegory of the 1938 and 1939 essays, the first published some six months before Kristallnacht, the second some four months before Germany invaded Poland.[33] (In 1944 Lewin learned that his mother had perished in a concentration camp in Poland.[34]) More than an urgent morality play, more than a refutation of Nazism and fascism and reminder of the virtues of democracy, Lewin offered a way to intervene, to take action. The Lewinians concretized democracy, as Hull has stressed. They materialized an intangible formation in the crucible of face-to-face interaction. They made it palpably small—a property of groups that you could gather and observe under the strictures of time-bound experimental protocol—which opened the possibility not just for knowledge and prediction, but also for control.

A Laboratory in the Wilds

If you knew what democratic life looked like and sounded like in the small group, what steps might you take to reproduce it? Of course, there were many opportunities to share knowledge in the usual ways. At the Chicago Rotary Club, for instance, the Lewinians discussed findings with film clips, charts, and graphs.[35] A more ambitious answer came in the form of a large annual training "laboratory" for group interaction that Lewin's center began holding in summers at an old private school in the fastness of Bethel, western Maine, a remote and seemingly idyllic village of some 2,000 located in the foothills of the White Mountains. To inculcate and spread democratic interaction widely, the lab would start from the top, with leaders—as many as you could get— from across the nation.

The National Training Laboratory on Group Development (NTL), as it was called, was sponsored by the United States Office of Naval Research and the National Education Association and had grown out of smaller-scale training events, which, in retrospect, had served as trial runs. One had been a conference for State Directors of Adult Education held at a hotel in West Point in September 1946.

The inaugural two-week lab at Bethel was held in 1947 and the center was not shy about its ideological commitments. One topic was "understanding and working in terms of an explicit democratic philosophy and ethics of change."[36] The lab ended on Independence Day.

A 1947 report outlined the mission: "(1) to provide research scientists with an opportunity to communicate scientific knowledge of group dynamics to key education and action leaders, (2) to provide an opportunity for observing, experiencing, and practicing basic elements of the democratic group process which are relevant to educational and action leadership, and (3) to provide an experimental laboratory for further research explorations." One hundred thirty-three delegates were invited and a little less than half came. They hailed from twenty-nine states and four foreign countries, and represented diverse domains and sectors: nutrition education, public health, food distribution, veterans' education, adult education, vocational education, public school curriculum, clinical psychology, home economics, child welfare, teaching labor relations, nursery school education, and more.[37]

The Bethel lab arose from many things and many people, yet in retrospect the germ of this experiment can also be traced to Lewin's own group. Years earlier, Lewin had started experimenting on his own group. Back in Berlin he had transformed his research team into one long experiment in democratic science by trying to cultivate an inclusive, non-hierarchical climate for free-flowing critical discussion.[38] At the heart of this experiment was a memorable discursive ritual. Called *die Quasselstrippe*—a playful colloquial term that can be translated loosely as "chatter box" or more literally as "chatter line" (the analogy here may be to the way people gab on the telephone), it was meant to be an incubator of creativity and open-mindedness.[39] He launched the ritual in Berlin in response to what he characterized as stifling hierarchical apprenticeships in which students studied at the feet of analysts like Freud and Adler. When you participated in the chatter line, it wasn't supposed to matter who you were. Existing roles and statuses were to be suspended to allow for the unfettered flow of discourse, a Habermasian ideal speech situation if there ever was one. His group did its heady chatting in a café located across the street from no less than the Berlin Psychological Institute.[40] When Lewin relocated to Iowa, he recreated this democratic ritual. Held on Tuesdays on the top floor of the Round Window restaurant to which his students would bring lunches, the group earned a new nickname, the "Hot-Air Club."[41]

Much as the Lewinians designed and modified experimentally the climate of the boy's club, so the Bethel lab would need a climate conducive to democracy as a lived interpersonal experience. "Each member of the laboratory would be a *change agent*," but making them so wouldn't be easy.[42] They had already experienced misfires during a trial run in Connecticut and were anxious to learn from their mistakes. You didn't want the delegates hanging on the words of scientific experts, for instance, nor should experts lord over delegates. You didn't want discussion to be one-sided or monopolized by a few.

In true ritual fashion, Bethel was a place set apart. This "intensive practice laboratory in human relations skills, isolated from the pressures of daily work and living, may prove to be the most effective means of learning how to bring behavior into line with the difficult demands of democratic ideology."[43] The pacific, retreat-like character of the Bethel lab, its freedom from everyday pressures—including the stresses of a hierarchical workplace at home—recalls Jamie Cohen-Coe's argument about the importance of leisure for the cultivation of liberal-democratic lifeways.[44] Bethel had its recreational activities like square dancing that "gave all delegates a chance to swing partners and *do-se-do*."[45] It had its "communal dining hall" and centralized living quarters that allowed participants to "live together."[46] "Informal singing" and music would break out spontaneously before and after meals.

Minor adjustments and renovations were needed to democratize the built environment. The private school had fixed desks. The organizers unbolted and removed them. In their place they found "beautiful oval oak tables that could seat about 20 persons."[47] Wherever possible, free-floating seats were arranged to form circles, and everyone would cultivate mindfulness about the inclusive power of the pronoun *we*. Visitors were discouraged from dropping by unannounced, "for much of the value of the experience would depend on the gradual development of intimate group relations and a very cohesive group structure."[48]

An informal daily log of one training session told the story of this cohesion. "Group level of morale in workshop lower today," the journal read just a few days in, though this was tempered by the glimmer of "good progress in strengthening group feeling." There was plenty of ups and downs, frustrations, even power struggles. Thursday into the retreat: "sometimes we had attempts at pretty autocratic or formalized leadership," but they "did not get away with it." Friday into the retreat: "two members had previously seemed to be vying for leadership role" and "today they seemed united against two members: less 'we-ness.'" One day the conveners felt the sting of criticism: "Got rather frank and personal in our evaluation today. We took it, but some of us felt a little sore." A week in, the meetings hit bottom, scoring their lowest rating, yet by "[getting] out a lot of aggression against each other and the leadership" this "cleared the way to move ahead." Indeed, by July 3, the "final evaluation session was almost a spiritual experience."[49]

"Spiritual" was only half the story. Bethel was a teetotaling town, and that wouldn't be conducive to "we-feeling." Martha Bradford—wife of Leland Bradford, the Director of Adult Education from DC who was both Bethel trainer and lab co-organizer—managed the lab's library. She also did the "Berlin Run"—Berlin, New Hampshire—twice a week by car in order to ferry booze across state lines. While the locals "usually retired around 9 p.m., our group often began drinking and singing into the early morning"—which predictably caused some strain with the community, and when "one participant drove his car around the academy's racing track, leaving deep ruts in the track and grass," the conveners were sure they'd never be invited back.[50]

How would you know if this lab had worked, beyond impressionistic notes in a journal and ruts in grass? The conveners had welcomed the delegates on the first Sunday with an "informal tea" and supper, but not long after, they subjected the delegates to "pre-measurements" so that you could later see if any change had come from this retreat. For practical reasons, only a handful of the participants underwent the full battery of individual psychological testing (and they did so along with the faculty), which included the Vigotsky test, the sentence-completion test, the Runner-Seaver, the Thematic Apperception Test (TAT), and an intelligence test. Projective tests designed for individuals were also retooled for groups, resulting in a group Rorschach and group TAT, so that a group, for example, collectively "composed a story around a picture of a somewhat ambiguous group situation."[51]

All delegates were assessed before and after on their ideology by means of a questionnaire and an interview, and these instruments got closest to the lab's mission. The First Ideology Questionnaire netted the demographics—age, religion, kinship, marital status, and various cultural indicators of class like, which magazines and periodicals do you read and which occupation would you choose if you had your druthers? Then came 74 statements to be evaluated on a five-point scale. Many were about the ethics and mechanics of group discussion. Do "group members have a responsibility to draw into the group discussion those who are not participating," for instance? Is it "all right to interrupt other people, if one has an important idea to put across"? Should "the more experienced group members . . . assume a greater share of the group discussion"? And the 74th and final issue to rate, "When disciplinary problems arise it is usually necessary to abandon democratic procedures."[52]

Then there was the interview. The First Ideology Interview got personal with 41 questions. "Do you have, or have you ever had, servants working in your home?" "How do you think servants ought to be treated?" "What traits should a good wife have?" "Should women have the same job opportunities as men?" "Do you think that character traits are fixed or changeable?" And so on. And, to the crux of the matter: "How should a leader behave in a democratic group?" What about its members? What should democratic decision-making look like? And then a hypothetical that left nothing to chance: "Suppose there was a dictator who would use the techniques of changing people without regard for their welfare"—"How would you feel about that?"

Near the lab's end came the "Final Ideology and 'Change' Interview," which probed the delegates' sense of change while soliciting feedback on the lab itself. It led with questions about whether there's been "any change in your feelings and attitudes toward dealing with groups and individuals," and whether there's been "a change in your skill dealing with groups and individuals." It quickly turned toward opinions of the faculty trainers: what were his "assets as a leader," compared to the other four faculty? "What do you consider his liabilities"—and, again, how does he compare with the other four? "What sort of relationship would you say exists between you and him?" And even, "What do you think of him as a person?"[53]

✳

Bales came with his wife to the first Bethel lab, not as a delegate but as one of several "interaction observers" within the research team. The lab would need to see how people behaved in groups, after all. Bales had come to a few of Lewin's seminars at MIT and once presented his own work.[54] Lewin saw enough promise in his methods that he recruited Bales to Bethel to supervise an observation team, an occasion Bales used to test and refine his coding system.

Group interaction took many forms at Bethel. Jacob Moreno's influential methods of psychodrama and sociodrama had popularized role-playing, and Bethel did much with this kind of improvisational theater.

"You, Jim Marston, are a man in your late thirties, a mechanical engineer by training," one hypothetical scenario began. The script was rich. You earn

$6,000 a year, are happily married, are Methodist and a Mason. And so on. The script colored in the town, dotted the landscape with clubs, shaded the population's political makeup, and last but not least, its resources for recreation. "Unfortunately for you"—and here came the complicating action— "there is no golf course near the town," and "you are very fond of golf." So Marston finds a few likeminded men and decides to "begin a campaign to get a course built." Here, now, is the problem. What steps do you take, what negotiations do you pursue? Before you can get far in your planning and scheming, other characters get in your way. One is George Wilcox, editor of the local newspaper: a "firm and vigorous character given to sharp, telling retorts if antagonized—a trifle bitter." "He does not drink and has not played golf in years." "He strongly believes in democratic principles and the common man."

Observers scored the role-plays with a form. How well did an individual inhabit and stay in character, for instance; how well did he or she communicate? And, of course, was the leadership style autocratic, democratic, or laissez-faire?

As for group discussions at Bethel, these usually occurred around the oval oak tables while a small observation team looked on. Bales's scorers did the observation. They assigned each person a number around the table to record who did what to whom, which they did by hand on gridded paper—as they didn't yet have Bales's interaction recorder. This resulted in the "interaction content record," a record that was understood to be microscopic in grain. Scorers were to code the "smallest discriminable act," Bales instructed, much as he later advised in his textbook.[55] His scorers scanned behavior for democratic and antidemocratic tendencies. At Bethel, Bales had been using a longer list of 20 communicative actions to score, and some were perfect for the task at hand. One category was "autocratic manner," which pinned governance style to observable behavior. It covered a family of acts, including "giving bald commands or directions, implying no autonomy for the other" as well as "denying permission, blocking, restricting, prohibiting, disrupting activity." This category didn't make it to his final list of 12 but gave the Bethel scorers a way to identify nondemocratic leadership.

At Bethel, Bales's methods were one of several ways to scrutinize group dynamics. Under the overarching goal of observing "group dynamics," each observation team would look at many things at once. Besides the Balesian interaction observers, there were "group observers" and an "anecdotal observer."[56] While Bales's scorers did the microscopic work, the group observers surveyed the behavior more coarsely, noting the content, who contributed it, and what the group "atmosphere" seemed like. Each team had one anecdotal observer, a generalist whose main job was to keep an eye on the "overall viewpoint" and to write up a short report. You needed to see the proverbial forest for the trees, so this observer would note apparent "goals," big and small, as well as the "techniques or strategy" used to accomplish them. And not to ignore the subjective and the intuitive, the page asked the birds-eye surveyors to rate how they felt the meeting went using a five-point scale that ran from "no good" to "swell," and a second five-point "progress" scale that ran from "nothing accomplished" to "great."[57] The colloquial register ("swell," "great," etc.) dialed down the scientistic tenor of these assessments, to ensure that they did not seem stuffy and clinical but light and informal—and, by implication, less hierarchical. Still, the delegates got annoyed at times by the technical jargon—sometimes called Bethelese—and, indeed, by the expert scrutiny.[58]

It wasn't only the observers who scrutinized. The participants also got their chance to rate what happened. Right after each discussion, participants filled out forms that probed how they felt things went. "Post-meeting reactions" were even plotted over time, so that you could see the changing "temperature" of the group as it warmed, cooled, and warmed again.[59] Right from the first days of the Bethel lab, the organizers also met regularly to talk about how things were going, how they were doing, what worked, and what didn't. They reflected on and listened to the delegates' reactions, the good and the bad.

In fact, it was critical that observation and assessment be shared with all as ongoing, multidirectional "feedback," because it was feedback that nurtured self-awareness and sensitivity, capacities deemed critical to democratic inter-subjectivity. (It was no accident that delegates had been asked in the preinterview about how "intuitive" and "sensitive" they thought they were, to create a self-reporting baseline.) They would soon learn how they actually behaved, both as leaders and as group members. The experts—the trainers—were as exposed to feedback as the delegates. Even the claims of these experts weren't insulated from critique. During their adult education training laboratory in Connecticut back in 1946, the Lewinians had learned how powerful it could be when participants were allowed to listen to and even participate in expert assessments of their own behavior. At a certain point, one "participant objected to a statement in one observer's report," while "another participant rushed to the defense of the observation," and this kindled such a spirited discussion that it improved their engagement with the training.[60]

After Bethel was over in August, the faculty leaders did this to themselves in an intense feedback review session. They reviewed evaluations of their performance and discussed how each trainer did. The reports were sometimes indicting. One found a trainer insensitive—"very self-assertive," "interrupts frequently," "argues often with one individual ignoring the effects on the group." Another as "very sensitive to wishes of others." Debate erupted at times over whether the assessments were fair, and each trainer got the chance to say how he thought things went. And all of this feedback on feedback was audio recorded and transcribed, so that there would be a good record for posterity. Perhaps if they had time in the future, they'd return to this transcript and go meta yet again in order to see what the flow and friction of these August discussions revealed about the individual styles and interpersonal dynamics of the group.[61] Endless reflection, feedback forever.

Democratic life wasn't easy. It wasn't simply a matter of doing some communicative actions and not others, because democracy, as an interactional culture, required reflexivity. Self-accountability, an openness to feedback and even criticism, a keen sensitivity to interpersonal action and reaction and the way that contributed to group climate—all this made up the communicative habits of a healthy, self-regulating democratic culture.[62]

The Bethel lab and its incessant multidirectional feedback, the studied informality and hierarchy flattening rituals that kindled we-ness—all this seemed mutually reinforcing, as if to position delegates as *like* these interpersonal scientists. It lowered the scientists a degree and raised the delegates, till they seemed to stand—nearly, anyway—on the same plane. It blurred the boundary between experimenter and subject, or such was the hope, as Lewin had been chipping away at this boundary for years. He had tried to break down knowledge–action and science–society antinomies to fashion new, hybrid roles and divisions of labor.

Levin passed away suddenly in 1947—just months before the first Bethel lab was to convene. After his death, his MIT center relocated to the University of Michigan, where it became a pillar of a new, soft-money-funded interdisciplinary social science hub, the Institute for Social Research (ISR). Dorwin Cartwright assumed the reins in Ann Arbor. In his five-year report, he reflected on their priority not simply to ensure "improved communication between social scientists and practitioners"—everyone aspired to that—but also to open up new "channels of communication" and afford "concrete coordination of research and action." This would allow for "a new social role—the social science consultant . . . paralleling that of a medical doctor."[63] (This ethic of consultancy was helped along by the center's dependency on soft money. The ISR had to serve society more strenuously than social scientists like Bales, after all. The federal government had supplied the largest share of the Michigan Center's support, its biggest contracts stemming from the Office of Naval Research, the National Institute of Mental Health [NIMH] and the US Air Force.[64] The University of Michigan did little more than host the center while collecting overhead on its contracts.)

At the first Bethel lab, the roles of experimenter and subject were mapped onto the action-roles of "changer" and "changee," but it would be ironic if not autocratic if the former told the latter what to do. As Fred Turner has chronicled, the social scientists of Washington's influential wartime Committee for National Morale thought hard about how to safeguard and spread a democratic culture at home, and that included ideas about how to reform mass communication. The committee worried about the antidemocratic affordances of mass media, notorious for their capacity to spread propaganda. The unidirectional, one-to-many vector that seemed to characterize media like radio and TV risked turning recipients into unthinking, intolerant masses. As an antidote, they imagined and eventually experimented with "multi-image, multi-sound-source media environments," what Turner calls "surrounds." A surround positioned a human not as the "receiver" of a single-sourced message, in the usual conduit model of communication, but rather as a subject who faced multiple messages from multiple directions, so that he could think and choose for himself.[65]

At Bethel, too, it had been tricky to train delegates in democratic interaction. They could not foist knowledge upon their guests, as it was not knowledge that they were there to impart. They had to train people democratically, because what they offered was not knowledge but a special way of being together with others. Democracy was an interpersonal culture and interaction a technology to bring it about. A serious obstacle was expert knowledge itself.[66] They couldn't maintain the usual asymmetry between observer and observed. Observers must come down from their high ground—even if their observations draw on expertise that their subjects lack. In the planning stages, Lippitt had stressed that the research team—which was big, more than a third of the whole Bethel community—must never look down on their subjects. The observers "cannot be seen as the adolescents of the culture," he pleaded. "There is to be no visible giggling or clustering about the sphere of their own social life, but rather, a joining in with the social life of the whole group." Another convener chimed in, adding "that any semblance to 'laughing at us from afar' should be eliminated."[67]

A Special Room

Along with this new intimacy between experimenter and subject came a revised relationship between laboratory and world. For the Lewinians, a lab wasn't a literal enclosure for capturing a phenomenon epistemically, but an environment—any environment, indoors or outdoors, big or small—designed for experimentation, and experimentation was as much for social change as knowledge. Back at Bethel, the MIT people sensed from the start that the Harvard observers like Bales had never fully embraced the commitment to democratic group cultivation nor the very idea of the lab at Bethel, and perhaps they were right.[68]

Despite his participation at Bethel, Bales remained comfortable only in the usual kind of lab. In 1947, the same year as Bethel's inaugural lab, Bales had created his own laboratory of sorts within the Laboratory of Social Relations—a "special room" as he first called it—expressly for observing human interaction. Just as he did with his machine and coding system, Bales went on to write a detailed guide on how to create rooms for studying small groups, which were soon being built around the country. In his lab in Emerson Hall, he maintained the usual strictures around experimenter–subject separation. He even physically removed himself and his interaction scorers from the scene by means of that emblem of unidirectional surveillance and epistemological distance, the one-way mirror.

Bales's special room was a generous 18 by 20 feet, its layout spare. It resembled a conference-room, outfitted with a table or two and some foldable chairs and a chalkboard. Bales wished to keep it a blank slate, not a space that would steer people's behavior this way or that. Yes, there were sweeping one-way mirrors and microphones delicately suspended from the ceiling that some people could and probably would spot; in fact, it's better if you expose the artifice to subjects in advance, Bales advised; in that way they could relax and interact freely without fear of surreptitious observation and recording.[69]

By comparison, consider for a moment again the neighboring world of interaction research on talk therapy, where scenographic naturalism was key, and where, as Zinn had demonstrated, stealth was fine. Over at Ohio State University, Carl Rogers and his students were at pains to ensure that the recording space of therapy felt so natural you'd never notice it. They produced an impressive corpus of recording-based transcriptions of their distinctive client-centered psychotherapy. A student of Rogers in 1942 published a list of suggestions that read like a beginner's guide to bugging a hotel room. You could take a goose-neck desk lamp and substitute the microphone and its cable for the bulb, socket, and cord, and then cover the face of the lamp with cheesecloth. "This disguise has been used in all of our interviews and the microphone has been detected by only 6 out of more than 130 clients." Or, you "mount the microphone in a dummy telephone," or "conceal it in a small radio."[70] In the 1950s, psychologist David Shakow launched an ambitious recording initiative on psychotherapy using 16mm sound film. The recording environment was laborious, and expensive, to create. Visitors irreverently referred to it as the "million-dollar toy," in no small part because of the cluster of special rooms Shakow needed. He needed a camera room and observatory, and, above all, a recording studio that would be a masterpiece in scenographic naturalism. The scenium, as Shakow called it, boasted elegant floor coverings, draperies, and furnishings that would avoid the chill of both

Chart 9. Pooled interaction profile for five four-person groups of 9th grade boys.

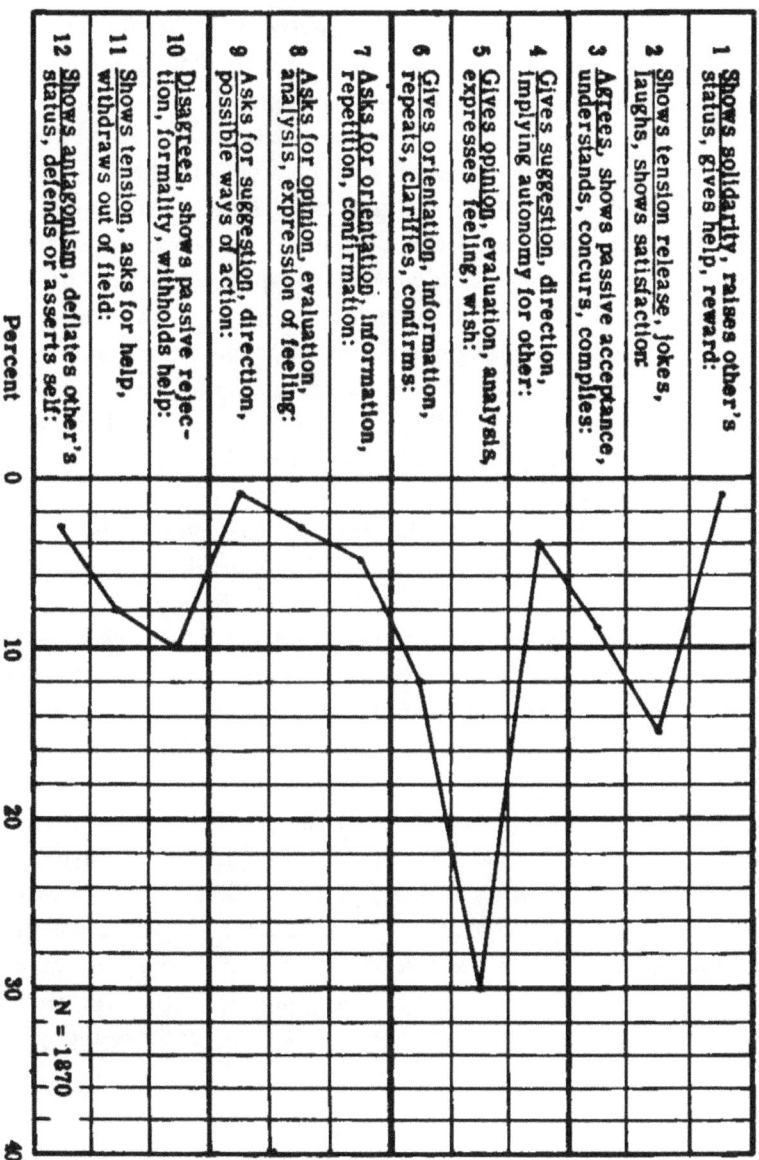

		Percent	0	10	20	30	40
1	Shows solidarity, raises other's status, gives help, reward:						
2	Shows tension release, jokes, laughs, shows satisfaction:						
3	Agrees, shows passive acceptance, understands, concurs, complies:						
4	Gives suggestion, direction, implying autonomy for other:						
5	Gives opinion, evaluation, analysis, expresses feeling, wish:						
6	Gives orientation, information, repeats, clarifies, confirms:						
7	Asks for orientation, information, repetition, confirmation:						
8	Asks for opinion, evaluation, analysis, expression of feeling:						
9	Asks for suggestion, direction, possible ways of action:						
10	Disagrees, shows passive rejection, formality, withholds help:						
11	Shows tension, asks for help, withdraws out of field:						
12	Shows antagonism, deflates other's status, defends or asserts self:					N = 1870	

F I G U R E 15. Bales's interactional profiling by pragmatic move type, 1950. Bales, *Interaction Process Analysis*, p. 23.

laboratory and recording studio. As one therapist who agreed to be recorded there recounted, "a couch, a few chairs, two small tables, one of which supports the microphone, a few books, two pictures, and a few growing plants have the task of making the room look like an ordinary office." The ambiance would feel so familiar that it would calm any recording anxieties by therapist or patient; yet at the same time the space was meticulously engineered for high-fidelity sound pick up and sharp cinematography.[71]

That his subjects were in a special room, Bales would freely share. But behind the one-way mirror was his observation room, and that was off-limits. What made small groups small was ultimately the fact that they fit in his special room, into which Bales could bring all kinds of groups: dyads like teacher–student, interviewer–interviewee, therapist–patient, mother–child, husband–wife; and larger groups of seeming infinite variety, such as "teams and work groups, family and household groups, children's play groups, adolescent gangs, adult cliques, social and recreational clubs." Each had its share of sociological troubles that small-group science might help illuminate, but the more immediate and pressing task for Bales was fine-grained observation, recording, and analysis.

Bales "profiled" his subjects, as he termed it. Chapple's profiles had been diagnostic and individual. His interaction chronograph revealed the interviewee's personality and temperament. Bales did sometimes chart how individuals behaved—what actions they tended to do—but he cared more about the dynamics of an event over time. It was groups that he profiled. By looking at five different four-person groups of ninth-grade boys, for instance, you could see that they tended to do a lot of opinion-giving (figure 15), whereas the action type that predominated in a study of five married couples was "*gives orientation* (information, repeats, clarifies, confirms)."[72]

To profile groups, it would help to standardize the task you gave them. If you handed the interactants a standard problem—Bales liked to use a chess task—then you could go on to adjust group size and "introduce experimental variables of almost unlimited diversity—variations in the problem, in the composition of personality types within the groups, in the social organization of members—with some prospect of being able to detect the resulting variations in interaction."[73]

Applying, Autonomizing

When it came to group dynamics, Bales hoped to do more than predict output from input. In addition, he hoped to learn something about interaction *itself*, about its dynamics as a whole, irrespective of who was interacting. If

FIGURE 16. Parody of interactional posturing at conferences. Robert Freed Bales, 1955, "How People Interact in Conferences," p. 32.

you looked carefully at change over time, at the changing densities and proportions of actions as they unfolded, perhaps you could find regularities if not laws. Deep in his 1950 textbook, Bales expressed this hope in a heady section, "dynamic tendencies of the interaction process," which concerned "tendencies or uniformities that may occur in the interaction over time within a given group, *without reference to the particular persons who initiate it or toward whom it is addressed*" (emphasis mine).[74]

Bales finally got the abstract knowledge he desired at RAND.[75] Collaborating with a member of the Systems Research Laboratory, Bales abstracted out seven decision-making steps—"information-processing operations"—that people went through to determine, from surveillance, whether an aerial object was friendly or unidentified, and, if unidentified, in which direction it was headed so that a fighter could be scrambled to intercept it.

You could find these seven in any problem-solving interaction, Bales came to claim. In a glossy 1955 essay written for the wide readership of the *Scientific American*, Bales argued that these seven were at work in a setting familiar to academics. In "How People Interact in Conferences," Bales suggested that those "interminable series of meetings around the conference table, international and otherwise" were "in many ways very like the operation of a large-scale communication and control system such as an air-defense network."[76] If this improbable analogy elevated the talk of intellectuals, if it seemed to put it on par with the life-and-death plane of national defense, the essay also poked at these chattering men. Cartoons added by the *Scientific American* jeered at their interpersonal posturing (figure 16). Whatever the motivation, this deflation insinuated that deliberation was never and would never be a sober, cerebral affair; it would always be worldly, because humans were interpersonal beings who acted and reacted; who were excitable, volatile, even; who formed coalitions and petty rivalries in a matter of minutes. You couldn't just analyze how humans rationally (or irrationally) linked premises to conclusions, for instance, nor could you ferret out an individual's psychological states or sociological conditions of life. You needed a dedicated science of interaction. You needed Bales.

Abstracting out rules and regularities of interaction may satisfy the nomothetic desire of a self-styled science of interaction, but it did not make social engineering easy. As the object interaction became loosened from its moorings, as it came to enjoy a life of its own, it became that much harder to "apply" knowledge of it—at least directly. Because now you needed additional personnel and the work of translation to concretize and fit this knowledge to the setting at hand. Compare with Chapple's technocratic science, which aimed for instant, relatively unmediated (if always proprietary) applicability. Ideally, Chapple's chronograph would require no outside labor to operate. In principle, anybody could use it. In this way Chapple's machine would function as an *embedded* technology, to be used on site without consultants or scientists. His machine would enter the circuit of institutional activity and function seamlessly. Bales's science may have made itself always and everywhere relevant, yet his mode of technologizing interaction took effort to apply. His knowledge of interaction would need to be tailored more to the situation. It would have to be brought down—*applied*—and Bales, unlike the Lewinians, didn't imagine himself as the person to do this.

*

The specialized interaction recorders of Chapple and Bales, then, did not just dedicate themselves to this new if intimately familiar object of knowledge, interaction. They also continuously affirmed interaction's ontological independence by the sheer promiscuity of their application. For the very fact that they could be used to record all *kinds* of human interaction suggested that interaction was a general thing, a type with many—perhaps indefinitely many—tokens. If you could apply the recorder widely, irrespective of situation or activity or category of participant, then surely what you recorded was not tethered to context. Hypostasized by promiscuous recording, interaction grew apart from its manifestations. It hovered on its own—autonomous—a thing to know, and to control.

From Chapple to Bales to Lewin and beyond, there were many ways and degrees by which you could technologize interaction, from relatively specialized applications to highly abstract knowledge that would take more work to "apply" but was nevertheless widely socially relevant. Regardless of how and with what effects small-group researchers technologized interaction, consider their industriousness: notice how they chase down forms of interaction everywhere, for as the Bethel lab conveners said of democratic interaction, it was relevant in "all areas of face-to-face living."[77]

How busy they were, these small-group scientists. In Ann Arbor, Lewin's relocated center celebrated its reach, its range of applicability. It could apply knowledge of group dynamics to anything—from the Boy Scouts and YMCA to the military. In his five-year report on the center, Cartwright listed "group productivity" as the first of several rubrics, for the "most frequent complaints about group enterprise is that it is inefficient or ineffective in 'getting things done.'"[78] Efficiency and effectiveness mattered everywhere, from factory floors to deliberative bodies including the United Nations.[79] About his MIT center, Lewin had noted how leaders in "government," "agriculture," "industry," "education," "community life" were starting to recognize the need for a science of group dynamics.[80] The vista was vast and dizzying. It was just as Fred Strodtbeck had forecast when he made his case for small-group research: interaction was everywhere with its problems, and this practical science would rush to understand and fix them so that small problems didn't become bigger.

Silence on Interscalarity

As interaction was discovered as a thing to know and grew ontologically independent, then, it seemed to show up everywhere, which made for a frenzied if unquestionably relevant science. There was no time to stop and ask why social science should care about small groups, and why, in particular, those like Chapple and Bales should bother to look at humans so carefully and microscopically. Did the discourse of small itself suggest something about the science's significance for society? Not directly or explicitly. Discursively, small at first was, again, a powerful, resonant gesture that condensed postwar virtues—rigor and hard science, social engineering and manageability. As small excited more than troubled its publics, people like Bales didn't need to explain much. There was little pressure to justify the focus on small groups because this science was too busy being relevant. Yet surely small groups still mattered as a topic only to the extent that these groups had *something* to do with the unmarked big groups to which the little ones were hitched.

This was the tease, for what *was* this something? Small-group analysis didn't collapse or erase distinctions between scales just because it spotlighted the small;[81] if anything, it sharpened the division between ontological scales by sweeping the big into the penumbral background; this left unsaid the precise manner in which the two scalar worlds coexisted. It created the conditions for worlds to become estranged, for interaction to break off into a paracosm.

This was a problem of interscalarity, which concerns *relations* between scales, whether epistemological or ontological.[82] It is with ontological scale that the problem of interscalar kinship—and in its extreme form, the problem of the paracosm—rears its head and forces one to figure out exactly how scales relate.[83]

When small-group science first sprang into action, there was no interscalar "problem" of kinship to solve. With the benefit of hindsight, we can anticipate their trouble and imaginatively suggest to them one of two well-rehearsed solutions for happy scalar coexistence. The first solution would be to say that small groups mattered because they were *microcosmic* in some way. Perhaps they allowed you to see more vividly patterns that looked indistinct and gauzy—or were invisible—at a macrosocial observational scale (which of course presumes that one is looking at the same reality more and less closely). Or, we might aver that interaction is not so much microcosmic as *constitutive* of the macrosocial in some way, such that small meant "elementary," as if one was peering into cells to learn something about the structures that encompassed them. (Unlike the microcosmic, here we do not need to assume that parts indicate or exhibit wholes or work exactly as they do, but only that the two are causally implicated in some fashion.) Note that in either case—the microcosmic and the constitutive—we face not one ontological scale but two, a matter of interscalarity.[84] This interscalarity typically turns on a mereological (part-whole) treatment of object domains, as if some objects (e.g., interaction) existed volumetrically "within" a hierarchically integrated domain (e.g., society).[85] Simply: when you study small groups in this light, you assume you've pried open society and are studying its parts. Wasn't this what small groups were, after all, parts of wholes, the outer reaches of which were the boundaries of "society" itself?

Bales did anticipate some interscalar trouble, but he entertained these concerns quietly, deep in his textbook. Bales said that when you coded, say, "solidarity," you should not jump directly from the solidarity of small groups—which seemed spatially and temporally bounded, which unfolded in his special room—to the solidarity of society.

A jump like that would be a "fallacy," for we must not be "misled by a similarity of words." We must distinguish "'solidarity' as a concept descriptive of an existing state or structural condition of a social relationship, and 'solidarity' as a concept descriptive of certain *immediate* emotional qualities of interaction" (emphasis mine). And as he elaborated, "In our field there are many problems where it is necessary to make a clear distinction between a more generalized state of being or structural condition of the system with which we are dealing, and a more *momentary* dynamic movement within that structure" (again, emphasis mine).[86] Immediate, momentary—these were qualities of interaction *itself*. Although interaction fit snugly "within" a larger structure (which presumably was the reason you studied it in the first place), Bales said that when you coded an action or observed a particular rate of action, you must not assume that it tells you anything "direct" about the social world of which it is a part.[87] Bales pried apart the face-to-face from the social world, to some degree and as a point of epistemological caution. To recognize interaction's true ontological kinship, to see its mereological place within the total social world of which it is a part, Bales said we'd have to wait. He gestured toward the future, to a time when we can muster all the social sciences—"economics, social anthropology, sociology, and psychology of personality."[88] Eventually, interaction process analysis would need to join hands with other fields and be reintegrated. In the meantime there was much interaction to record.

That he buried these reflections suggests that Bales didn't think he needed to defend his science. On rare occasions he did come out and address interscalarity, but tellingly, his comments were brief and rather predictable.

In *Family, Socialization, and Interaction Process*, for instance, a volume he coedited with Talcott Parsons, it was Parsons who led with a brief interscalar argument about why we should care about small-group analysis. In his preface, he trumpeted the "importance of the fact that the family—the 'nuclear' family, that is—is everywhere a *small* group." And as a small group, it is "relatively a very simple social system," so that if you understand how it serves as an "agency of socialization and of personality stabilization," then you can learn about an enduring issue for social scientists, the relationship between social system, personality, and culture.[89] Families were at once microcosmic and constitutive. A nuclear family qua small group was not itself a whole, not "an independent society," but a part—a "differentiated subsystem of society."[90] And not just *any* part of society but a part critical to socialization, so critical that you could say that families were partly *constitutive* of these larger social formations. Families were *microcosmic*, too, because they offered you a glimpse of the same world that the macrosociologist cared about. If you examined the small groups experimentally and microscopically, you could see the same patterns, only more clearly: "it should be easier to discern certain fundamental relationships between them [family members] than it is on the more complex levels where for example problems of 'national character' arise."[91]

In his own chapter Bales echoed Parsons. In his study of role differentiation—how interactants in small groups assume different social roles in interaction (e.g., who is "proactive" and "reactive," who becomes the "best liked man" and who the "idea man")—the aim "is to catch role differentiation 'in the making' from some minimal level, in the hope that the character of the minimal phenomena may give clues as to very general forms and reasons for development of role differentiation."[92] Hopes like these amounted to atmospherics. They were framing comments, and little more. Parsons and Bales made the case for small groups briefly and effortlessly, because nobody forced them to try very hard.

Of course, there were many subtle and implicit ways in which Bales did link his small groups with culture, society, and history, but the point is that he never saw ontological interscalarity as a problem to address. Where was his effort to connect so-called micro and macro? Where was his response to critics who might hear the "small" of small groups as evidence of narrowness and limited significance? Indeed, by stressing that interaction could have its own dynamics, and by not clearly tying his science of the small to the science of big groups, Bales created the conditions for his science to seem remote and for interaction as an object to float off into a paracosm. In a snap, independence can become isolation, which is what arguably befell small-group science in the late 1960s and early 1970s when its object's autonomy became a liability. For some critics, it became evidence of the field's aloofness, an aloofness confirmed by its distanced scientism, and of a conservative if not reactionary stance on urgent social ills that you could plainly see. Small became proof, in a word, of this science's irrelevance.

PART III

Micropolitics

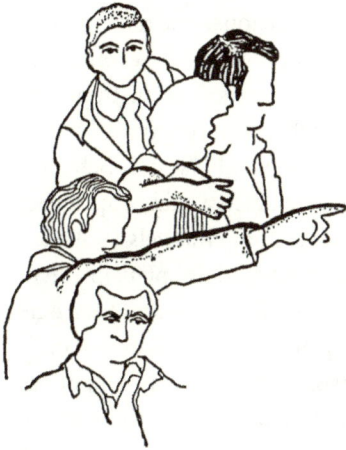

Gestures of dominance.

Gestures of submission—lowering eyes, cuddling, smiling.

FIGURE 17. Illustrations by Deidre Patrick that conjure the pervasiveness of embodied acts of gender dominance and submission. Nancy Henley, *Body Politics*, 185, 186.

Small-group science experienced a precipitous decline in the seventies. Many within its fold weren't quite sure what happened. "All who have written on this topic . . . agree that group research suffered a system crash within North American social psychology in the late sixties and early seventies."[1] There were surely many reasons for the crash, but one was that a politically mobilized vanguard in sociology—the discipline that represented a core constituency for small-group science—had a hard time seeing progressive let alone revolutionary potential in its distanced, postwar scientism and its liberal, patient, technocratic posture.

Which isn't to say that all those who studied social interaction and embraced "the small" or microscopy were being written off by those who saw themselves as part of a political vanguard, because, as we shall see, "small" in some circles took on new subversive significance around the same time.

Outside the academy, a new and different kind of "small group" was forming in the late 1960s, that of radical feminist consciousness raising (CR), which at first was sometimes called a "small group." More importantly, for some second-wave feminists, "the interpersonal" emerged as an important ideological site of gender politics. Unwanted touches, interruptions by men, unequal terms of address, were called out as comparatively "small" behaviors that were nonetheless important in the daily battle against male supremacy. These behaviors were pernicious because they were comparatively subtle and thus harder to notice and report—and easier for men to claim plausible deniability. They were also pernicious because they were frequent, and hence not really small at all. They could happen anytime you interacted with a man.

This feminist politicization of the interpersonal inspired scholars of language and interaction within the academy, who tried to mobilize their science to pinpoint patriarchy in everyday interactions between men and women. In a parallel scene, much as Chester Pierce called out a pernicious, steady, microscopic racism with his notion of "microaggression," a new wave of young "microsociologists" and "microethnographers" began to scrutinize what happened in schools—an institution notorious for its anti-Black racism and now a place where integration made interracial interaction a critical thing to study. They began to look for discriminatory verbal and nonverbal behaviors in classroom interaction with teachers, in standardized testing environments, in guidance counselor interviews with students. They would catch racism in the act—subtle, tacit, but chronic racism—and show teachers and policymakers how to intervene.

In this way, influenced by converging streams of social justice movements, in this last story we will see how the interpersonal got political. Within the academy, this imbued interaction with fresh importance. It made sense why you might want to analyze interaction closely, especially when these interactions might reveal sexism and racism.

Still, questions arose. What exactly was this new interpersonal "micropolitics," as a self-consciously scalar object of knowledge—and action? How did this micropolitics relate to a politics elsewhere, and what was its relative importance? Would scholars of language and communication be able to produce actionable knowledge of this micropolitics just from their mediatic recordings and transcripts of talk? If they got too fine grained, wouldn't that draw them into thinking about perplexing details and have them forget why this all mattered? Could their knowledge complement the social movement activism that had helped give interaction its renewed relevance and urgency? Or was the whole enterprise misguided? Perhaps all this attention toward interaction in general amounted to a distraction from the ideological sites where, in the case of the women's liberation movement, male supremacy mattered most. After all, if daily face-to-face interaction was always "just" a matter of a few people at a time, stuck in little places here and there, conversing and then departing after a short while, wasn't this less pressing to understand, and undo, than the "larger," "systemic" inequalities—legal and institutional—that ultimately kept women down and that probably explained *why* patriarchy reared its head in interaction in the first place?

That is, inside and outside the academy, new questions erupted over the scale of interaction, questions that animated and vexed scholars of the face-to-face—and shouldered them with the burden of explaining themselves. The politicization of scale raised the problem of the paracosm, forcing those who studied interaction to address it and to thereby confront what had become a scalar truism: that interaction was an intrinsically small-scale level of social reality. Up for debate was no less than the reality of interaction and its relation to the rest of the world, as interaction's ontological scale (and sometimes also its accompanying epistemological scale) became sharply contested. As scholars took sides and tried to sort out what interaction's true scale was, critiques—and defenses—formed and these set the terms for the future of this object.

8

The Interpersonal Gets Political

Social interaction is the battlefield where the war
between the sexes is fought daily, minute by minute.
NANCY HENLEY, 1970[1]

In the San Francisco Bay Area radical feminist newsletter, *It Ain't Me Babe*, Lynn O'Connor began her searing 1970 essay, "Male Dominance: The Nitty-Gritty of Oppression," with a shot at leftist men. "Many men would like us to believe that oppression takes place in some vague, amorphous abstraction called 'institutions' over which they have no control," when in truth, "the nitty-gritty of oppression occurs in the one-to-one relationship, most often in the form of nonverbal communication."[2]

This oppression operating in the shadows of overt communication between voice and ear suggested that face-to-face interaction was fiercely political. Communicative behavior—not just talk but also gestures and postures and embodied signals of all kinds—could count as political in the sense of involving the exercise of power, in this case by men over women. It took several years and the convergence of communication science and second-wave feminism for arguments like O'Connor's to crystallize within the academy. As taken up by scholars in fields such as social psychology, sociology, linguistics, and anthropology, second-wave feminism helped give interaction as an object of scientific knowledge a new if contested politics of scale, a certain "micropolitics" as it was sometimes called.[3] It was this convergence that added the prefix *inter-* to *personal* in the memorable second-wave precept, "the personal is political."

I spotlight here only a couple of the many feminist linguists and communication scholars of the 1970s whose work argued for an interpersonal micropolitics and was catalyzed by a dialectic between scholarship and social movement activism. This is not a representative sample of feminist communication science writ large let alone a window onto movement politics. I select this writing because it reveals some of the many imaginative efforts to rethink the stakes of studying social interaction in the academy and to reimagine the possibilities of harnessing this knowledge for purposes of social transformation. In a way, this was again a case of interactionalization, of interaction constituted as method and technology and not just as an important thing to know. The scholarship foregrounded here can especially help us appreciate the questions—and the troubles—that ensued when you tried to argue that face-to-face interaction was deeply political. Indeed, feminist scholars of the interpersonal inherited the widespread assumption that interaction was an intrinsically small-scale level of reality, so if interaction did have a politics, this politics would need to be reconciled with a politics elsewhere, and that wasn't so easy.

The very idea of the interpersonal as a battlefield if not *the* battlefield for women, a trope evoked by Nancy Henley in the epigraph, was, of course, contentious. Like other feminist interventions that addressed language, speech, and embodied interaction, such a claim could elicit, as Elise Kramer writes, "a particularly vicious and enduring hostility whose legacy persists in the commonly held linkages between feminism, political correctness, and censorship."[4] But centering interpersonal communication was also not without some controversy within the women's movement, and this had much to do with scale. Among the different and competing currents of feminist thought of the period, some disagreed with what they saw as a misplaced emphasis on the interpersonal; many liberal feminists focused on reversing legal and institutional discrimination much as socialist and Marxist feminists insisted on keeping capitalism in the crosshairs. As we shall later see, such tensions over the relative importance of the interpersonal was not unlike tensions faced by social science scholars who had made a specialty of social interaction.

If, as Erving Goffman argued in the 1950s, face-to-face interaction really was a "little social system with its own boundary-maintaining tendencies,"[5] if this object did require a kind of "microsociology"—as many sociologists in the 1970s came to label work like his—then what relation did this little world have with "the social" of so-called macrosociology, many wondered? That is, what did "micro" here entail? In the 1970s, when feminist researchers of conversation began to pore over transcripts of talk, suspecting that they would find women's oppression there—in language choice and language use, in turn taking, in topic control, in interruptions, in how male interlocutors responded to women's talk or fell silent—were they looking for *evidence* of "sexism" or "male supremacy" or "patriarchy" *in* interaction, as if interaction were one more place in which these pernicious, entrenched ideological formations revealed their effects? Was interaction, that is, only one in a long list of ideological sites where women's oppression could be seen, and, if so, was the interpersonal truly as important as, say, the family or the school or the courtroom? Or was there something special, something primary if not constitutive about interpersonal gender violence against women? Could it be that interaction was, as Henley sometimes suggested, *the* premier site for women's liberation, perhaps because it occurred all the time, because interaction served as a necessary condition for nearly every imaginable kind of concerted human action? This kind of interscalar stance inverted things. It flipped the scaled universe. It made it seem as if the "small" world of interaction mattered more, that it demanded more attention precisely because of its ubiquity. Under dispute among scholars, as in the women's movement, was the ontological question of interscalar kinship, of exactly *how* the politics of the interpersonal was connected to a politics elsewhere.

Into the Nitty-Gritty

An influential Bay Area activist, O'Connor helped found a San Francisco branch of *Redstockings*, launched a newsletter, and penned essays in feminist criticism. She remembers her awakening as sudden. In 1969, on the heels of the months-long strike at San Francisco State, where she had been enrolled as a student, it took just one feminist consciousness-raising (CR) session for her to spring into activism. As she recounted it, her intellectual influences had featured work in sociology, notably a heavy dose of Marxism—her paternal grandfather had been a revolutionary near Odessa, her first husband a scholar of the Cuban revolution—and, by the late '60s, human ethology. As for her interest in ethology and the nonverbal, she credited her father, I. Arthur Mirsky. An interdisciplinary medical scholar who contributed to psychosomatic medicine and later trained in psychoanalysis, Mirsky did research in the late '50s and early '60s on the nonverbal communication of affect in rhesus monkeys.[6]

Human communication depends on both verbal and nonverbal signs, one of his articles began. "Every therapist is aware that although attitudes, moods and feelings may be conveyed not only through content but also through the tone of the words used in communication between therapist and patient, of even greater significance may be the communication of affects through some consciously or unconsciously perceived behavior." Mirsky and his coauthors repeated here the truism about the communicative unconscious, that when people interact, they give off telltale, indexical signs that the sensitive, receptive clinician should pick up. And just as Lasswell, Sullivan, and others had earlier argued, how people used their body—and not only their talk—indexed what their speech meant, clinically speaking, even though, Mirsky and his coauthors lamented, "little is known about the mechanisms of non-verbal communication."[7]

O'Connor's synthesis of Marxism, feminism, and ethology offered a startling and disquieting view of "nonverbal communication." She adopted the tooth-and-nail language of ethologists to expose power in conversations that on the surface may look placid and unremarkable. Using ethology to grasp social interaction was not unusual. Albert Scheflen, for instance, wrote in 1965 of seemingly innocent "quasi-courtship" displays in psychotherapy sessions, by both female patients and male psychotherapists: preening hair or a tie or socks, for instance, tensing leg muscles, drawing closer, mirroring posture.[8] Ethology informed ideas about how humans managed their bodies in public—in Goffman's *Behavior in Public Spaces* (1963) and E. T. Hall's *Hidden Dimension* (1966), for example. Goffman's 1969 seminar in "Public Order" had devoted an entire section to animal studies.[9] Gregory Bateson ventured far beyond the humans, into the communication systems of whales and dolphins, for instance. Ethology ran through Michael Argyle's *Social Interaction* (1969), just as it did through Desmond Morris's popular ethological provocations in *The Naked Ape* (1967), *The Human Zoo* (1969), and *Intimate Behavior* (1971).[10]

O'Connor's stance on these vestigial dramas was anything but clinical. Her concern was gender violence and what should done about it. Though ethology was not his inspiration, Harvard psychiatrist Chester Pierce would soon publish on what he called racial "microaggressions," which he, too, envisioned as prototypically nonverbal. "Racial respect is usually conferred non-verbally. Hence most racism may be kinetic." "Racism," he continued, "is the brusque way change is returned to the Black customer, or the recoiling, resigned grimace and haughty disdain a white passenger demonstrates when taking a seat on an airplane next to a Black [passenger]." Of course, interpersonal racism did often involve talk, but talk was only part of the story and by itself no reliable guide to racist pragmatics. Pierce's appeal to the "nonverbal" and "kinetic" was, in a sense, a way to call attention to a basic epistemological problem, namely, that the most frequent forms of racist behavior can be hard to notice as such.[11]

Ethology and the nonverbal did something similar for O'Connor, for whom the nitty-gritty of women's oppression also hid in plain sight. Ethology revealed oppression in the most prosaic of interactions. In O'Connor's ethology, dominance displays exercised by men over women weren't natural biological reflections of differences of sex but rather the result of a long history of economic oppression. Nonverbal dominance occurred "against the backdrop of the male-supremacist economy which ensures the dependency of women on men and maintains a powerful army ready to move if needed." The historical materialisms of both Marxism and ethology allowed O'Connor to concretize and localize power, to take it out of the head and see it transpiring between individuals, in interaction. Male domination became immanent, always here and now, never only "out there" as those New Left men implied when they pointed at power and absolved themselves of any responsibility in reproducing it.

Nancy Henley's Multimodal "Micropolitics"

O'Connor's provocation on the nitty-gritty of oppression had been excerpted from a longer essay written in 1969. "Male Supremacy: A Theoretical Analysis," authored under the pseudonym Nicole Anthony, had elaborated on the materialist underpinnings of patriarchy. The full essay was reprinted and circulated, and both pieces found their way into the hands of Nancy Main Henley (1934–2016). A newly minted social psychologist who was becoming a feminist activist in her own right,[12] Henley too was interested in the nitty-gritty of communication, though she didn't know O'Connor and for years thought O'Connor and Nicole Anthony were two different people.[13] Henley came slowly to the women's movement, and to graduate school. She dropped out of college to have a child and managed to graduate a dozen years later. Henley's dissertation in psychology at Johns Hopkins had been an experimental study of the semantic field for animal terms in English.[14] It had nothing to do with gender or power or nonverbal behavior. In 1968, as she began her first teaching job at the new Baltimore County branch of the University of Maryland, she began to meet monthly with faculty to talk about social justice issues at people's homes. There she noticed interpersonal gender dynamics in the discussions. She was struck by the use of nonverbal behaviors, notably nonreciprocal touch—where one touches and the other doesn't touch back—as a dominance display by men over women, a subtle threat, it seemed, that reminded women of their inferior status. She was also surprised that there was virtually no literature on this topic in social psychology.

And so she designed a study. Henley trained an undergraduate research assistant to observe touch in public interactions between men and women outdoors. On data sheets, her assistant hand-recorded instances of touch, which Henley later correlated with demographic variables—principally sex, but also age, race, and occupation. By 1970, at an annual meeting of the American Psychological Association, Henley delivered a paper on the politics of touch as part of a panel on "Social Psychology and Women's Liberation" and continued research on this topic at a postdoc at Harvard in 1971.[15]

Touch wasn't only or even primarily about intimacy, not when you considered who got touched. Here Henley adapted an argument by Harvard social psychologist Roger Brown and Boston University's Albert Gilman. In their influential 1960 essay, "The Pronouns of Power and Solidarity," Brown and Gilman had argued that nonreciprocal pronoun exchange—a French employer says *tu*, for instance, while an employee responds with *vous*—signals unequal relations and is an indicator of the universal "power" dimension of conversation; reciprocal exchange, by contrast, indicates "solidarity."[16] Henley extended this to the asymmetries of touch. Men touched women nearly twice as often as women touched men.

She reported her findings soberly in one article but adopted a more activist register when she reiterated her argument in an essay called "The Politics of Touch," which was published as a chapter for *Radical Psychology* and also reprinted and circulated by *Know, Inc.*, a feminist alternative press. Here, in prose that was by turns clinical and cutting, she charged that men used unsolicited, nonreciprocal touch—an arm draped over the shoulder, a hand placed casually on the back—as a gesture of dominance, particularly over women. Stylistically, she imbued scholarly argument with feminist activism. For one, she told a story—an anecdote about herself getting touched. She drew on personal experience as a source of knowledge, much as women did in feminist CR sessions. Yet she also displayed her best agentless passive and provided summary statistics and citations of scholarly literature. Juggling scholarly and activist commitments was not always an easy synergistic relationship. The divide could be too wide to straddle, forcing you to make a choice, not just in what you said but in how you said it. Would you pen your argument as a sober social scientist, or smuggle in some of the irreverent wit and playful snark found in alternative feminist media, for instance?

The stakes of such choices could be high. Navigating the activist-scholarly divide had been notoriously perilous for those involved in other struggles. Monica Heller and Bonnie McElhinny note how the field of sociolinguistics, which began to coalesce in the 1960s, got its start a decade earlier as part of a push for "development" and decolonization. In the United States, "the field of sociolinguistics emerge[d] in this period as a means to construct engagement with social inequalities in the face of the promises of progress in the postwar period," and while many of its scholars directed their energy internationally toward curing former colonies from the ills of past imperialism, they also turned their attention homeward, targeting inequality in America (even if this turn homeward could also be seen as neocolonialist, as Heller and McElhinny suggest). Many leading scholars who worked under the big tent of "sociolinguistics," such as John Gumperz, William Labov and Dell Hymes in the United States, lent their expertise to social movements at home. This included offering expert testimony, demonstrating that Black English was just as logical as any other language, and defending indigenous rights.[17] Yet all the while these sociolinguists had to manage—sometimes quite carefully—the perception of just how "political" they were and which movements they supported. As Heller and McElhinny suggest, much of this delicacy was spurred by the lingering and painful legacy of McCarthyism when many linguists were investigated and disciplined and, in some cases, fired.[18] In this light, stylistically, Henley's admixture was not subtle. She practically trumpeted her plan to incite revolution, if only within her field, and she continued her experimentation at synthesizing activism and scholarship as she expanded her argument about touch into a full-length book, *Body Politics* (1977).

✶

But politicizing touch also raised some serious conceptual, and, indeed, political questions. From the start Henley wrestled with the scale of what she observed. Nonreciprocal touch may look "little"—the scare quotes are hers—yet it is "one more tool used by a male-supremacist society to keep women in their place." Here she echoed O'Connor. Men reproduced male supremacy in interaction (for the most part, unknowingly), and they needed to stop. As she expanded on this in *Body Politics*, interaction became a site for a multimodal micropolitics: "The 'trivia' of everyday life—touching others, moving closer or farther away, dropping the eyes, smiling, interrupting—are commonly interpreted as facilitating social intercourse, but not recognized in their position as micropolitical gestures, defenders of the status quo—of the state, of the wealthy, of authority, of all those whose power may be challenged."[19]

Let us pause to consider Henley's curious interscalar stance on the small, which, after all, was hardly small at all. It only looked this way when you counted bodies and weighed them against big groups—understood as quantitative aggregations of human individuals into agencies like crowds, masses, movements, unions, constituencies, parties, and so on. And yet this communicative micropolitics eclipsed these groups: spatially, it was "pervasive," cross-cutting social domains; temporally, it was continuous, occurring "daily."

Micropolitics cut deeper, too, as its prefix *micro-* could often imply. Communicative micropolitics operated under the surface of behavior, with little or no awareness by humans (or at least with plausible deniability); "these minutiae find their place on a continuum of social control which extends from internalized socialization at one end to sheer physical force at the other." A form of "covert control," as she saw it, communicative micropolitics operated on and through the body and hence didn't rely on the "content" of *what* people said nor even on *how* they spoke. As for causation, micropolitics wasn't "merely" symbolic: "Nonverbal power gestures provide the micropolitical structure, the thousands of daily acts through which nonverbal influence takes place, which underlies and supports the macropolitical structure."[20] While granting poetic equivalence to micro and macro—each substantialized as its own structure, as so many sociologists began to do in 1970s—Henley distinguished the former by its causal, and, we might add, feminized role: micropolitics acts daily in a thousand unnoticed ways; it "supports" and reproduces the dominant order from below.

In her earlier work on touch, Henley had largely refrained from making this strong claim about the reproduction of patriarchy. In the closing words of Politics of Touch, she conceded that nonreciprocal touch was ultimately a sociological symptom, an "indicator,"[21] yet by *Body Politics* behaviors like touch had become more than this. While in *Body Politics* she stressed that the true cause of women's oppression wasn't communication—its "roots" were political and economic—you couldn't explain the persistence of male domination without the micropolitical. The nonverbal was pernicious not simply because it was subvisible but because it played a critical role in reproducing women's oppression in daily life.[22]

As a scaled and gendered object, the interpersonal–political amalgam that Henley fashioned was a practical thing to know. "Understanding this pervasive process [of micropolitics] will suggest ways we can *begin* dealing with our interaction on a personal level, to begin to change our and others' opportunities" (emphasis in original). Knowledge of communicative micropolitics could spur interactional activism. It could encourage you to be political in daily life, whenever and wherever you wished. Unlike small-group CR sessions, which often saw their work as preparatory, a pedagogy based on communicative micropolitics had *pragmatic immediacy*. It gave you a way to act on the interpersonal level as a "first step." "Changing nonverbal behaviors will not eliminate prejudice or oppression—these must be attacked at their political and economic roots," and that takes time and effort and, to be sure, lots and lots of people. But communicative micropolitics did, indeed, offer a way to "begin," a way to localize and concretize the personal as a target for political action.[23] Interaction could become a technology for feminist social transformation.

Henley herself experimented with interactional activism. If men touched her, she'd grab them back in order to foreground the practice as a dominance display—"something I try to do now whenever men lay their hands on me—really scares them."[24] (Compare with "experiments in hostility," which appeared in a section on manners in several issues of the feminist newsletter *Off*

Our Backs. One installment discussed hissing as a "good method of attacking sexism in public." In another report: "We have . . . written some graffiti, made a few genuine obscene calls, heckled men in the streets and hissed in movies. In addition, we have refused to submit graciously to intimidation or witty dismissals of women in our personal lives.")[25] Henley took part in provocations and guerrilla theater, especially at conferences, which were her grounds for feminist networking and activism. At one meeting, she protested a restaurant that excluded women. At another she helped target an exhibition booth with images of scantily clad women. In her 1970 talk on body politics, when a man voiced skepticism, a friend of Henley's performed a stunt: she went over and touched him.[26] At the close of *Body Talk*, Henley advised that women "should train themselves . . . not to submit to another's will because of the subtle implication of his touch, and—why not?—start touching men, if the situation is appropriate, in order to break through the sexist pattern of tactual interaction." For their part, she listed steps men should take to stem their patriarchal habits: "*Men can stop*: invading women's personal space; touching them; excessively interrupting; taking up extra space; sending dominance signals to each other; staring."[27]

Interaction as Micropolitical Site: The Consciousness-Raising Group

As for the dialectic between scholarship and activism, it was not that the interpersonal became political because feminist social psychologists, linguists, and others made it so, but because their efforts were already supported by a conviction that had been building for some years, namely, that everyday interaction between men and women mattered critically, that it was a *site* for gender politics.

About sites of ideological work, Susan Gal and Judith Irvine stress their semiotic and interactional constitution. Sites are defined not by their literal socio-spatial location and extension, as the site metaphor can imply, but rather by the way they involve and invite "joint attention," by the way actors *mutually orient* toward some object of interest, in this case, toward the object of social interaction, which can occur anywhere.[28]

That one had to argue that interaction was a site for feminist micropolitics at all implied that this could be disputed, that this couldn't be taken for granted. Indeed, to be recognized as a site of feminist scrutiny and reform, social interaction would need to be compared, if only implicitly, with other sites, such as the patriarchal family or the sexist workplace or discriminatory law. Could interactional signs of male supremacy rival these in importance? Was the gender politics of the face-to-face as urgent to address as, say, wage discrimination or sexual violence? As a newly proposed site for feminist joint attention, interaction would need to be compared to domains of social life *elsewhere*, just as its micropolitics would be compared with a politics *elsewhere*, and there was no easy consensus on the results of this comparison.

The grounds for arguing that interaction was a micropolitical site had already been prepared, but not by social scientists of communication. By the late '60s in America, it is true that interaction was already a familiar object of knowledge for many social scientists and had enjoyed this status after the Second World War. True, too, that quite a few social scientists of interaction saw their object as a site for a kind of micropolitics—notably, a place where authoritarian and democratic lifeways were at stake in how people behaved— yet few outside the academy knew of this view. The women's liberation movement helped give visibility to the idea that interaction was an ideological site, even if those within the movement disagreed about how important this site was relative to other sites of struggle.

As is well known, the feminist foregrounding and politicization of the interpersonal came as a response to women's acute sense of marginalization during their participation in the civil rights, New Left, and anti-war movements of the '60s. The complaints ran the gamut but included frustration at not be listened to and taken seriously; being interrupted by men; being forced into secondary, supportive roles rather than leadership positions. (As O'Connor flippantly put it late in life: she got "sick of making tuna fish sandwiches for pompous [and somewhat stupid] lefty men.")[29]

A cumulative effect of these frustrations was a heightened recognition that power and domination could play out in interpersonal encounters and would need to be addressed there too. But how did this recognition take hold? Interaction was not a site for gender micropolitics until this recognition spread, and it spread thanks to a new feminist institution that ritually tried to counter entrenched practices of masculinist interpersonal exclusion. The story of how the interpersonal emerged as a contested micropolitical site begins in the late '60s as women who grew alienated from their participation in the New Left adopted what would soon become a practice central to second-wave feminism: the CR group. To appreciate the micropolitics created through a fusion of feminism and mediatic communication science, we must therefore first take one step backward and appreciate how interaction became a site for gender politics in the first place.

As an interaction ritual, the carefully orchestrated "small group," as CR was often called early on, featured ostentatiously inclusive methods of participation. The group would be a "safe" space, a "free" space, in which women got a chance to speak and nobody would be judged. With its special methods, the feminist small group foregrounded interaction itself as a domain of social life, making its usual expectations stick out so that they could be critiqued and ritually transformed.[30] Interdiscursively, the feminist small group contrasted poetically with "ordinary" (androcentric and patriarchal) conversation in which women experienced subordination and marginalization. The success of CR—its dissenting feminist voices notwithstanding—increased stock in the basic idea that a few human interacting together could be politically potent. Of course nobody wished to confuse the small group for mass protest or formal political engagement—or worse, think that the small group could serve as a substitute for these—yet discussions among a clutch of women once a week, in a home, could matter a lot.

The idea that interaction could be a micropolitical site had plenty of precedent from earlier in the sixties. Witness, for instance, Mary Hamilton's civil rights activism in which she insisted on being addressed as *Miss*—a respect term denied Black women like herself. At the close of the decade, Hamilton's former roommate, Sheila Michaels, went on to agitate for the use of *Ms.* as an alternative for *Miss and Mrs.*, as this address term didn't broadcast a woman's marital status.[31]

As for CR, feminists claimed it as their own while acknowledging that its influences were many. Some credited the Maoist practice of "speaking bitterness" as a source of inspiration, and despite early disavowals by feminists promoting CR, the practice drew deeply on a therapeutic sensibility. Less acknowledged at the time was CR's indebtedness to the discursive practices of the New Left circles of the early '60s, such as Students for a Democratic Society (SDS), with their desire to democratize participation—including how people interacted at meetings.[32]

Yet it was the upsurge of feminist CR that spread the basic conceit, that a small group could matter—a lot. Irrespective of what women talked about, the very fact that they met together presupposed the efficacy of a microcommunity in a political struggle. CR was used in varied and sometimes conflicting ways, and its functions changed over time as it spread, yet the practice helped build support for the idea that interaction was a site for gender politics.

Communication researchers like Henley enriched and expanded on this view, arguing that small-scale interactions of all kinds—not just at home, not just among women—mattered for their subvisible micropolitical dimensions. As the '70s unfolded, new scholarship by feminist researchers turned this site into an object of knowledge and began to explore how patriarchy and power operated *sub rosa* in conversation. Some even empirically studied CR groups themselves as part of an effort to understand whether men and women talked and interacted differently. By the mid to late 1970s, it became possible to think that a transformative if not liberating gender politics was compatible with the fine-grained analysis of interpersonal life; this, despite the many disclaimers and qualifications by feminist microanalysts that betrayed how contested the "micro" of their micropolitics was.

Subversively Small Groups, 1969

In 1969, just before feminism and communication science began to entwine, Harvard's Robert Freed Bales released a new textbook on small groups. At over 500 pages, his updated science had absorbed much since *Interaction Process Analysis*. Influenced by his new training in psychoanalytic theory and technique, he had turned from studying "task-oriented groups" toward free-flowing, naturalistic, "self-analytic" discussion groups. By self-analysis he meant group members who study themselves to understand why an interaction went well, or poorly. The Harvard class he developed for this was Social Relations 120, "Analysis of Interpersonal Behavior." Here was a chance to learn about "personality and interpersonal behavior, including your own, through firsthand experience in a laboratory setting."[33] The new book incorporated his behavior coding categories, albeit in revised form and with somewhat diminished importance, and an appendix even mentioned his old interaction recorder. Yet his "special room" had grown into a vast laboratory theater with a reception area, a group meeting room capable of accommodating a class of 25, and an observation area where just as many could watch behind a one-way mirror in tiered amphitheater seats. More than an introduction to group processes, his book was a how-to guide for creating your own SR 120.

Bales's rebooted science was as much a pedagogy for interpersonal life outside the classroom as it was for academic learning. For its salubrious effects on social cohesion, such a course might even be "introduced in the regular liberal arts curriculum." As his syllabus promised, and cautioned, "you should take the course only if you are prepared to participate and try to improve your understanding of yourself as an individual person."[34] In place of the steely, distanced, top-down technocratic posture of value-neutral postwar small-group scientism, Bales now extended a direct hand. He provided a therapeutically framed bottom-up cure for social relations in which group members would be both observers and observed. With some expert guidance, group members could analyze and fix themselves.[35] In this, Bales came to resemble the hopeful Lewinians whose laboratories for interpersonal democracy had harnessed the force of small-group science to make humans catalysts for social change. Indeed, the Lewinian T-groups, buoyed by popular "human potential" theorists like Abraham Maslow, made therapy a technology for the nation.[36]

However, an altogether different small-group pedagogy and technology was beginning to take off in 1969, the "small group" of women's liberation—a false-friend if there ever was one. While drawing on a therapeutic sensibility, the group was not to be confused with "therapy," its early promoters insisted.[37] The feminist small group went by other names: "rap group," "cell group," and most indelibly, the "consciousness-raising" (CR) group. With no men present, women would be free to explore issues each week. ("Why did you marry the man you did? How do you feel men see you? How do you feel about housework? . . . What did you want to do in life?").[38] By sharing and probing feelings and personal experiences, members would learn about their collective condition and ready themselves for political action.

While ferreting out the indexical meaning of feelings, much as one might do in therapy, this anti-therapy therapy reversed the directionality of this indexicality. Feelings supplied insight into the political, pointing not inward toward endogenous mental states but outward toward patriarchal social relations. "Our politics begins with our feelings," O'Connor titled a 1970 essay she presented to *Redstockings West.* "Our first task is to develop our capacity to be aware of our feelings and to pinpoint the events or interactions to which they are valid responses."[39] When one follows the indexical route from feelings to sources, these sources are not individual pathologies like "masochism, self-hate, or inferiority" but rather "a response to some behavior that was in fact designed to humiliate, hurt and oppress us."

CR groups were largely white and tended to draw women of class and educational privilege, which meant that the intense homosocial intimacy that CR members could experience was not simply an effect of intersubjective talk and discovery. Their sense of connection and shared plight was aided by real similarity—similarity based not on being members of a monolithic, universally oppressed class called "women" but on being a raced and classed subgroup whose commonalities were created in part by postwar suburbanization and redlining, which ensured that these women looked alike, and shared a lot, well before they set foot in each other's homes. CR groups could also shut their doors whenever they felt they got too big, which, in practice, could be used for gatekeeping.[40] Their contradictions and exclusions notwithstanding, by 1970 feminist small groups populated major cities across the United States and rapidly became the celebrated interaction technology of second-wave feminism, the "backbone," the "cornerstone," the "heart and soul" of the whole movement.[41]

CR's "origins" were discussed and disputed at the time it was popularized, and the practice itself was a moving target as CR underwent changes as it spread. It started in radical feminist circles, yet after 1970 liberal organizations like the National Organization for Women (NOW) started to use CR largely as a means of recruitment, and CR often started to look more like a "support group" or a "study group" for women, to the dismay of CR's early architects and promoters.[42] As Anne Enke stresses, given how decentered the women's movement was, CR was flexible and could be tailored for local contexts.[43]

But let us simply consider the early discourse of scale that accompanied its formation. As a discourse about scale, the "small" of the second-wave feminist small group was just as resonant as it had been for small-group science of the early '50s, if for very different reasons. At its most literal, small again meant size—reckoned quantitatively in terms of discrete, countable individuals. Bales put a rough number on his small groups, between two and twenty. CR groups, which met weekly not in labs but in members' homes, ranged from as few as five or six to as many as twelve or fifteen.[44] As a CR guide in *Ms.* magazine noted in 1972, "Larger groups make individual participation difficult." Or as Georg Simmel had put it in his reflections on the importance of numbers, "smaller groups have qualities, including types of interaction among their members, which inevitably disappear when the groups grow larger."[45]

For CR enthusiasts, small numbers mattered crucially. Small groups had affordances that made certain forms of participation possible. Groups were to consist exclusively of women and meet weekly in a group member's home. Focusing on a topic of concern to women, they would allow everyone to speak, to create a "safe" space for discussion, to speak in terms of one's personal experiences, and to listen and learn from each other.[46] As the small-group practice spread and evolved, its participation structure experienced ideological elaboration, regimentation, and contestation. Normatively, CR group institutionalization tried to make the practice ever more finely equalitarian. As an early essay noted, the small group form experimented with "internal democracy," which involved settling a topic of discussion in advance, ensuring that everyone got a chance to speak. "Some of the rules include no leadership, speak in circles, no one talks a second time until everyone has had her turn, no challenges of the veracity of members' statements, theoretical analysis of a topic only after all have spoken."[47] In some cases, speaking tokens were distributed, to be cashed in whenever one talked and counted at the end of the session to see who had talked more, and less. Just as one must speak from personal experience, one should only ask clarifying questions of others, thus never "challenging another woman's experience."[48] Great care was taken to ensure that each member respected a woman's autonomy and her inviolable personal experience, that each listened well and validated others.[49]

CR had crystallized as a method. Kathie Sarachild, who had chartered feminist CR in late 1968, had contempt for what she saw as such procedural fetishism. Plus, giving unconditional support to others was never the point, she wrote. The aim had been to learn from others empirically so that you could generalize and produce knowledge that would inform and incite political action. In fact, Sarachild's own small-group facilitation style reportedly could feel "confrontational," as "she did not hesitate to challenge . . . testimony." Her remarks hint at debates over what feminist small-group participation should look like, with some within the movement using the gender binary to distinguish "soft" from "hard" CR.[50]

The soft variety won out. Its variation in form and function notwithstanding, CR became a self-consciously feminized organizational form (even as men and others experimented with the genre). It was feminized not simply because of the "absolute dictum" that men be excluded[51] but especially due to the semiotic design of the ritual. The inclusiveness, the epistemic personalization, the attentiveness, and the validation of feelings—all amounted to a prefigurative politics. The practice forged an image of who women, writ large, wished to be. Indeed, some of the new social science research on sex differences in communication in the 1970s went on to suggest that the CR small group had incorporated communicative habits from women's interactional "culture," as if CR groups really did have something essential in common with feminized practices like coffee klatches.

As O'Connor had declared, "the political unit in which we can discover, share, and explore our feelings is the small group." At its most utopian, the CR small group became a feminist counter-institution—the mirror-image of all the competitive, hierarchical, androcentric organizations that demeaned, subordinated, and silenced women. Women would "develop a group process not predicated upon dominance and subordination."[52] As Pamela Allen's influential essay branded it, CR aspired to be a "free space": "the small group is especially suited to freeing women to affirm their own view of reality and to think independently of male-supremacist values."[53]

The smallness of the second-wave CR group was contested both within and outside the movement. Was a CR group itself truly a political unit? Could you build "mass" political action—as early small-group architects insisted— from a clutch of conversing humans? Even if hundreds or even thousands of such little groups existed here and there, how would they pool their efforts when they often opposed the very idea of stable hierarchical leadership?

What is more, some inside and outside the women's liberation movement complained that the topics women discussed in CR groups were too small in a different sense—in the sense of "personal" and "private." Could intimate talk about life in the home and bedroom help dismantle sexist institutions and structures? The liberal feminist flag bearer Betty Friedan derided small groups for their "navel-gazing."[54] If women were an exploited class, where was attention to the "system"—to macrostructures of exploitation, to capitalism? New Left Marxists wondered. "Other critics insist[ed] that CR is simply another therapy fad, something like group encounters and nude marathons."[55] Wasn't the small group merely a support group for individuals, akin to group therapy or just another iteration of politically disengaged "coffee klatches, hen parties, or bitch sessions"?[56]

It was in defense of the then embryonic feminist small group that Carol Hanisch penned her watershed 1968 essay bearing the title—and indelible slogan—"The Personal Is Political." Hers was a defense of the small group, which wasn't apolitical therapy, she countered, because the feminist small group didn't pathologize individuals for failing to adjust to the status quo. Sloganized, the alliterative poetics of "the personal is political" made this surprising equivalence into a speech act, a performative. And when applied to the small group, it baptized interaction as a technology for women's liberation.

As a precept, "the personal is political" was rich in meanings. It could mean that a woman's personal knowledge made her an expert in her own condition, even if this knowledge remained latent and had to be drawn out through discussion and probing. It often meant that the realm of personal life—sex, marriage—needed to be recognized as a site for male domination—and hence gender politics. Closely related to this reading was yet another inflection of the slogan. Here the scope of the "personal" came to include social interaction—how someone talks to you, touches you, treats you in daily encounters: the *interpersonal* is political, just as O'Connor and Henley had argued. In *Body Politics*, Henley rightly noted that knowledge of embodied communication added new depth to the feminist precept. By attending to the nonverbal you could appreciate "just how much of the seemingly personal is truly political."[57] For their part, women had learned to accede interactionally to male domination in daily life. A woman's "smile," for instance, was an embodied indexical convention that "indicates acquiescence of the victim to [their] own oppression," as Shulamith Firestone wrote in her 1970 radical feminist classic, *The Dialectic of Sex*. ("My 'dream' action for the women's liberation movement: a smile boycott, at which declaration all women would instantly abandon their 'pleasing' smiles, henceforth smiling only when something pleased *them*.")[58]

This interpersonal reading of the precept did not coalesce all at once for students of communication, however. While it was a reading nurtured by the radical feminist tendency to expect male supremacy in *all* domains of social life, and especially by the spread of CR groups with their heightened attention to small-group behavior, it became epistemologically rich and vivid and sharp only after feminist linguists and interaction researchers in the mid-to-late 1970s began to record, transcribe, and identify signs of male supremacy in language and discursive life.

In her introduction to Erving Goffman's 1976 photographic book, *Gender Advertisements*, Vivian Gornick recognized the parallel between the fine-grained microsociology of everyday life and the fine-grained feminist interrogation of everyday patriarchy.

> The contemporary feminist movement, with all its clamor about the meaning of the little details in daily life, has acted as a kind of electric prod to the thought of many social scientists, giving new impetus and direction to their work, the very substance of which is the observation of concrete detail in social life. Because of the feminists the most ordinary verbal exchange between men and women now reverberates with new meaning; the most simple gesture, familiar ritual, taken-for-granted form of address has become a source of new understanding with regard to relations between the sexes and the social forces at work behind those relations. Operating out of "a politics that originates with one's own hurt feelings," the feminists have made vivid what the social scientists have always known: It is in the details of daily exchange that the discrepancy between actual experience and apparent experience is to be found.[59]

About this convergence of feminism and communication science, Gornick credits the feminists for politicizing the interpersonal and making it possible to study power relations—patriarchal or otherwise—in something as seemingly small-scale as face-to-face interaction. As an ideological site of scrutiny, interaction owed much, she claimed, to the women's liberation movement. As a scaled object of knowledge, however, interaction was already small and had been for years. Feminist communication researchers like Henley had assumed, just as nearly everyone else did, that interaction was an intrinsically small-scale level of social reality that often required microscopic and frequently mediatic methods of recording and playback. Scholars like Henley elaborated on this scale in new ways, arguing for a communicative micropolitics that was both an object for empirical investigation and a site for activism.

9

Interruption—and Male Supremacy

The spread of feminist consciousness raising (CR) reveals how interaction became a scaled *site* for gender micropolitics in social movement activism before it became a scaled *object* of empirical knowledge in the sciences of language and communication. The questions that plagued CR—How exactly did it contribute to a politics elsewhere? To "mass" mobilization? To the elimination of institutional sexism?—questions that had to do with the contested scale of the interpersonal, vexed feminist communication scientists as well, as we shall see.

Consider *interruption*, a communicative behavior that began to attract feminist and later feminist social-scientific scrutiny. Cat calls and violent, misogynist slurs stood out as spectacular verbal manifestations of male dominance, but what about verbal practices that were insidious because they occurred more often and under the radar?

Interruption was of course already a canonical conversational offense. Some etiquette manuals considered it a symptom of the "conversational bore," who failed to take turns symmetrically, failed to listen and respect another's needs. Interruption here was not so much proscribed for polite society as left a prerogative of those of status. Interrupting down was fine, so long as you respected the inviolable turns of those equal and above your station. In *Body Politics* Henley had repeated this common sense but stressed the sociological asymmetries of interruption and its role in domination of all kinds: "Not saying 'sir,' interrupting, contradicting, and bullying are all privileges of the superior, not the subordinate. . . ." In an activist pamphlet titled "Facing the Man Down," Henley acidly enumerated twenty-five tips on how to confront men in power. "Never smile, never laugh, never hesitate," for "there are no jokes except against them." "When taking seats, infiltrate" by sitting among them. And point 18 read, "Don't let them interrupt you. Keep talking; you may lose, but at least they don't win." (Her epigraph dedicated this guide "to the Executive Committee of the Board of Directors of the American Psychological Association, without whose opposition it might never have been written.")[1]

Interruption could be a slippery charge, though, because of its wide range of application and because its meaning depended on context—not the least on who was doing it, when, and where. In the narrow verbal sense, interruption could seem deceptively straightforward. Wasn't interruption acoustically overlapping speech? Could you say that interruption occurred whenever, in a focused conversation, someone started talking while another was already talking—the implication being that this violated turn-taking etiquette and was evidence of disrespectful, uncooperative, even hostile intent? Yet the term "interruption" was awfully expansive. As a pragmatic category it was never limited to speech. Speech interruptions could sometimes be likened to nonverbal "interruptions," and both could be understood to violate a person's autonomy. "Mother's time, like mother's space, can always be interrupted," Henley had written. "She is less likely to have a time to call her own within the family (or a 'night out') than is father."[2]

Interruption, in all its resonant polysemy, became an important pragmatic category. Second-wave feminists seized upon verbal interruption as a gendered offense—a tactic used by men to curtail women's right to speak and keep them down. While not a common topic of discussion in feminist alternative media like newsletters, the moralization and politicization of interruption was on full display in CR groups—especially the so-called softer varieties—which usually saw interruption as a problem to manage.

Interruption as Sexism

In the early '70s, interruption also became an empirical problem. Was it true that men interrupted women in conversation and that this was an exercise of patriarchy? Were all speech overlaps "interruption," and, if not, how can we distinguish the two? And how does interruption operate alongside other gendered conversational behaviors, such as the signals we emit when we listen (*mm*, or head nods to show we're involved) or how we respond to stances expressed by another, or how we handle the flow of topics—all of which are taken to constitute a self-discipline of "listening" well—a term that never meant only aural receptivity?

A handful of feminist communication scientists beginning in the '70s began to resolve interruption into a series of empirical questions, and they did so through mediatic microscopy: they turned to recording technologies and fine-grained transcripts of talk.

In *Body Politics*, Henley had complained that interruption was understudied. She wondered aloud whether "a hierarchy of power in a group could be plotted by ordering people according to the number of successful interruptions they achieve. . . ."[3] A promising recent study that Henley did mention in *Body Politics* was the empirical work of two ethnomethodologically oriented sociologists from the University of California at Santa Cruz, Don H. Zimmerman and his then graduate student Candace West.[4]

During a seminar with Zimmerman in 1971, West audio recorded casual conversations in public settings and found that men overwhelmingly interrupted women more. This discovery matured into a master's thesis, "Sexism and Conversation," and into articles that she coauthored with Zimmerman and that culminated with her 1978 dissertation. Her first article with Zimmerman appeared in 1975 in a volume Henley helped edit. There she came armed with transcripts of those audio-recorded campus conversations—everyday "chit chat"—among same-sex and mixed-sex dyads in "coffee shops, drug stores, and other public places in a university community."[5]

Not all simultaneous speech was interruptive—in its disruptive sense—so how could you distinguish true interruptions from mere overlapping speech? Their answer evolved over time, but Zimmerman and West drew heavily on an understanding of turn taking drawn from the then new area of sociology that came to be called conversation analysis, or CA for short. Inspired by the ethnomethodology of Harold Garfinkel (with whom Zimmerman had studied at UCLA), its principal architects were Harvey Sacks and Emanuel Schegloff—also based in Southern California—and Gail Jefferson, who started as Sacks's secretary but quickly became a co-originator of CA (even if it took years before she was recognized for this).[6] Turn taking in conversation was usually locally managed, CA emphasized. No third-party referee decides who gets to speak and for how long, and conversationalists do not have at their disposal unambiguous turn-completion signals to tell others when they're done or when they want a chance to talk.

So how do people accomplish fast and fluid and often seamless turn changes? In large part because interlocutors follow tacit turn-taking rules, which CA tried to draw out. Turn taking ran so smoothly not only because of hidden rules but because of the way interlocutors monitored each other and made inferences about the beginnings and ends of turns. In the absence of dedicated turn signals, interlocutors—speakers and hearers—had to actively *anticipate* when a turn might be plausibly over. Speakers had to orient toward upcoming points of possible turn completion and adjust their behavior accordingly. They might speed up their speech, for instance, or utter a long filled pause (*uhh*) to hold onto their turn. To time their own bid to speak, hearers, for their part, anticipate points of possible completion as speech unfolds.[7]

Zimmerman and West proposed a simple way to know an interruption when you hear it. If person B overlaps with speaker A *before* A has reached a transition place, it's an interruption; it's a "violation" of the rules "which provide that the proper place for transition between speakers is at the terminal boundary" of what in later CA would be called a turn constructional unit. If B overlaps A *at* a possible turn boundary (what later CA would call a transition-relevance place), then B's behavior was an innocent, unintentional "overlap"—an error of timing—and not a violation of the one-at-a-time turn-taking rule of conversation. For example: "I know what 'cha mean . . . we went camping in Mojave last—" The first speaker clearly isn't done, and so when the other speaker overlaps with "[Oh] didja go with Mark in August?", that counts as an interruption.[8]

Operationalized neatly in this way, you could pinpoint interruption in a transcript. You could count up instances as discrete acts—which the authors did, revealing a stark gender asymmetry in terms of who interrupted whom. In effect they confirmed what feminists knew well. Men interrupted women, a *lot*. In same-sex conversations, men and women interrupted each other roughly equally, while in mixed-sex groups, men initiated interruptions of women 96 percent of the time—an indicting statistic that found its way into a short *Time Magazine* column in 1978. What is more, they noted how interruptions seemed to work in concert with other gendered behaviors, notably minimal responses and topic shifts. "Minimal responses" (sometimes also called "backchannels") are conversational vocalizations like *mm* produced by hearers to show their continuing involvement in a conversation as it progresses. Men offered fewer minimal responses while listening; in mixed-sex conversations this slowness to convey active listenership can be seen as slowness to encourage or "support" women to keep talking. And as for topic shifts, they noted that in cases where a male interlocutor repeatedly interrupted a woman, he also usually went on to change the topic to something he wanted to talk about.

Taken together, transcripts revealed evidence of sex-based domination that looked homologous to other domains. "We view the production of both retarded minimal responses and interruptions by male speakers interacting with females as an assertion of the right to control the topic of conversation reminiscent of adult-child conversations where in most instances the child has restricted rights to speak and to be listened to." Interactionally, men treated women like children—a homology whose significance had been stressed and probed elsewhere, as in Firestone's *The Dialectic of Sex*.[9] Indeed, in a follow-up essay from 1977, "women's place in everyday talk," Zimmerman and West expanded on the similarity between the way men interrupt women and parents interrupt children.[10]

In their initial work, Zimmerman and West imagined the scale of interruption in a particular way. They characterized their findings as evidence of a superordinate ideological formation, sexism. Unlike Henley's micropolitical argument, where interruption was seen as part of daily sexist praxis that girds oppression constantly and quietly from below, the authors here stressed a different and basic point: that sexism exists in conversation and manifests itself—just as certain feminists had alleged—in everyday behavior. They pointed to a phenomenon and supplied evidence, yet without any rousing call to reform or for the counter pragmatics of interrupting back.

Interruption as Rape

A very different stance on interruption appeared a few years later, notably in a 1979 essay solo-authored by West that drew on her dissertation and was provocatively titled, "Against Our Will: Male Interruptions of Females in Cross-Sex Conversation." Back in 1975 Zimmerman and West noted in passing that interruption involved *penetration*—"penetrating the boundaries" of someone's speaking turn. While they left no hints to suggest that this was meant to invite a parallel with sexual violence, her dissertation, and especially her 1979 essay which drew on that research, made this parallel. She analogized sexual violence and verbal violence, suggesting that "male intrusions into [women's] turns" were . . . like rape. "Male dominance in conversation might be likened to our cultural (and sometimes legal) conceptions of rape."[11]

In the summer of 1977, West had driven cross-country to Tallahassee to take a position at Florida State University for what would be two eventful years that intensified her feminist activism. One afternoon, after stepping out from the building in which she had been teaching, she heard the roar of helicopters overhead from which rained pink anti–Equal Rights Amendment (ERA) leaflets bearing the image of the big bad wolf and listing all the unsavory groups that supported the ERA—from the Black Panthers to the Young Communist League. In a visit to shore up support for the ERA, Bella Abzug visited Tallahassee. In the wake of her visit, a "take back the night" march was organized, during which two women were dragged off and raped. West's choice of title, "Against Our Will" recalled Susan Brownmiller's 1975 bestseller about rape that bore the same main title.

Justifications for rape and interruption sounded similar. West reported in her essay "Against Our Will" that in response to her earlier studies showing that men interrupted women more, some (she didn't reveal who, but these were real people) wondered whether women played a role in "creating, sustaining or inviting men's interruptions of their utterances"; to West, this sounded very much like the way women get blamed for inviting assault by virtue of what they wear, how they comport themselves, and, most notoriously, by not resisting. "I have observed females falling silent for longer and longer durations after repeated interruptions by males," so was this "dropping out . . . tantamount to 'not putting up a fight' "?[12]

West had tested this in her dissertation. Her first study in 1971 had recorded conversations surreptitiously in public—conversations among people who already knew each other. And that posed a problem, she came to realize. Since the interactants knew each other—in some cases romantically—and as the setting was "casual," some might argue that the interruptions flowed more freely, that the usual norms limiting simultaneous speech had been suspended. In her dissertation West recalled "the traditional view of interruption," which "suggests that it is largely a function of intimacy and the relaxation of usual rule for conduct." Or as Goffman wrote, and here she quoted him: "When a set of persons are on familiar terms and feel that they need not stand on ceremony with one another, then inattentiveness and interruptions are likely to become rife, and talk may degenerate into a happy babble of disorganized sound."[13]

To control for this, her dissertation research focused on strangers getting to know each other. Her strangers were recruited from a pool of sociology students, and as a distractor she screened them with a questionnaire that hinted that her study was about bicycle ownership and policy. Two at a time, the student subjects were led into a waiting room, where they were separated to discourage premature interaction. Then, wired with lavalier microphones, the dyads—some same sex, some mixed sex—were brought to a room outfitted with two large one-way mirrors whose presence was minimized with curtains. Through an intercom and bell West gave start and stop cues and instructions. She audio-recorded a collection of 12-minute-long conversations, and then transcribed them using the transcription conventions developed by conversation analyst Gail Jefferson. This gave West 1,119 instances of simultaneous speech.

In her new laboratory-based study of interruption, West became more granular and more processual than in her first study. Rather than only count up who interrupted more and less, she inspected how men and women *reacted* to simultaneous speech, in same-sex and in mixed-sex groups. She also added nuance when it came to identifying interruptions. At first she and Zimmerman had defined interruptions by focusing on whether simultaneous speech occurred at a terminal boundary. She now conceded that some overlaps that occurred well before this boundary may be supportive and affiliative—and hence not interruptive at all. (For example, "saying the same thing at the same time" may serve to ratify—rather than disorganize—the utterance being produced by a current speaker.") West focused on what she dubbed "deep interruptions," which had two criteria: (1) deep interruptions were "more than two syllables away from the terminal boundaries of a possibly complete utterance (a word, phrase, clause, or sentence depending on its context)"; (2) there was evidence in the transcript that this interruption disrupted the speaker. These, in effect, were true interruptions.[14]

Her findings confirmed, though somewhat less dramatically than before, that men committed deep interruptions a lot more frequently than women, yet in her dissertation and "Against Our Will" essay especially, the question was: How did women react? When West looked at what women did next, in the face of simultaneous speech, she found signs of struggle, not passivity. True, only rarely did women explicitly complain *about* interruption, yet they reacted tacitly in ways that were just as telling. In general, speakers can do various things when interrupted rather than just "drop out" when the violation occurs. A speaker might restart, repeating what she was trying to say, only louder than before. Or she might persist and continue speaking, as if the intrusion hadn't occurred. Or she might focus on the other person and "retrieve" portions of her interlocutor's overlapping talk or try to repair the interruptive moment with a question about what the interruptive person was trying to say. Women *did* respond actively to interruptions and often put up a struggle, which confirmed that they experienced interruption as a violation. Interruption was, indeed, against their will.

Interscalar Stances on Interpersonal Life

Let us sharpen the contrast between these two stances on interruption. West's dissertation featured an intensified processualism and granularity along with higher political stakes. Indeed, an activist sensibility was on full display in the title of her 1979 essay as she placed herself within the "our" of "against our will." In her first article with Zimmerman, she had only adduced interruption as evidence of sexism. Cooler and legalistic in tone, the coauthors had oriented toward their epistemic object through a kind of *evidentiary* type-tokenism: they showed that interruption counted as—served as a token of—evidence of the "larger issue of sexism in American society," and, in so doing, they demonstrated the reciprocal creep of sexism into everyday life. Sexism could manifest itself in the form of interruption, but interruptions were not said to constitute or reproduce this ideological formation in any strong sense.[15]

Not so in West's dissertation and in the "Against Our Will" essay that arose from it, which resembled O'Connor's stance and Henley's in *Body Politics*. West now adopted a *pragmatic* rather than an evidentiary type-tokenism. Interruption was not some exhibit held up in the court of scholarly or public opinion but was *itself* framed as a problem. Especially in "Against Our Will," interruption by men was meant to stoke outrage in readers. In exposing interpersonal violence, it obliged you to take a stance, lest you remain complicit. Here was the white-hot immediacy and urgency of a pervasive, continuous sexism, where women faced verbal violence constantly in conversation, much as Henley suggested when she spoke of social interaction as a battlefield.

And West had more to say about gender politics in this interpersonal microworld. She had disabused her readers of the view that women invited interruptive violations by virtue of "submissive" behavior. She pushed back not only against rape discourses that blamed victims but against those scholars of language and gender who reified gender differences with the construct of "women's language"—a construct that implied that there was something distinctive and contrastive about women as a category that could help explain their plight. "Females in cross-sex conversations are no more likely to do bootlicking than are males when deeply interrupted." As she noted in her dissertation, this made calls for "assertiveness" training for women misguided. Women weren't interpersonally submissive in the first place. Assertiveness training was misguided for a second reason, because as her findings also showed, men never seem bothered when women did deep interruptions of them; interruptions felt threatening only when they came from other *men*, and this, West speculated, was likely due to the fact that men did not see women as equals. Men tolerate interruptions by women much as parents tolerate interruptions by their unsocialized children who do not share the same liberal-discursive rights and responsibilities. It wasn't difference that explained what men did. It was domination.[16]

West's pragmatic stance on interruption also made a stronger argument about why the interpersonal mattered in the first place. Whereas the evidentiary stance asked only that you recognize a truth, the pragmatic stance had the potential to make interruption actionable and to make *you* accountable for your response. These stances configured micropolitics very differently. They offered competing visions of and for interpersonal gender politics.

The evidentiary stance interscaled interaction as if the face-to-face world sat comfortably within a vast encompassing macrosocial world of institutionalized

sexism. It contained interaction as a microcosm, in which you could see recapitulated in miniature the familiar shapes of patriarchy. Causally, interruption
indexed—presupposed—this larger world of oppression but was not *itself* a
cause of that world, except in the way a noxious symptom can erupt on the
body's surface. Interruption reflected trouble *elsewhere*.

The pragmatic stance inverted this. It grew this little world of interaction
till it rivaled this larger world in extent—and importance. "I contend that
these patterns [of interruption] cannot be explained by simple reference to
'the sexist nature of our language'; nor can they be reduced to mere *reflections
of* the social hierarchy," she stressed. For conversationalists, these patterns of
male dominance "considerably constitute the hierarchy; they are the shadow
and the substance," again quoting Goffman.[17] Interpersonal life *continually* reproduced oppression, and did so *proximally*, right where you stood. Interaction perpetuated oppression in daily life. Foregrounded so, interpersonal life
could even seem to encompass the patriarchal order, even though this order
was still said to be the root cause and remained the target for eradication in
the longue durée. But what mattered day to day, hour to hour, interaction to
interaction, was the interpersonal–political—not as symbol or symptom of
oppression elsewhere but as a struggle in its own right. Indeed, because interaction occurred everywhere and often, encountering other people required
immediate attention and constant vigilance. Talking about a problem "from
afar" versus confronting it "up close"; patient, critical reflection on oppression
versus urgent, impassioned activism; the scholarly field, the battlefield: Here,
in short, were two very different interscalar stances on the same conversational violation, interruption.

I spotlight this sharp difference in interscalar stance on interruption, in
part, as a reminder that there was no singular feminist "micropolitics" of the
interpersonal, that different arguments could be made about the small, sometimes by the same author. These stances framed and enacted the *micro* of interaction very differently. But more important than the mere fact of variation
is the contestation that especially haunted the activist scalar stance implied
by West and advocated explicitly by Henley, for by making the interpersonal
so big and important, it raised the question of *where* power was to be found.

Power and the Paracosm

In the 1970s, power—its forms, how to "locate" it, and the capacity of individuals to resist it—became familiar concerns. Should power still be conceived mechanistically, for instance, a "discrete quantum of energy" exercised
by some over others who resisted it?[18] Was power diffuse, making its full reach

and effects difficult to see? Did power operate on subjects through an array of subtle, unremarkable practices (what Foucault famously referred to as the "microphysics of power," or what, in a different vein, Bourdieu called habitus: embodied habits—how to walk, talk, hold your body—that served as moves in an agonistic contest over forms of capital)? And what degrees of freedom, critical distance, and resistance were possible for human agents?

Feminist interactionists claimed to be able to put their finger on power. A close look at the fleeting, subtle, elusive signs of interaction would allow you to see power in action and do something about it. This shared much in spirit with what would coalesce later as "practice," "praxis," and "performance" in social theory. For feminist interactionists such interest was fueled by an activist sensibility. About social theory, Sherry Ortner wrote in the '80s, this new "practice theory" "express[ed] . . . an urgent need to understand where 'the system' comes from—how it is produced and reproduced, and how it may have changed in the past or be changed in the future."[19] Henley could hold men accountable and teach them how to behave, just as she could train women to recognize, disrupt, and reform social life from below. Here was a semiotic practice theory *ante litteram* compatible with feminist social transformation and pedagogy.

Just as rituals can condense and materialize the cosmological in the electric here and now of ritual performance, allowing participants to see, touch, hear, and, crucially, operate on otherwise intangible things, so the diffuse and abstract formations of "sexism," "androcentrism," and "male supremacy" could be concretized, concentrated, and localized, so that you could take political action. West's blend of empiricism and activism in works like "Against Our Will" did two seemingly incompatible things at once: it shrank interruption into something "small"—making it epistemologically knowable as well as pragmatically manipulable—while inflating its synecdochical enormity as a sexist act, not unlike a good laboratory experiment or, perhaps better, the targeting of cells to kill off something from below. Because social interaction was everywhere and always, she arguably inverted the interscalar universe such that it was interaction that demanded attention.

The emphasis on the sheer pervasiveness of gender violence can be experienced as a rousing call to action. The everydayness can spur you to be vigilant in places where you might not expect it. Yet this pedagogy, which suggested that you could become an activist in daily conversation, also invited questions.

Consider how "Against Our Will" elevated the seemingly "minor" speech offense of interruption, placing it, improbably, toward the top of the list of sexist offenses. Didn't this alleged similarity between interruption and rape minimize the gravity of the latter and fail to distinguish degrees and kinds of gender violence? We may recall Gal and Irvine's discussions of *rhematization*, which involves semiotic and ideological processes that stipulate a *likeness* between objects in a way that can alter what they mean. If interruption violated the boundaries of a woman's speaking turn *just like* rape violated the boundaries of a woman's body, this invited you to rethink what interruption meant and did. West did not spell out what exactly this analogy entailed, but by analogizing interruption and rape, she *anchored* the former in the latter.[20] That is, she explained the relatively unfamiliar gender violence of interruption in terms of a paradigmatic violation of women's bodies. For some audiences, no doubt, this stipulated likeness did more than ground something unfamiliar in terms of the familiar. It made interaction matter, as if to place it on a continuum of violence that led all the way up to rape. Moreover, the imputed likeness also mobilized you to *act* by raising the stakes of interruption—albeit at the cost, critics might aver—of failing to distinguish *among* tokens of gender violence as more serious and less serious, more and less consequential.

Indeed, neither of these interscalar stances on the "small" of interaction, the evidentiary or the pragmatic, that of the feminist empiricist or that of the activist, seemed very worried about the *different* contexts of interaction. West's concern, and Henley's, was rather with undifferentiated "everyday" interaction, which was everywhere and nowhere. (This was no surprise in the case of West, as the tradition of CA she and Zimmerman followed had committed itself uncritically to the study of everydayness, just as ethnomethodology did, as we will later see.) And while West would later turn to studying institutional interactions, notably doctor–patient interactions, in her laboratory-based studies of interruption she did not dispense guidance on how to assess how one communicative action, event, or encounter might matter more than another. Not surprisingly for a laboratory study, no distinctions were made in terms of when, where, how, or with whom interruption might *differentially* matter in terms of pragmatic, personal, or, indeed, political effects. This could be taken to suggest that these were all the same. If taken to an extreme, this would result in a categorical exercise in tokenism: for the evidentiary stance, something was an instance of sexism, or it wasn't; for the pragmatic stance, something counted as a sexist act, or it didn't. And, from the pragmatic and activist point of view, if everything was equally consequential in terms of reproducing male supremacy in society, then what difference, if any, did "context" make? We will see next that other scholars at the time studying racism in schools were more concerned with the when and where of power and domination in large part because they worked in, and with, institutions, and they felt pressed to identify what to fix.

As a feminist activist and scholar, Henley knew the interscalarity of her object was contested. This is evident in how careful she was in justifying her focus and qualifying its relation to a politics elsewhere. In the '70s and '80s, scalar tropes surfaced repeatedly in debates over what posture feminist social critics should adopt. In the 1980s, for instance, Nancy Fraser and Linda Nicholson wrestled with scale as they charted a postmodern feminist social criticism. While sympathetic with postmodernism, they challenged its "suspicion of the large." With Lyotard as their representative, they underscored how, for him, Marxism's "story is too big, since it spans virtually the whole of human history." In place of metanarratives and grand theory, Lyotard seemed to promote a social criticism that is "smallish, localized narrative," which risked "cast[ing] critique as strictly local, ad hoc, and ameliorative, thus supposing a political diagnosis according to which there are no large-scale, systemic problems which resist local, ad hoc, ameliorative initiatives." A postmodern feminism, the authors countered, "need not abandon the large theoretical tools needed to address large political problems."[21]

Scalar ideas and tropes manifested themselves variously in the social criticism of the late '60s, '70s, and '80s, but the point here is simply that feminist communication scholars knew they couldn't take the idea of power in interaction for granted—not even within their own fields. Indeed, the male-dominated fields of these authors had tended to sever the objects "conversation" and "interaction" from the messy world of the political, purifying them in a bid to study them scientifically. Some came to charge that this purification *depoliticized* interaction, which made interaction science incompatible with social movement activism. Of course, it had been possible to be intensely "political" *while* autonomizing an object of knowledge. That had been plain from Chomsky, whose anti-capitalist and anti-fascist activism coincided with his construction of language as a rule-governed system unto itself, shorn cleanly from "context."[22] Yet for critics autonomy was now a damning trope, as if walling off the thing you want to know—treating it as free of the contingencies of history and society—was proof that you had cocooned yourself from the truth of pervasive injustice, that you had retreated into a distanced, reactionary science that refused to get involved.

As for seeming to keep politics out of it, Harvey Sacks, after all, had spent a lot of time thinking about interruption, yet only in terms of what interruption revealed about the underlying dynamics of turn taking and about what airing a complaint about being "interrupted" does as an action in its own right. His reflections on interruption were not rousing calls to study "micropolitics." Schegloff was infamous for chafing at those who read too much context into interaction and failed to anchor claims in observables. Where

was gender, really, "in" the transcript? You had to *show* that gender was relevant for the people themselves rather than presume that demographic facts
about participants always mattered to *them*. You couldn't just look at whether
"men" and "women" interacted differently. In print, Schegloff's skeptical reception of Zimmerman and West is evident indirectly, in the way that these
authors, while basing themselves in CA, did not feel entitled to claim that
they were doing basic science. Theirs was an *applied* CA, not pure: "We wish
to make it clear that we do not view our efforts as a contribution to CA per
se but rather as an attempt to apply it to a particular problem."[23] CA's stance
on conversational interaction had been to treat it as an autonomous object
that could be studied apart from "context." West quietly challenged this in her
dissertation. Conversation analysts had argued that the "turn-taking model
operates independently of the identities of any particular conversationalists,"
yet she showed "that one particular type of simultaneous speech is related to
particular identities of speakers and conversational occasions." As Marjorie
Goodwin would later term it, this was the making of a "feminist conversation
analysis."[24]

To some scholars of language and communication, it was not at all clear
whether fields like CA were compatible with social justice movements. At one
workshop, a young female linguistic anthropologist pressed Schegloff on the
way he methodologically bracketed context so austerely in the name of rigor
and basic science that, in effect, he shut down applied inquiries into problems
of social inequality. In frustration, she told him, "We can't wait." At the end of
a two-day workshop on film and communication at the American Anthropological Association in 1970, after Ray Birdwhistell gave the closing remarks, a
woman in the audience raised the issue of gender. Birdwhistell laughed and
quipped, "this is the first time in my life I've ever been accused of leaving
women out of my life."[25] Whatever tensions existed across generational and
gender lines, they did not erupt in print. Henley cited and paid deference to
elders like Ray Birdwhistell and especially to Erving Goffman, and she even
found a way to build on the work of researchers like Robert Bales—much as
West did.[26] Yet among those who studied communication in interaction, there
was no longer an easy consensus about what kind of object—autonomous or
contextually entangled—interaction was, nor on what kind of science—basic
or applied, empiricist or activist—interaction science could or should be.

Tempest in the Transcript

In "Interactional Shitwork," a potent case study that fused interaction scholarship and feminist activism, Pam Fishman argued that it was women who did the brunt of conversational labor, and got little recognition for it. She had set up her portable UHER 4000 sound recorder in the apartments of three male–female couples, which were tiny enough to pick up conversations from everywhere—even from the bathroom. Fishman studied and transcribed their talk and found that women worked to "fill silences and keep conversations moving." They sustained conversation with buoyant signals of listener involvement—minimal responses like *yeah, umm, huh*. They elicited talk from men and evaluated them encouragingly (e.g., "that's really interesting"). They used *y'-know* tag questions and sentence-final rising pitch on statements, which made them sound like questions, to keep men engaged. While men controlled the conversation, by deciding and steering topic flow, women did the "support work": a sexual division of conversational labor akin to women's unpaid—and devalued—domestic labor that reflected, and reproduced, their position of powerlessness.[1]

Fishman, who started in the same sociology cohort as West at Santa Barbara, drew broader conclusions about interaction that resonated with other dissident interactionists from the Southern California scene. "Power is usually analyzed macrosociologically," she reflected, yet it was no "abstract force operating on people." "Power must be a human accomplishment, situated in everyday interaction." Hugh (Bud) Mehan, another student of ethnomethodology from the area who, like Fishman and West, drew from the breakaway field that would soon become conversation analysis (CA), had activist commitments of a different kind, yet he sounded remarkably similar. "Politics are always the politics of everyday life," he declared. "Where else could

In my opinion, to dismiss efforts at radically modifying everyday interactions at the microscopic level is not only inaccurate but ultimately self-defeating. For it is to misread the way students and teachers, men and women, whites and blacks interact if one reads it merely as a *symptom* of a politics whose real locus is exclusively on a scale that plumbs the depths of history and spans the breadth of the western world. Everyday interactions are a cause as well as a symptom, and a logical place for struggle . . . and a struggle it is.

JEFFREY KITTAY,
"Reader's Forum: Body Politics and the Body Politic: An Afterword," *Kinesis Report* 3, no. 1 (1980): 14

political forces be found?" "Abstract categories like 'alienation,' 'capitalism,' etc. must be tied to everyday events." Mehan had returned from Vietnam an ardent anti-war activist and came to train his mediatic science of interaction not on sexism but classism and racism in schools.[2]

These pronouncements about power drew on distinct if entangled social movements, yet they articulated a similar sentiment about scale and interaction: that interaction is a site for micropolitics, that looking closely at interaction offered a way to concretize, pinpoint, and *act on* forces that otherwise seemed intangible and intractable. In fact, if you ignored interaction, if all you did was point outward at institutions and systems and forces beyond your control, you were guilty of a kind of complacency about which O'Connor had complained when she indicted leftist men for railing against the System while overlooking the interpersonal, namely, how they treated women hour to hour, day to day, interaction to interaction. In this critical science of conversation, Fishman and Mehan, like West, had no doubt that they could exploit mechanical recording, playback, transcription, and fine-grained analysis. Their mediatic science would muster the epistemological rigor that microscopy implied in order to contribute to social justice activism.

Indeed, just as feminist communication scientists envisioned an urgent, interactional micropolitics, so, too, did scholars like Mehan, who belonged to a small but growing band of education researchers that studied the micropolitics of schools. As sites, schools were notorious. For their racist segregation and gross inequities in resources, schools had been in the crosshairs of civil rights activists for years. The 1966 Coleman report suggested inter alia that parents' education was correlated with school success, a finding that some sociologists took to mean that schools were complicit in class stratification. Schools weren't the great meritocratic leveler that ignored what you looked like and where you came from and rewarded only individual talent and performance; in effect, they maintained the status quo, though exactly how remained unclear. This became a kernel argument in an emerging critical sociology of education that in the early 1970s, inflected especially by the rediscovery of Marx, charged that schools "reproduced" divisions in society, principally those of class.[3]

Interactionists like Mehan shared this critical, revisionist stance on schools, but unlike their sociology colleagues, they wanted to see more "closely" within school walls. In terms of observational scale, this meant looking at interaction with the aid of recording technologies and fine-grained analysis. Mehan showed, for instance, that when kids took intelligence tests they were attuned to and subtly cued by the test givers in ways that affected their performance. He went on to interrogate how schools perpetuated social stratification in all the ways they sorted kids by ability, classifying some as "learning disabled," for instance, shuttling some into "special education"—all with the help of purportedly objective diagnostics and assessment.[4]

This chapter begins by spotlighting a couple of these new interactionists of education who trained their mediatic microscopic on interpersonal behavior in schools and did so believing in the transformative potential of their science for liberal institutional reform. Theirs was a science that they felt was compatible with social movement activism. These parallel streams of research on the face-to-face—interactionists working in schools, feminist researchers on everyday talk—anticipated concerns with power, domination, and conflict that came to assume great importance for social science scholars of language and communication in the decades to come.

As this chapter unfolds, we will fan outwards from education to reconsider the movement called ethnomethodology, which was never quite comfortable with "micro" as a label but whose practitioners often opposed mainstream sociology in scalar terms and came to be seen as "microsociology." We will remember how a range of sciences in the '70s started getting corralled as micro as part of the rapidly intensifying scholarly debates about scale, including about the scale of interaction. These new politicized iterations of the microscopic and the small became fraught not long after they came about, and became so even by critics who shared the same political commitments but didn't believe the best way to transform the world was by scrutinizing how humans interacted.

By the chapter's end, I bring us in effect to the cusp of the notorious scale wars that roiled many fields in the 1980s and that affected scholarly life long after the rancor died down. By revisiting moments from the 1970s, moments of experimentation, ferment, and contestation over interaction's scale, we can sense similarities with debates that animate scholarship today, as many now ponder the importance of the interpersonal as a political site. We can recognize how recent debates over issues of harmful speech, microaggressions, and the like, frequently turn on questions of scale, especially questions about interscalar kinship and the problem of the paracosm, not unlike the way they did more than a half century ago. All these debates, then and now, creative and thoughtful as they have been, presume that there is something basically, ontologically small about this object and proceed to "solve" the problem by spelling out how interaction relates to a wider world.

Frederick Erickson's Microethnography

At first these activist communication scholars of the small, at least in education studies, did not worry much about being labeled micro, either in how finely they observed or in how little they examined. A few even proudly displayed the prefix.

Take "microethnography," which was the coinage of Frederick Erickson, a young urban ethnographer of education based in Chicago. He proposed the term in 1971, in a conference in Detroit.[5] Observationally, *micro* in microethnography meant the usual inverse correlation of grain and extent: "the detailed description and interpretation of a small sample of behavior." To get this granular you needed technological prosthesis—a mediatic microscope akin to those created by other fine-grained analysts of interaction who belonged to the Natural History of an Interview (NHI) network and with whom Erickson had some contact at Northwestern when he began graduate studies in 1966. Microethnographic samples were "audiovisual behavioral records," which could be videocassettes, Erickson noted, whose recording and playback technology had just surfaced in the consumer market; or they could be the familiar—if expensive, laborious, and fussy—film recording and playback technologies like those the NHI network had used.[6]

Yet there was a difference from NHI. In terms of collection, Erickson's microethnography sought "audiovisual records of behavior *at critical points along the cycle of situational frames*" (emphasis mine). This long locative phrase was important. Unlike the unstructured way NHI had gotten its data, Erickson wanted to find interactions that affected the biographies of people, and not just any people but minoritized people—principally, poor Black urban youth.

Erickson borrowed "situational frames" from his teacher E. T. Hall, for whom it meant "the smallest viable unit of a culture that can be analyzed." Situational frames "numbered into the hundreds if not thousands" and included "greeting, working, eating, bargaining. fighting, governing, making love, going to school, cooking and serving meals, hanging out, and the like." Each had its norms—including norms of communication—which meant that the enculturated had competency in many "situational dialects."[7] In this cosmopolitan anti-essentialism, humans seemed ever adaptable—as the Boasians had insisted—ever capable of learning the codes of comportment that governed each little clime of the social world. But by speaking of a *cycle* of such frames, Erickson processualized Hall, in a way. Hall, like sociolinguist John Gumperz and others like him, had marveled at the mercurial shifts that people performed as they moved across settings, whereas Erickson was after their sinuous movement as a whole, as one big processual unit. That is, rather than merely pluralize situational frames, Erickson wanted to trace an individual's "daily round," their circuit of *repeated* movements across a subset of situations. (A rather literal inspiration for this method was *One Boy's Life: A Specimen Record of Behavior* [1951]). Pedagogically, Erickson would teach this to students by adapting an exercise he learned from Hall. Armed with 50 to 60 3″ × 5″ index cards, students would spend a half day stopping "each time you sense yourself intuitively to be in a different social situation," and noting "the time, location, participants, and activity in that situation. . . ."[8] The daily round had practical urgency for the urban ethnographer. Cities had density and sprawl, which made them impossible to encompass synoptically. You had to thread your way through, and the routes taken should not be yours but those of the people you want to know.[9]

To be sure, as the anthropologists had stressed, people came from different cultures and subcultures that inflected how they talked—and even how they managed their bodies, as Hall and Birdwhistell had detailed. But during the hopscotch of a day, as humans skipped from scene to scene, they adjusted how they communicated along the way. Among other things, microethnography could show you this adjustment.

A couple weeks before his Detroit talk, in a conference presentation titled "The Chicano in a Black Mask: A Microethnography of Communication Behavior," Erickson shared slow-motion films of pairs of undergraduates from Chicago who differed ethnically and racially and were getting to know each other for the first time. He noted how "the Mexican American students accommodated to the ethnic others kinesically, in the ways they held their upper bodies, and with gaze, and when talking with Black students the Mexican American students style switched in the direction of Black English." They adjusted not only to the situation but also to the perceived identities of their interlocutors. They could do this, Erickson added, because Mexican American students "had more everyday experience with Black students—in high school and living in neighborhoods that adjoined Black neighborhoods."[10] Not only did Erickson's microethnography depart from NHI in its quest to find "critical points" but also in its wish to retain conventional ethnography, to incorporate "information about individuals, neighborhoods, and daily rounds in Chicago." His tropic microscopy got its social relevance by being yoked to urban ethnography.

Finding critical points had everything to do with Erickson's political commitments. While an undergraduate music student at Northwestern in the early 1960s, where he double majored in music history and composition, Erickson was stirred by the civil rights movement. He organized fellow music students to offer free music lessons at a YMCA on weekends in a Black inner-city neighborhood in Chicago, and after matriculating, he created an after-school music education program to teach Black kids African American History in Music—a subject informed by his ethnomusicological studies. He was moved by the way the students shuffled in each day looking profoundly dispirited, and how they became animated and restored only as they interacted with each other outside school walls. It seemed as if whatever was happening in school was making it hard for them to thrive.

By the time of Martin Luther King's visit to Chicago in 1965, Erickson had already joined a Black church and had participated in marches, protests, and the development of a local community organization that was modeled after those started earlier by Saul Alinsky. He volunteered for the Southern Christian Leadership Conference's "northern initiative" in Chicago, where he met Bernard Lafayette and James Bevel. As his activism intensified, music receded and education came to the fore. To understand urban life and its troubled schools, he rejoined Northwestern in 1966 as a graduate student of education with a strong interest in anthropology and in interaction.

His 1969 dissertation critiqued deficit theories of Black children that had argued that their culture and language impeded school success. He focused again on Chicago's poor inner-city Black youth and compared them with white middle-class kids from the suburbs. In the spirit of small-group analysis, Erickson got them to talk among themselves, and he kindled their casual talk with what he knew best, music. Lacking a Balesian special room, he invited his small groups to various YMCAs in the city and suburbs. As a stimulus, a discussion leader would play a popular tune for each group— "Bernadette" by the Four Tops, "Tobacco Road" by Lou Rawls, and more— and invite commentary on the lyrics. The kids sat around a table as three microphones captured their conversation on a Wollensak tape recorder. Then came transcription, which was hard, as the kids—especially the inner-city kids—didn't develop topics individually, with neat, one-at-a-time speaking turns; "a comment could provoke a chorus of mutual assent or dissent," or what he dubbed "echoing." With transcripts of busy, quick-fire talk in hand, Erickson examined quantitatively the relationship between "language style" and "inquiry style."[11]

The basic need for this research was plain. If schools were to integrate, if diverse students were to live and learn under the same roof, it would be important to understand their differences. In his dissertation's literature review, Erickson surveyed the history of assimilationist school policies that had harmed racialized and minoritized groups, including those from lower socioeconomic classes. He noted, with approval, how many schools now wished to experiment with embracing cultural pluralism, a pluralism that didn't just mean better demographic representation in terms of teachers and administrators but also curricular diversity in terms of what got taught—such as Black History—and *how*, including the medium of instruction and the dialects allowed. Case in point, Black English, whose beauty was surely in the eye of the beholder, Erickson quipped, then added clinically that "it is conceivable that the use of nonstandard English in the school is more of a problem for the teacher who hears it than for the child who speaks it." "One proposal"—and this is the one he supported—was to "include the language and lifeways of the ghetto in the classroom, together with 'standard English' and a modified standard curriculum."[12]

Meeting the Man

Erickson's research continued to build in social relevance. After his dissertation, he charted an ambitious, multisite project on "gatekeeping" encounters. With Hall's encouragement, he applied for a grant from the Center for Studies of Metropolitan Problems at the National Institute of Mental Health (NIMH), "for a study of interracial and interethnic relations in urban job interviews and academic advising interviews." Here would be the "critical points" in people's lives. Gatekeeping encounters were chokepoints for minoritized people, where institutions impinged upon life trajectories. Recalling his social movement activism, "I learned quickly that daily living for people in the neighborhood involved an inside-outside polarity: children learned at a young age that they had 'to meet the Man'—the white outsider—each day. As they grew up they recognized that white people had power and influence and that Black people did not."[13]

The solutions were not simple, even if the commonplace was probably true: that the gatekeeper favored those he took to be most similar in background. Still, the observer mustn't pigeonhole people into demographic categories and neglect what happens when people interact. "There is no way that skin color, accent or demeanor can be ignored in face-to-face encounters," but it was not obvious when and how these differences mattered; what is more, almost anything could become grounds for comembership. "It is clear that ethnicity and race cannot be viewed simply as background variables which constantly affect interaction in the same ways across all encounters. . . .

Background factors that are relevant outside the encounter may, or may *not*, be relevant in it." You had to understand when and how differences mattered, and that required research on communication. If you could understand how exactly people attended to and responded to difference in these encounters, if you could notice the subtle work of affiliation and disaffiliation, perhaps you could take corrective action and make gatekeeping fairer.[14]

As for gatekeeping, in *The Educational Decision-Makers* (1963), sociologists Aaron Cicourel and John Kitsuse had already shown how to pinpoint discrimination in a high school—a school located, in fact, in the Chicago area. Against the meritocratic assumptions that individual capacity and performance explained school success, they argued that routine administrative practices did much to "differentiate" students into college-ready and not college-ready. Erickson would do the same, in a way, except that he would pay attention to social interaction with video recording, playback, transcription, and fine-grained analysis. Unlike the sociologists who had "largely allowed the internal workings of school to remain a 'black box,'" he represented a new kind of education researcher who was after practice.[15]

In his dissertation, Erickson had relied on transcripts made from sound recordings, but he got a taste of what film could offer in late 1967, and it changed him. He decided to bring one of his groups of middle school kids to a recording studio that had been used for microteaching—a method pioneered in the early 1960s in which you filmed a short teaching session and then allowed the novice instructor to review it to improve their craft. The video astonished him. "One single videotape seemed marvelously illuminating; I could see who the speakers were addressing as they spoke—a particular individual, a subset of the group, or the whole group." How surprising it was, especially for a student of music, to discover that sound alone could be so impoverished. With the visual added, he could now follow the play of gaze and bodily movement, the balletic coordination through which humans interacted.[16]

A gatekeeping encounter that became of special interest was that of guidance counseling in junior colleges. Erickson placed a videorecorder in the corner of the office where the school counselor met students and operated it remotely from another room.[17] Rather than rush to code and quantify, Erickson experimented with playback. Sometimes he and his assistants pored over paper transcripts of talk. Sometimes they returned to the audiotapes and listened anew. As for film, they watched "with sound and without" as well as "at regular speed and slow motion." Because the capacity to notice was limited, because the senses were blinkered, you had to keep adjusting how you observed; you had to work across and against modes of seeing and hearing.

You had to estrange yourself from the interaction and continue at this until you knew the interaction well.

It was not that Erickson tried to touch bottom and arrive at a definitive account of what had happened. Nor was this defamiliarization allowed to continue aimlessly. Whereas NHI engaged for years in an open-ended empirical exploration of communication, Erickson maintained a tight focus that matched the urgency of public and policy relevance. In 1975, Erickson relayed some of his findings in "Gatekeeping and the Melting Pot," where he "tested the hypotheses that the more alike counselors and students were in terms of social identity and communication style, the more smoothly the counseling interaction would proceed and the more special help counselors were likely to give students."

Empiricism in educational studies of the day demanded backing from statistics, and so, early in his career, Erickson shored up his claims with p values and quantitative summary tables and a steely presentation of hypotheses and methods. At times, he relied on demographic categories that were the coin of both the social scientist and social movement activists—principally race and ethnicity—yet at other times Erickson examined subtleties that were not evident from identity alone. He would assess the "interactional character" of a gatekeeping encounter, for instance. To operationalize this, he developed three indices, including the "overall behavioral smoothness" of the event. He scored smoothness with the "Overall Behavior Symmetry Coefficient," "which counted the total number of uncomfortable moments, asymmetric verbal interruptions and symmetric verbal overlaps within each encounter."[18]

The point of such scrutiny was to provide objective measures of how well or poorly the interaction was going, but Erickson also used interpretive playback sessions to tap how participants felt. He held open-ended viewing sessions. He separately showed each participant the video and invited them to pause playback whenever they felt something significant happened, and then comment on the moment.

One revealing vignette, one that Erickson returned to over the years, featured a white counselor and Black student. Asked about his plans, the student divulges that he hopes to go into counseling. The response he gets from the counselor is long and circuitous.[19]

COUNSELOR: . . . as far as next semester . . . why don't we give some thought to what you'd like to take there. . . . (Leans forward) Do you plan on continuing along this PE major?

STUDENT: Yeah. I guess so. I might as well keep it up . . . My PE, and
(Shifts in chair) I wanna go into counseling too, see . . . you know, to have
two way . . . like equal balance.
COUNSELOR: I see, Ah . . . What do you know about counseling?
STUDENT: Nothing. (Smiles and averts eyes, then looks up)
COUNSELOR: Okay . . .
STUDENT: (Shifts in chair, smiles and averts eyes) I know you have to take
psychology courses of some sort . . . and counseling.
COUNSELOR: (Leans back) Well, . . . (Student stops smiling, looks directly
at counselor and sits almost immobile while counselor talks and shifts
in chair repeatedly) it's this is a . . . It'll vary from different places to different
places . . . But essentially what you need . . . First of wall you're gonna need
state certification . . . state teacher certification . . . in other words you're
gonna have to be certified to teach in some area . . . English or history, or
whatever happens to be your bag . . . PE. Secondly, you're gonna have to
have a master's degree . . . in counseling . . . which as you know is an advanced degree. (Short laugh) That's what you have to do
to get a counseling . . . to be a counselor.

In a playback session, the student paused the video here. He reported feeling discouraged and suggested that the counselor was trying to thwart his
career goals.

> I guess he didn't think I was qualified, you know. That's the way he sounded
> to me. . . . This guy here seems like he was trying to knock me down, in a way,
> you know. Trying to say no . . . I don't think you can handle anything besides
> PE. You know he just said it in general terms, he just didn't go up and POW
> like they would in the old days, you know. This way they just try to use a little
> more psychology . . . they sugar coat it this way.[20]

The student "inferred an implicit meaning from the relatively convoluted
way of explaining used by the counselor, who was white," Erickson reported.[21]
The counselor saw things differently. He was only providing information to
a student that didn't know the steps to take and seemed a "little bit ahead of
himself." Erickson did not definitely resolve for his readers the question of
what exactly caused this apparent disconnect. He used the segment more to
show that interaction mattered but was a messy affair. Inferring pragmatic
intentions from what people said wasn't straightforward, not the least because
"communicative style" varied across groups, but as his essay unfolded, he
made it clear what the effects of such moments were, what discouragement—
inferred correctly or incorrectly—did to junior college students.

FIGURE 18. "Irish Counselor–Black Student" (*top*), "Italian Counselor–Italian Student" (*bottom*). From "Interethnic Communication Study Project," 1970, Frederick Erickson. Illustration from original video stills by Karson Schenk.

That junior colleges didn't offer what traditional colleges did, everyone knew. They did not launch students—save for the lucky few—into the upper echelons of the economy but instead prepared them to accept less. On this Erickson summoned a damning argument made earlier by sociologist Burton Clark. Clark drew on Goffman's essay on confidence artists, "On Cooling the Mark Out." Cooling out was slang for the work the con did to calm irate victims, by convincing them that they were somehow to blame for their victimization. This is what junior colleges did. Here, analogously, was an institutional cooling out, and a basic correlation held up: the stronger the comembership, the less likely cooling out happened. "In our data," Erickson reported, "we saw a few instances of cooling out in intraethnic encounters, more instances in interethnic encounters and even more in encounters with low comembership."[22]

Animated by civil rights activism, and by the liberal optimism that it was possible to fix institutions, Erickson's microethnography in this way tried to operate just where power was likely to be exercised. Applying interaction science to critical institutional junctures, to times and places where interactions were likely to matter to individuals, soon became a standard method to mobilize the science of face-to-face talk and make it matter. In the 1970s, notably, Gumperz, during his time in England, collaborated to produce *Crosstalk: A Study of Cross-Cultural Communication*, which aired on the BBC in 1979 as part of a series on multiracial Britain.[23] *Crosstalk* dissected real and dramatized workplace interviews as they went well or went awry, in order to teach audiences the small but consequential ways that cultural differences manifested themselves in talk and interaction; if gatekeepers weren't careful (and they usually weren't), they would draw the wrong conclusions about job seekers, and job seekers would assume the worst about the gatekeepers. This initiative became part of a wave of research and teaching on what often called itself interethnic and intercultural "(mis)communication." Gumperz's interest in gatekeeping was inspired directly from Erickson.[24] Erving Goffman had exchanged letters with Erickson and liked his work on gatekeeping. In his final address to his field of sociology in his role as president, Goffman stressed how important gatekeeping was and mentioned school counselors as an example. Such "people-processing encounters" showed how interactional events can be consequential in all the usual ways that mattered to "macrosociology."[25]

Erickson's own microethnographic gatekeeping studies did not embody the "liberal practicality" derided by C. Wright Mills, where social scientists had complexified things so intently, had broken their studies up into such fine problems, that they contented themselves with small, gradual reforms. "For if everything is caused by innumerable 'factors,' then we had best be very careful in any practical actions we undertake." "[As] practical men, we must be piecemeal reformers of milieux."[26] While a reformer rather than a revolutionary, Erickson had only contempt for the status quo, and said as much toward the close of his 1975 essay. Although he complicated simplistic arguments about gatekeeping—as if sameness or difference of identity alone was all that mattered—he concluded that "charges of 'institutional racism' and 'cultural genocide' brought by Third World peoples against white Americans and of 'effete snobbery' brought by white ethnics against predominantly English American, upper-class whites should not be dismissed."[27]

As Erickson began to envision his craft of microethnography, he teamed up with a few fellow travelers, which included Hugh (Bud) Mehan, Ray McDermott, and Jeffrey Shultz, Erickson's student and collaborator from Harvard. Together they began to hold viewing sessions at professional meetings. "Because the equipment we carried through airports on the way to academic meetings was so cumbersome (reel-to-reel video playback decks, slow-motion

FIGURE 19. Frederick Erickson (*left*) and Jeffrey Shultz presenting video data from a study of children's interaction at home and school. Conference at the University of Pennsylvania, 1978.

16mm cinema projectors, and big speakers for sound)," Shultz "came up with a whimsical name for our group—the SHLEPPERS," which punned on the Yiddish with an acronym as cumbersome as the equipment they lugged: "The Society for the Hermeneutic Location of Everyday Practices, Primarily in Educational Research Settings."[28]

Erickson was comfortable using "micro" in the early 1970s, but in just a few years, Mehan advised him to drop the prefix. Otherwise, they'll come after you, just as critics had come after me, he warned. Scale was fast becoming a problem.

Ethnomethodology and the Subversive Smallness of "the Everyday"

Smallness of many kinds entered a state of pitched contestation, of valorization and counter-valorization, in the social sciences of the '70s. If the small of "small-group" science became ethically and politically suspect, if it could be criticized by some politically awakened social science critics for its distanced scientism and technocratic posture, new iterations of the small became alluringly subversive. Like the small of feminist "small-group" consciousness raising (CR), or the very idea of micropolitics. The Shleppers had no special allegiance toward any one of the scholarly circles that specialized in talk and interaction in the early 1970s, yet "hermeneutic location of everyday practices" cued ethnomethodology, an area to which Mehan especially was devoted.

Ethnomethodology had a curious and seemingly ambivalent commitment to the small. Spearheaded by Harold Garfinkel against much of what sociology had to offer, ethnomethodology came to be pegged as "microsociology" even though most of its practitioners disliked or even disavowed the prefix.

Ethnomethodology's own prefix had been made familiar by anthropologists. In midcentury American anthropology, *ethno-* evoked the kaleidoscopic diversity of man in the spirit of cultural relativism. For anthropologists interested in cognition and language, "ethnoscience," for instance, meant the study of diverse words, the terminologies of different groups that revealed how they conceptualized their world. As method, "ethnography" meant a commitment to studying human diversity firsthand, through fieldwork, which would reveal differing forms of life with no expectation, or promise, of extracting universal laws. In nomenclature, ethnomethodology drew from both sensibilities.

As Garfinkel chartered it, ethnomethodology set out to explore tacit meaning-making practices. It would explore commonsense knowledge, the background assumptions that people take for granted and make manifest with each other as they interact. These assumptions were not a trove of invisible rules or norms that determined or steered social action either from below ("mind") or from above ("society"). The orderliness of intersubjectivity was, instead, an artifact of members' local labor—an ongoing, contingent, precarious accomplishment, as ethnomethodologists liked to say. Moment by moment, it was members *themselves* who strained to produce and reproduce a mutually intelligible world, and who held each other morally "accountable" to this achievement.[29] They were not usually aware of this labor; they were not analytic philosophers of the everyday because their lives were intensely routinized and usually unproblematic. Still, the point of stressing their interpretive freedom and agency was to counter that pernicious fiction that Dennis Wrong had called the "oversocialized conception of man" and that Garfinkel called the "judgmental dope." This was the subject of social science that Parsons got blamed for propagating: a passive, unreflective subject, a subject who would toe the line and never resist, which "over-stresses the stability and integration of society."[30]

Garfinkel's early ethnomethodological investigations ran the gamut: juror deliberations, quotidian social interactions, a trans person who learns to pass in a world devoted to a gender binary. The sheer variety demonstrated the reach of the program, even if it risked appearing scattered and incoherent.

Ethnomethodologists did not brand what they did or studied as small, yet from both within their fold and from without, an implicit smallness of a kind helped define their renegade mission. For one, they often declared that they would study "everyday" reality. When they invoked the everyday, they liked to underscore not just its constructedness but its immediacy as an *event* that the analyst could experience, if only vicariously: the everyday was "situated," "here and now," an "ongoing achievement." Words like these operated indexically. They were like pointing gestures for the ethnomethodologist, except that they didn't pick out concrete objects or features of a landscape you could readily see and know. Rather, they steered attention toward a gossamer-like context that was all around you but hard to see: an encompassing yet elusive world, intimately felt yet hiding in plain sight. (In a different and explicitly philosophical way, Garfinkel adapted the notion of indexicality from philosophers of language, to stress how people's talk and actions were irreducibly tied to context.)[31]

What made all this pointing reminiscent of feminist provocations of the small was the ethnomethodologist's interscalar antagonism. Whatever the genealogical roots were—and most shined a light on influences from phenomenology—expressions like "situated" and "here and now" rhetorically suggested a world right in front of your nose, which the whole of sociology had somehow overlooked. Mainstream "macrosociology"—now a term of derision—had become alienated from this manifold of lived experience. Not only did this mean that this sociology misapprehended reality; it also suggested complicity with the status quo, because if you could not see how everyday reality was made and how this reality impinged upon you, you were likely to follow its dictates no matter where those led.

For its anti-establishment spirit, its drive to expose artifice, to denaturalize the most hardened, taken-for-granted social realities, ethnomethodology attracted many feminist and New Left social scientists. Gouldner's *The Coming Crisis in Sociology* (1970) noted how ethnomethodology appealed to the rebellious and to "the counterculture" writ large even if, in his analysis, this movement was just a symptom of sociology's crisis and hardly a cure.[32]

Not Micro?

Although the ethnomethodologists liked to stress and point to the everyday real and distinguish themselves from mainstream "macrosociology," it is telling that they did not embrace the discourse of "micro." For some in sociology, micro was redolent of the wrong kind of empiricism, the kind practiced by those postwar social scientists whose technocratic science seemed uncritically committed to the status quo and for this could be dismissed for its liberal practicality.

Mill's *The Sociological Imagination*—a veritable manifesto for vanguard
sociologists in the late '60s—had pathologized sociology's scalar extremes
well before scale surfaced as a theoretical and methodological problem. At
one end stood the imperious "Grand Theorists"—epitomized by Harvard's
Talcott Parsons—who operated at such an abstract level that they erased "the
facts of power and indeed of all institutional structures, in particular the economic, the political, the military." At the other toiled the "abstracted empiricists," who were blinded by their dedication to methods and had lost sight of
theory and of why things mattered.[33]

That scale helped define ethnomethodology's revolutionary mission was
evident from its early enthusiasts. In *Understanding Everyday Life* (1970)—a
self-styled revolutionary collection of essays in ethnomethodology and
phenomenology—editor Jack Douglas called for nothing less than a whole-
scale "reconstruction of sociological knowledge," as the subtitle read. Mainstream sociology is a sociology of "macroanalysts" who think that "there exist
higher levels of order in social phenomena" and "use this argument to justify
their going directly to an analysis of the society as a whole or the institutional
groups as a whole, rather than starting with an analysis of the lower-level
orderings found in everyday life and proceeding to an analysis of higher levels of social ordering only when they have solved the problems of the lower
levels." Macrosociologists treat the macro as if it were a separate world—a
paracosm—due, no doubt, to a science envy that seduces them into thinking that what they do resembles the "ways in which natural scientists can
study and analyze molecular interactions (higher levels of order) independently of atomic interactions (lower levels of order) and atomic interactions
independently of the interactions of subatomic particles (an even lower level
of order)." Macrosociologists fell for the "fallacy of treating society *as if* it is
somehow a separate level of existence, outside of the hearts and minds of live-
and-breathing human beings."[34]

And this was no innocent error of thought. It betrayed the hubris of "presumed social omniscience." Despite all their clamoring for mechanical objectivity, these analysts had imposed *their* preconceived ideas on the social world
"without any reference to concrete instances of empirical observations." Such
an "absolutist conception of objectivity" went hand and hand with an "absolutist perspective on society," for such "'experts' have increasingly used their
scientific rhetoric to control our lives through their growing effect on government policies."[35]

If absolutist social science was top down, epistemologically and technocratically, a democratically inflected science countered by lowering the analyst. It put him on the same plane as the people he studied. And it would treat

any setting, no matter how humble, as equally the product of human labor, as equally an artifact of local meaning-making "methods"—*ethno-methods*. Ethnomethodology democratized the manifold of social life. Everything and everyone deserved attention. In principle, all empirical sites were endowed with equal significance. The most ordinary scene was as valuable to investigate as the proverbial star chamber or corridor of power. (In his cutting 1975 presidential address to sociology, Lewis Coser charged that this led to jargon-addled essays on the banal, like one by David Sudnow on the way passers-by glance at each other. In "Temporal Parameters of Interpersonal Observation," Sudnow offered a meditation on how people cross the street that Coser summarized by advice he'd give to his four-year old grandson: "Always watch for passing cars.")[36] Nor was science exempt from scrutiny, as ethnomethodology insisted that sciences of all kinds were entangled in this everyday world and as unaware of their own ethno-methods as anyone else—a sentiment that would nurture sociologists of science like Bruno Latour and Karin Knorr-Cetina.

For all this it is no wonder that ethnomethodologists came to be cast as "microsociologists." While wary of embracing micro as a caption for how they worked or what they studied, the ethnomethodologists had protested against macrosociology through their emphasis on the everyday, which they often characterized as if it were an order of social reality somehow more elementary or at least empirically immediate. The macrosociologists, in effect, then struck back with scale. Tagged as *micro*, the ethnomethodologists were hoisted up with their own petards.

I will not rehash the debates and delicate philosophizing and textual exegesis that surrounded the question of what kind of sociology ethnomethodology "really" was; the relevant point is only that there was a scalar aspect to arguments about how ethnomethodology differed from the rest of sociology. Outside the fold of this upstart tradition, there was a growing consensus that ethnomethodology belonged under the umbrella of "microsociology" along with traditions such as symbolic interactionism and the writings of Erving Goffman. As ethnomethodologists got positioned as microsociologists, they seemed reluctant if not resistant to the term. Neither Garfinkel—nor Goffman for that matter—seemed all that eager to embrace the prefix.[37]

As "mainstream macrosociology" called out ethnomethodology for its thinly veiled scalar pretensions, even audiences sympathetic to ethnomethodology were troubled by what these scalar commitments suggested about

> It is a somewhat special sociological world on which this book dwells—a world without history and largely without institutions or social concretions or precipitates from past human actions.
> Review of Erving Goffman's *Behavior in Public Places*, by Louis Schneider, *American Sociological Review* 29, no. 3 (1964): 427

the ability to diagnose and act on power. Ethnomethodology may be anti-establishment in spirit, but this rebellious movement seemed too aloof. It seemed to lack political nerve.

Reflecting on her years as a young sociologist, Pam Fishman noted how she joined the women's movement during her first year as a sociology student at Santa Barbara. She credited ethnomethodology, her specialty, for showing her "the importance of everyday interactions, that they are not simply a reflection of reality but the means by which people construct and maintain their understanding of the world and of themselves." Yet for a movement that relished invoking the here and now, that could expose the constructedness of social life, ethnomethodology made for a strangely gauzy, unfocused politics.

It would seem to me, that we deal here with a massive cop-out, a determined refusal to undertake research that would indicate the extent to which our lives are affected by the socioeconomic context in which they are embedded.
On ethnomethodology, by
LEWIS A. COSER,
"Presidential Address: Two Methods in Search of a Substance," *American Sociological Review* 40, no. 6 (1975): 698

Fishman, who like Henley and West and others had become convinced that the interpersonal was political, put it flatly: "This approach did not deal with power" and so it could not advance the aims of feminism.[38] Or as Roslyn Wallach Bologh later wrote in her feminist critique of ethnomethodology, "The discovery or uncovering of members' practices is not meant to affect members (such as himself) or to change them in any way. Garfinkel does not see his work as contributing to 'raising consciousness,' which is a political act." Ethnomethodology "lacks a political dimension."[39]

This alleged neglect of power became a rote critique of ethnomethodology and of the phenomenology on which it drew. It echoed what Gouldner had written dismissively back in 1970, that ethnomethodology appealed more to the counterculture than political radicals, that it had no teeth.[40] Despite educational ethnomethodologists like Mehan who would argue otherwise, ethnomethodology did not seem keen to pinpoint specific time-spaces, to identify specific junctures where the construction of reality allowed you to see how human lives were subjected to the asymmetrical violence of class, race, ethnicity and gender. In this ethnomethodology differed from feminist iterations of micropolitics, because even though feminist micropolitics also at times constructed interpersonal life as if it were one sweeping site for gender politics, a site

We have argued that the theoretical and methodological premises of ethnomethodology, symbolic interactionism, and phenomenology are essentially similar. We have indicated that the image of man which they offer, and the means by which they study him, leads to a conservative, astructural, ahistorical, situational perspective. . . . Everyman is not in control of his own destiny. The supposed liberation they would offer him—- by giving him a glance at the strings by which he is controlled—is a false liberation.
SCOTT G. MCNALL AND JAMES C. M. JOHNSON,
"The New Conservatives: Ethnomethodologists, Phenomenologists, and Symbolic Interactionists," *Critical Sociology* 5, no. 4 (1975): 64

that was left undifferentiated, it never wanted to isolate "the interpersonal" as the only or primary domain in which politics happens. Even when feminists foregrounded the interpersonal, even when this emphasis made the background blur, they knew this was a social movement with multiple fronts. Even though they could argue internally about the relative importance of the interpersonal, for feminists who stressed how urgent the interpersonal was to their liberation, they never wanted this emphasis to come at the expense of collective actions, including actions that so-called liberal feminists had prioritized. Even those feminists who thought interpersonal micropolitics was important wanted to retain a concern with those "big" formations—sexism, patriarchy, and male supremacy—to which interpersonal micropolitics was always hitched, even if they wrestled with the questions of how the two worlds of politics connected, with what caused what, and what deserved priority. Likewise, for most of the "new" sociologists of education who had turned toward the study of conflict and power, the usual ethnomethodologist seemed unfocused. He let power slip through his fingers. "His rebellion, though radical in its rejections of the routines of daily life, avoids direct confrontation with the status quo."[41]

In Defense of the Mediatic Microscope

Among those who drank deeply of ethnomethodology, it was conversation analysts who seemed least concerned with the charge that they ignored power relations. To be sure, some within their ranks—including West herself who owed much to CA—would develop ways to study power by studying interactions that mattered, especially in what they broadly considered institutional contexts. But in general, as CA got ensnared in the scalar skirmishes of the 1970s, skirmishes that grew into what became referred to politely as the micro–macro problem, they tended to stand their ground, largely unfazed and rarely defensive.

Let us accumulate many microscopic studies; slowly and minutely, like ants dragging many small crumbs into a great pile, we shall "build up the science."
C. WRIGHT MILLS,
The Sociological Imagination
(New York: Oxford University Press, 1959), 127

Indeed, while ethnomethodologists struggled to respond to the critics that poked at their diminutive scale, most conversation analysts did not bother to mount much of a defense. In his influential synthesis, *Garfinkel and Ethnomethodology* (1984), John Heritage made it seem like CA *was* ethnomethodology, pure and simple. Having stitched together the two traditions seamlessly, CA was not only a natural outgrowth of ethnomethodology but perhaps its finest expression. (As Schegloff reportedly quipped about ethnomethodology, what this tradition lacked was *method*, which was what CA could offer.) In his epilogue's parting paragraph, Heritage enjoined readers to peer with him through CA's mediatic microscope. "The research of the last twenty years or so has resulted in the creation of the sociological equivalent of the microscope," he wrote. "The use of this instrument is yielding glimpses of previously unimaginable levels of social organization in human conduct and it is clear that major findings at the molecular and submolecular levels of social structure are there to be made."[42]

This trope was not lost on ethnomethodological purists. Citing the offending passage, Pollner lamented how far CA had strayed. It had devolved into yet another vulgar form of empiricism.[43] To be sure, you could tell the story of CA's betrayal only because its historiographers had ignored or downplayed the fact that CA was never only an outgrowth of ethnomethodology; instead, it was indebted to other ideas and movements—not the least, to Chomsky's cognitivist vision of a universal grammar. While notoriously hostile toward empiricism, the Chomskyans chased the underlying, hard-wired, generative code of language, not unlike the way CA pursued a conversational "grammar" beneath everyday *parole*.[44]

As ethnomethodologist Richard Hilbert lamented, CA did not help the case of ethnomethodology by "focusing on tiny pieces of conversation as taped and transcribed in minute detail," which only seemed to confirm that ethnomethodology really was microsociology. "Ethnomethodologists' concern with such detail . . . appears to document a 'one-sided' emphasis on micro issues at the expense of everything else."[45] For his part, Hilbert tried to rescue CA—and, in turn, the legacy of ethnomethodology—from its misadventures with micro. CA, like ethnomethodology, should be seen as "indifferent to structure at any level," he wrote. It was neither micro nor macro. True, Hilbert conceded, both CA and ethnomethodology did like to stress the "local" "here and now" of social life, but this was only meant to emphasize the importance of studying what was empirically available, to "account for . . . observations solely from the empirical data at hand": this way of talking should *not* be taken to mean that conversation is some separate, ontologically scaled *level* of social reality.[46] Epistemological scale and ontological scale must be pried apart, once again.

Hilbert tried to upend common sense, but he was late. Few doubted that ethnomethodology—and certainly CA—were instances of microsociology, and by the mid-1970s being called micro was a charge that now required a defense. A decade earlier, in the mid-1960s, CA architect Harvey Sacks didn't seem all that bothered by the suggestion that what he did was microscopic. "Now, the way I work has been called 'microscopic' with, then, the usual sociology as 'macroscopic.' And it's not a bad distinction." What bothered him was only the further suggestion that "social events are not closely enough ordered so that we can get results at the 'microscopic' level of investigation."[47] By the 1980s, "micro" had become morally and politically freighted as sociologists of all stripes became preoccupied with problems of interscalar kinship. The answer to this problem mattered because of its implications for who scholars themselves were relative to each other. Sorting out the micro–macro would sort out scholars, too.

The conceptual solutions to this interscalar chestnut were many. In his grand synthesis, Anthony Giddens in the 1980s famously integrated micro and macro so tightly that he claimed he could drop the antinomy and replace it with a single, new processual idea that transcended both, "structuration." Sociologists were wrong to treat micro and macro as opposed, as if they named different levels of social reality—as different ontological scales—in which one was "more fundamental than the other."[48]

Debates over micro and macro represented a "phoney war if there ever was one." And so Giddens lent a hand to the newly corralled "microsociologists"—a term that was mostly an exonym pinned on these scholars by others—whose ranks had grown and included Goffman, Garfinkel, and the whole of CA, among others. Giddens would rescue them from the charge that they couldn't account for structural constraints on interaction.[49] He offered a truce, albeit on his terms. Others were less charitable, and some spoiled for a fight. Bourdieu sided with critics who dismissed ethnomethodology and conversation analysts as head-in-the-sand situationists who failed to see the objective structures that shaped dispositions and produced rampant inequality—in uneven distributions of economic, symbolic, and cultural capital. Contrary to "the occasionalist illusion which consists in directly relating practices to properties inscribed in the situation," "'interpersonal' relations are never, except in appearance, *individual-to-individual* relationships and that the truth of the interaction is never entirely contained in the interaction." "This is what social psychology and interactionism or ethnomethodology forget," Bourdieu chided, "when, reducing the objective structure of the relationship between the assembled individuals to the conjunctural structure of their interaction in a particular situation and group, they seek to explain everything that occurs in an experimental or observed interaction. . . ."[50]

> I think it is a mistake to regard encounters in circumstances of copresence as in some way the basis upon which larger, or "macrostructural," social properties are built. So-called "microsociological" study does not deal with a reality that is somehow more substantial than that with which "macrosociological" analysis is concerned. But neither, on the contrary, is interaction in situations of copresence simply ephemeral, as contrasted to the solidity of large-scale or long-established institutions.
>
> ANTHONY GIDDENS,
> *The Constitution of Society: Outline of the Theory of Structuration*
> (Berkeley: University of California Press, 1984), xxvi

For Bourdieu, and for many others, microsociology alone was incapable of studying power and domination. Most microsociologists were put on their heels.

The analysis of ever more refined minutiae of reality construction, and the assertion that one cannot possibly understand larger social structures before all these minutiae have been exhaustively mapped, irresistibly brings to mind Dr. Johnson's pregnant observation that, "You don't have to eat the whole ox to know that the meat is tough."

LEWIS A. COSER,
"Presidential Address: Two Methods in Search of a Substance," *American Sociological Review* 40, no. 6 (1975): 698

Mehan went on the offensive. He rebranded "microethnography" as "constitutive ethnography." "The term microethnography can unwittingly perpetuate the unfortunate micro–macro distinction in sociology by suggesting that only minutiae are under study, while larger social structures are being ignored." As all "social structures are social accomplishments," this meant interactional realism made sociological abstractions empirically manifest—and that included abstractions of great political importance. "There are no things in the sensuous world like 'bourgeois consciousness' or 'class' or 'the capitalist system,' there are only people doing their lives in a succession of here-and-nows." This processualist science of the everyday was compatible with Marx, he insisted. It didn't drop power and domination as topics of concern, as Fishman and others alleged; no, it had localized, concretized, and concentrated these processes, not unlike the way radical feminists like O'Connor and Henley made male supremacy immanent in interpersonal relations. And because ethnomethodology was skilled in exposing artifice, it could pierce the social constructedness of the world. It could liberate "the masses of people . . . forced to live in worlds they did not create." Ethnomethodology could open up humans to alternative futures, allowing them to remake the world into a different and better place. "Ethnomethodology displays the everyday practices of this alienation and provides a means to transcend it, thus making Marx a forefather of ethnomethodology."[51]

Mehan's activist interactional realism remained committed to the ontological unity of scalar worlds. Interaction wasn't a paracosm. Unlike Schegloff's separatist vision for CA, Mehan did not wish to wall off conversation as its "own" order even though he did want to make discursive interaction into something primary, something constitutive—something, in a word, that mattered. If you wanted to understand power relations, he argued, you needed to study interaction, because this is where the world was made and remade. In this way he mounted a counterargument about what was primary and what wasn't, while tearing up—or trying to, anyway—the map of social reality that had apportioned out to him so little territory.

Other interactionists were eager to drop micro and macro, as the distinction didn't serve them well. Ray McDermott, another activist educational researcher and fellow Shlepper, defended the relevance of his science while also declaring that it was time to get "beyond micro and macro."

There were two reasons why interaction analysis was not "merely" micro. First, you could *see* the macro world vividly and immediately in interaction, as he discovered early on with Super 8 recordings of classroom interaction: "the astounding finding is that the institutional constraints which we usually address with broad 'macro' generalities are actually observable at the behavioral level of immediate interaction," in the sense that the "specifics of such socially pervasive facts as gender, ethnicity, status, and role are, to use Sapir's phrase, 're-animated or creatively affirmed' from one moment to the next. . . ." Though he did not spell out the practical and political implications of this immediacy, this suggested that you could find—pinpoint—the exercise of power and domination in ways that would allow reformers to do something about it.

Interactional analyses often are referred to as micro. On the surface, the designation seems to stem from the fact that interactional analysts work on short strips of behavior, often only a few seconds at a time. At a more profound level, however, the diminutive carries the additional bias that interactional analyses are not about much, that they do not address the real constraints on people's lives in ways which macro studies of whole cultures or market systems do.

R. P. MCDERMOTT
AND DAVID R. ROTH,
"The Social Organization of Behavior:
Interactional Approaches," *Annual
Review of Anthropology* 7 (1978): 322

A second reason was scientific. Macro studies "need to be verified by an interactional record," which implied that there was something concrete about interaction as evidence, that it was a level needed to ground claims. Again, here was a critical science that was at once rigorous and activist.[52]

Conversation: Autonomous and Alone

Some social theorists sympathetic with the small sciences of interaction did not protest the micro–macro divide so much as the nature of the relationship. They largely accepted the interscalar ontology that posited distinct but related "levels" of social reality but countered that interaction was "elementary" or "primary" or "constitutive" in a way that made it important. Sociologists such as Randall Collins, Gary Fine, and Ann Rawls, among others, would all make arguments in this vein. In their own ways, they would insist that

Some sociologists become so absorbed in words as to fail to renew their relation to actual contexts. Admittedly, it is fascinating to discover the richness of speech, coming from a disciplinary background that has neglected it; but it is a bit absurd to treat transcribed tapes of interaction as if they were the Dead Sea Scrolls.

DELL H. HYMES,
*Foundations in Sociolinguistics:
An Ethnographic Approach*
(Philadelphia: University of
Pennsylvania Press, 1974), 81

understanding interaction was necessary for understanding the macrosocial and for filling out social theory.[53]

Frustrating the efforts of these interscalar synthesists were many conversation analysts. Of all the strains of interaction science from the 1970s, it was CA, or at least its most vocal proponents, that seemed comfortable being positioned as microsociology and went the furthest in making interaction paracosmic. CA tended to autonomize its object strongly. For this it came under fire, not only by outsiders but also by other scholars of discourse and interaction, including some who worked largely within the terms of CA.[54]

Emanuel Schegloff staked out a strong position on conversation's autonomy. He insisted that scholars of conversation should resist imposing their assumptions about "context" on the interactions they were studying. They should instead ground interpretive claims in what was in front of them, which, in this mediatic science, meant a paper transcript created from a sound-recorded conversation using transcription conventions that Gail Jefferson helped develop and standardize.

In an edited book from the '80s dedicated to the "micro–macro link," Schegloff spelled out his position. He began by complaining about the "utter relativity and likely hopelessness of [the] terms" micro and macro," while accepting that CA would of course be considered "microanalysis."[55] Schegloff challenged the very idea of micro–macro links and promoted his own science in the process. He went further than most. He questioned the compulsion to explain interaction by such staples as class, race, ethnicity, and gender without demonstrating how these actually become relevant *to participants themselves*. To make his point, he went back and challenged none other than the feminist conversation scholarship on interruption by West and Zimmerman.

For an interaction between men and women, gender may—or may not—be relevant, Schegloff cautioned. This was not an unusual caution for interactionists. In his gatekeeping work, Erickson had reminded his audience that social identities were not automatically relevant but had to be *made* so by participants themselves in the way they talked and responded to each other. This had also been a basic ethnomethodological point. Schegloff took this further. To show that gender was evident to the participants themselves, gender had to appear "in" the transcript in some way. Gail Jefferson, a co-architect of early CA, was a stanch supporter of West but agreed with Schegloff's assessment.[56]

"It may well be that women are interrupted more than they interrupt," Schegloff argued, "but the introduction of such an 'external' attribute early in the research process or the account can deflect attention from how the outcome of the conversational course of action is determined *in its course, in real time.* Once this process has been explicated, much of the interest it had may well have been 'secularized' and appear anonymous rather than gender-specific." Maybe what's going on is not about gender at all, Schegloff mused. "Whether gender per se will turn out to be a macro-relevant attribute relating to these is not clear. Perhaps it is one 'proxy' for high/low power or status."[57]

For Schegloff, there was no tempest in the transcript, because the transcript was not some microcosm in which ideological formations like sexism showed up in miniature. Miniaturism reduced interaction to an echo as it forced you to concede that it is the macrosocial that is the font of all things important. Schegloff credited Goffman for having taught him that "there was a world here . . . in these little scenes of interaction," that interaction was an object in its own right, that it was its own order.[58] A transcript may reveal trouble and turbulence, but further study might show that these tensions stem from something else. Maybe it's a struggle over status that isn't limited to interaction between men and women. Maybe upon further analysis such tension will resolve into a struggle of a different kind, perhaps something specific to face-to-face interaction. Schegloff's hedges and cautions about too-easily seeing gender in transcripts broadcast more than epistemological care but also a commitment to basic science—even if, to his critics and to researchers with activist sensibilities, this could make CA look reactionary. Didn't Schegloff discourage scholars from bringing the struggles of the street into the study of transcripts? Didn't he risk depoliticizing the study of interaction?

Like Giddens, albeit for very different reasons, Schegloff wanted to drop the micro–macro distinction. Rather than think of interaction as made of "micro-level phenomena" and "context" as something that looms from without, *"modes of interactional organization might themselves be treated as contexts."*[59] Trying to drop ontological scale wouldn't be easy, though, because, in practice, Schegloff was never indifferent to scale. His mediatic microscopy, with its system of sound recording and playback, with its discipline of faithful transcription and patient fine-grained analysis, had made conversation into a scaled object of knowledge no matter what he professed. CA, at least as Schegloff and his students envisioned it, was known for its commitment to a mediatic microscope, and proud of it.

CA may have enacted a version of conversational interaction as a separate world, but officially they were cautious about theorizing it this way and instead sometimes tried to pry apart epistemological and ontological scale. They did not really want to say that conversation was its own irreducible thing, akin to Saussure's la langue or Durkheim's "society." The autonomy they ceded to their object was supposed to be provisional, and practical. It was supposed to be in the service of epistemology. Thinking about the "autonomy" of conversation was supposed to help the analyst hold at bay—bracket—the rush of intrusive and potentially irrelevant facts from the familiar "macro" world.[60] The analyst must learn to notice only what is empirically sensible under the mediatic microscope. They should be guided only by what is on the page (even if the transcripts used are densely mediated artifacts, structured by conventions, inflected by ideology, created by human labor, and indebted to mechanical recording and playback—as CA's critics stressed).[61]

But for outsiders, there was little doubt about what CA had done, and that was to autonomize their object and embrace its troubled scale. Schegloff recognized the growing public pressure to explain CA's position. If CA was indeed *micro*-sociology, as charged, then to remain relevant they'd have to prove their contribution to macrosociology. It is "only by linkage to macro themes that microanalysis becomes 'respectable' and finds its *raison d'être*."[62]

Schegloff tried to resist this push for respectability. Others relented, even as they were no less committed to a mediatic microscopy. Some even cited Schegloff deferentially and professed allegiance to ethnomethodology and to CA. It was only that they were concerned not to depoliticize the science of interaction, as they saw Schegloff at risk of doing. Feminist communication scientists who drew deeply on CA, such as West and Zimmerman, exemplified this stance, as did microethnographers of education like Erickson and Mehan who used video and transcripts to address racial and ethnic discrimination in schools.

As CA practitioners like Schegloff made conversation an autonomous and scaled object of knowledge, others staked out similar but less extreme positions. Erving Goffman, who was famously critical of CA, ended his career by doubling down on the basic idea that interaction was a world unto itself, an "interaction order." "The interaction order" was the title of his 1982 presidential address to the American Sociological Association and was proposed as a distillation of decades of writing on face-to-face encounters, encounters that transpire in "environments in which two or more individuals are physically in one another's response presence." Unlike Schegloff, Goffman did not want to circumscribe interaction too tightly. He allowed for a "loose coupling" with the macrosocial—a minor concession but a concession nonetheless.[63]

And concessions abounded, as interactionists began to scramble to show that the world they studied wasn't cut off from the world everyone knew and cared about. Interaction was no longer comfortably, unproblematically small. Was the microscopic gaze still laudable for its laser focus and rigor, or was it myopic and the details it generated gratuitous? As for "micropolitics," could a mediatic discipline of fine-grained noticing nail furtive truths about humans, catching them in the act? Or had these microscopists gotten distracted. Had they become so absorbed in their craft and allowed their pride in scrupulous observation to swell, that they lost all perspective? Was it a true tempest that roiled in the transcript, or just a patch of rough current that they magnified so monstrously that it allowed them to indulge in the ultimate of delusions, that what hung on the page was of grave consequence, that it, and *they*, mattered?

11

Conclusion

After chartering "microethnography" in the early 1970s and practicing it for some three decades, Frederick Erickson tried to set the record straight. In 2004, in *Talk and Social Theory*, he did what many other interactionists felt inspired, and obligated, to do: to reconcile the "problem" of multiple scalar worlds, to explain how an ontologically distinct domain of interaction, visible and audible in its fullness through a mediatic microscope, related to the surface world known to social science. "Economy, history, and the distribution of power" *did* matter crucially, Erickson stressed, putting to rest—or trying to— the claim that interactionists had somehow ignored all this. Interaction was no paracosm.[1] Like many other interactionists, he argued that this vast context both "constrained" and "enabled" interaction, and that if you understood this embeddedness well, you'd appreciate the importance of face-to-face life and understand why scholars chose to study it carefully.

As for what interaction could offer social science, Erickson went on to suggest—and others made similar arguments—that what close attention to interaction gave you was an unparalleled appreciation for *process*.[2] Process was made manifest in part through mediatic transcripts thick with details that you could not otherwise perceive, details that added so much grain and texture to action that they disrupted the reader's ability to make easy inferences about what was happening. Which was the point, as interaction was not how it seemed. The pervasive unexpected qualia of roughness that Hooke saw under the optical microscope disrupted the impression that human-made things had smooth, taut, familiar surfaces. This estrangement made the epistemological feat of microscopic discovery possible, and palpable. Mediatized processualism restored a kind of roughness, in a way. Its granularity roughened up the impossibly smooth surfaces of social theory, making "room for deviation," for "wiggle room," Erickson wrote. It allowed you to account for change over time, change that had been left a mystery under top-heavy—the old polemical word was deterministic—theories of social life that smoothed over the complexities of what humans actually did to, for, and with each other in "practice."

Indeed, practice—a notion and trope that attracted widespread interest—was something that interactionists could claim to study well, if not better than most. This and cognate notions like performance had often been prized for its promise to restore agency to subjects and unsettle all those totalizing generalizations about social life, yet to scholars of language and interaction it was not clear whether ethnographies claiming to get at practice had truly succeeded. As Charles Zuckerman reflects, from the vantagepoint of mediatic scholars of interaction, most ethnographies had ironically bleached out and smoothed over practice because, simply put, they had failed to look carefully enough. Video recording and playback could help. Because of the sensorial excess that comes from the "bundled" signals of mediatic replay—there was always more to see and hear than you expected—video review could disrupt the quick-forming interpretations and generalizations that threatened to make discursive practice a static and stereotyped thing. In this and in other ways, those who studied interaction with recording and playback technologies have felt they can study practice thickly—as ethnographers desire—so long as they do not get too distracted, so long as they remember the contextual fullness of their object, for interaction *must* be studied in relation to society, culture, and history, much as Erickson insisted.[3]

And yet, as an interscalar argument, this commitment to study interaction-in-context remained comfortably and ecumenically monistic. It retained the familiar micro–macro division but now used it to cinch the world together. In this it prefigured interdisciplinary cooperation: an invitation for fields to come together, to get along, to recognize that each had something to offer. As if all the fuss and factionalism over scale had just been the result of different observational perspectives. Yes, observational scales narrowed what you saw, but no, the world itself was not so divided. Though Erickson did not put it in these terms, the problem was that you needed to pry apart epistemological and ontological scale because the two had once again gotten conflated.

Disciplines of Scale

Undoing this generative conflation would not be easy. No declaration could undo this, even when repeated many times, because the effects of this conflation had been sedimented over many years, so much so that scalar distinctions live on even though it is now rare to see scale debated so explicitly.

Let me be clear: as with other objects of knowledge, social interaction has no intrinsic ontological scale,[4] nor does it necessarily demand a "microscopic" epistemological scale. And yet, even as many have tried to reconfigure interaction in ways that escape this scaling, this has proved to be hard. It has been hard because the problem of scale birthed new scholarship, so that even as the passionate debates over scale quieted down, the problem came to live on in institutionalized convictions about what makes fields and their objects and methods similar and different. Again, who hasn't imagined face-to-face interaction as a relatively small object that epistemologically demands microscopy of some kind? And once you think this, there comes the reflex— atavistic though it may now seem—for students of interaction to need to explain themselves. The justifications they provide are now rote and predictable, as rote and predictable as the criticism used to dismiss these sciences of the small.

Trying to solve or shake off the problem of scale has not made scale go away. In a familiar irony, the concerted resistance just made scale burrow deeper. Scholars in fields as diverse as gender studies, sociology, science and technology studies, and social anthropology have repeatedly exposed scalar assumptions baked into notions ranging from person to body to nation-state, and many over the past few decades have either worked to resolve scale's antinomies such as micro–macro and local–global or have tried to drop these in favor of alternatives, from the dizzying rhizomes of Deleuze and Guattari to the multidirectional dialogicality of Bakhtin to the flat ontology of actor network theory. Yet what a zombie analytic scale is, for even as scale has been subjected to critique after critique, most of the things we claim to know—language, mind, society, state, economy—remain differentially scaled in forms of scholarly life. For many, "political economy" and "the state," for example, are still thought to encompass, influence, and for some, even determine the objects that occur "within" their scope and jurisdiction, including objects like human interaction. Contemporary cultural anthropology may pride itself on having transcended the old, coarse micro–macro divide, but hasn't this divide persisted in its prized practice and sensibility, ethnography? Don't we tend to praise the capacity to move from "sweeping" contexts of one kind or another to fine-grained detail involving events, movements, discourses, and narratives? Big and small, at once—is this not still the dominant integrative epistemology and aesthetic that owes much to anthropology's legacy of holism?[5]

Ideas about the scales of objects and the methods needed to know them have showed up in the restless play of disciplinary positioning and counterpositioning, and this is hardly new. (Remember how Auguste Comte tried to groom sociology for a position at the peak of a hierarchy that ran from the "simple" [or "elementary"] disciplines, like astronomy and physics, to sociology, which he touted as the most "complex" of all; and how his sociology had to settle for "rag-picking on the periphery of the intellectual market-place,"[6] inheriting what the more established traditions discarded—like the study of domestic cities where criminality and social ill were said to breed?) Fields often vie with each other through an idiom of scale. Sometimes big tries to eat small; sometimes small eats big from micro "up," through a form of downward causation or reduction that makes "microfoundations" of one sort or another matter most.[7]

Fields disagree internally just as vociferously, usually by replaying the same debates with roles now filled by their colleagues. Some time ago, Strathern called out entrenched ethicopolitical stances on scale, such as when "anthropologists alternate between accusing one another now of myopia, now of panoptics."[8] Even within the fold of linguistic anthropology, a subfield that often gets treated by skeptics as uniformly devoted to small things and fine-grained analysis, its scholars have sometimes redirected the scalar critiques used on them toward each other, calling out peers who have supposedly gotten distracted and lost sight of what matters most. Like anthropology, historians have used scale on themselves. Movements like microhistory in the 1970s, for instance, magnified units such as events and individuals, which many took to be a rejoinder to mainstream historiography which they charged with blindly doing the bidding of power. Somewhat like earlier "histories from below," microhistory would recover and amplify marginalized voices lost in the historical record.

Or take literary criticism, which, as Heather Love discusses, has experienced great ferment over the question of what should replace its once cherished commitment to the institution of "close reading." Some have chosen to go big, eschewing hermeneutic deep dives into infinitely rich, singular texts in favor of "thin," "surface," or "distant" readings. The results include studies in sociological registers, such as large-scale quantitative views of book production and consumption. Others, Love reports, steer in the opposite direction, toward what Mark Seltzer has called "the new incrementalism." In terms of the novel, they promote "minor characters," "minor feelings," "little resistances." At issue is a politics of scale. While some, for instance, argue that the new down-scaled incrementalism reflects a loss of political nerve, Love reminds us that works like Claudia Rankine's 2014 *Citizen: An American Lyric* demonstrate how a fine-grained, microanalytic gaze can effectively expose everyday racial violence in a manner as forceful as Chester Pierce's attention to microaggressions.[9]

Not all fields have such a vivid and explicit politics of scale, or have had it always and to the same degree, and I certainly do not wish to collapse differences across fields by suggesting that the crises chronicled in this book, which largely concern the social sciences of language, interaction, and communication, are the same as those encountered elsewhere. Still, we should not overlook the many family resemblances. Nor should we miss the basic fact that at least in the humanities and social sciences, scale is often treated as if it were ideologically inflected. The very existence of passionate scalar contestation within and across fields—from anthropology to sociology to history—reminds us that these methodological stances on how to know can become moralizing stances on how to study and live in the world.

As scholars have come to dig in their heels, scalar commitments and even durable dispositions have formed; in closing, let me once again disclose mine. This book can be read as a critical history of scale from within and from below, insofar as the little sciences—trained on putatively small things, favoring seemingly "microscopic" modes of analysis—have been quite often challenged to explain themselves. It is not that I want to defend microscopy and its putatively small objects, which would risk leaving our scalar commitments intact. Nor do I want to dissolve scale, a feat I cannot achieve. For now, at least, I only want to insist that we consider—with more care, focus, and acuity—how scale manifests itself in and around our disciplinary practices of knowing and being. Not surprisingly, my own orientation toward scale shares much in spirit with the various disciplines of close reading, thick description, fine-grained analysis in which I trained; by turning scale on itself, I hope to restore a measure of roughness to our reflexive understanding of scale, to see what can be revealed.

What all this suggests is that the effort to avoid settling scale in advance, as Latour and others urged, seems, in retrospect, naive, because we cannot willfully drop scale. Scale *has* been settled for us in advance, by self and by others, through institutionalized forms of life that have made scale a stubborn thing in our disciplines.

Microfoundations, Strong and Weak

Where better to appreciate this institutionalization than in economics, where scale seems particularly stubborn? Whatever ambivalence this field expresses about scale, its courses, textbooks, jobs, journals, centers—to say nothing of research and theory—remain devoted to a distinction between micro and macro that, as their in-house historiography has it, Norwegian economist Ragnar Frisch first floated in the early 1930s. If, as Frisch imagined, the economy as a whole did have its "own" dynamics, then how should we reconcile this with smaller-scale dynamics, such as the manner in which agents like firms and households behave?[10]

For economic theorists wrestling to explain historical change, scale has sometimes been both problem and solution. Case in point, the stagflation of the early 1970s surprised most economists with the simultaneous rise in both inflation and unemployment. Mainstream Keynesian economics had expected these to be inversely correlated. In reflecting on this surprise, some came to blame macroeconomic theory itself. Robert Lucas's eponymous "Lucas critique" from the mid-1970s highlighted how government policy had affected macroeconometric statistics. This meant you can't just view these statistics as if they offered a direct window onto economic life. Macroeconomic theory had gone astray by failing to base itself in microeconomic behavior, its "foundation." Indeed, since the early '70s at least, economics' micro–macro divide has most often been resolved (at least officially) by a form of downward causal reduction that claims microeconomics as the economic real. Around 1970, "microfoundations" came to name this anti-realist stance toward macro-level econometrics. As Lucas famously put it, though, micro and macro are but provisional labels. Once economists grasp the full nature of microfoundations, "the term 'macroeconomic' will simply disappear from use and the modifier 'micro' will become superfluous."[11] The age of unified "economic theory" will dawn again. The economy will become whole, the language of scale will vanish.[12] Given how institutionalized scale is, if this ever did happen, it would end the world of disciplinary economics as we know it.

If we shift from the economy to interaction, we find an object whose microfoundations, as it were, are anything but secure.[13] For decades now, as we have seen, interactionists in fields like sociology and anthropology have been put on their heels for their *micro*-methodological commitments and, as minority research traditions, they have usually felt compelled to respond. Skeptics have wondered what their seemingly blinkered research can tell us about the "wider" world. (It is tiresome to use scare quotes on every scrap of scalar language, but I cannot overstate how habitual and unquestioned this language is.) If poring over the detailed transcript of a recorded conversation is a kind of microsociology, as many scholars historically termed the enterprise, then why, indeed, should (macro)sociology care? Worse, what if interaction is a paracosm, an irreducible world whose distinctive dynamics cannot be understood using the theories and methods of macrosociology? If interaction does have "a life of its own," as Erving Goffman famously wrote, if it is "a little social system with its own boundary-maintaining tendencies," "a little patch of commitment and loyalty with its own heroes and its own villains," then can we expect anything more than tenuous ties—"loose coupling"[14]—to the macrosocial? Or perhaps interaction is microcosmic but only in the sense of offering a higher resolution image of something we already see if only in "broad strokes," as we sometimes say. This would imply—and some have argued this—that microsociology (or however we should now term this scholarly sensibility) is, at best, a bundle of methods. These methods might help give us insights into data that we can't get through other means and instruments, but even if microsociology were widely accepted as a methodological complement to sociology (it currently isn't), can we expect it to generate new social theory and help adjudicate among competing ideas about how the world works? (Most would say no.)

Even the odd transcripts of the interactionists have not been spared in these disputes. Many, if not most, scholars of interaction remain devoted to this transductional craft and class of text, which do various things for them, more than they realize. One function is evidential. Anticipating that their readers may want to check their work, transcripts can serve as backing for claims made about a swatch of discursive interaction. Transcripts do much else, too. They may have helped the author with analysis, but expositionally, in a publication, they may also be set off and framed in such a way that they show, illustrate, or teach something that the author wants readers to notice. Design—as Keith Murphy has shown—has been a critical aspect of transcription, even if it has only rarely been recognized or valued as such. The question of how to do transcription "well" (e.g., rigorously, efficiently, elegantly) has generated a minor literature.[15]

To be sure, not everyone leans heavily on transcripts. Another kind of analyst insists on returning to source media through repeated playback. The need for mediatic returns is usually premised on an acute awareness of what transcripts leave out—the fact that they necessarily exclude a lot.[16] Nevertheless, for many if not most interactionists, transcripts remain important. Epistemologically, as I suggested at the outset, they are even treated as an analog of the optical microscope's glass slide with specimen mounted on it. In this respect, transcripts represent a technique of observational scale. By adding details from recordings, these then break up the deceptively smooth contours of talk as pure denotational text—the literal "what-is-said" of talk, as it is usually termed. Transcripts in this way unsettle and ideally estrange you from the misleading surface of talk in order to show you how discursive interaction really is. Akin to the careful atmospherics and scene-evoking descriptive writing that ethnographers often use to conjure a place, time, action, or occasion (and the sense of *being there*, as Geertz wrote),[17] so too can transcripts construct a vicariously experienceable naturalism that turns a fine-grained observational scale into something you can encounter, feel, and inhabit.

And yet no matter how naturalistic these transcripts have tried to be, aesthetically, these texts lack immediacy. This is by design, because these are not texts to be "read" in the usual way. Instead, they foreground features of discourse, such as speech overlaps and pause lengths, so that they can be noticed. Critics outside the fold sometimes complain that these strange transcripts betray life—the sensory feel of it, the affective charge, the pace and intensity, the colors and textures—even if the betrayal is ultimately the result of being accustomed to different conventions for representing conversational life on paper.[18] Presumably they'd prefer something more familiar. They find these specialized transcripts of the interaction analysts to be too dense (or too granular, if you accept the observational scale of this craft). Plus, if it takes so much time to create these microanalytical transcripts and if it places such a burden on non-initiates to read them, you could wonder whether these peculiar texts were worth the trouble.

Linguistic Anthropology and the Total Interactional Fact

All this wrangling over scale has made for a flurry of distinctions, within and among fields, including for scholars dedicated to interaction. At one corner stood stalwart conversation analysts who tended to treat their object as autonomous and rest content with fine-grained methods. Conversation analysis (CA) had grown a lot since the early '70s, and changed too. Some critics came to lament what they saw as an arc of routinization in which CA's early ethnomethodological openness contracted after Harvey Sacks's untimely death in the '70s. According to this story, after his loss, the field hardened into Kuhnian normal science as it came to pride itself on its proprietary methods, methods that too often look like canned techniques of noticing that ironically undermined CA's commitment to *ethno*-methods—all the ways people make meaning together—which we should never presume to know in advance.

Another concern afflicted its early practitioners, as we saw, and it had to do with political relevance. Although CA largely treated conversation as an autonomous object, early on some within its fold desired a more relevant science, and for that an autonomous object would not do. They too had embraced mediatic techniques that circumscribed interaction spatially and temporally, but they sought more than knowledge of abstract structures and the mechanics of conversation. While early CA had been content to study "everyday" conversational life, which seemed diffuse and undifferentiated, those within CA who sought relevance felt they should choose their interactions more carefully. After her early work on the gender micropolitics of interruption, Candace West turned to study doctor–patient interaction, for instance, much as others turned to institutional sites in which interaction was suspected to matter, from courtrooms to classrooms to workplaces. Much as Erickson's microethnography sought "critical points" in the trajectories of people's daily lives, so some within CA did the same with the hope that they could reconnect conversation to the world.

For rivals, CA became a foil and scale was part of their criticism. John Gumperz's "interactional sociolinguistics," as it often came to be called, offered its own style of "conversational analysis" after all—wording that suggested that there were other ways to study conversation than only CA. This competing claim to conversation was made without fanfare, as Gumperz himself was not polemical. It was just that he would, as he would sometimes say, "listen more to Erving [Goffman] than to Manny [Schegloff]," as one former student from the 1970s reported. Gumperz did not like the way Schegloff had stripped down and autonomized interaction to the point that you could no longer appreciate how culture and "context" came to inflect conversation.

Those with one or both feet in anthropology agreed with this criticism but were more vocal and pointed. The late Michael Silverstein, a lead figure in what would soon coalesce as linguistic anthropology, opposed autonomized views of language. Silverstein sought what he called the "total linguistic fact" (cf. Mauss's "total social fact") against a mainstream disciplinary linguistics that, in a genealogy stretching from Saussure to Bloomfield to Chomsky, had tried to sever language from context—society, culture, history, and all else—in a bid to constitute it as an autonomous, unalloyed thing to know. This became a defining antagonism, and it was an antagonism that had been building for some time.

Let us recall briefly how linguistic anthropology came to care about scale so much, which in turn explains how it feels about interaction. Linguistic anthropology became a recognizable field only slowly as it got disentangled from overlapping approaches to the study of language-in-context. It became institutionally distinct in the early 1980s, and in America, as one of anthropology's four subfields. According to the subfield's own history of itself, it could claim belonging in anthropology thanks especially to Boas's holistic "science of man," which had encompassed cultural, archaeological, biological, and indeed linguistic life. Agitation for recognition—sometimes as "anthropological linguistics," sometimes as "linguistic anthropology"—was led by Dell Hymes in the early and mid-1960s in collaboration with Gumperz and others. In the '60s and early '70s, Hymes, Gumperz, and others also marched under the banner of "sociolinguistics," an even more expansive term that could include everything from quantitative urban dialectology to philosophical accounts of speech as social action. Scholars of language-in-context, their many differences notwithstanding, joined hands in opposition to the so-called Chomskyan cognitivist revolution, which represented the apogee of a view of language as an autonomous, irreducible object that could be shorn from context.[19] Hymes and Gumperz simultaneously made efforts to introduce ethnography to the study of language. They chartered an "ethnography of speaking" (which was soon stretched into a broader "ethnography of communication"), which featured a shift from studying language as a static object to a focus on speaking as a dynamic activity tethered to its social and cultural setting.[20] Language so conceived seemed more contextually entangled than ever. This new expansive orientation toward language became a point of distinction against a disciplinary linguistics that walled language off.

All of which is to say that the questions of whether language was bounded or porous, autonomous or embedded, in need of a science of its "own," or not— were points of serious contestation, and distinction, and it was within this state of ferment that anthropologists of language came to discover who they were.

As Constantine Nakassis observes, linguistic anthropology grew in the interstices between fields. "By being critically engaged with, and ambivalently situated between, linguistics and sociocultural anthropology, linguistic anthropology has made its interventions by, on the one hand, arguing that social life can't be thought of independently of the workings of language; and, on the other hand, by arguing against any account of language that would excise social and cultural context (however construed)." Given this positionality, no purified, autonomous, irreducible view of language would do, and "ultimately linguistic anthropological inquiry has attempted to base itself less on 'language' as its foundational object of study . . . than on articulating a space beyond 'language' precisely through a study of it(s limits)."[21]

Over and over, linguistic anthropologists would demonstrate, with increasing conceptual refinement, the hybridity and embeddedness of an ever hyphenated "language-in-context," an amalgam whose hyphens kept coming, agglutinating more and more things, expanding, encompassing. When we faced our wider publics in print, we chose our titles carefully. In many of our essays and books and seminars, we would often remind the world of our relevance and reach through a simple but bold titular formula, "Language and X," where x could be anything (and the more that thing was something other social scientists cared about or claimed as their own, the better). Language and . . . affect, gender, identity, race, materiality, media, nationalism, personhood, politics, political economy, power, religion, sexuality, social justice, technology, and so on.[22] And inevitably the *and*, which seemed to cleave neatly the two sides, was revealed to be an illusion, for in fact language was complexly enmeshed and not separate at all.

For linguistic anthropologists fascinated by discursive interaction in particular—social interaction mediated by language use—the same hybridizing
sensibility applied. We disliked CA's classic view of conversation as some
crypto-Chomskyan analog of language, as if conversation was the output of a
context-independent, rule-governed system. Against such a baptismal move
that tried to separate and purify this object of knowledge, the anthropologists
of interaction embraced what they took to be the inescapable hybridity and
embeddedness of face-to-face life. We sought the equivalent of what we might
call "the total interactional fact." About CA, Silverstein wrote acidly about
what he took to be their epistemological naivete. At a conference in the '90s, he
dismissed CA as a "surviving scientistic atavism in the study of discursive interaction," faulting it for its "fetishization of the moment-of-interaction frozen
in vitro by transcriptional techniques" which failed to see just how freighted
this whole science was with cultural intuitions and "context," and which tried
in vain to purify "conversation" of all this embeddedness.[23] It is telling that
even as the linguistic anthropologists drew deeply from Erving Goffman—
who himself had critiqued CA—many could not brook Goffman's own commitment to the autonomy of interaction. In the twilight of his career, Goffman
had cast what he had studied as "the interaction order," a "domain whose preferred method of study is microanalysis."[24] Even as Goffman was careful not to
wall off interaction, instead allowing for a "loose coupling" between micro and
macro orders, many anthropologists felt that he had treated interaction too
much like a world of its own, and this made them uncomfortable.

For linguistic anthropologists, then, there were quite a few reasons to reject the view that interaction was an ontologically distinct, scaled order. One
reason, again, had to do with sub- and inter-disciplinarity. It had to do with
the fact that this had been an interstitial field committed to an equally interstitial object. Another reason stemmed from an old ethnographic sensibility
that had advocated studying social life holistically, which linguistic anthropology inherited from cultural anthropology. But beyond these field-specific
motivations was the dialectic of social movement activism and scholarship
catalyzed in the late '60s and early '70s, which made interactionists of all
stripes worry anew about how their "small" object related to a wider world, a
worry that reached a fever pitch when the micro–macro wars later broke out.

A lot more trouble was on its way, too. Fields that embraced the small were
put on their heels once again as interests in globalization and transnational-
ism swept over disciplines in the 1990s. All this talk of movement, circula-
tion, and flows only made matters worse for the interactionists, whose subject, especially when it was called "conversation" or "face-to-face" interaction,
now looked smaller than ever. How blinkered these interactionists seemed.

It looked as if they had holed themselves up on spatiotemporal islands, as *extent*—as an aspect of observational scale—erupted into a serious methodological problem. To be sure, extent had been a problem many times before, as when some critics complained that the natural history–style fine-grained analysts—scholars like Ray Birdwhistell and others in the Natural History of an Interview (NHI) network—had been too casual if not reckless about sampling. In looking at so little data, how could they possibly *generalize*? Now the critique of extent was different: how could scholars of face-to-face interaction recognize the connections and commerce *among* sites, when they spent so much time stuck in only one or a few?

Many responded by dutifully adding sites, sometimes literally. If a "site" in a literal, fieldwork sense was a place for the researcher to be at or to sample from, then it would seem to have spatiotemporal extension, which meant that you could multiply sites to expand your epistemological reach. Through careful, "multisited" research design—a methodological push that came from many quarters in anthropology at the time—the linguistic anthropologists of discursive interaction found imaginative ways to study things that would have seemed beyond their reach, from the far-flung assemblages of global commodity chains to the transnational flow of cultural forms such as hip-hop.[25] Other stayed spatially focused on a few sites but looked across multiple instances of "the same" event or kind of event, as if to stretch the temporal envelope in order to see a larger trajectory or history of interaction. Stanton Wortham, for instance, experimented at tracking *meso*-level historical shifts in the formation of student identity across a single school year, examining how identities came together and either changed or got reinforced as classroom interactions built on each other, one after another.[26]

Along with other linguistic anthropologists, Wortham also simultaneously stretched the boundaries of events without doing so literally through fieldwork and data collection. Like many others he challenged the very idea that these events were as bounded as assumed. Collectively, linguistic anthropologists began to interrogate their units. They stressed their porosity and plasticity. As Asif Agha wrote, the effort was to break from an earlier scalar ontology of discursive interaction, present in influential notions such as the "speech event" and in Goffman's notion of the interaction order, which had envisioned "bounded episodes of social history in which persons encounter each other through communicative behaviors amenable to recording- and transcript-based study. . . ." This push for porosity and plasticity was not unlike what the cultural anthropologists were doing when they strained to break through the boundedness of the groupings and units that they too had once taken for granted.[27]

This was no end in itself. The point was not to throw up our hands and accept a messy congeries of crisscrossing signs that resisted analysis; instead, this was intended to open up for investigation the careful study and careful theorizing of event-to-event relations, of what was sometimes called interdiscursivity. In this, linguistic anthropologists found inspiration in the rediscovered writings of Mikhail Bakhtin and those in his circle. We began to marvel at all the ways that even a "single" instance of language use, which seemed tethered spatially and temporally to the immediate context of utterance, summoned or gestured toward speech from other times and places and people—which we studied with the help of concepts such as dialogism, heteroglossia, voicing, interdiscursivity, and intertextuality.

It wasn't only the anthropologists of talk and interaction who were busy finding solutions to the problems of scale. Solutions came from neighboring fields as well. In his late-'90s introduction to discourse analysis, for instance, sociolinguist James Gee leaned into the criticism and proposed a distinction between two kinds of discourse analysis that needed to be combined. There was "little-d discourse," which referred to everything the sociolinguists had been busy studying all along with their mediatic recordings and transcripts of spatiotemporally situated language use. To this he then added "Big-D" discourse—a D redolent of Foucauldian "discourse." Whatever else Big D did, it functioned as a sweeping conciliatory gesture toward *everything else* that the little-d scientists had observationally missed. Discourse analysis, in Gee's version of it, would do both at once, for only by yoking d/D would this science achieve its full relevance. The late sociolinguist and linguistic anthropologist Jan Blommaert found ways to domesticate the problem of scale by showing how you could study the way scalar experience gets created, negotiated, and transformed by actors themselves, by their language choices and language use; at the same time, he also pressed sociolinguistics to rethink itself in light of the global.[28]

Still, it was the linguistic anthropologists who for several reasons felt great urgency to address the problem of scale and demonstrate the truth of the total linguistic and total interactional fact.

Think that "political economy" and "language" are really worlds apart? Or that conversation and history necessarily exist at different ontological scales? The field's influential notion of "language ideology" and more recent framings such as "raciolinguistics" exposed the folly of thinking you could ever wall off language as an irreducible object. Asif Agha demonstrated both theoretically and empirically how you could dissect a temporally and spatially situated discursive text with acuity and care without ever getting stuck in either "micro" or "macro." "Things that last for seconds can have effects that last for years. Even physical tokens of discourse that have a fleeting durational existence (such as spoken utterances) can order and shape social relations of a much more perduring kind, ones that persist far longer than the initial speech token itself, whether through uptake in the subsequent activities of others, by incorporation into widely routinized practices that rely on and replay them, or by conversion into artifacts of a more durable kind."[29] Distinct observational scales exist, sure, but any scalar ontology that tries to put language at one scale and social relations at another is misguided.[30]

Besides the steady stream of theory and research detailing links and dialectics of various kinds between micro and macro, local and global, and cognate distinctions, the linguistic anthropologists of discursive interaction enacted a defense against scalar critics in print again and again. We'd remind them how our objects mattered. One expositional strategy was elegant in its simplicity. First, alight upon a "little" discrete chunk of language, which we usually transcribed so that it seemed smaller still and trapped on a page: a sitting target, it would seem, an illustration of everything wrong with this narrow science. But this was bait. Just when you thought we had trapped ourselves, through some scale-defying feat of analysis we would wriggle free, performatively showing how this fleeting, short stretch of discourse was in fact indexically far reaching, how it escaped its illusory confinement, how it was made up of signs that pointed this way and that and linked up with much, much more.[31] (Though our transcriptional performativity differed in purpose and effects from the conversation analysts, most of us have been just as invested in these texts.) What the linguistic anthropologists had hoped to adduce on a page with the help of mediatic recordings and transcripts was nothing less than embeddedness incarnate, the total discursive fact. It is hardly a surprise that a subfield accused of being narrow should commit itself to exploding this misconception time and again.

In a deeper and positive sense, the linguistic anthropologists of the total interactional fact would demonstrate to the humanities and social sciences how we could concretize and grasp what many scholars sought—the *linguistic* of the "linguistic turn," the *practice* of "practice theory"—through close attention to discursive interaction. We would be able to see what others had hoped to see, and we would do so in sharper, more vivid detail—often with the aid of recordings and transcripts and fine-grained analysis.

More than merely an empirical feat, the linguistic anthropologists thus often positioned themselves in this way as semioticians of practice who leaned into their observational scale as a strength, for if you ignored the pervasive linguistic and semiotic dimensions of power, hierarchy, and so on, you'd see a forest, sure, but it would remain hazy, indistinct. Not unlike certain feminist inflections of communication science, it was as if some had argued that only through knowledge of the "nitty-gritty"—as Lynn O'Connor put it—would you be able to see how power is exercised interpersonally, which then also made it possible to intervene, if that is what you wished to do. Even as this argument has taken many different forms and has not always assigned the same weight to interactional life, it has remained a vital way to justify scholarship. In a recent, provocative theme issue on language and white supremacy, for instance, coeditors Krystal Smalls, Arthur Spears, and Jonathan Rosa curate essays that demonstrate "how carefully attending to language, discourse, and signs provides particular ways of grabbing hold of White supremacy's slippery logics, organizing principles, dynamic infrastructures, and diverse practices."[32] The promise, again, is that a close look—sometimes with the help of transcripts of talk—can reveal what we might otherwise miss about the pervasive logics and sweeping formations that cause such harm, not only so that we can understand them better but also so that we can intervene. Here again is a science of discursive life fully compatible with social justice activism.

Even as linguistic anthropologists of all stripes have learned to counter the charge that we pore over intrinsically small things with excessive granularity, privately, in grant writing, we tend to be more conciliatory. We tend to reassure reviewers that the significance of our study does not of course stem from our microanalytic methods alone and that we will compensate by means of addition. Methodologically, we promise to "combine" our close, fine-grained styles of analysis with more expansive ethnographic methods, for instance. Scholars of interaction in other fields, again, not just in anthropology, have similarly inherited a basic defensiveness about their subject matter and methods, which alternates from very public arguments against scalar critics to quiet concessions that suggest they secretly recognize their own epistemological limits.[33] All this proactive and reactive posturing suggests how the problem of scale has lived on.

I will not continue trying to recount here all the imaginative responses and solutions to the challenges of scale, because that would require surveying no less than the entire landscape of contemporary scholarship. It is no exaggeration to say that social science research on interaction in fields like anthropology remains so indebted to these challenges that if we were to somehow subtract this preoccupation with scale, little would remain.

And some have tried very hard to subtract scale. There have always been interactionists who critiqued the idea that their methods and object were narrowly micro, and, as we have seen, some have tried to dismiss the micro–macro problem as no real problem at all. Outside their fold, too, past critics have gone after scalar discourse before. In the late 1980s, for instance, the sociologist Stephan Fuchs questioned the alleged "concreteness" of interaction, which had often been part of the pitch for studying interaction mediatically—with recordings and transcripts—against all those gauzy macrosocial "abstractions" that you could never really see. As Fuchs wrote pointedly, "the concepts of 'individual' or 'interaction' for example, are in no sense less abstract and more empirical than, say, the concept of 'state' or the Watson-Crick model of DNA."[34] Early in the '80s, Erving Goffman himself was already leaning in this direction, writing that he did *not* "subscribe to the notion that face-to-face behavior is any more real, any less of an arbitrary abstraction, than what we think of as the dealings between two corporations. . . ."[35]

Bruno Latour brought the matter to a head: "people are only too ready to accept that . . . abstractions like structure, context, or society should be criticized," but they are convinced that there is something concrete and local and micro about the abstraction called interaction. In a characteristically mischievous exercise, a series of "gymnastics," as he called it, he went on to pick apart intuitions about the scale of interaction until you were not sure how small or large, local or nonlocal, micro or macro interaction was. No interaction is "isotopic," because "what is acting at the same moment in any place is coming from many other places, may distant materials, and many far-away actors." No interaction is "synchronic," because the pieces it comprises did not all begin at the same time. Interactions are not "synoptic" either, says Latour, in the sense that only some participants are visible and focal at any given point. Those who inhabit participant roles like "speaker" and "hearer" make up only the official roster of actors present. Nor are interactions "homogeneous," his fourth and related gymnastic. The kinds of agents that make up interactions are not necessarily the same type, and some aren't even human. The "relays through which action is carried out," he writes, "do not have the same material quality all along," but instead there is a "crowd of nonhuman, nonsubjective, nonlocal participants who gather to help carry out the course of action. . . ." Interactions are not, finally, "isobaric"—a meteorological trope, Latour's attempt to speak of the varied "pressures" exerted by the manifold agents of action. Taken together, these gymnastics suggested that it is "impossible to start anywhere that can be said to be 'local.' "[36]

Latour wanted us to be "indifferent" to scale, not because scale is illusory but because he did not want to "settle scale in advance"; he wanted to provide actors "enough space," he wrote, "to deploy their own contradictory gerunds: scaling, zooming, embedding, 'panoraming,' individualizing, and so on." When his negative propositions are applied to interaction, they are supposed to function as theoretical "clamps" to prevent the analyst from prematurely jumping scale, so that the scale-jumping virtuosity of participants can become something we study.

For their part, linguistic anthropologists had tried indifference before and had engaged in their own gymnastics for years. Again and again, they had challenged assumptions about the scalar dimensionalities of language, discourse, and interaction. I too have done this, and more than once,[37] and yet none of this could eliminate the trouble with scale because all of this effort had been a response to a problem that we, and others, continued to presume. As linguistic anthropologists would be primed to admit, with due deference to Bakhtin, our responses were replies that interdiscursively kept the old conversation about scale going.

⋆

My point of all this genealogical reflection is not to try to uproot some pernicious idea holed up deep in scholarship, as if scale itself were an illusion to be dispelled. I offer this critical reflection on scale ultimately so that we can better study scale-making as part of knowledge practices, not just in the world but in our fields, for we cannot do the former if we don't look more carefully at ourselves. Indeed, none of the attempts thus far at razing scale has succeeded in making the debates and troubles over scale go away, because we have not appreciated just how generative scale has been for *us*, in terms of defining our objects of knowledge and offering a platform for debate, for distinction and counter-distinction, for envisioning how we can and should relate to each other.

As with most forms of critique, I do hold onto the hope that such reflection can open up alternative futures, but this can only occur if we take more seriously the scalar projects to which we have been committed and the troubles scale has often caused us. I have tracked in these pages many kinds of struggles—practical, epistemological, ontological, moral, political—and have invited us to consider how these struggles have sometimes resulted in durable dispositions for fields as they emerge, quite often agonistically, in relation to each other. Mind, body, interaction, text; state, economy, infrastructure, institution—all ready-made objects that tend to be scaled differentially and that, in turn, differentiate those committed to them. The same for observational scales, whose paired and usually morally imbued terms, "thick" and "thin," "close" and "distant," and so on, are still very much with us. Unsettling the scale of one object, interaction, may well unsettle all the objects defined in relation to it, because scale has been a means of differentiation and contestation within the humanities and social sciences.

Even as fields both internally and externally distinguish themselves by scale, scale has very often promised to hold everything together; at times, it has even been used to argue for collaborations in which all parties accept or at least tolerate different scalar commitments. These efforts usually rest on two concessions. First, that epistemological scales do limit what we know. (Try studying hominin phylogeny with a shallow time depth, for instance, and your study goes nowhere.) Second, that there is no one scale that offers a totalizing, synoptic view. What follows from these two premises is the problem of scalar "mismatches" and scalar "multiplicity." That is, what happens when the scale of observation isn't appropriate for the realities you seek to know, and, ontologically, what happens when the realities you seek to know "require" that you combine or alternate among several different observational scales? Might these problems be solved by "collaboration" and by coordinating and calibrating diverse findings?

In the philosophy of science, there is an area of thought called the "unity of science." To simplify brutally, its unenviable task is to reconcile the claims of different sciences with the assumption that they address the same reality. In the past, such metascientific synthesis made use of visual and textual technologies like tree diagrams and encyclopedias that arranged and showed relations among knowledges. In many quarters, scale has been recruited to do this labor of unification, offering a way to coordinate and calibrate disciplines—to show how each can do its part and interact "well."

More than most, for instance, political ecologists of late have rallied diverse sciences with scale. Stressing that imminent environmental disaster in the Anthropocene requires that sciences work together by working across multiple scales, they have rushed to create new forms of collaboration—not necessarily utopian forms, but new nonetheless.[38] Or take many recent interpersonal experts in anti-racist or trauma-informed pedagogy, who hope to find new ways for students to talk, listen, and respond to one other. To transform what they take to be a diffuse "culture" of a college campus, they sometimes team up with organizational sociologists who specialize in how institutions work. In the past and even now, we may remember that the micro-macro distinction itself has been proposed as a way to hold together, under one roof, scholars with very different sensibilities. As we turn our reflexive attention toward the study of scale at home, within and across disciplines, we may well wonder what forms of scholarly interaction—and predicaments—await us.

Acknowledgments

The momentum to write this book began to build during a spirited multi-year collaboration that I had the pleasure of co-leading with E. Summerson Carr from the University of Chicago. Our collaboration started with talks and workshops and culminated in a 2016 book, *Scale: Discourse and Dimensions of Social Life*. I remain indebted to these conversations.

I began research on *A History of Scale* in 2015–2016 at Stanford's Center for Advanced Study in the Behavioral Sciences (CASBS) through a Lenore Annenberg and Wallis Annenberg Fellowship in Communication. There I learned especially from the historians. On the history of science, I owe a special debt to Nicholas Rasmussen. I am grateful as well to historians Louis Hyman and Dan Rodgers, and from others in our cohort, especially philosopher Andrew Chignell and sociologist Elisabeth Clemens. During 2018–2019, I made progress on this book as a Richard and Lillian Ives Fellow at the Institute for the Humanities, University of Michigan, and thank Peggy McCracken for cultivating such a stimulating and supportive interdisciplinary community there. At the start of this research, and its end, I found inspiration in conversations with the historian of science Rebecca Lemov.

In addition to the Michicagoan group and *Scale* volume, two other collaborations have shaped this book. When I started reading in media history for this book in 2016, I began a collaboration with Miyako Inoue, a linguistic anthropologist whose brilliant scholarship on media technologies in Japan continues to be an inspiration. Matthew Hull regularly joined our conversations and taught me much about the intersection of semiotic anthropology and science and technology studies. Under the banner of technosemiotics, we co-organized sessions and workshops designed to bring linguistic anthropology into closer dialogue with science and technology studies, media anthropology, and media history.

In 2021 I received astute feedback on a chapter draft in a Michicagoan faculty seminar hosted by Constantine Nakassis, which included Richard Bauman, E. Summerson Carr, Susan Gal, Matthew Hull, Judith Irvine, Alaina Lemon, Webb Keane, Bruce Mannheim, Barbra Meek, Susan Philips, and Kristina Wirtz. For comments on other excerpts from the book, I thank Miyako Inoue for a reading session she convened in 2019 at Stanford, which included Ilana Gershon, Matthew Hull, and Kabir Tambar. In 2022, I benefited enormously from a book workshop with Monica Heller, Matthew Hull, Miyako Inoue, Rebecca Lemov, and Jack Sidnell.

For reading and commenting on portions of the book, I thank Frederick Erickson, Richard Handler, Hugh (Bud) Mehan, Seth Watter, and Charles Zuckerman. I must especially thank Seth Watter, who has conducted his own illuminating research on the history of media in the interaction sciences and was generous in sharing archival leads and materials.

I am indebted to many other people for conversations and correspondence over the last few years, including Molefi K. Asante, Richard Bauman, Don Brenneis, Carlton Cornett, Scott Curtis, Martha Davis, Patrick Feasters, Susan Gal, John S. Gilkeson, Charles Goodwin, Marjorie (Candy) Goodwin, Monica Heller, Arlie Hochschild, Judith Irvine, Webb Keane, Alice Beck Kehoe, Adam Kendon, Stuart Kirsch, Wendy Leeds-Hurwitz, Heather Love, Bruce Mannheim, Hugh (Bud) Mehan, Marlyn Merritt, Yasmin Moll, Lynn O'Connor, Susan U. Philips, Anita Pomerantz, Nathan Sayre, Jack Sidnell, Michael Silverstein, Benjamin Smith, Jürgen Streeck, Deborah Tannen, Fred Turner, Naoko Wake, Jim Weil, Candace West, and Kathryn Woolard.

As always, I remain indebted in so many ways to my former teachers in anthropology from the University of Pennsylvania: Asif Agha, Greg Urban, and Stanton Wortham, as well as Fred Erickson, who first introduced me to the study of interaction. I thank colleagues and students here at the University of Michigan, who recently served as an invaluable audience for me as I shared the book's argument through the Roy L. Rappaport Lectures. Portions of the book's argument were shared through many other talks. I especially wish to thank Henning Engelke and Sophia Gräfe for an invitation to present at "The Movement Movement: Histories of Microanalysis at the Intersection of Film, Science, and Art," convened at Philipps-Universität Marburg, Germany, in 2021.

I am grateful for access to various archives, including at the Cummings Center for the History of Psychology at the University of Akron; the De-Witt Wallace Institute for the History of Psychiatry at Weill Cornell Medical

College; the University of Chicago; at Harvard, Baker Library Special Collections at Harvard Business School, Countway Library's Center for the History of Medicine, Harvard University Archives, and Tozzer Library Special Collections; the Alan Mason Chesney Medical Archives at Johns Hopkins University; The Library of Congress; Maryland State Archives; the Commonwealth of Massachusetts State Archives; University of Michigan's Bentley Library; the National Anthropological Archives; the National Anthropological Film Collection; Rockefeller Foundation Archives; University of California, Santa Cruz; University of Pennsylvania's Museum of Archaeology and Anthropology; University of Pittsburgh's Falk Library, Rare Book and Special Collections; Stanford University Archives and archives for CASBS at Stanford; and Yale University's Sterling Memorial Library.

Before and during the pandemic, archivists and librarians offered invaluable assistance, including Lizette Barton, Maria A. Day, Meredith Eliassen, Jason Gonzales, Margaret Hogan, Len Levin, Hailey Mooney, Alexa Pearce, Alex Pezzati, Marisa Shaari, and Mark White. For granting me access to the Bateson Papers, I also thank Phillip Guddemi of the Bateson Idea Group. For their superb research assistance, I thank Alex Forrest, Nichole Grimes, Scott Ross, and Charles Zuckerman. Karson Schenk produced lovely illustrations from old video frame grabs, and Isabella Furth offered an insightful editorial pass.

The University of Michigan supported this book at various stages, through the Associate Professor Support Fund and an Advance Faculty Summer Writing Grant, and especially through generous funding to publish this book as open access.

Portions of part 1 appeared as a 2019 article, "Fine-Grained Analysis: Talk Therapy, Media, and the Microscopic Science of the Face-to-Face," *Isis* 110 (1): 24–47. Chapter 3 includes adapted material from a 2019 article, "What is an Anthropology of Gesture?" *Gesture* 18 (2–3): 173–208 (published in a special issue edited by Heather Brooks and Olivier Le Guen). Chapter 7 includes sections from a 2025 chapter, "Free Speech, without Listening? Liberalism and the Problem of Reception," from *Freedoms of Speech: Anthropological Perspectives on Language, Ethics, and Power* (Candea, Matei, et al. [ed.]), Toronto: University of Toronto Press.

Several remarkable scholars of interaction passed while I was working on this book, including, most recently, Janet Bavelas and Adam Kendon, but I must single out two losses: Charles (Chuck) Goodwin, one of the most vital scholars of social interaction whose infectious curiosity and professional vision made us all look *again*. And Michael Silverstein, whose scintillating brilliance and tireless institution building in a real sense made the contemporary field of linguistic anthropology and whose scholarship continues to inspire us all.

I thank my family—Yasmin, Zayn, and Zadie—for their love and patience, and my parents Rhoda and Theodore Lempert for a lifetime of unconditional support for someone who fell far from the tree.

Notes

Preface

1. See Jef C. Verhoeven, "An Interview With Erving Goffman, 1980," *Research on Language and Social Interaction* 26, no. 3 (1993): 317–48.

Chapter One

1. Ibram Kendi, *How to Be an Antiracist* (New York: One World, 2019), 46; Chester Pierce, "Offensive Mechanisms," in *The Black Seventies*, ed. Floyd B. Barbour (Boston: P. Sargent, 1970), 266; "microscopic fashion" of racism, "A Theory of Racism," 8, Chester M. Pierce, Chester M. Pierce Papers, Harvard University, Countway Library of Medicine, box 06, folder 24. In theorizing racism, the micro prefix in microaggressions indicates not only a "subtle" racist behavior but a behavior which, taken individually, is a relatively "*minor* insult or put down" (emphasis mine). "By itself a single verbal and/or kinetic microaggression is relatively innocuous," yet "with cumulative, never-ending accretion of microaggressions, the result is to render the victim defeated, demoralized and tyrannized" (ibid., 17).

2. Kendi, *How to Be an Antiracist*, 46–47.

3. Pierce, "Offensive Mechanisms," 268.

4. Ruha Benjamin, *Viral Justice: How We Grow the World We Want* (Princeton: Princeton University Press, 2022), 29; Matthew Claire, "Public Thinker: Ruha Benjamin on Uprooting Oppression and Seeding Justice," *Public Books* (April 11, 2023), https://www.publicbooks.org/public-thinker-ruha-benjamin-on-uprooting-oppression-and-seeding-justice/.

5. Richard Bauman, *Let Your Words Be Few: Symbolism of Speaking and Silence among Seventeenth-Century Quakers* (New York: Cambridge University Press, 1983), 52–53.

6. C. H. Lüthy, "Atomism, Lynceus, and the Fate of Seventeenth-Century Microscopy," *Early Science and Medicine* 1, no. 1 (1996): 3.

7. *Oxford English Dictionary*, 2nd ed., (Oxford: Oxford University Press, 1996). It would be wrong to get overinvested in any divide between the literal and figurative, because in contemporary usage, tropic microscopy is not necessarily hitched interdiscursively to the instrument of the microscope.

8. This was no simple mediatic repurposing, especially as camera operators, photographers, and filmmakers joined research teams. Historians have started to examine how this incorporation

led to the emergence of "behavioral film." This scholarship resists any easy separation between "aesthetic" from "epistemological" demands—art here, science there. In his reanalysis of the famous "Doris" film used by the "Natural History of an Interview" group (see part 1), for instance, Henning Engelke examines "how the separated practices of filmmaking and analysis were still entangled with each other, and how, in the perceived gap between these practices, epistemological assumptions about interaction and film developed." Engelke, "Perception, Awareness, and Film Practice: A Natural History of the 'Doris Film,'" in *Holisms of Communication: The Early History of Audio-Visual Sequence Analysis*, ed. James McElvenny and Andrea Ploder (Berlin: Language Science Press, 2021), p.112. See also Bernard Dionysius Geoghegan, "The Family as Machine: Film, Infrastructure, and Cybernetic Kinship in Suburban America," *Grey Room* 66 (2017): 70–101; Seth Barry Watter, "Scrutinizing: Film and the Microanalysis of Behavior," *Grey Room* 66 (2017): 32–69; and for other sciences, see work such as Lisa Cartwright *Screening the Body: Tracing Medicine's Visual Culture* (Minneapolis: University of Minnesota Press, 1995) and Scott Curtis *The Shape of Spectatorship: Art, Science, and Early Cinema in Germany* (New York: Columbia University Press, 2015).

9. E. Summerson Carr and Michael Lempert, *Scale: Discourse and Dimensions of Social Life* (Oakland: University of California Press, 2016).

10. See, for instance, Kelty's reflections on the mereology of most liberal theory, with its underlying assumption of what he terms the "contributory autonomy" of individuals. *The Participant: A Century of Participation in Four Stories* (Chicago: University of Chicago Press, 2019), 62 et passim.

11. In *Scale*, Carr and Lempert, we discussed such conversions as one manifestation of *interscalarity*, on which see part 3, "Micropolitics."

12. Ecologists, Sayre adds, do not usually distinguish observational from operational scale. As for grain and extent, he draws on definitions like this: "Grain refers to the finest level of spatial or temporal resolution available within a given data set. Extent refers to the size of the study area or the duration of the study" (M. G. Turner, V. H. Dale, and R. H. Gardner, "Predicting across Scales: Theory Development and Testing," *Landscape Ecology* 3, no. 3–4 [1989]: 247; cited in Nathan F. Sayre, "Ecological and Geographical Scale: Parallels and Potential for Integration," *Progress in Human Geography* 29, no. 3 [2005]: 281).

13. Nathan F. Sayre, "Scales and Polities," in *The Routledge Handbook of Political Ecology*, ed. Thomas Albert Perreault, Gavin Bridge, and James McCarthy (London: Routledge, Taylor & Francis Group, 2015), 507.

14. In her essay on thin description and the politics of scale, Heather Love recalls Greenblatt's trope of "foveation" which he used to think through issues of scale in the hermeneutics of literary reading. (Love, "Close Reading and Thin Description," *Public Culture* 25, no. 3 [2013]: 401–34); Greenblatt, S., "The Touch of the Real," *Representations*, Summer, no. 59 [1997]: 14–29.)

15. Clifford Geertz, "Thick Description: Toward an Interpretive Theory of Culture," in *The Interpretation of Cultures* (New York: Basic Books, 1973), 21–22; Gilbert Ryle, *Collected Papers Volume 2: Collected Essays 1929–1968* (London: Routledge, 2009 [1971]).

16. Lily Hope Chumley, "Qualia and Ontology: Language, Semiotics, and Materiality; an Introduction," *Signs and Society* 5, (2017), S1; see also Lily Hope Chumley and Nicholas Harkness, "Introduction: QUALIA," *Anthropological Theory* 13, no. 1–2 (2013): 3–11. See also Webb Keane's discussion of Peircean qualisigns (Keane, "Semiotics and the Social Analysis of Material Things," *Language & Communication* 43 [2003], 414ff.)

17. Bruno Latour, *Reassembling the Social: An Introduction to Actor-Network Theory*, (Oxford: Oxford University Press, 2005), 185.

18. In cultural anthropology, see especially Robert Oppenheim's actor-network theory (ANT) inspired ethnography of place-making in Korea, *Kyŏngju Things: Assembling Place* (Ann Arbor: University of Michigan Press, 2008). On scale in social anthropology itself, see Marilyn Strathern's *The Relation: Issues in Complexity and Scale*, (Cambridge, UK: Prickly Pear Press, 1995). See also Carr and Lempert (*Scale*, Introduction), where we take note of many efforts beside our own to study scale-making ethnographically.

19. Gabrielle Hecht, "Interscalar Vehicles for an African Anthropocene: On Waste, Temporality, and Violence," *Cultural Anthropology* 33, no. 1 (2018): 114.

20. Erving Goffman, *Behavior in Public Places: Notes on the Social Organization of Gatherings*, (New York: Free Press, 1966 [1963]).

21. In speaking of scalar ontologies and multiple versions of interactional reality, I gesture with appreciation to Annemarie Mol ("Ontological Politics. A Word and Some Questions," *Sociological Review* 47, 1 [1999]: 74–89; *The Body Multiple: Ontology in Medical Practice* [Durham, NC: Duke University Press, 2002].) While I cannot develop this here, it is worth considering whether her analytic tropes of "performance" and "enactment"—especially with their suggestions of locatability—reinstates a familiar, spatiotemporally bounded scalar ontology of practice even as she wishes to make ontological multiplicity ethnographically manifest.

22. Here there is a whole literature in linguistic anthropology and adjacent fields on matters of "interdiscursivity" and "intertextuality," which was inspired by the rediscovery of the Bakhtin circle. See chap. 11, "Conclusion."

23. John Durham Peters, *Speaking into the Air: A History of the Idea of Communication* (Chicago: University of Chicago Press, 1999), 21. Peters argued that experiences with "long distance" communication technologies were tropically incorporated into ideologies of communication in the form of a "gap." Normatively, such a gap must be crossed or otherwise closed for intersubjective communication to occur. On gaps and efforts to close them, see Alaina Lemon's "Touching the Gap: Social Qualia and Cold War Contact," *Anthropological Theory* 13, no. 1–2 (2013): 67–88; Lemon, *Technologies for Intuition: Cold War Circles and Telepathic Rays* (Oakland: University of California Press, 2018). Other media histories have similarly identified shifting conceptions of speech and communication. See, for example, Jennifer Petersen's account of changing construals of "speech" in US First Amendment rulings. (Petersen, *How Machines Came to Speak: Media Technologies and Freedom of Speech* [Durham, NC: Duke University Press, 2022]). See Miyako Inoue's work on the way inscriptional technologies in Japan helped produce the idea of public speech and speaking. (Inoue, *The Stenographer's Invisible Hand: How Did Speech Become Language in Modern Japan?* [Unpublished]; Miyako Inoue, "Stenography and Ventriloquism in Late Nineteenth-Century Japan," *Language & Communication* 31, no. 3 [2011]: 181–90).

24. Hannah Landecker, "Creeping, Drinking, Dying: The Cinematic Portal and the Microscopic World of the Twentieth-Century Cell," *Science in Context* 24, no. 03 (2011): 381–416.

25. In the eighteenth century, this kind of argument blossomed into physicotheology, where "the hand of God was recognized in the intricate construction of the smallest living beings." Marian Fournier, *The Fabric of Life: Microscopy in the Seventeenth Century* (Baltimore: Johns Hopkins University Press, 1996), 29.

26. Catherine Wilson, *The Invisible World: Early Modern Philosophy and the Invention of the Microscope* (Princeton: Princeton University Press, 1995), 228.

27. Strathern, *The Relation*, 6. I write of "level" and "scale" as if they were synonymous, only because this represents a familiar ontological stance on scale.

28. Wilson, *The Invisible World*.

29. There were exceptions. Hooke waxed poetic about seaweed, for instance, noting how the "plant is cover'd over with a most curious kind of carv'd work, which consists of a texture much resembling a Honey-comb." In a famous, grand illustration, he showed off the fantastic regularities of the drone fly's eye, as if to reassure readers that as you ascend the great chain of being from minerals to vegetables to animals, things do get more orderly, more geometrically intricate.

30. Wilson, *The Invisible World*, 244 et passim. It bears repeating that microscopy, like other forms of technologically mediated scrutiny, does not automatically engender a world. Telescopes in the latter part of the sixteenth century, in England and Italy, for instance, were often sought because they folded ordinary space—as in military operations where one spies an enemy from afar. No world is disclosed. One simply sees the target object as one would see it were one standing closer (see, for example, Lüthy, "Atomism, Lynceus, and the Fate of Seventeenth-Century Microscopy"). Compare with natural philosophers who argued, as Hooke did, that by means of the telescope "the Heavens are open'd."

31. Landecker, "Creeping, Drinking, Dying," 385.

32. Landecker, "Creeping, Drinking, Dying." Hooke's *Micrographia* dwelled on this dissonance between magnified and unmagnified appearances for other reasons, arguably, to demonstrate the very need for an empirical science whose instruments could overcome limited human senses. See Fournier, *The Fabric of Life*, 98–99; see also, for example, Christa Knellwolf, "Robert Hooke's Micrographia and the Aesthetics of Empiricism," *The Seventeenth Century* 16, no. 1 (2001): 177–200.

33. Walter Charleton, *Physiologia Epicuro-Gassendo-Charltoniana* (1654), 97 cited in Wilson, *The Invisible World*, 57.

34. Fournier, *The Fabric of Life*, 167.

35. Malebranche, *Search after Truth*, 31. cited in Wilson, *The Invisible World*, 185. See especially Wilson's discussion of Pascal, ibid., 190.

36. Wilson, *The Invisible World*, 190–91.

37. Indeed, Wilson (*The Invisible World*, 61) argues that "subvisible material causes of the most obscure phenomena drove out explanations that involved spiritual entities or correspondences."

38. See Asif Agha's *Language and Social Relations* ([Cambridge, UK: Cambridge University Press, 2007], 11 et passim) for a discussion of the way mereological relations in social theory are commonly thought to map onto the micro–macro distinction.

39. As for contention, we can think, for instance, of twentieth-century debates among realists and antirealists over the ontology of groups. On the mereology of "part" and related words, see introductions such as by Giorgio Lando, *Mereology: A Philosophical Introduction*, (London: Bloomsbury, 2017), chap. 1. See also Strathern's discussions of what she has called the "merographic," a notion inspired by but distinct from philosophical mereology (Strathern, *After Nature* [Cambridge, UK: Cambridge University Press, 1992].)

40. Some historians of science may wish to subsume scale and its troubles within a broader history of "observation" (on which, see an important volume, by Lorraine Daston and Elizabeth Lunbeck, *Histories of Scientific Observation* [Chicago: University of Chicago Press, 2011].). Scale does lurk in histories of scientific observation, but not all scalar troubles center on or start with observation; sometimes ontological scales (local–global, interpersonal–structural, etc.) come apart for other reasons.

41. On "deep time," see a volume by Andrew Shryock and Daniel Lord Smail, eds., *Deep History: The Architecture of Past and Present* (Berkeley: University of California Press, 2011), and compare with an edited volume from the same year that revisits the synchronic, spatial vastness

of the "world system," by David Palumbo-Liu, Bruce Robbins, and Nirvana Tanoukhi, *Immanuel Wallerstein and the Problem of the World: System, Scale, Culture* (Durham, NC: Duke University Press, 2011).

42. The names for this object of knowledge vary, and this variation matters. "Face-to-face interaction," "social interaction," "conversation," "small groups," "talk-in-interaction"—these and others have telling differences that often reveal contestation over what exactly is being studied and how best to study it. I do not treat such terms as substitutes for each other, as if lurking behind it all were some stable referent called interaction. At several points in the stories that follow, I will pause and note some of these competing framings. Needless to say, even when fields settle upon a shared name, this guarantees nothing about their similarity. We need only recall the wildly resonant term "discourse," with its rich scholarly—and polemical—life during the so-called linguistic turn of decades past. As this term took off, various brands of "discourse analysis" arose, each laying claim to discourse even as they disagreed over what discourse meant, why it mattered, and how to understand it best.

43. Talcott Parsons, cited in Paul Erickson et al., *How Reason Almost Lost Its Mind: The Strange Career of Cold War Rationality* (Chicago: University of Chicago Press, 2013), 115.

44. I thank an anonymous reviewer for proposing this fitting, parallel caption, interactionalization.

45. For an illustration of this processual sensibility in linguistic anthropology, see Silverstein "'Cultural' Concepts and the Language-Culture Nexus," *Current Anthropology* 45, no. 5 (2004): 621–52. Evidence of this sensibility can be seen generally in the field's desire to processualize analytic terms, turning from "text" and "context," for instance, to "entextualization" and simultaneous "co(n)textualization" (Michael Silverstein and Greg Urban, *Natural Histories of Discourse* [Chicago: University of Chicago Press, 1996]). For recent reflections on processualization in linguistic anthropology, see Charles H. P. Zuckerman, "Don't Gamble for Money with Friends," *American Ethnologist* 47, no. 4 (2020): 432–46. Compare with processualism in sociology, which also owes much to the legacy of American pragmatism, as Andrew Abbott suggests (*Processual Sociology* [Chicago: University of Chicago Press, 2016]).

46. Judith T. Irvine, "Going Upscale: Scales and Scale-Climbing as Ideological Projects," in *Scale*, 213–31.

47. Peter Harrison, "Angels on Pinheads and Needles' Points," *Notes and Queries* 63, no. 1 (2016): 45–47.

48. "White Supremacy Culture—Still Here," 2021, accessed August 28, 2023, https://www .whitesupremacyculture.info/, 26.

49. In linguistic anthropology, see, for example, theme issues on racialization (Hilary Parsons Dick and Kristina Wirtz, "Racializing Discourses," *Journal of Linguistic Anthropology* 21 [2011]: E2–E10) and on white supremacy (Krystal A. Smalls, Arthur K. Spears, and Jonathan Rosa, "Language and White Supremacy," *Journal of Linguistic Anthropology* 31, no. 2 [2021]: 149–311) as well as numerous articles and books.

Part One

1. David Shakow, "The Recorded Psychoanalytic Interview as an Objective Approach to Research in Psychoanalysis," *Psychoanalytic Quarterly* 29 (1960): 90.

2. See Sigmund Freud et al., *The Standard Edition of the Complete Psychological Works of Sigmund Freud*, 24 vols. (London: Hogarth Press, 1966), 1414; Shakow, "The Recorded Psychoanalytic Interview as an Objective Approach to Research in Psychoanalysis," 83.

Chapter Two

1. This chapter can be read alongside recent scholarship on psychiatry, recording technologies, and the sciences of communication. See Seth Watter who examines scholars like Eliot Chapple (discussed in part 2) who leveraged his proprietary interaction recorder for psychodiagnosis. (Seth Barry Watter, "Interaction Chronograph: The Administration of Equilibrium," *Grey Room*, no. 79 [2020]: 40–77.) For a recent survey of recording technologies in psychiatry, see Hadar Levy-Landesberg and Amit Pinchevski, "The Recording Cure: A Media Genealogy of Recorded Voice in Psychotherapy," *Theory, Culture & Society* 40, no. 6 (November 30, 2022): 125–46, https://doi.org/10.1177/02632764221135553. See also Katie Joice, "Mothering in the Frame: Cinematic Microanalysis and the Pathogenic Mother, 1945–67," *History of the Human Sciences* 20, no. 10 (2020): 1–27; see as well, Felix E. Reitmann, "Mother-Blaming Revisited: Gender, Cinematography, and Infant Research in the Heyday of Psychoanalysis," *History of the Human Sciences* (forthcoming). On the indexicalized receptivity of machines in clinical psychodiagnostics, see, for example, Beth M. Semel, "The Body Audible: From Vocal Biomarkers to a Phrenology of the Throat," *Somatosphere*, September 24, 2020, http://somatosphere.net/2020 /the-body-audible.html/; and Beth M. Semel, "Listening Like a Computer: Attentional Tensions and Mechanized Care in Psychiatric Digital Phenotyping," *Science, Technology, & Human Values* 47, no. 2 (2022): 266–90. On the way videographic testimony can preserve indexicalized markers of collective trauma, see Amit Pinchevski, *Transmitted Wounds: Media and the Mediation of Trauma* (New York: Oxford University Press, 2019), chap. 2.

2. Freud et al., *The Standard Edition*, 4619. On Freud's personal memory: Gail S. Reed, Howard B. Levine, and Jorge L. Ahumada, *On Freud's "Screen Memories"* (London: Karnac Books Ltd, 2015). Strachey's remark is cited in Mikkel Borch-Jacobsen and Sonu Shamdasani, *The Freud Files: An Inquiry into the History of Psychoanalysis* (Cambridge, UK: Cambridge University Press, 2012), 195.

3. Sigmund Freud, "Recommendations to Physicians Practicing Psychoanalysis," in *The Standard Edition* (1912): 112. Freud's "actual" receptivity is another matter, as is the whole question of how "listening" has been variously configured as technique, ideal, and semiotic ideology. On Rogerian listening, see, for instance, Katja Guenther, " 'Um, mm-h, yeah': Carl Rogers, Phonographic Recordings, and the Making of Therapeutic Listening," *History of Psychology* 25, no. 3 (2022): 191–210. For a recent ethnography of psychoanalytic listening, see Xochitl Marsilli-Vargas's *Genres of Listening: An Ethnography of Psychoanalysis in Buenos Aires* (Durham, NC: Duke University Press, 2022).

4. Freud et al., *The Standard Edition*, 3508.

5. On semiotic ideology, which Webb Keane glosses as "underlying assumptions about what signs are, what functions signs serve, and what consequences they might produce," see Keane's "On Semiotic Ideology," *Signs and Society* 6, no. 1 [2018]: 64–87), as well as related discussions by Susan Gal and Judith Irvine, *Signs of Difference: Language and Ideology in Social Life* (Cambridge, UK: Cambridge University Press, 2019).

6. Published posthumously, Harry Stack Sullivan, "The Psychiatric Interview," *Psychiatry* 14, no. 4 (1951): 362.

7. Again, I use indexicalization not as a caption for what is actually happening semiotically but rather as a label for a key facet of a semiotic ideology. I intend this as an ethnographic shorthand and approximation of what actors themselves desired and experienced when it came to understanding therapeutic talk and, later, talk in general. Semiotic anthropologists would prefer *dicentization*. As Ball writes, this Peircean inspired notion invites us to consider a basic

ethnographic and semiotic question, "How do actors make indexical connections where before they were not present, only latent, or invisible?" (Ball, Christopher, "On Dicentization," *Journal of Linguistic Anthropology* 24, no. 2 [2014]: 125). For a different use of "indexicalization" that is also historical, see Joel Kuipers, *Language, Identity, and Marginality in Indonesia: The Changing Nature of Ritual Speech on the Island of Sumba*, (New York: Cambridge University Press, 1998). I leave many other Peircean distinctions at bay, including those that distinguish conventionalized from unconventionalized indexicals (e.g., the deictic expression "I" versus smoke as an index of fire). Nor do I raise the intimately related issue of "likeness" through Peircean notions of iconicity and rhematicity. Indexicality overlaps empirically with iconicity, especially as interaction analysts care not just about the fact *that* a sign in a transcript indicates an object (e.g., a psychodynamic dimension of the analysand), but also with the way that a sign exhibits qualities of the object such that one can glean information from it. This is important insofar as the transcript is understood to represent an earlier, originary therapeutic session.

8. Freud, "Recommendations to Physicians Practicing Psychoanalysis," 115–16.

9. Compare with Kittler's stronger reading of the telephonic analogy that arguably imputed unidirectional influence and causality (Kittler, *Gramophone, Film, Typewriter* [Stanford, CA: Stanford University Press, 1999], 88). Freud experimented with tropes other than the telephonic, as in his sustained meditation on a novelty item called a mystic pad.

10. Sarah Franklin, "Analogic Return: The Reproductive Life of Conceptuality," *Theory, Culture & Society* 31, no. 2–3 (2014): 244, 245, 248.

11. Lorraine Daston and Peter Galison, *Objectivity* (New York: Zone Books; Distributed by MIT Press, 2007), 256 (emphasis mine).

12. Daston and Galison, 256.

13. I use "inscription" for familiarity, recalling influential works such as Timothy Lenoir, *Inscribing Science: Scientific Texts and the Materiality of Communication*, (Stanford, CA: Stanford University Press, 1998). As an analytic, inscription is arguably better conceptualized as technosemiotic *transduction*.

14. Robert M. Brain, "Representation on the Line: Graphic Recording Instruments and Scientific Modernism," in *From Energy to Information*, ed. D. Clarke and D. Henderson (Stanford, CA: Stanford University Press, 2002), 159. Analogies abound in the ethnographic record. As Webb Keane notes, with haruspicy (entrail divination) one may seek in a dead animal a visible response to a verbal question. In this way "denotational language" is answered "with indexical (and sometimes iconic) signs" (Webb Keane, "On Spirit Writing: The Materiality of Language and the Religious Work of Transduction," *Journal of the Royal Anthropological Institute* 19, no. 1 [2013]: 3). Keane calls this crossmodal semiosis "transduction" and, indeed, the technosemiotic conversions I trace here—especially from sound to wax-cylinder to paper—may be termed this way. On transduction in relation to translation, see especially Michael Silverstein, "Translation, Transduction, Transformation: Skating 'Glossando' on Thin Semiotic Ice," in *Translating Cultures: Perspectives on Translation and Anthropology*, ed. Paula G. Rubel and Abraham Rosman (Oxford: Berg Publishers, 2003), 75–105; see also Susan Gal, "Politics of Translation," *Annual Review of Anthropology* 44, no. 1 (2015): 225–40; see also Steven P. Black, "Anthropological Ethics and the Communicative Affordances of Audio-Video Recorders in Ethnographic Fieldwork: Transduction as Theory," *American Anthropologist* 119, no. 1 (2017): 46–57; on transduction in STS, see Stefan Helmreich, "Transduction," in *Keywords in Sound Studies: Towards a Conceptual Lexicon*, ed. David Novak and Matt Sakakeeny (Durham, NC: Duke University Press, 2015): 222–31; Jennifer C. Hsieh, "Piano Transductions: Music, Sound and Noise in Urban Taiwan," *Sound Studies: An Interdisciplinary Journal* 5, no. 1 (2019): 4–21.

15. Brain, "Representation on the Line."

16. See Kris Paulsen, "The Index and the Interface," *Representations* 122, no. 1 (2013): 83–109. See also Jonathan Sterne, *The Audible Past: Cultural Origins of Sound Reproduction* (Durham, NC: Duke University Press, 2003). For an influential introduction to indexicality in sociocultural life, see Parmentier, "The Pragmatic Semiotics of Cultures," *Semiotica* 116–1 (1997): 1–114.

17. On epistemological desire, see Karin Knorr-Cetina, "Sociality with Objects: Social Relations in Postsocial Knowledge," *Theory, Culture & Society* 14, no. 4 (1997): 1–30. In this case, the epistemological longing toward indexicality came from the lure of a communicative unconscious and from a growing sense that humans and machines had parallel capacities for indexical receptivity. Compare with Hans-Jörg Rheinberger's argument about an internal dialectic whereby "epistemic things" that start off as things to know may later become backgrounded as unproblematic "technical objects" (Rheinberger, *Toward a History of Epistemic Things: Synthesizing Proteins in the Test Tube,* [Stanford, CA: Stanford University Press, 1997], 105–11).

18. See chap. 5 of Sterne, *The Audible Past.* See discussions of "intertextual fidelity" in Richard Bauman and Charles L. Briggs, *Voices of Modernity: Language Ideologies and the Politics of Inequality* (Cambridge, UK: Cambridge University Press, 2003), 212 et passim; and Miyako Inoue, "Word for Word: Verbatim as Political Technologies," *Annual Review of Anthropology* 47 (2018): 217–32.

19. Emily Thompson, "Machines, Music, and the Quest for Fidelity: Marketing the Edison Phonograph in America 1877–1925," *Musical Quarterly* 79, no. 1 (1995): 171.

20. See Lisa Gitelman, *Scripts, Grooves, and Writing Machines: Representing Technology in the Edison Era* (Stanford, CA: Stanford University Press, 1999).

21. Gitelman, 137.

22. Gitelman, 138, 135.

23. Amanda Weidman, "Sound and the City: Mimicry and Media in South India," *Journal of Linguistic Anthropology* 20, no. 2 (2010): 294–313. For a critical discussion of media "newness," see Ilana Gershon, "Language and the Newness of Media," *Annual Review of Anthropology* 46 (2017): 15–31. Compare with Lukas Rieppel, who describes divergent orientations to dinosaur bones at the American Museum of Natural History. When curators created multimedia exhibits, they had a dicentized orientation to bones, stressing their auratic indexicality as traces of the past (Rieppel, "Bringing Dinosaurs Back to Life: Exhibiting Prehistory at the American Museum of Natural History," *Isis* 103 (2012): 460–90).

24. Walter Benjamin, "The Work of Art in the Age of Mechanical Reproduction," in *Illuminations,* ed. Hannah Arendt (New York: Schocken Books, 1985).

25. Eitan Y. Wilf, *School for Cool: The Academic Jazz Program and the Paradox of Institutionalized Creativity* (Chicago: University of Chicago Press, 2014): 137.

26. Watter, "Scrutinizing"; Watter, "Ray L. Birdwhistell, 'Lecture at American Museum of Natural History, October 4, 1980.'" See also Scott Curtis, "Tangible as Tissue: Arnold Gesell, Infant Behavior, and Film Analysis," *Science in Context* 24, no. 03 (2011): 417–42.

27. Paul Kockelman, "Gnomic Agency," in *Distributed Agency,* ed. N. J. Enfield and Paul Kockelman (Oxford: Oxford University Press, 2017), 16; see N. J. Enfield and Paul Kockelman, *Distributed Agency,* (Oxford: Oxford University Press, 2017), introduction. As Kockelman rightly stresses (16), "There is no interesting account of agency that is not simultaneously an account of those agents who are trying to account for agency," which is why we must not decide the allocation of agency in advance and fail to recognize its status as an ethnographic problem. For an important discussion of historical shifts in German media theory from postwar to present, which touches on contestation over the human and posthuman in relation to the very idea

of "media," see Bernhard Siegert's introduction in *Cultural Techniques: Grids, Filters, Doors, and Other Articulations of the Real* (New York: Fordham University Press, 2015).

28. By affordances I mean Gibson's familiar ecological notion, which stressed the potentiality of a material feature of an environment in relation to an organism's behavioral dispositions (James J. Gibson, "The Theory of Affordances," in *Perceiving, Acting, and Knowing: Toward an Ecological Psychology*, ed. R. Shaw and J. Bransford [Hillsdale, NJ: Lawrence Erlbaum, 1977], 67–82.) On affordances in social theory, see especially Webb Keane, *Ethical Life: its Natural and Social Histories* (Princeton: Princeton University Press, 2016), 28ff; Webb Keane, "Perspectives on Affordances, or the Anthropologically Real: The 2018 Daryll Forde Lecture," *HAU: Journal of Ethnographic Theory* 8, no. 1–2 (2018): 27–38.

29. From the standpoint of Daston and Galison's chronology, mechanical objectivity arrived late for psychoanalysis, a practice that was often seen as a holdout against empirical science.

30. In child development research, cinematography was applied early, first when John Watson used a hand-cranked camera in 1919 to record infant reflexes, then extensively by Arnold Gesell, as Scott Curtis examines. Gesell had constructed at his Yale Clinic an impressive "observational dome rigged with a variety of still and motion picture cameras" (Curtis, "Tangible as Tissue," 424). While panoramic, the sensory modalities he surveyed remained narrowly visual. He did not wire the dome to catch sounds of human growth. Even in his educational sound films from the 1930s, Gesell did not include vocalizations; the sound included was only his, laminated over the visual as non-diegetic voice-overs. Personal communication, Scott Curtis, 2016.

31. Patrick Feaster, "Reconfiguring the History of Early Cinema through the Phonograph, 1877–1908," *Film History: An International Journal* 21, no. 4 (2009): 311.

32. Through "phonomanipulation," in which one sped up or slowed tinfoil phonographs, linguists in 1878 had tested hypotheses about vowel sounds, for instance. Patrick Feaster, "'A Compass of Extraordinary Range': The Forgotten Origins of Phonomanipulation," *ARSC Journal* XLII (2011): 1167.

33. Thomas A. Edison, "The Perfected Phonograph," *North American Review* 146, no. 379 (1888):648–9. Thanks to Richard Bauman for this reference.

34. For a recent essay on photographic indexicality, see Christopher Ball, "Realisms and Indexicalities of Photographic Propositions," *Signs and Society* 5, S1 (2017), S154–S177. On Peirce's view of photography, see Alexander Robins, "Peirce and Photography: Art, Semiotics, and Science," *Journal of Speculative Philosophy* 28, no. 1 (2014): 1–16. While focusing on the cinematic rather than photographic image, see Constantine Nakassis's *Onscreen/Offscreen* (Toronto: University of Toronto Press, 2023), where he adapts Mol's notion of ontological politics to argue that we need to study the contestation that surrounds the very question of what a filmic image is, which has often centered on questions of indexicality.

35. See Richard Bauman on speech memorialization and mechanical recording. "Better than Any Monument: Envisioning Museums of the Spoken Word," *Museum Anthropology Review* 5, no. 1–2 (2011): 1–13; *A Most Valuable Medium: The Remediation of Oral Performance in Early Commercial Recordings* (Bloomington: Indiana University Press, 2023). On fidelity and salvage ethnography, see, for example, Walter J. Fewkes "On the Use of the Phonograph in the Study of the Languages of American Indians," *Science* 15, no. 378 (1890): 267–69; Erika Brady, *A Spiral Way: How the Phonograph Changed Ethnography* (Jackson: University Press of Mississippi, 1999): chap. 3. To save the "fast disappearing languages of races" ("Use of the Phonograph," 267), Fewkes did praise the phonograph's indexical fidelity (it could capture "inflections, gutturals, accents, and sounds in aboriginal dialects" [ibid., 267–68]), but this was meant to assist with preservation—salvage anthropology—rather than with making the close analysis of discourse possible.

36. S. D. Lamb, *Pathologist of the Mind: Adolf Meyer and the Origins of American Psychiatry* (Baltimore: Johns Hopkins University Press, 2014), 150–52.

37. On early psychoanalytic case notes, see Elizabeth Lunbeck and Bennett Simon, *Family Romance, Family Secrets: Case Notes from an American Psychoanalysis, 1912* (New Haven, CT: Yale University Press, 2003).

38. Inoue, "Word for Word." Importantly, Inoue uses "verbatim" not simply as a name for an historically specific set of sociotechnical practices and ideologies. Analytically, she also wants us to think about verbatim practices comparatively, inviting us to consider forms of speech-to-speech transductions (as in the oral transmission of ritual texts) in contrast to various kinds of text-to-speech and speech-to-text replications.

39. As language ideology, "verbatim" was not a unitary and uncontested category. Despite the general consensus that verbatim transcripts could be produced without machines, some debated what "verbatim" entailed and whether it was always "objective." In one spirited debate from 1928, Chicago sociologist Ernest Burgess argued in favor of verbatim reporting in social work records. "Verbatim" here meant that you couldn't substitute your own words for those of a subject, but you *could* judiciously select from this discourse without compromising the record's status as both verbatim and objective. See Ernest W. Burgess, "What Social Case Records Should Contain to be Useful for Sociological Interpretation," *Social Forces* 6 (1928), especially p. 528. The sociologist Frank Bruno countered that such selectivity would undermine objectivity. (Bruno, "Some Case Work Recording Limitations of Verbatim Reporting," *Social Forces* 6 [1928]: 532–34.) While he overlooks the contested status of the "verbatim" as a textual ideology, Raymond M. Lee offers a useful early survey (Lee, "Recording Technologies in Sociology, 1920–2000," *Sociology* 38 [2004]: 869–89). See Miyako Inoue "Word for Word" for a more incisive interrogation of "verbatim" and similar semiotic-textual ideologies.

40. Social Science Research Council (US), *The Social Science Research Council, Fifth Annual Report 1928–1929* (New York: Social Science Research Council, 1929), 11.

41. Robert Yerkes Papers (hereafter Yerkes Papers), MS 569, ser. I, box 54, folder 1043, letter from Zinn to Yerkes, March 14, 1926, Yale University.

42. Yerkes Papers, ser. II, box 77, folder 1471, NRC Committee on Sex, Fourth Annual Report 1925–1926; Report on Research in Sex Problems in Europe, Earl F. Zinn, exhibit B, 36.

43. Advisory Committee on the Family, 1928–1932 (hereafter Advisory Committee), Minutes of the Committee on Problems & Policy, Executive Committee Council, 14, April 6, 1929, accession 1, ser. I, Committee Projects, Social Science Research Council, box 152, folder 855, subseries 19, Rockefeller Foundation Archives.

44. Advisory Committee. See app. XVI, Familial Relations; app. "Report of the Committee on Research in Familial Relations" (June 4, 1929), "Report of the Subcommittee on Familial Relations."

45. Advisory Committee, app. X, 103–4. "Report of the Subcommittee on Familial Relations," Mr. Earl F. Zinn, May 31, 1929.

46. Advisory Committee, Minutes of the Committee on Problems & Policy, Executive Committee Council, 28, 36, August 23, 1929.

47. Advisory Committee, Letter from Zinn to Wissler, 2 August 1929, app. I, 34.

48. Advisory Committee, "Report of the Subcommittee on Familial Relations," Mr. Earl F. Zinn, May 31, 1929, app. X, 103–4, Rockefeller Archive Center, accession 1, ser. 1, Committee Projects, box 152, subseries 19, folder 855.

49. Letter from Zinn to Wissler, August 2, 1929, app. I, p. 34, Advisory Committee on the Family 1928–1932, Minutes, Rockefeller Archive Center, accession 1, ser. 1, Committee Projects, box 152, subseries 19, folder 855.

50. When recording efforts expanded in the 1940s and 1950s, experts shared tips on how to make recording inconspicuous. See chapter 7 and, for example, Bernard J. Covner, "Studies in Phonographic Recordings of Verbal Material: I. The Use of Phonographic Recordings in Counseling Practice and Research," *Journal of Consulting Psychology* 6 (1942): 105–13.

51. Speak-O-Phone Recording Studies, Inc. to David Shakow, April 13, 1932, David Shakow papers (Hereafter Shakow Papers), Drs. Nicholas and Dorothy Cummings Center for the History of Psychology at the University of Akron, box M1501, folder: "Speak-O-Phone."

52. Correspondence with Adolf Meyer, Key 11317, folder 1, unit I/4149, The Adolf Meyer Collection (hereafter Meyer Papers), The Alan Mason Chesney Medical Archives of Johns Hopkins Medical Institutions, Letter from Earl F. Zinn to Adolf Meyer, May 20, 1930.

53. Yerkes Papers, ser. I, box 54, folder 1043, Letter from Zinn to Yerkes. February 6, 1930.

54. Social Science Research Committee Records, box 9, Local Community Research Committee, University of Chicago, Annual Report 1929–1930 to the Rockefeller Foundation, University of Chicago Special Collections.

55. Harold D. Lasswell, "Psychoanalytic Interview as a Method of Research on Personalities," in *The Child's Emotions: Proceedings of the Midwest Conference on Character Development, February 1930* (Chicago: University of Chicago Press, 1930), 138. For an earlier iteration, see Harold D. Lasswell, "The Problem of Adequate Personality Records: A Proposal," *American Journal of Psychiatry* 85, no. 6 (1929): 1057–1066.

56. Lasswell, "Psychoanalytic Interview," 138.

57. Department of Anthropology Records, box 9, folder 1, Letter from Lasswell to Sapir, 1929.

58. Lasswell, "Problem of Adequate Personality Records," 1057.

59. Lasswell, "Problem of Adequate Personality Records," 1066.

60. Lasswell, "Problem of Adequate Personality Records," 1061.

61. Arnold A. Rogow, ed., *Politics, Personality, and Social Science in the Twentieth Century: Essays in Honor of Harold D. Lasswell* (Chicago: University of Chicago Press, 1969), 9.

62. Rebecca Lemov, *Database of Dreams: The Lost Quest to Catalog Humanity* (New Haven, CT: Yale University Press, 2015), chap. 8.

63. Social Science Research Committee Records, box 9, Local Community Research Committee, University of Chicago, Annual Report 1929–1930 to the Rockefeller Foundation, University of Chicago Special Collections.

64. Harold D. Lasswell, *Psychopathology and Politics* (Chicago: University of Chicago, 1930), 239.

65. See Freud et al., *The Standard Edition*, 1414.

66. Harold D. Lasswell, "Verbal References and Physiological Changes During the Psychoanalytic Interview: A Preliminary Communication," *Psychoanalytic Review* 22 (1935): 13–14.

67. Rebecca Lemov, "X-rays of Inner Worlds: The Mid-Twentieth-Century American Projective Test Movement," *Journal of the History of the Behavioral Sciences*, 47, no. 3 (Summer 2011): 270. See also Lemov, *Database of Dreams*, 194; and Otniel E. Dror, "The Scientific Image of Emotion: Experience and Technologies of Inscription," *Configurations* 7, no. 3 (1999): 355–401. Rebecca Lemov notes how Lasswell's turn to the body anticipated the fusion of Freudianism and behaviorism synthesized in the 1930s. Rebecca M. Lemov, *World as Laboratory: Experiments with Mice, Mazes, and Men* (New York: Hill and Wang, 2005).

68. Social Science Research Committee, box IX, folder 4, Local Community Research Community, University of Chicago, Annual Report 1929–1930 to The Rockefeller Foundation, 7–8, University of Chicago Special Collections.

69. Jamie Cohen-Cole, "The Creative American: Cold War Salons, Social Science, and the Cure for Modern Society," *Isis* 100, no. 2 (2009): 219–62; Jamie Nace Cohen-Cole, *The Open*

Mind: Cold War Politics and the Sciences of Human Nature (Chicago: University of Chicago Press, 2014).

70. Lasswell, "Verbal References," 11–12.

71. Lasswell, "Verbal References," 19–20.

72. Lasswell, "Verbal References," 19.

73. Personality Committee Budget Recommendations, 1931–1932, Department of Anthropology Records, box 9, folder 1, University of Chicago Library.

74. Social Science Research Committee, Meeting, March 2–3, 1932, Social Science Research Committee, box I, folder 7, University of Chicago Library.

75. Memorandum to the Social Science Research Committee, May 11, 1933, Harold D. Lasswell, Social Science Research Committee Records, box 15, folder 23, University of Chicago Library.

76. The Prolonged Interview, Budget 1934–1935, Social Science Research Committee Records, box 12, folder 3, University of Chicago Library.

77. Social Science Research Committee Minutes, April 24, 1934, Social Science Research Committee Records, box II, folder 1, University of Chicago Library.

78. Yerkes Papers, MS 569, ser. I, box 54, folder 1043, Letter from Earl F. Zinn to Robert Yerkes, September 16, 1931.

79. Letter from Earl F. Zinn to Adolf Meyer, October 19, 1933. Correspondence with Adolf Meyer. Key 11318. ser. I, unit I/4149, Meyer Papers.

80. Zinn did shorter recordings at Worcester and Yale as well. His work was remembered as pioneering but it made no headlines at Worcester. Given the prevailing somatic view of mental illness, few thought talk alone could treat serious pathologies like schizophrenia. Zinn's research never made the hospital's annual reports, even though chief psychologist and director of research David Shakow was sympathetic. On Zinn serving as analyst for Shakow, "The Contributions of the Worcester State Hospital and Post-Hall Clark University to Psychoanalysis," in *Psychoanalysis, Psychotherapy, and the New England Medical Scene, 1894–1944*, ed. George Edmund Gifford (New York: Science History Publications/USA, 1978), 38.

81. Shakow recounted that Zinn "used a microphone in the head of the couch which transmitted to a pair of Dictaphone machines in an adjacent room. His secretary serviced the machines and transcribed the cylinders after each session." (Shakow, "The Contributions of the Worcester State Hospital and Post-Hall Clark University to Psychoanalysis," 81.) Zinn's inventory of items shipped to Yale lists only one dictation machine, and given the success of his prior setup, it is likely that Zinn used the same double-mandrel recorder from New York. At Yale he placed an order for a second recorder. If he did link two recorders, it likely happened there.

82. Earl F. Zinn, "A Psychoanalytic Study of a Schizophrenic," (New Haven, CT: Institute of Human Relations, Yale University, 1939), Vol. 1, iii.

83. Zinn, "Psychoanalytic Study of a Schizophrenic," Vol. 1, ii.

84. On ideologies of transcription, see especially Elinor Ochs, "Transcription as Theory," in *Developmental Pragmatics*, ed. E. Ochs and B. B. Schieffelin (New York: Academic Press, 1979), 43–72; Mary Bucholtz, "The Politics of Transcription," *Journal of Pragmatics* 32, no. 10 (2000): 1439–1465; Mary Bucholtz, "Captured on Tape: Professional Hearing and Competing Entextualizations in the Criminal Justice System," *Text & Talk* 29, no. 5 (2009): 503–23; Inoue, "Word for Word."

85. Zinn, "Psychoanalytic Study of a Schizophrenic," iii.

86. Zinn, "Psychoanalytic Study of a Schizophrenic," 26.

87. Zinn, "Psychoanalytic Study of a Schizophrenic," iii.

88. Lasswell, "Verbal References."

89. Harold D. Lasswell, "A Provisional Classification of Symbol Data," *Psychiatry* 1, no. 2 (1938): 197.

90. Lasswell, "A Provisional Classification of Symbol Data," 197.

91. On referential and nonreferential indexicality, see Michael Silverstein, "Shifters, Linguistic Categories, and Cultural Description," in *Meaning in Anthropology*, ed. Keith H. Basso and Henry A. Selby (Albuquerque: University of New Mexico Press, 1976), 11–55.

92. See Nathan G. Hale, *The Rise and Crisis of Psychoanalysis in the United States: Freud and the Americans, 1917–1985*, (New York: Oxford University Press, 1995).

93. Rachael I. Rosner, "Psychotherapy research and the National Institute of Mental Health, 1948–1980," in *Psychology and the National Institute of Mental Health: A Historical Analysis of Science, Practice, and Policy*, ed. Wade E. Pickren, Stanley F. Schneider, and American Psychological Association. (Washington, DC: American Psychological Association, 2005), 113–50.

94. I use "communication science" broadly for various fields that had epistemological investments in language and human semiotic behavior rather than narrowly for postwar communication studies. On "communication" and "language" as different objects of knowledge in midcentury America, see Monica Heller and Bonnie S. McElhinny, *Language, Capitalism, Colonialism: Toward a Critical History* (Toronto: University of Toronto Press, 2017).

95. Edward Sapir, "Speech as a Personality Trait," *American Journal of Sociology* 32 (1927): 892, 893, 898.

96. American Psychiatric Association. Committee on Relations with the Social Sciences, *Proceedings of the Second Colloquium on Personality Investigation*, November 29–30, 1929, New York City (Baltimore: Johns Hopkins Press, 1930), 39.

97. Edward Sapir to L. D. White, Executive Secretary of the Local Community Research Committee, February 25, 1930, Department of Anthropology Records, box 9, University of Chicago Special Collections, Chicago, Illinois. Sapir's 1927 essay "Speech as a Personality Trait" has been seen as an early inspiration for what is now a substantial body of literature on the indexicalities and semiotics of "voice." For a review, see Amanda Weidman, "Anthropology and Voice," *Annual Review of Anthropology* 43 (2014): 37–51.

98. Naoko Wake, *Private Practices: Harry Stack Sullivan, the Science of Homosexuality, and American Liberalism* (New Brunswick, NJ: Rutgers University Press, 2011). My thanks to Naoko Wake for discussing her research with me. Some have suggested that Sullivan used mechanical recording in the 1920s, but this seems unlikely. Still, there were important changes in Sullivan's transcription practices. Earlier transcripts of psychiatric interviews featured talk only from the patient, whereas later transcripts included Sullivan himself as questioner, suggesting a more interactional orientation toward the event. Although the dates on his transcripts are difficult to determine, some came to include parenthetical inserts in which Sullivan included behaviors that seemed to be of indexical interest. For example:

s: That is very fortunate. Tell me about it.
Tell me about it. I don't think you know.
(Movement of lips continues, with only brief periods of quiescence.)
s: I don't think you have the faintest idea who I am.
p: I know you are a policeman, all right.
(Grins.)

(Clarence G. Schulz, "Sullivan's Clinical Contribution During the Sheppard Pratt Era—1923–1930," *Psychiatry* 41, no. 2 [1978], 120.) It may seem that such insertions demanded mechanical recording, yet Wake (personal communication) cautions that Sullivan often added inserts *after* interviews, based strictly on his memory. They cannot be taken to imply the existence of mechanical recording.

99. Harry Stack Sullivan, "Affective Experience in Early Schizophrenia," *American Journal of Psychiatry* 83, no. 3 (1927): 471.

100. "Proposal for a Unit on Personal Social-Synthesis," Dr. Harry Stack Sullivan, box 9, folder 2, 1-2, University of Chicago Special Collections.

Chapter Three

1. Harry Stack Sullivan, "Psychiatry: Introduction to the Study of Interpersonal Relations, I.," *Psychiatry: Journal of Interpersonal Relations* 1, no. 1 (1938): 133.

2. Pittenger, Hockett, and Danehy, *The First Five Minutes: A Sample of Microscopic Interview Analysis*.

3. NHI was not one seamless collaboration but several linked ones based at different institutions, forming an "informal network" (Wendy Leeds-Hurwitz and Adam Kendon, "The Natural History of an Interview and the Microanalysis of Behavior in Social Interaction," in *Holisms of Communication*, 146); on NHI, see also Wendy Leeds-Hurwitz, "The Social History of *The Natural History of an Interview*: A Multidisciplinary Investigation of Social Communication," *Research on Language & Social Interaction* 20 (1987): 1–51; Wendy Leeds-Hurwitz, "Frieda Fromm-Reichmann and the Natural History of an Interview," in *Psychoanalysis and Psychosis*, ed. Ann-Loiuse S. Silver (New York: International Universities Press, 1989), 95–127; Adam Kendon, *Conducting Interaction: Patterns of Behavior in Focused Encounters* (Cambridge, UK: Cambridge University Press, 1990), chap. 1. Although publication fell through, the resulting five-volume work was microfilmed and stored at the University of Chicago where it lived on in the classroom and beyond. Norman A. McQuown, ed., *The Natural History of an Interview*, Microfilm Collection of Manuscripts on Cultural Anthropology (Chicago: University of Chicago Library, 1971).

4. *The First Five Minutes* reanalyzed sound recordings from Merton Gill, Richard Newman, and Fredrick C. Redlich, *The Initial Interview in Psychiatric Practice, with phonograph records available to professional persons and institutions* (New York: International Universities Press, 1954). For a history that traces how the group settled on its filmed material, see Henning Engelke, "Perception, Awareness, and Film Practice," in *Holisms of Communication*, ed. McElvanny and Ploder.

5. The distinction between the verbatim and indexically saturated transcript is heuristic; in practice, indexicalization was never categorical and always gradient, admitting of degrees. Nor was it sudden. Indeed, this tendency developed over time for Zinn and Lasswell.

6. Pittenger, Hockett, and Danehy, p. 8.

7. Robert E. Pittenger, "The First Five Minutes—Its Significance in Mental Health," *Journal of Communication* 13, no. 3 (1963): 142.

8. Erving Goffman, *The Presentation of Self in Everyday Life* (Garden City, NY: Doubleday, 1959), 13–14.

9. Theodore Schwartz, review of *The First Five Minutes: A Sample of Microscopic Interview Analysis* by Robert E. Pittenger, Charles F. Hockett, and John J. Danehy, *American Anthropologist* 64, no. 6 (1962): 1315.

10. Pittenger, Hockett, and Danehy, 211.

11. Zinn, "Psychoanalytic Study of a Schizophrenic," vi.

12. Lasswell, "Psychoanalytic Interview," 139.

13. Lasswell, "Psychoanalytic Interview," 154.

14. Harold Garfinkel, "Evidence for Locally Produced, Naturally Accountable Phenomena of Order, Logic, Reason, Meaning, Method, etc. In and as of the Essential Quiddity of Immortal Ordinary Society, (I of IV): An Announcement of Studies," *Sociological Theory* 6, no. 1 (1988): 103–9.

15. William James and Rouben Mamoulian Collection (Library of Congress), *The Principles of Psychology*, 2 vols. (New York: H. Holt and company, 1890), 314.

16. Pittenger, Hockett, and Danehy, 211.

17. Pittenger, Hockett, and Danehy, 212. Although they speak of tacit, group-relative, sociocultural conventions, the analysis tends to trace signs to speaker interiority (e.g., emotion) and interpersonal meaning without establishing that these signs are conventional.

18. Lemov, "X-rays of Inner Worlds: The Mid-Twentieth-Century American Projective Test Movement," 257; Lemov, *Database of Dreams*.

19. *The First Five Minutes*, 215.

20. Norman McQuown "Linguistic Transcription and Specification of Psychiatric Interview Materials," *Psychiatry* 20 (1957), Note 10, page 80.

21. Pittenger, Hockett, and Danehy, *The First Five Minutes*, 30–32.

22. Edmund Bergler, "On the Resistance Situation," *Psychoanalytical review* 25 (1938): 182–83. On the indeterminacy of indexicality, see especially Constantine V. Nakassis, "Indexicality's Ambivalent Ground," *Signs and Society* 6, no. 1 (Winter) (2018): 281–304.

23. Wilf, *School for School*, 137.

24. Pittenger, Hockett, and Danehy, 6.

25. On accuracy versus precision, see M. Norton Wise, ed., *The Values of Precision* (Princeton: Princeton University Press, 1995); Theodore M. Porter, "Speaking Precision to Power: The Modern Political Role of Social Science," *Social Research* 73 (2006).

26. Shakow Papers, box M1501, folder: "Speak-O-Phone."

27. Compare with a quote by Bateson, cited in Engelke ("Perception, Awareness, and Film Practice," 110): "It is necessary again to insist upon the *unconscious* character of most communication. [. . .] We are commonly unaware also of many characteristics and components of the messages themselves." Gregory Bateson, "Communication," in *The Natural History of an Interview*, ed. Norman A. McQuown (Chicago: Microfilm Collection of Manuscripts on Cultural Anthropology, University of Chicago, Joseph Regenstein Library, 1971), 24.

28. G. L. Trager, "Paralanguage: A First Approximation," *Studies in Linguistics* 13 (1958); Ray L. Birdwhistell, *Introduction to Kinesics: An Annotation System for Analysis of Body Motion and Gesture* (Louisville 8, Kentucky: University of Louisville, 1952).

29. Erving Goffman has a complicated place in this history, because he rejected mechanical recording and transcription along with the technophilic and technocratic aspects of what were then the influential traditions of interaction analysis.

30. Carlo Prevignano and Paul J. Thibault, *Discussing Conversation Analysis: The Work of Emanuel A. Schegloff* (Amsterdam: John Benjamins, 2003), 57.

31. Ruesch, Jurgen, and Gregory Bateson. *Communication: The Social Matrix of Psychiatry.* (New York: W. W. Norton & Company, 1951).

32. On Bateson's research on the family, see Geoghegan, "The Family as Machine: Film, Infrastructure, and Cybernetic Kinship in Suburban America." Bateson later expressed regret about such research: "it was from psychiatry that we got our money, and we let ourselves be strongly and disastrously influenced by the need to apply our science in that field." Cited in Carol Wilder, "The Palo Alto Group: Difficulties and Directions of the Interactional View for Human Communication Research," *Human Communication Research* 5, no. 2 (1979): 171. Compare with remorse expressed by Carl Rogers late in his career over his early efforts to record and study

therapeutic talk "microscopically." Carl R. Rogers, "Empathic: An Unappreciated Way of Being," *Counseling Psychologist* 5, no. 2 (1975): 2–10. I thank Benjamin Smith for this reference.

33. On "sociolinguistics" as a category, see Alessandro Duranti, "Linguistic Anthropology: History, Ideas, and Issues," in *Linguistic Anthropology: A Reader*, ed. Alessandro Duranti (Malden, MA: Blackwell Publishers Inc., 2001), 5–8; for a critical history, see Heller and McElhinny, *Language, Capitalism, Colonialism*. As Gumperz argued, people used language to construct the relevant "context" of their own talk (a topic Bateson had opened up as "metacommunciation" and Goffman wrote about as "framing"). "Contextualization cues," as Gumperz came to call them, were non-denotational indexical signs that usually operated behind people's backs. Gumperz's scholarship on contextualization cues has often been compared to Michael Silverstein's writings on metapragmatics in linguistic anthropology. Both contributed to an influential early volume on contextualization, Peter Auer and Aldo Di Luzio, *The Contextualization of Language* (Amsterdam: Benjamins, 1992); in linguistic anthropology, see A. Duranti and C. Goodwin, *Rethinking Context: Language as Interactive Phenomenon* (Cambridge, UK: Cambridge University Press, 1992). On Gumperz's notion of contextualization cues, see especially his influential volume John J. Gumperz, *Discourse Strategies* (Cambridge, UK: Cambridge University Press, 1982). For his own late-career reflections on interactional sociolinguistics, see John J. Gumperz, "Interactional Sociolinguistics: A Personal Perspective," in *The Handbook of Discourse Analysis*, ed. Deborah Schiffrin, Deborah Tannen, and Heidi Ehernberger Hamilton (Malden, MA: Blackwell Handbooks in Linguistics, 2001), 215–28.

34. Compare with Miyako Inoue's writings on stenography and subject formation in late nineteenth and early twentieth-century Japan, where she traces how gendered practices of transcription helped produce linguistic modernity (Inoue, "Stenography and Ventriloquism in Late Nineteenth-Century Japan").

35. Gregory Bateson, "Language and Psychotherapy—Frieda Fromm-Reichmann's Last Project," *Psychiatry* 21 (1958): 97.

36. Covner, "Studies in Phonographic Recordings of Verbal Material: I. The Use of Phonographic Recordings in Counseling Practice and Research," 112–13. Bernard J. Covner, "Studies in Phonographic Recordings of Verbal Material. II. A Device for Transcribing Phonographic Recordings of Verbal Material," *Journal of Consulting Psychology* 6, no. 3 (1942): 149–53; Bernard J. Covner, "Studies in Phonographic Recordings of Verbal Material: III. The Completeness and Accuracy of Counseling Interview Reports," *Journal of General Psychology* 30, no. 2 (1944): 181–203; Bernard J. Covner, "Studies in Phonographic Recordings of Verbal Material: IV. Written Reports of Interviews," *Journal of Applied Psychology* 28, no. 2 (1944): 89–98. See also Bernard J. Covner, "A Note on Postwar Phonographic Recording Equipment," *Journal of Consulting Psychology* (1945): 194–95.

37. Covner, "Studies in Phonographic Recordings of Verbal Material: IV."

38. William U. Snyder, "An Investigation of the Nature of Nondirective Psychotherapy," *Journal of General Psychology* 33, no. 2 (1945): 193–232.

39. Robin L. Cautin, "A century of psychotherapy, 1860–1960," in *History of Psychotherapy: Continuity and Change*, ed. John C. Norcross, Gary R. VandenBos, and Donald K. Freedheim (Washington, DC: American Psychological Association, 2011), 29; Rosner, "Psychotherapy Research and the National Institute of Mental Health, 1948–1980."

40. On the way "clinical psychology," based in psychology rather than in medicalized psychiatry, did not constitute itself as autonomous until after the war, see, for example, Donald K. Routh, "Clinical Psychology Training: A History of Ideas and Practices Prior to 1946," *American Psychologist* 55, no. 2 (2000): 236–41.

41. In scholarship on language and social interaction, a significant body of literature has co-alesced around therapeutic talk. For an early and influential sociolinguistic volume, see William Labov and David Fanshel, *Therapeutic Discourse: Psychotherapy as Conversation* (New York: Academic Press, 1977). For more recent synoptic views of this topic and its literatures, see, for example, Benjamin Smith, "Language of Therapy," in *The International Encyclopedia of Linguistic Anthropology*, ed. James M. Stanlaw (John Wiley & Sons, 2021), 1–5; James M. Wilce, "Medical Discourse," *Annual Review of Anthropology* 38 (2009): 199–215.

42. Emphasis in original, *The First Five Minutes*, 229.

43. Pittenger, "The First Five Minutes—Its Significance in Mental Health," 144.

44. *The First Five Minutes*, 5.

45. Daston and Lunbeck, *Histories of Scientific Observation*, 1.

46. This observer effect was not left unquestioned. See, for example, Rae Shifrin Sternberg, Jean Chapman, and David Shakow, "Psychotherapy Research and the Problem of Intrusions on Privacy," *Psychiatry* XXI (1958): 195–203.

47. Redlich, Dollard, and Newman, "High Fidelity Recordings of Psychotherapeutic Interviews." *American Journal of Psychiatry* 107, no. 1 (1950): 43.

48. Richard E. Renneker, "Microscopic Analysis of Sound Tape: A Method of Studying Preconscious Communication in the Therapeutic Process," *Psychiatry* 23, no. 4 (1960): 350.

49. Freud, "Recommendations to Physicians Practicing Psychoanalysis," 115–16.

50. Redlich, Dollard, and Newman, "High Fidelity Recordings10," 42.

Chapter Four

1. Pittenger, "The First Five Minutes—Its Significance in Mental Health," 142, 140.

2. "The first-year medical student fails to see anything significant when he first looks down his microscope barrel, but in time he learns to use the instrument to make important diagnoses. Microscopic interview analysis is also a new tool for its users. Its resolving power seems to be excellent. Let us hope, now, that we can discover something with it." Eric H. Lenneberg, "Review of *The First Five Minutes: A Sample of Microscopic Interview Analysis* by Robert E. Pittenger, Charles F. Hockett and John J. Danehy," *Language* 38, no. 1 (1962): 73.

3. *The First Five Minutes*, 249.

4. *The First Five Minutes*, 249.

5. *The First Five Minutes*, 248–49.

6. Emanuel A. Schegloff, "The First Five Seconds: The Order of Conversational Opening" (PhD diss., University of California, Berkeley, 1967).

7. Schegloff, "The First Five Seconds," 37–38.

8. Prevignano and Thibault, *Discussing Conversation Analysis*, 17.

9. Pittenger, 1963, 45. Schegloff occasionally included phenomena like filled pauses "uh" and "simultaneous" (overlapping) talk. He noted select pauses here and there parenthetically: "(pause)" (p.81), and, in one case, a contrast between "(pause)" and "(longer pause)." Still, his own transcription conventions were not structured around recovering indexical dimensions of the interaction.

10. Pierre Bourdieu, "Erving Goffman: Discoverer of the Infinitely Small," in *Erving Goffman*, ed. Gary Alan Fine and Gregroy W. H. Smith (London: Sage Publications, 2000), 3–4.

11. On Goffman's writing style, see a thoughtful engagement by Richard Handler, "What I'm Reading. What's Up, Doctor Goffman? Tell Us Where the Action Is!" *Journal of the Royal Anthropological Institute* 18 (2012): 179–90. For Goffman's critique of CA, see Erving Goffman, "Replies and Responses," *Language in Society* 5, no. 3 (1976): 257–313. As Schegloff recounted, for instance,

his early experience of Goffman's work was that it "brought into view a much more proximate sense of social context . . . by several orders of magnitude." (Prevignano and Thibault, *Discussing Conversation Analysis*, 21.) In Goffman's corpus, one can find considerable interest in the indexical dimensions of communication, as with his famous distinction between what people "give" and what they "give off" and his late discussion of "response cries" (Erving Goffman, "Response cries," *Language* 54 [1978], 787–815.)

12. W. S. Condon and W. D. Ogston, "A Segmentation of Behavior," *Journal of Psychiatric Research*. 5 (1967): 221. While Ogston was technically coauthor, it was Condon who was very much the principal here (Seth Watter, personal communication 2022).

13. Condon and Ogston, "A Segmentation of Behavior," 223, 224. While I do not provide a historical ethnography of playback here, needless to say, "frame-by-frame" is not itself an adequate description of the practices it captions.

14. On Birdwhistell's scholarship, see Adam Kendon and Stuart J. Sigman, "Ray L. Birdwhistell (1918–1994)," *Semiotica* 112, no. 3/4 (1996): 231–61; Kendon, *Conducting Interaction*, ch. 1; Martha Davis, "Film Projectors as Microscopes: Ray L. Birdwhistell & Microanalysis of Interaction (1955–1975)," *Visual Anthropology Review* 17, no. 2 (2001–2002), 39–49; Wendy Leeds-Hurwitz, "The PENN Tradition," in *The Social History of Language and Social Interaction Research: People, Places, Ideas* (Cresskill, NJ: Hampton Press, 2010), 235–70. For a history that covers the full sweep of Birdwhistell's career and work, see Watter, "Scrutinizing."

15. Henry W. Brosin, "Studies in Human Communication in Clinical Settings Using Sound Film and Tape," *Wisconsin Medical Journal* 63, no. 11 (1964): 503–6.

16. See Henning Engelke's "Perception, Awareness, and Film Practice," that traces the very emergence of "behavioral film" and its desired properties.

17. See a late public lecture by Birdwhistell introduced by Seth Watter, "Ray L. Birdwhistell, 'Lecture at American Museum of Natural History, October 4, 1980.'" Here Birdwhistell narrates the influence of his father, who had worked with a literal microscope as a virologist and apparently seeded passion for the instrument in a young Birdwhistell.

18. See Martha Davis's aptly titled essay, "Film Projectors as Microscopes," and Farnell "Theorizing "the Body" in Visual Culture," in *Made to be Seen: Perspectives on the History of Visual Anthropology*, ed. Marcus Banks and Jay Ruby (Chicago ; London: University of Chicago Press, 2011), 146.

19. Gregory Bateson and Margaret Mead, *Balinese Character, a Photographic Analysis*, (New York: New York Academy of Sciences, 1942).

20. Goffman reportedly quipped about Birdwhistell's turn to methodology and suggested that this was a sign he recognized his science of kinesics had failed. Yves Winkin, ed., *Erving Goffman: Les Moments et Leurs Hommes* (Paris: Seuil/Minuit, 1988), 232 cited in Kendon and Sigman, "Ray L. Birdwhistell (1918–1994)," 245, 256 n. 16.

21. Martha Davis, Personal Communication. See also Davis, "Film Projectors as Microscopes."

22. Kendon and Sigman, "Ray L. Birdwhistell (1918–1994)," 231.

23. Birdwhistell imagined the linguistic analogy breaking down or one day giving way to something else. Tellingly, he left a parenthetical question mark next to "kineme" in his 1952 introduction. Later, he even imagined that kinesics would need to be reconsidered. "All of the emerging data seems to me to support the contention that linguistics and kinesics are infracommunicational systems," and that "only in their interrelationship with each other and with comparable systems from other sensory modalities is the emergent communication system achieved" (Ray L. Birdwhistell, *Kinesics and Context: Essays on Body Motion Communication* [Philadelphia: University of Pennsylvania Press, 1970], 127.)

24. On the constituency-like structure of embodied communication, Birdwhistell, *Kinesics and Context*, 115. On the entanglement of communication science with filmic techniques and visual aesthetics, see chapter 1, note 8.

25. On "shorthand notation," Birdwhistell, *Kinesics and Context*, 220; Kendon and Sigman, "Ray L. Birdwhistell (1918–1994)," 247; on use of term gesture, Birdwhistell, *Kinesics and Context*, 119.

26. Birdwhistell, *Kinesics and Context*, 79–80.

27. Birdwhistell, *Kinesics and Context*.

28. In another context he stressed how gestures were akin to bound morphemes. Birdwhistell, *Kinesics and Context*, 119.

29. What exactly this "integration" entailed was a serious problematic, as Birdwhistell recognized. See, for example, his discussion of the relation between kinesic and linguistic stress in Birdwhistell, *Kinesics and Context*, 237–50.

30. When Birdwhistell zoomed out to place his kinesics within a wider science of capital-C communication, he imagined a comprehensive, "multichannel" semiotics. Not unlike the way Saussure envisioned his linguistic science of la langue within a vast semiology (Saussure, *Course in General Linguistics* [La Salle: Open Court, 1983]), so Birdwhistell declaimed that "communication is not just what happens in one channel" but consists of multiple channels that may be "ultimately inseparable." We are most familiar with "the audio-acoustic (vocal) channel" and "kinesthetic-visual," but Birdwhistell—now looking forward—adds the "odor-producing-olfactory channel," "the tactile" channel," "and so on." Birdwhistell, *Kinesics and Context*, 71.

31. Letter from Henry Brosin to Ray L. Birdwhistell, Norman A. McQuown, and Henry Lee Smith. November 11, 1963, 2, Norman A. McQuown Papers, box 690, folder 4 (NHI correspondence), University of Chicago Special Collections.

32. Birdwhistell, *Kinesics and Context*, xiii. Birdwhistell alludes here to Goffman "The Neglected Situation," *American Anthropologist* 66, no. 6–2 (1964): 133–36.

33. Birdwhistell later dropped socials kinesics in favor of "macrokinesics," which then paralleled "macrolinguistics."

34. Ray L. Birdwhistell, "Background to Kinesics," *ETC: A Review of General Semantics* 13, no. 1 (1955):12.

35. Cf. Kendon and Sigman, "Ray L. Birdwhistell (1918–1994)," note 22, 257.

36. Birdwhistell, *Kinesics and Context*, 101ff.

37. Birdwhistell's student Stuart Sigman reports that, at Penn, Birdwhistell treated Pike's work with enormous deference (Leeds-Hurwitz, "The PENN Tradition," 246) much as he did with his former colleague Scheflen. Deference notwithstanding, Birdwhistell's work differed from both men in very important ways.

38. A Pikean confidence in the hierarchical structure of behavior can be found in the microinteractionist work of Albert E. Scheflen with whom Birdwhistell worked closely at EPPI. (Scheflen, *How Behavior Means*, [New York: Gordon and Breach, 1973], 27–28.) Scheflen credited Birdwhistell as a key influence, yet Scheflen's understanding of hierarchy resembled Pike better than Birdwhistell, who remained more guarded about the linguistic analogy and about the extent of hierarchal constituency. Scheflen even suggested that one could "synthesize a picture of the structure by first examining the small units and then saying how these are put together to form larger integrations at higher levels" (ibid., 27). As Kendon and Sigman note, Birdwhistell came to appreciate the "limits of the 'bottom-up' hierarchical view offered by structural linguistics" (Kendon and Sigman, "Ray L. Birdwhistell [1918–1994]," 253.)

39. On "wheels within wheels," Kenneth L. Pike, *Language in Relation to a Unified Theory of the Structure of Human Behavior*, vol. 1, Preliminary Edition, (Glendale, Calif: Summer Institute of Linguistics, 1954), 32 et passim; on "molecular level," ibid., 1, 50.

40. Ray L. Birdwhistell, "Research in the Structure of Group Psychotherapy," *International Journal of Group Therapy* 13 (1963): 491. As he wrote, "the most comprehensive knowledge of linguistics and kinesics (qua linguistics and kinesics) will not permit us to analyze the precise social meaning of the content of an interactional sequence" (Birdwhistell, "Research in the Structure of Group Psychotherapy," 490.)

41. On "total context," see Birdwhistell, "Background to Kinesics," 24. On the three scenes, ibid., 23ff.

42. Birdwhistell, *Kinesics and Context*, 177.

43. For an early review, see M. Catherine Bateson, "Review: Microcultural Incidents in Ten Zoos," *American Anthropologist* 74, no. 1–2 (1972): 191–92.

44. Ray L. Birdwhistell, "Kinesic Analysis of Filmed Behavior of Children," in *Group Processes: Transactions of the Second Conference. October 9, 10, 11, and 12, 1955, Princeton, NJ*, ed. Bertram Schaffner (New York: Josiah Macy, Jr. Foundation, 1956), 143.

45. Consider, for example, an essay such as, "The American Family: Some Perspectives" Ray L. Birdwhistell, "The American Family: Some Perspectives," *Psychiatry: Interpersonal and Biological Processes* 29 (1966): 203–12. This incorporated findings from his earlier, pre-kinesics ethnological work yet Birdwhistell did not draw on kinesic fine-grained noticing, so we do not see how the ethnological and the kinesic could be combined.

46. I neglect here Birdwhistell's important corpus of behavioral film, such as his *Microcultural Instances in Ten Zoos*, produced during his time at EPPI.

47. The Body Motion chapter was first drafted in the late 1950s and was revised and expanded over the following decade into a pair of chapters, the second of which addresses the Doris-Gregory film of NHI.

48. Birdwhistell, *Kinesics and Context*, 173.

49. Martha Davis's "Film Projectors as Microscopes" essay on Birdwhistell is aptly titled, as microscopy was, indeed, a live trope that was materialized by means of recording and playback technologies.

50. Birdwhistell, *Kinesics and Context*, 174.

51. On zooms, see Latour, *Reassembling the Social*.

52. Birdwhistell, *Kinesics and Context*, 178.

53. Compare this presentation of data with his initial examples of social kinesics in his 1952 charter, where there was no well-ordered zoom nor even a fuller, socially enriched reading.

54. In his teaching, Birdwhistell was famous for acting out the way embodied habits could index social and cultural information. He "demonstrated the possibility that mannerisms and behavioral details—such as styles of walking, handling a cigarette, and the like—could be analyzed as if they were social rituals" (Kendon and Sigman, "Ray L. Birdwhistell [1918–1994],":235–36; see Winkin, *Erving Goffman: Les Moments et Leurs Hommes*.)

55. Mary Moore Goodlett and Barbara Lynch, "Making Entrée to Communication through the (Family) Living Room" (Twenty-Ninth Annual Conference of The International Communication Association, Philadelphia, Pennsylvania, 1979; unpublished manuscript), 1–17. The exercise had roots long before PENN, as it was purportedly a retooled version of an exercise Birdwhistell had first experienced at the University of Chicago.

56. On "machinaphobic" instructions, R. L. Birdwhistell, "The Use of Audio-Visual Teaching

Aids," in *Resources for the Teaching of Anthropology*, ed. Rexford S. Beckham et al. (Berkeley: University of California Press, 1963), 53. On selecting a room, ibid., 56–57.

57. Birdwhistell, "The Use of Audio-Visual Teaching Aids," 57.

58. Birdwhistell, "Kinesic Analysis of Filmed Behavior of Children," 144. Compare with his late reflections on mechanical recording and its hazards in Birdwhistell, *Kinesics and Context*, chap. 19, written in 1969; Ray L. Birdwhistell, "Some Discussion of Ethnography, Theory, and Method," in *About Bateson: Essays on Gregory Bateson*, ed. Mary Catherine Bateson and John Brockman (New York: E. P. Dutton, 1977), 108–10. On such issues see Birdwhistell's recently uncovered public lecture from 1980. Watter, "Ray L. Birdwhistell, 'Lecture at American Museum of Natural History, October 4, 1980.'" I do not attempt to reconstruct here a history of Birdwhistell's evolving views toward film as a scientific instrument, nor do I try to situate his arguments in relation to midcentury contestation over the photographic and cinematic image. In broad terms the naivety against which he cautioned was based on an assumption that cameras were unmediated, mechanically objective recording instruments. Against this view Birdwhistell sometimes stressed how practices of recording and viewing were influenced by acquired habits, practices, and assumptions that escaped awareness—a stance that arguably reflected an anthropological sensibility that showed up as a generalized resistance toward postwar scientistic empiricism with its fetishization of special tools, on which, see Joel Isaac, "Tool Shock: Technique and Epistemology in the Postwar Social Sciences," *History of Political Economy* 42, no. Supplement 1 (2010): 133–64. As for contestation from the period, within visual anthropology of the 1970s, see especially the memorable debate between Margaret Mead and Gregory Bateson on photography. Gregory Bateson and Margaret Mead, "Margaret Mead and Gregory Bateson on the Use of the Camera in Anthropology," *Studies in Visual Communication* 4, no. 2 (1977): 78–80; see also earlier, important essays by Paul Byers, "Still Photography in the Systematic Recording and Analysis of Behavioral Data," *Human Organization* 23, no. 1 (1964): 78–84; "Cameras Don't Take Pictures," *Columbia University Forum* 9, no. 1 (1966): 27–32. For thoughtful discussions of the history of photography in anthropology, see Elizabeth Edwards, "Tracing Photography," in *Made to Be Seen*, 159–89; and Farnell, "Theorizing 'the Body' in Visual Culture."

59. Goodlett and Lynch, "Short Making Entrée to Communication through the (Family) Living Room," 2. Emphasis in original.

60. Marcel Mauss, *The Gift: Forms and Functions of Exchange in Archaic Societies* (Glencoe, IL: Free press, 1954 [1925], 3).

61. Kendon and Sigman, "Ray L. Birdwhistell (1918–1994)."

62. Ray McDermott, "Profile: Ray L. Birdwhistell," *Kinesis Report: News and Views of Nonverbal Communication* 2, no. 3 (1980): 3–4. Birdwhistell did not follow his peers who saw this immanence as a chance to domesticate context, to make it manageable. Birdwhistell did not shift his footing from self to ethnographic subject to see how *they* (the native interactants, as it were) delimited context in interaction, how *they* put action under a description. That is, if contextualization (n.b. the processualization) were studied from the standpoint of communicating social actors, as ethnomethodologists and conversation analysts sought to do, and as interactional sociolinguists and linguistic anthropologists began to do, then a seemingly infinite context could be held at bay; context could become a local, practical, semiotic problem that is to be solved not by the analyst who enjoys a God's-eye view, but rather by what Silverstein (" 'Cultural' Concepts and the Language-Culture Nexus," 631) called a "sign's-eye view." This redirected attention to local semiotic practices of contextualization that you could detect empirically, if only indirectly or implicitly, in a good transcript (see, for example, Duranti and Goodwin, *Rethinking Context*).

Conversation analysis, for instance, viewed response behavior as a source of evidentiary backing for its claims about sequential pragmatics. Simply put, if someone reacts to an utterance in a manner that suggests that a "request" was just issued, then that's indirect evidence that a request was indeed just issued—at least from that respondent's perspective. Scholars inspired by Batesonian "metacommunication," Goffmanian "frames," Silversteinian "metapragmatics," Gumperzian "contextualization cues" and "conversational inference" all tried in their own way to specify how interlocutors *themselves* locally signal and infer relevant context linguistically and paralinguistically, so that the analyst can know "when enough [context] is enough," as Silverstein once put it. Michael Silverstein, "The Indeterminacy of Contextualization: When is Enough Enough?" in *The Contextualization of Language*, ed. Peter Auer and Aldo Di Luzio (Philadelphia: John Benjamins Publishing Company, 1992), 55–76. Birdwhistell did take Bateson's metacommunication to heart and thought often about what Bateson called the "cross-referencing" capacity of communication, the way signs could reflexively point to other signs at other levels to help settle what they mean, on which, see Lempert, "What is an Anthropology of Gesture?" Nevertheless, this was not used to make contextualization itself into an object of microanalytic attention.

63. Kendon and Sigman argue that it would be incorrect to say that Birdwhistell "gave up kinesics," but only that he "laid increasing emphasis on the larger sociocultural contexts in which any of the several 'partial' or 'infracommunicational' systems must operate, including the kinesic system" (Kendon and Sigman, "Ray L. Birdwhistell [1918–1994]," 250.) Even if we want to argue that Birdwhistell remained confident about the explanatory power of his science, never flagging, never seriously modifying his views—this, despite his trademark tentativeness—we must still explain his dramatic shift in emphasis.

64. On Goffman's trajectory, see, for example, Heather Love's *Underdogs*.

65. Leeds-Hurwitz, "The PENN Tradition," 246.

66. Birdwhistell's unconventional chapter was licensed by the fact that this was a volume to honor Bateson, who was famous for blurred and experimental genres like the "metalogue."

67. Birdwhistell, "Some Discussion of Ethnography, Theory, and Method," 116–17.

68. Birdwhistell, "Some Discussion of Ethnography, Theory, and Method," 140. Much more could be said about the tensions and paradoxes of a cybernetic structuralism of communication.

69. Birdwhistell, *Kinesics and Context*, 88.

70. Davis, "Film Projectors as Microscopes," 44.

71. See, for example, Birdwhistell, "Kinesic Analysis of Filmed Behavior of Children," 142.

72. Leeds-Hurwitz and Kendon, "The Natural History of an Interview and the Microanalysis of Behavior in Social Interaction"; Leeds-Hurwitz, "The Social History of *The Natural History of an Interview*," 8; Watter, "Scrutinizing," 54. Again, I do not attempt to reconstruct here the practices of repeated playback, which obviously cannot be taken for granted and are only hinted at by terms like "soaking" and "frame-by-frame."

73. On wholes nowhere to be found, see, for instance, Hannah Landecker, "Microcinematography and the History of Science and Film," *Isis* 97, no. 1 (2006): 121–32. Compare, again, with Pike. Invoking the photographic notion of depth of focus, Pike imagined he could see behavioral units both finely *and* synoptically at once. "Depth of focus seems to be increased if the observer has a longer time to study the activity—that is, if he can study a record of it a number of times by seeing movies repeated. . . . Not only does the unit as a whole remain in top focus, but much more of the intricate details of the activity and the inter-relationships between those details can then be brought under attention without losing the simultaneous focus on . . . the activity unit as a whole" (Pike, *Language in Relation to a Unified Theory of the Structure of Human Behavior*,

v. 1, 51.) Pike seemed sanguine about the possibility of reaching a proverbial God's eye view on behavioral complexity, a view that, in effect, rejected the conventional wisdom about observational scale, which assumed an inverse correlation between grain and extent: The finer you look, the less expansively you can see. On holism in relation to the sciences of interaction, see McElvenny and Ploder, *Holisms of Communication*. On holism in anthropology, see especially Ton Otto and Nils Bubandt, eds., *Experiments in Holism Theory and Practice in Contemporary Anthropology* (Chichester, UK: Wiley-Blackwell, 2010).

74. On the familiar irony in which microscopy produces more complexity, see, for example, Strathern, *The Relation*, 6; Marilyn Strathern, "Environments Within: An Ethnographic Commentary on Scale," in *Culture, Landscape, and the Environment: The Linacre Lectures 1997*, ed. Kate Flint and Howard Morphy (Oxford: Oxford University Press, 2000), 44–71. Compare with those disciplines of fine-grained phonetic transcription that advised transcribers *not* to listen to the whole of sound data first but instead to proceed piecemeal, so as to avoid biases from one's native phonological distinctions. Thanks to Bruce Mannheim (personal communication) for this point. It must be noted that Birdwhistell's method did ensure that he retained the sense of a gestalt, of pattern. He did not work inductively from the bottom up (cf. Kendon and Sigman, "Ray L. Birdwhistell [1918–1994]," 252–53.) In this light, it may be no surprise that he remained committed to the idea of a unified, cohesive, visual-kinesthetic channel, because he would have been accustomed to finding that unity through the very way he worked with his visual data. He refused to separate out hands and feet and heads and so on, because, from that purportedly grosser if more holistic vantagepoint, these were "interdependent systems." In that interview with McDermott late in his career, Birdwhistell insisted that the "body is not made up of a set of parts." "It seems to me ridiculous and inappropriate to subdivide an organismic system or social system and to act as though we're a little red wagon with wheels, tongues, or other replaceable parts that can be studied one at a time" (McDermott, "Profile: Ray L. Birdwhistell," 14–15.)

75. Ray L. Birdwhistell, from a double conference session on "Film Analysis of Culture and Communication" held at the 1970 meetings of the American Anthropological Association, San Diego, California, December 20–21. National Anthropological Film Collection at the Smithsonian, Washington, DC. Recordings SR 002, SR 003. For access to audio recordings, many thanks to Scott Ross and to Human Studies Film Archives (HSFA) archivists Daisy Njoku and Mark White.

76. On the over-extension of linguistic structuralism, Stephen Murray, for example, writes: "The forms of body motion and other nonverbal signaling are not organized hierarchically, as linguists of the 1950s—with their view of distinct 'levels' of language—had hoped." Murray, *American Sociolinguistics: Theorists and Theory Groups* (Amsterdam; Philadelphia: J. Benjamins, 1998), 44. See Birdwhistell's late interview with McDermott, in which Birdwhistell offers an alternative analytic trope for context, that of a "rope" whose tightly twisted fibers can be isolated out as discontinuous threads even as they function as a whole. McDermott, "Profile: Ray L. Birdwhistell," 4–5.

77. See, for example, Ekman, Paul, and W. Friessen. "The Repertoire of Nonverbal Behavior: Categories, Origins, Usage and Coding." Semiotica 1 (1969): 57. Davis suggests that the debates between Ekman and Birdwhistell intensified in the '70s and that "Ekman replaced Birdwhistell in the important role of arbiter of NIMH grants for nonverbal communication research." Davis, "Film Projectors as Microscopes," 46.

78. We may recall here Jason Throop's phenomenological recuperation of the notion of experience for anthropology. Throop, "Articulating Experience," *Anthropological Theory* 3, no. 2 (2003): 219–41.

79. Christiane Frey, "The Art of Observing the Small: On the Borders of the subvisibilia (from Hooke to Brockes)," *Monatshefte* 105, no. 3 (2013): 382.

80. Anna Lowenhaupt Tsing, *The Mushroom at the End of the World: On the Possibility of Life in Capitalist Ruins* (Princeton: Princeton University Press, 2015).

81. P. 2. Hockett began collaborating with Pittenger and Danehy at Syracuse after he began to withdraw from the NHI group in 1957—the year Freida Fromm-Reichmann died. He stopped attending the NHI meetings altogether when the group shifted its meetings to Pittsburgh in 1958 (Leeds-Hurwitz, "The Social History of *The Natural History of an Interview*," 10–11). The resemblance of *The First Five Minutes* to NHI was due not only to Hockett's participation but also to the fact that NHI members Birdwhistell, Smith, and Trager served as consultants (ibid., Leeds-Hurwitz, 25.)

82. Library of Congress Manuscript Division, ACLS (American Council of Learned Societies), I:559, box 53.1, folder "Language Programs: Subcommittee on Language and Psychotherapy."

83. *The First Five Minutes*, 210, 211.

84. Augusta F. Bronner, "The objective evaluation of psychotherapy round table, 1948," *American Journal of Orthopsychiatry* 19 (1949): 472. Much like the authors of *The First Five Minutes*, Shakow was quick to qualify his argument, adding that he did recognize the benefits of top-down hypothesis testing and was not encouraging aimless, unfettered data collection:

"I am not advocating a grubbing, compulsive, scavenging collection of observations as ends in themselves; nor am I advocating activity of a merely taxonomic kind. I recognize the importance of hypotheses for helping one to see clearly, and their generally great liberating character. But in our hurry to deal with problems, I am afraid that a most important step has been skipped" (ibid., 472).

Among researchers on interaction, debates over experimental and naturalistic methodologies intensified and acquired arguably even higher stakes in the 1960s. See for example, Louis A. Gottschalk and Arthur H. Auerbach, *Methods of Research in Psychotherapy*, (New York: Appleton-Century-Crofts, 1966).

85. Rosner, "Psychotherapy research and the National Institute of Mental Health, 1948–1980"; H. Stam, R. Radtke, and I. Lubek, "Strains in Experimental Social Psychology: A Textual Analysis of the Development of Experimentation in Social Psychology," *Journal of the History of the Behavioral Sciences* 36, no. 4 (2000): 365–82; Kurt Danziger, "Making Social Psychology Experimental: A Conceptual History, 1920–1970," *Journal of the History of the Behavioral Sciences* 36, no. 4 (2000): 329–47. What won out was a very specific sense of the "experimental" (see Danziger, *Constructing the Subject: Historical Origins of Psychological Research*, [Cambridge, UK: Cambridge University Press, 1990]; Danziger, "The Project of an Experimental Social Psychology: Historical Perspectives," *Science in Context* 5 [1992]: 309–28). See also Lemov, *World as Laboratory*. Rosner argues that there was a politicization of epistemology here, where the top-down style of hypothesis testing was argued to be less open and democratic than more naturalistic approaches. On this, see also Cohen-Cole, *The Open Mind*. This debate was locally inflected, so that when psychotherapeutically minded researchers spoke up against experimentalism, they were also defending the capacity of human "intuition." Shakow and others saw a parallel between the receptive psychoanalyst and the inductive empiricist; the two epistemologies had a certain affinity. The former's openness and sensitivity to the world resembled that of the naturalist. As Rosner writes, this debate persisted. (Rosner, "Psychotherapy research and the National Institute of Mental Health, 1948–1980," 114.)

Part Two

1. In their influential textbook, *Introduction to the Science of Sociology* (Chicago: University of Chicago Press, 1924 [1921]), Park and Burgess dedicated a chapter to "social interaction," but

by this they did not mean what this expression would often later mean, namely, situated human interaction in groups of two or more characterized by reciprocal, mutually responsive communication. Park and Burgess cared about "social interaction" in this narrower sense but placed this within a separate chapter on "Social Contact," where "face-to-face relations" (280) was one elementary kind of "interaction." On balance, they used "social interaction" only secondarily for face-to-face interaction. Instead, social interaction was used more expansively. It was used to call attention to the mutual, "reciprocal" influence of humans upon each other, which is ultimately what society was: "A person is a member of society so long as he responds to social forces; when interaction ends, he is isolated and detached; he ceases to be a person and becomes a 'lost soul.' This is the reason that the limits of society are coterminous with the limits of interaction, that is, of the participation of persons in the life of society" (341).

2. For debates over how Cooley should be situated in relation to pragmatism, see especially Glenn Jacobs, "Charles Horton Cooley, Pragmatist or Belletrist? The Complexity of Influence and the Decentering of Intellectual Traditions," *Symbolic Interaction* 35, no. 1 (2012): 24–48. Mead's student Herbert Blumer went on to canonize Mead as founder of "symbolic interactionism." Herbert Blumer, "Society as Symbolic Interaction," in *Human Behavior and Social Processes: An Interactionist Approach*, ed. Arnold M. Rose (Boston: Houghton-Mifflin, 1962), 179–92; Herbert Blumer, "Sociological Implications of the Thought of George Herbert Mead," *American Journal of Sociology* 71, no. 5 (1966): 535–44; Herbert Blumer, *Symbolic Interactionism: Perspective and Method* (Englewood Cliffs, NJ: Prentice-Hall, 1969).

3. Charles Horton Cooley, *Social Organization: A Study of the Larger Mind* (New York: C. Scribner's sons, 1909), 48, 23–24. Cooley, ibid., 23. Cooley's investment in interaction ran deep, as interaction in primary groups helped nurture the social and moral self. More, the primary group was the cradle for a natural democracy where liberal ideals of freedom and autonomy took root; the durable intimacy of the primary group was perhaps even a cure for the social fragmentation and anomie of capitalist modernity. Critics later charged, fairly or not, that all this betrayed a white Protestant liberal nostalgia for "small town" American life. The charge that Cooley's work uncritically reflected a provincial American ideology was first leveled at Cooley after his death by George Herbert Mead. George Herbert Mead, "Cooley's Contribution to American Social Thought' [Foreword]," in *Human Nature and the Social Order*, ed. Charles Horton Cooley (New York: Schocken, 1964 [1930]), ix–xxxviii.. For a later, influential critique that continued in this vein, see, Philip Rieff, "Cooley and Culture," in *Cooley and Sociological Analysis*, ed. Albert J. Reiss (Ann Arbor: University of Michigan Press, 1968). On Mead's distortions of Cooley's thought, see G. Jacobs, "Influence and Canonical Supremacy: An Analysis of How George Herbert Mead Demoted Charles Horton Cooley in the Sociological Canon," *Journal of the History of the Behavioral Sciences* 45, no. 2 (Spring 2009), 117–44; Hans-Joachim Schubert, "The Foundation of Pragmatic Sociology," *Journal of Classical Sociology* 6, no. 1 (2016): 51–74; Natalia Ruiz-Junco and Baptiste Brossard, *Updating Charles H. Cooley: Contemporary Perspectives on a Sociological Classic* (London: Routledge, Taylor and Francis Group, 2019).

4. As for mechanical recording, Cooley imagined these tools could deliver incomparably rich, detailed behavioral records ("If we had a film of George Washington, with phonograph accompaniment, taken when he was conducting the raid on the British at Germantown, it would add more to our precise knowledge of him than all the measurements imaginable"). Yet he did not insist that sociologists build a mediatic microscope to know interaction so "precisely," as many midcentury sciences of interaction would urge. On microcosmic aspects of the primary group, Cooley, *Social Organization*, 26–27. On the epistemological immediacy of the primary group and indexical fidelity of recording technologies Charles Horton Cooley, "Case Study of

Small Institutions as A Method of Research," in *Sociological Theory and Social Research; Being Selected Papers of Charles Horton Cooley*, ed. Robert Cooley Angell (New York: H. Holt and Co., 1930), 318ff, 314.

5. Albion Small, in his sweeping 1905 *General Sociology*, wrote that "the term 'group' serves as a convenient sociological designation for any number of people, larger or smaller, between whom such relations are discovered that they must be thought of together." And so, "a family, a mob, a picnic party, a trade union, a city precinct, a corporation, a state, a nation, the civilized or the uncivilized population of the world, may be treated as a group." Even as he scaled groups in terms of "larger" and "smaller" aggregations of discrete, countable individuals, nothing about small groups made them ripe for a new science. Albion W. Small, *General Sociology: An Exposition of the Main Development in Sociological Theory from Spencer to Ratzenhofer* (Chicago: University of Chicago Press, 1905), 495.

Chapter Five

1. Robert Freed Bales, *Interaction Process Analysis: A Method for the Study of Small Groups* (Cambridge, MA: Addison-Wesley Press, 1950), i. Writing especially about John Roberts's approach to Navajo households in 1951, Joel Isaac notes how small groups seemed "experimentally and theoretically tractable" relative to larger social units (Isaac, "Epistemic Design: Theory and Data in Harvard's Department of Social Relations," in *Cold War Social Science: Knowledge Production, Liberal Democracy, and Human Nature*, ed. Mark Solovey and Hamilton Cravens [New York: Palgrave MacMillan, 2012], 83.) Though it was not experimental tractability that he had in mind, Cooley, too, for example, had suggested that the "small"-ness of the primary group gave it a certain epistemological immediacy compared to larger groupings (Cooley, "Case Study of Small Institutions as A Method of Research").

2. We can see here an ideological elaboration of the negative correlation of grain and extent, which shows up time and again in methodological disputes of various kinds.

3. See especially Mark Solovey, *Shaky Foundations: The Politics-Patronage-Social Science Nexus in Cold War America* (New Brunswick, NJ: Rutgers University Press, 2013), 4; Brett Gary, "Communication Research, the Rockefeller Foundation, and Mobilization for the War on Words, 1938-1944," *Journal of Communication* 46, no. 3 (1996): 125; Joel Isaac, *Working Knowledge: Making the Human Sciences from Parsons to Kuhn* (Cambridge, MA: Harvard University Press, 2012). On this sense of objectivity, see Theodore M. Porter, *Trust in Numbers: The Pursuit of Objectivity in Science and Public Life* (Princeton: Princeton University Press, 1995). An analogous technocratic sensibility characterized the interwar period, when private funders such as the Rockefeller Foundation and Carnegie Corporation figured prominently. As Solovey chronicles, there was no seamless, unproblematic continuity stretching from the interwar period into and through the Cold War. Social scientists in the 1930s, for instance, faced pitched battles from many quarters over their alleged objectivity and value neutrality, and some academics were either ambivalent about or hostile toward the value neutrality demanded of them (Solovey, 11–12). On the '20s and '30s, see, for example, Mark C. Smith, *Social Science in the Crucible: The American Debate over Objectivity and Purpose, 1918–1941* (Durham, NC: Duke University Press, 1994). On not exaggerating the discontinuity of the Cold War, see David C. Engerman, "Social Science in the Cold War," *Isis* 101 (2010): 393–400.

4. This rebranding argument is made by Pooley "A 'Not Particularly Felicitous' Phrase: A History of the 'Behavioral Sciences' Label," *Serendipities: Journal for the Sociology and History of the Social Sciences* 1, no. 1 (2016): 38–81.

5. Joel Isaac, "Tool Shock: Technique and Epistemology in the Postwar Social Sciences," 137; Engerman, "Social Science in the Cold War," 396. Jamie Cohen-Cole has suggested that the boundary object of interaction, which demanded collaboration from different fields, recapitulated and reciprocally affirmed the cultural virtues of democratic life. As he details, getting along well within the academy via interdisciplinarity was quite often a method to exhibit liberal-democratic and pluralist virtues (tolerance, respect for diversity, democracy, anti-authoritarianism) to and for funders and for wider publics. See Cohen-Cole, "The Creative American" and *The Open Mind*. For a different perspective on interdisciplinarity, specifically at Harvard, see Isaac's discussion of the "interstitial academy" in *Working Knowledge*, 23 et passim, chap. 1.

6. On Bales, see also Erickson et al., *How Reason Almost Lost Its Mind*, chap. 4; Rebecca Lemov, "The Laboratory Imagination: Experiments in Human and Social Engineering, 1929–1956" (PhD diss., University of California, Berkeley, 2000), 337–52.

7. See Isaac, *Working Knowledge*, chap. 5, on the emergence of the Department of Social Relations within what he terms the "Harvard Complex."

8. I am grateful to Seth Watter for our correspondence in 2019, during which time he shared useful archival leads and material. This chapter discusses Chapple's work only until the 1950s and is profitably read in concert with Watter's "Interaction Chronograph" essay, which moves into the 1960s and 1970s. On the full arc of Chapple's career in relation to anthropology as a field, see also Alice Beck Kehoe and Jim Weil, "Eliot Chapple's Long and Lonely Road," in *Expanding American Anthropology, 1945–1980: A Generation Reflects*, ed. Alice Beck Kehoe, Paul L. Doughty, and Nancy K. Peske (Tuscaloosa: University of Alabama Press, 2012), 94–103.

9. I say "styled," because these dedicated machines were not as faithful to interaction as advertised. Bales later recognized that his recorder was practically indistinguishable from a whole class of "auto-instructional devices" that worked very much like his. These machines even had their own trade magazine. One scholar who wrote to Bales out of interest in his machine later said he didn't need one because he had found a stenographic machine used in courtrooms that did pretty much the same thing. As for Chapple's machine, as Watter describes and as noted below, at least one of Chapple's early machines (which existed until his patent filing in 1942) borrowed more than a little from an existing event recorder called a Marsto-Graph.

10. Rebecca Lemov, "'Hypothetical Machines': The Science Fiction Dreams of Cold War Social Science," *Isis* 101 (2010): 404. See also Erickson et al., *How Reason Almost Lost Its Mind*, chap. 4; Isaac, "Tool Shock."

11. Lemov, *Database of Dreams*, 199–200.

12. On human versus mechanical recording in relation to photography, Elizabeth Edwards suggests that "the body became a sort of camera" for ethnographers, in the sense that ". . . the source of the photograph, the anthropologically creating eye, became as significant as the mechanically inscribed content . . ." (Edwards, "Tracing Photography," 161). As for the history of mechanical sound-recording technologies, the trajectory of displacement that Lemov notes, in which confidence in human recording gives way to confidence in machines, did have its exceptions. One was sociologist Erving Goffman who seemed to reject everything that the dominant postwar small-group researchers cared about. Goffman famously rejected mechanical recording along with the technophilic and technocratic aspects of interaction analysis while also simultaneously insisting on interaction's autonomy (albeit on Durkheimian grounds). In a note from 1961, he quipped that "'small-group' experimenters have certainly stood up close to their data but have used a considerable amount of this opportunity to adjust their equipment" (Erving Goffman, "Role Distance," in *Encounters: Two Studies in the Sociology of Interaction* [New York: Bobbs-Merrill Company, Inc., 1961], note 46, 143.)

13. See Chris Kelty's *The Participant*, an imaginative historical ethnography that also touches on matters of interaction—specifically, on the very idea of "participation"—and includes a sustained discussion of Kurt Lewin.

14. Bales, *Interaction Process Analysis*, i. Beyond size, his definition invoked a certain intimacy of copresence and mutual awareness: "A small group," wrote Bales, "is defined as any number of persons engaged in interaction with each other in a single face-to-face meeting or a series of such meetings, in which each member receives some impression or perception of each other member distinct enough so that he can, either at the time or later questioning, give some reaction to each of the others as an individual person, even though it be only to recall that the other was present" (ibid., 33).

15. Robert F. Bales and Henry Gerbrands, "The 'Interaction Recorder': An Apparatus and Check List for Sequential Content Analysis of Social Interaction," *Human Relations* 1 (1948): 456.

16. Bales did note the need for other data but in practice and in terms of how he presented his science, what mattered most was his coding methods, which immediatized interaction.

17. See, for example, Stam, Radtke, and Lubek, "Strains in Experimental Social Psychology." On the changing sense of the experimental in social psychology, see Danziger, "The Project of an Experimental Social Psychology" and "Making Social Psychology Experimental."

18. Danziger, "Making Social Psychology Experimental," 334. See also John D. Greenwood, *The Disappearance of the Social in American Social Psychology* (Cambridge, UK: Cambridge University Press, 2004).

19. Max Weber, *The Theory of Social and Economic Organization*, trans. A. M. Henderson and Talcott Parsons (New York: Free Press, 1947), 118.

20. Sullivan, "The Psychiatric Interview," 364.

Chapter Six

1. In industry, see, for example, Vinzenz Hediger and Patrick Vonderau, *Films that Work: Industrial Film and the Productivity of Media*, (Amsterdam: Amsterdam University Press, 2009).

2. Bales, *Interaction Process Analysis*, 38–39, 37.

3. Eliot D. Chapple, "Measuring Human Relations: An Introduction to the Study of the Interaction of Individuals," *Genetic Psychology Monographs: Child Behavior, Animal Behavior, and Comparative Psychology* 22, no. 1 (1940): 5.

4. Chapple, "Measuring Human Relations," 12. Chapple's conversion was not his alone. The sensibility he embraced was being embraced by many, and in some quarters it seemed positively contagious. As Watter notes, for instance, one doctrine Chapple adopted was Bridgman's operationalism. This doctrine was one of many that had a family resemblance, and kindred ideas included those of logical positivists and other members of the Vienna Circle.

5. Chapple, "Measuring Human Relations," 6.

6. See Richard Bauman and Charles L. Briggs, "Making Language and Making It Safe for Science and Society: From Francis Bacon to John Locke," chap. 2 in *Voices of Modernity: Language Ideologies and the Politics of Inequality*, 19–69; cf. Michael Losonsky, *Linguistic Turns in Modern Philosophy* (Cambridge, UK: Cambridge University Press, 2006).

7. Watter, "Interaction Chronograph."

8. See Peter Burke, *The Art of Conversation* (Ithaca: Cornell University Press, 1993).

9. Chapple "Quantitative Analysis of the Interaction of Individuals," *Proceedings of the National Academy of Sciences of the United States of America* 25, no. 2 (1939): 59.

10. Compare with the counterdirectional drive that Lemov *Database of Dreams* describes as the "subjective turn" in the social sciences, where researchers tried to access rather than wall off interiority using methods that were often redolent of the rigor of the harder sciences.

11. Chapple, "Measuring Human Relations," 24.

12. Using the behaviorist metalanguage of stimulus and response, Chapple described the mechanics: "When one or more quanta of action q_i manifested by Individual A, are followed by one or more quanta of action p_i, manifested by Individual B, the quanta q_i may be regarded as the stimulus s_i, and the quanta p_i as the response r_i. Such a succession $s_i r_i$ will be defined as constituting interaction between the individuals A and B." (Ibid., 24.)

While unidirectional, the directionality may then reverse itself. For if A then acts after B's response, B's action becomes the stimulus and A's action the response. Chapple's argument read like a behaviorist domestication of John Dewey's "reflex arc" critique. Dewey had argued against the discrete, linear, unidirectional logic of stimulus-to-response, in part by stressing the counterdirectional and the co-constitutive: a response is also—simultaneously, not sequentially—a stimulus for ongoing action. For Dewey, the then nascent behaviorists had broken up actional wholes into "a patchwork of disjointed parts, a mechanical conjunction of unallied processes," and *then* puzzled over what-caused-what; their "disjointed psychology" had failed to see the intricate state of organic interdependence and constant interplay. "In its failure to see that the arc of which it talks is virtually a circuit, a continual reconstitution, it breaks continuity and leaves us nothing but a series of jerks." (John Dewey, "The Reflex Arc Concept in Psychology," *Psychological Review* 3 [1896], 358, 360, 360.) Chapple made interaction into a circuit, of sorts, whose bidirectional current ran from A to B and B to A, yet this was a circuit whose actions were discrete, linear, and sequential—a series of jerks. Actions were also monofunctional—they did one thing at a time—just as they did for Bales, as we shall later see.

13. Danziger, "Making social psychology experimental," 333.

14. For Chapple's own account of his machine's development, see Eliot D. Chapple, "The Interaction Chronograph: Its Evolution and Present Application," *Personnel* 25 (1949): 296ff; see also Eliot D. Chapple and Donald Jr. Gordon, "A Method for Evaluating Supervisory Personnel," *Harvard Business Review* Winter (1946): 200. While Chapple was busy with his first prototype in 1938, Arensberg wrote a long teacherly letter to Solon Kimball, whom Arensberg mentored. "Reserve your real work for recording," he advised, and offered instructions: "Get (perhaps) a large daybook, in which you can make entries day by day or even hour by hour. In this daybook, record events, putting down what you . . . see and nothing more. Disregard what was done, the kind of action, for you want that only literary use. But record religiously Who Began It, Who Took it Up, When. You can run a scheme of events in parallel columns, as in book-keeping. . . ." Conrad Arensberg to Solon Kimball, February 14, 1938, Conrad M. Arensberg Papers, ser. 3, box 31, Letters of Eliot Chapple and Solon Kimball, National Anthropological Archives.

15. Narrating things this way may make it seem as if machines arrived to satisfy human epistemic needs; but, of course, the story wasn't linear and the relationship not one of simple "use."

16. Watter, "Interaction Chronograph."

17. See Watter "Interaction Chronograph" and the discussion of the Marsto-Graph below.

18. Chapple, "Quantitative Analysis of the Interaction of Individuals," 59.

19. Chapple, "Measuring Human Relations," 34; Eliot D. Chapple, " 'Personality' Differences as Described by Invariant Properties of Individuals in Interaction," *Proceedings of the National Academy of Sciences of the United States of America* 26, no. 1 (1940): 11.

20. See Watter, "Interaction Chronograph."

21. Its name stuck publicly, but he retained the name "interaction recorder" for purposes of his patent.

22. Watter, "Interaction Chronograph."

23. See discussions of Daston and Galison, *Objectivity*, in part 1.

24. Lawrence C. Kelly, interview with F. L. W. Richardson and Eliot D. Chapple, 48, Washington DC, December 6, 1980, tape, box 3, item 33. Lawrence "Larry" Kelly Papers (hereafter Kelly Papers), University of North Texas Special Collections. Thanks to Seth Watter for this. A second medical study by Chapple appeared in 1944, as Eliot D. Chapple and Warren T. Vaughan, "A Clinical Method for Studying the Factor of Human Relations in Disease," *Journal of Laboratory and Clinical Medicine* 29, no. 1 (1944): 1–18.

25. Kelly Papers, 63.

26. Kelly Papers, 27.

27. Letter from Eliot D. Chapple to William J. Crozier, 2. Thanks to Seth Watter for drawing my attention to this letter. In an issue on small groups, editor Fred Strodtbeck paid Chapple a backhanded compliment: "Chapple, in his hard-headed positivistic conviction that the fallibility of the observer should be eliminated, created in his interaction chronograph a milestone in the growth of small-group techniques." Fred L. Strodtbeck, "The Case for the Study of Small Groups," *American Sociological Review* 19, no. 6 (1954): 652–53.

28. See Cohen-Cole's *The Open Mind* and his earlier essay, "The Creative American."

29. For a sense of Chapple's view of human relations, see Eliot Dismore Chapple and Carleton S. Coon, *Principles of Anthropology* (New York: H. Holt and Company, 1942), iii. Compare with the interdisciplinary embraced by the Department and Laboratory of Social Relations. Anonymous, *Department and Laboratory of Social Relations, Harvard University: The First Decades 1946–1956* (Cambridge, MA: Harvard University Press, 1956). Tozzer Library Special Collections, Harvard University.

30. Erickson et al., *How Reason Almost Lost Its Mind.*

31. Bales and Gerbrands, "The 'Interaction Recorder.'"

32. Bales, *Interaction Process Analysis*, pp 5–6, v. His machine may not have been obligatory, but it was not subordinate to commercially available recording technologies. Bales used sound recording in his lab alongside his interaction recorder but only for "insurance against accidental loss"; in principle, "sound recording is not an absolute necessity" (Bales, v).

33. Bales, in effect, brushed aside the whole issue of what ordinary language philosopher John Austin introduced as speech-act performativity, that is, how exactly you get from what people say to what they do (*How to Do Things with Words* [London: Oxford University Press, 1962]). Instead, he cut through language with inference and then shored up the validity of pragmatic inferences through tests of intercoder reliability.

34. Monofunctional didn't mean that Bales saw all acts as equally discrete and comparably sized units in respect of time. He distinguished acts that were relatively compact from those that were "diffuse," for example. Bales, *Interaction Process Analysis*, 190ff.

35. His universe of twelve actions was riddled with assumptions too numerous to draw out here, but let us consider some features of its architecture. Divide by three and the twelve fall cleanly into four superordinate categories (A, B, C, D). A and D represent "positive reactions" and "negative reactions" respectively, while B and C represent "Attempted Answers" and "Questions" respectively. Zoom out more, and now A and D together make up "social-emotional" actions whose polarities run positive (A) and negative (D). (A positive act might be to "show solidarity"; a negative one might be to "show antagonism.") The social-emotional sets A and D contrast with the instrumental, task-oriented sets B and C. As Bales took cybernetics to heart, he

came to see these two sets as dynamically related in which group members provide "more or less constant feedback on the acceptability of the problem-solving attempts." (Robert F. Bales, "How People Interact in Conferences," *Scientific American* 192, no. 3 [1955], 32.)

36. Chapple, "The Interaction Chronograph," 173.

37. Bales, *Interaction Process Analysis*, 35, 85.

38. Bales, *Interaction Process Analysis*, 7.

39. ". . . The essential operation is still one of inference as to the meaningful or functional content of behavior. This feature specifically and radically differentiates the present method from all methods of analyzing interaction on the basis of purely spatiotemporal characteristics, such as that of Chapple or various types of time-and-motion studies" (Bales, *Interaction Process Analysis*, 6).

40. On the gendering of the human–machine interface, specifically with respect to the typewriter, see Jensen "Women as Typewriters," *Turn-of-the-Century Women* III, no. 1 (1986): 43–50. See her discussion of "touch typing," which may be compared with the discipline required of Bales's operators. "Touch typing involves adopting a rigid posture, with arched wrists, fingers hovering on the home keys, and eyes on the copy to be typed, not on the typewriter keyboard. The touch typist's fingers fly while she scans the words to be typed without 'understanding' them . . ." (46).

41. On the legacy of Mead, see the testy exchange in the mid-1960s between Bales and symbolic interactionist Herbert Blumer. Blumer, "Sociological Implications of the Thought of George Herbert Mead"; Robert F. Bales, "Comment on Herbert Blumer's Paper," *American Journal of Sociology* 71 (1966): 545–47; Herbert Blumer, "Reply," *American Journal of Sociology* 71 (1966): 547–48.

42. Bales, *Interaction Process Analysis*, 39.

43. Bales, *Interaction Process Analysis*, 42.

Chapter Seven

1. Gustave Le Bon, *The Crowd: A Study of the Popular Mind* (New York: Penguin Books, 1977): whole bigger than parts, pg. 1; collective mind, unconsciousness reigns, 7–8; crowd members like "savages" and laborers, 12.

2. Strodtbeck, "The Case for the Study of Small Groups."

3. Strodtbeck, "The Case for the Study of Small Groups," 652.

4. Mary E. Roseborough, "Experimental Studies of Small Groups," *Psychological Bulletin* 50, no. 4 (1953): 279.

5. In feedback Margaret Mead once gave Chapple, she brought up his lack of interest in group dynamics. "You haven't allowed for or more or less interaction—*as a whole*, and for the extent to which a large amount of interaction or a small amount as certain properties for all participants" (emphasis in original), Letter to Eliot Chapple, August 19, 1966, box C76, folder 5, Margaret Mead Papers and the South Pacific Ethnographic Archives, Manuscript Division, Library of Congress, Washington, DC.

6. Chapple, "Measuring Human Relations," 34.

7. In the patent description, the activity curve was, more precisely, "the patient's actions, minus his silences or inactions." The second showed "the patient's interruptions of the physician, minus his failures to respond to the latter, and is customarily referred to as the 'adjustment' curve." The third showed the same as the second, but did so for the physician. Eliot D. Chapple. Interaction recorder. United States Patent Office, Patent No. 2,387,563. October 23, 1945, 3.

8. See Chapple, "The Interaction Chronograph," 295 and Chapple, " 'Personality' Differences as Described by Invariant Properties of Individuals in Interaction."

9. In a manual for his chronograph from 1956, Chapple used language that helped map interactional behavior onto other characterological attributes, such as "impatience." See Watter, "Interaction Chronograph."

10. Eliot D. Chapple and Gordon Jr. Donald, "An Evaluation of Department Store Salespeople by the Interaction Chronograph," *Journal of Marketing* 12, no. 2 (1947): 173–85.

11. For details on the standard interview, aptly called a "stress" interview, see Watter, "Interaction Chronograph."

12. Chapple and Donald, "An Evaluation of Department Store Salespeople by the Interaction Chronograph," 176.

13. Eliot Dismore Chapple and Edmond F. Wright, *How to Supervise People in Industry: A Guide for Supervisors on How to Understand People and Control Their Behavior* (Chicago: National Foremen's Institute, Inc., 1946), 8.

14. Chapple and Donald, "An Evaluation of Department Store Salespeople by the Interaction Chronograph," 173.

15. Gerard Piel, "Your Personality Sits for Its Photo," *Nation's Business* 35, no. 4 (1947): 51; Herbert Yahraes, "Machine Probes your Personality," *Popular Science* 152, no. 4 (1948): 148–53.

16. Chapple and Gordon, "A Method for Evaluating Supervisory Personnel," 197.

17. Chapple, "The Interaction Chronograph," 298.

18. Jacob E. Finesinger et al., *An Investigation of Prediction of Success in Naval Flight Training.*

19. Bales, *Interaction Process Analysis*, 20.

20. Frederick Turner traces out how Lewin's project articulated with other scholars who hoped to discover and promote a distinctively "democratic" mode of communication (Turner, *The Democratic Surround: Multimedia & American Liberalism from World War II to the Psychedelic Sixties* [Chicago: University of Chicago Press, 2013].) Lewin has attracted a considerable literature, not the least because he became important in fields such as organizational psychology, organizational sociology, and organizational development, as well as in "intergroup relations" within communication studies.

21. Discursively Levin did not name his object in scalar terms ("small"), as Bales and others did.

22. Kurt Lewin, "The Research Center for Group Dynamics at Massachusetts Institute of Technology," *Sociometry* 8, no. 2 (1945): 131.

23. Lewin, "The Research Center for Group Dynamics at Massachusetts Institute of Technology," 133–34.

24. On the Lewinians at Harwood, see especially Kelty's recent, insightful discussion in *The Participant*. The MIT Center opened at the same time that the American Jewish Congress created its Commission on Community Interrelations, and Lewin hoped for a synergy between his new center and this commission. (Alfred J. Marrow, *The Practical Theorist: The Life and Work of Kurt Lewin* [New York: Basic Books, 1969].) For a biographical account of Lewin's early experiences of antisemitism and their effect on his political sensibilities, see Miriam Lewin, "The Impact of Kurt Lewin's Life on the Place of Social Issues in His Work," *Journal of Social Issues* 48, no. 2 (1992): 15–29.

25. Roseborough, "Experimental Studies of Small Groups," 281.

26. As Hull writes, technologizing is "an attempt to stabilize a sociomaterial process (speaking practices), to 'black box' . . . it in texts, procedures, inscriptions and so forth, so it can be said to have determinative effects independent from the actual situations in which it occurs"

Matthew Hull, "Democratic Technologies of Speech: From WWII America to Postcolonial Delhi," *Journal of Linguistic Anthropology* 20, no. 2 (2010): 259.

27. Kurt Lewin, Ronald Lippitt, and Ralph K. White, "Patterns of Aggressive Behavior in Experimentally Created 'Social Climates,'" *Journal of Social Psychology* 10 (1939): 271–99. During the mid-1930s Lewin shifted from the study of human dyads to small groups, which had dynamics of their own. Mitchell G. Ash, "Cultural Contexts and Scientific Change in Psychology: Kurt Lewin in Iowa," *American Psychologist* 47, no. 2 (1992): 202. For a closer history of this research, see Leland P. Bradford, *National Training Laboratories: Its History, 1947–1970: Originally National Training Laboratory in Group Development and Now NTL Institute for Applied Behavioral Science* (Bethel, ME: Bradford, 1974); see also Ralph K. White and Ronald Lippitt, *Autocracy and Democracy: An Experimental Inquiry*, (New York: Harper, 1960).

28. Kurt Danziger, *Constructing the Subject*; "The Project of an Experimental Social Psychology: Historical Perspectives," *Science in Context* 5 (1992): 319.; "Making Social Psychology Experimental."

29. Danziger, "The Project of an Experimental Social Psychology."

30. Lewin, "Experiments in Social Space," 25. To assess different climates, the Lewinians drew together a kaleidoscopic array of data. Stenographic records were made by hand, to get at speech, but these were only one data point among many. In a 1939 article, Lewin noted how "we-centered" statements occurred more frequently in democratic climates and "I-centered" in autocratic climates (Lewin, "Experiments in Social Space," 26). The attention to deictic expressions "I" and "we" may seem reminiscent of Lasswell's 1938 proposal for a generalized discourse analysis (Lasswell, "A Provisional Classification of Symbol Data"), but the Lewin group did not privilege communication as a special object worthy of careful recording and investigation.

31. Bradford, *National Training Laboratories*, 9.

32. Lewin, "Experiments in Social Space," 273, 271.

33. On the dramaturgy of experimentation that treads on somewhat similar issues, see Ian Nicholson, "'Shocking' Masculinity: Stanley Milgram, 'Obedience to Authority,' and the 'Crisis of Manhood' in Cold War America," *Isis* 102 (2011): 238–68.

34. Marrow, *The Practical Theorist*, 141.

35. White and Lippitt, *Autocracy and Democracy*, 10.

36. *Preliminary Report of the First National Training Laboratory on Group Development, Held at Gould Academy, Bethel, Maine* (Bethel, ME, 1947), 69.

37. *Preliminary Report of the First National Training Laboratory on Group Development*, 6.

38. On Lewin's early experiences with academic hierarchy, see Lewin, "The Impact of Kurt Lewin's Life on the Place of Social Issues in His Work," 20.

39. See Marrow, *The Practical Theorist*.

40. Ash, "Cultural Contexts and Scientific Change," 201.

41. Marrow, *The Practical Theorist*, 88.

42. *Preliminary Report of the First National Training Laboratory*, 6. While the Lewinians' early focus on the boy's clubs suggested a familiar gendering of the political as a male-coded domain, women were invited to the first national training laboratory, and these participants were not all wives of male invitees. See Directory of Participants, *Preliminary Report of the First National Training Laboratory*. I thank Matthew Hull for alerting me to the gendering of the political in Lewin's science.

43. *Preliminary Report of the First National Training Laboratory*, 15, iii.

44. See Cohen-Cole's "The Creative American" and *The Open Mind*.

45. *Preliminary Report of the First National Training Laboratory*, 31.

46. *Preliminary Report of the First National Training Laboratory*, 30, 4–5.

47. Bradford, *National Training Laboratories*, 44.

48. Bradford, *National Training Laboratories*, 16.

49. Bradford, *National Training Laboratories*, 139–42.

50. Bradford, *National Training Laboratories*, 48.

51. Bradford, *National Training Laboratories*, 45.

52. Bradford, *National Training Laboratories*, app., 107–11.

53. Bradford, *National Training Laboratories*, app., 105.

54. Robert F. Bales, "Cooley-Mead Award 1983: Robert F. Bales," *Social Psychology Quarterly* 47, no. 1 (1984): 99.

55. *Preliminary Report of the First National Training Laboratory*, 127.

56. Another category of observer was residually titled, "overall observation and sociometric." This was done by Richard Sheldon, a social anthropologist from Harvard.

57. *Preliminary Report of the First National Training Laboratory*, on group observation, 46. On the anecdotal report, 137, and app., 97.

58. Bradford, *National Training Laboratories*, 158.

59. Bradford, *National Training Laboratories*, 138.

60. Bradford, *National Training Laboratories*, 35.

61. Bradford, *National Training Laboratories*, 160.

62. As Chris Kelty writes, when the Lewinian democratic technology was trained on the workplace, and not on cultivating leaders, you could see this effort as a form of "governing through freedom," to use Peter Miller and Nikolas Rose's expression, specifically, as "the crafting of a new kind of subject" who was "exhorted to be democratic, independent, autonomous, and eventually entrepreneurial." Kelty, *The Participant*, 96; Peter Miller and Nikolas Rose, *Governing the Present: Administering Economic, Social and Personal Life* (Cambridge, UK: Polity Press, 2008).

63. Dorwin Cartwright, *The Research Center for Group Dynamics: A Report of Five Years' Activities and a View of Future Needs* (Ann Arbor: Institute for Social Research, University of Michigan, 1950), 6, University of Michigan Bentley Library, Institute for Social Research, box 25.

64. Cartwright, 26.

65. Turner, *The Democratic Surround*, 3.

66. On such expertise and its mitigation, see E. Summerson Carr, "Enactments of Expertise," *Annual Review of Anthropology* 39 (2010): 17–32.

67. Bradford, *National Training Laboratories*, 59.

68. Bradford, *National Training Laboratories*, 151.

69. See Robert F. Bales and Ned A. Flanders, "Planning an Observation Room and Group Laboratory," *American Sociological Review* 19, no. 6 (1954): 771–81. Erickson et al. propose to think of Bales's special room eventfully and processually as the spatial aspect of what was often called a "situation"—a Cold War category of quasi-experimental method that could occur indoors or outdoors and make *anything* tractable. (Erickson et al., *How Reason Almost Lost Its Mind*, chap. 4, 112.)

70. See Covner, "Studies in Phonographic Recordings of Verbal Material: I. The Use of Phonographic Recordings in Counseling Practice and Research," 107–8.

71. Paul Paul Bergman, "An Experiment in Filmed Psychotherapy," in *Methods of Research in Psychotherapy*, ed. Louis A. Gottschalk and Arthur H. Auerbach (New York: Appleton-Century-Crofts, 1966), 40. For Shakow's reflections on how best to record, see Shakow, "The Recorded Psychoanalytic Interview as an Objective Approach to Research in Psychoanalysis." See also Allen T. Dittmann, Seymour N. Stein, and David Shakow, "Sound Motion Picture Facilities for

Research in Communication," in *Methods of Research in Psychotherapy*, ed. Louis A. Gottschalk and Arthur H. Auerbach (New York: Appleton-Century-Crofts, 1966), 25–33. "Million-Dollar Toy," undated, handwritten letter from Rae Shifrin Sternberg to David Shakow, Shakow Papers, box M1646, folder 9.

72. Bales, *Interaction Process Analysis*, 23, 25.

73. Bales, *Interaction Process Analysis*, 29.

74. Bales, *Interaction Process Analysis*, 126ff. Apart from Parsons's systems theory, certain sociologies and social psychologies of groups had argued this for years. In the 1930s, Lewin, pace Allport, claimed that "any dynamical whole has properties of its own" (Lewin, "Experiments in Social Space," 22–23.) As Lewin's student Cartwright reflected: "It was Lewin's conviction that laws of group behavior could be established independently of the purposes or the specific activities of the group. Thus, it would be possible to study a group's productivity as a phenomenon whether it be in the committee-room, factor, or classroom. Further, one would be able to specify the determinants of friendship or hostility between groups whether they be formed on the basis of race, religion, sex, or nationality." (*The Research Center for Group Dynamics*, 5–6.)

75. A precursor to the seven stages can already be detected in embryonic form as early as 1947. See *Preliminary Report of the First National Training Laboratory*, 120.

76. Bales, "How People Interact in Conferences," 32, 35.

77. *Preliminary Report of the First National Training Laboratory*, 1.

78. Cartwright, *The Research Center for Group Dynamics*, 10.

79. Cartwright, *The Research Center for Group Dynamics*, 10.

80. Lewin, "The Research Center for Group Dynamics," 129.

81. Pace Jamie Cohen-Cole, who writes that "the most important innovations in social science in the postwar years were designed to erase distinctions between forms and scales of social life. These included game theory and small-group studies" (Cohen-Cole, *The Open Mind*, 107).

82. In *Scale*, we used "interscalarity" in at least three distinct ways. First, interscalarity reminded us of the unavoidable relationality of scale (small-scale implies large-scale, etc.), which meant that even when actors focused on one end of a scalar divide, we needed to tease out the unstated, contrasting term and ask how the two were being related in a given case. Second, interscalarity reminded us to explore *conversions* among distinct senses and operations of scale. We noticed that sometimes distinct kinds of scale got chained together. On this, see especially a chapter by Barbra Meek (*Scale*, 70–88) on Kaska language revitalization in Canada's Yukon Territory. Third, we used interscalarity to refer to dense *laminations* of mutually reinforcing scalar practices, as described by Susan Philips (112–32), who peeled back Tonga's "Higher" and "Lower" court system to reveal its infrastructure. (Compare with another ostentatiously scaled institution, the state, whose "nested system of jurisdictions, statutes, and regulatory and fiscal agencies produces manifold observable effects on social reality" Sayre, "Scales and Polities," 506.)

83. Anthropologist Gabrielle Hecht has written recently of "interscalar vehicles": *things* that invite and afford leaps of scale, which, in her case, were uranium rich rocks in Gabon that became the center of contestation (Hecht, "Interscalar Vehicles for an African Anthropocene: On Waste, Temporality, and Violence"). Hecht's essay resonates with E. Summerson Carr and Brooke Fisher ("Inter-scaling Awe, De-escalating Disaster," in *Scale*, ed. E. Summerson Carr and Michael Lempert), who focus on the interscalar significance of a Japanese dock that suddenly landed on an Oregon beach. The geographer Neil Smith wrote about a literal interscalar vehicle, detailing how homeless people in New York City defied the scaled urban landscapes that tried to constrain them using a technology, the Homeless Vehicle. (e.g., "Contours of a Spatialized Politics: Homeless Vehicles and the Production of Geographical Scale," *Social Text* 33 [1992].)

84. Carr and Lempert, *Scale*.

85. See Oppenheim's discussion of actor-network theory's critique of this "volumetric inclusion," in Oppenheim, "Actor-Network Theory and Anthropology after Science, Technology, and Society." *Anthropological Theory* 7, no. 4 (2007): 471–93.

86. Bales, *Interaction Process Analysis*, 118ff.

87. Bales, *Interaction Process Analysis*, 119.

88. Bales, *Interaction Process Analysis*. 120.

89. Talcott Parsons and Robert Freed Bales, *Family, Socialization, and Interaction Process* (Glencoe, IL: Free Press, 1955), vii-viii.

90. Parsons and Bales, *Family, Socialization, and Interaction Process*, 356.

91. Parsons and Bales, *Family, Socialization, and Interaction Process*, ix.

92. Parsons and Bales, *Family, Socialization, and Interaction Process*, 260.

Part Three

1. McGrath, Joseph E. "Small-Group Research, That Once and Future Field: An Interpretation of the Past with an Eye to the Future." *Group Dynamics: Theory, Research, and Practice* 1, no. 1 (1997): 7. As McGrath goes on to note, some of these small-group traditions "flourished in a number of adjacent disciplines (e.g., organizational behavior, speech communication, political science)," even as they declined in the fields that first embraced them.

Chapter Eight

1. Nancy M. Henley, "The Politics of Touch," in *Radical Psychology*, ed. Phil Brown (New York: Harper & Row, 1973), 421.

2. Lynn O'Connor. "Male Dominance: The Nitty Gritty of Oppression." *It Ain't Me Babe*, v. 1: 8 (June 11–July 1), 1970.

3. For early surveys of the language and gender literature, see Barrie Thorne and Nancy Henley, *Language and Sex: Difference and Dominance*, (Rowley, Mass: Newbury House Publishers, 1975). Susan U. Philips, "Sex Differences and Language," *Annual Review of Anthropology* 9 (1980): 523–44.

4. Elise Kramer, "Feminist Linguistics and Linguistic Feminisms," in *Mapping Feminist Anthropology in the 21st Century*, ed. Ellen Lewin and Leni M. Silverstein (Rutgers: Rutgers University Press, 2016), 65.

5. Erving Goffman, "Alienation from Interaction," *Human Relations* 10, no. 1 (1957): 47–60.

6. Interview, June 12, 2020. Lynn E. O'Connor, "How to Think Like a Clinician: Evolution of a Theory," 2019. Unpublished manuscript in possession of Lynn O'Connor.

7. I. Arthur Mirsky, Robert E. Miller, and John V. Murphy, "The Communication of Affect in Rhesus Monkeys: I. An Experimental Method," *Journal of the American Psychoanalytic Association* 6, no. 3 (1958): 433.

8. Albert E. Scheflen, "Quasi-Courtship Behavior in Psychotherapy," *Psychiatry* 28, no. 3 (1965): 245–57.

9. Syllabus accessed from Bios Sociologicus: Erving Goffman Archives, Dmitri N. Shalin, ed. (UNLV: CDC Publications, 2009).

10. Desmond Morris, *The Naked Ape: A Zoologist's Study of the Human Animal*, (New York: McGraw-Hill, 1967); Desmond Morris, *The Human Zoo*, (New York: McGraw-Hill, 1969); Desmond Morris, *Intimate Behaviour* (London: Cape, 1971).

11. "A Theory of Racism," 17, Chester M. Pierce, Chester M. Pierce Papers, Harvard University, Countway Library of Medicine, box 06, folder 24, identifier H MS c523. It is common to distinguish "verbal" from "nonverbal" microaggressions, and while Pierce would soon make this distinction, he gave special importance to embodied interpersonal behavior. He later developed the notion of "kinetic" racism, which he argued was the mode of anti-Black racism that predominates in America.

12. Henley's writings here may seem to reflect a "radical" feminist sensibility, yet my concern, again, is not to locate her relative to social movement politics. Many recognize the historiographic troubles that come from trying to use contested labels such as "radical," "liberal," and "cultural" feminism. Similar tensions have surfaced in the "language and gender" literature. For instance, as linguist Robin Lakoff became canonized, scholars asked how to place her within the women's movement. See Robin Tolmach Lakoff and Mary Bucholtz, *Language and Woman's Place: Text and Commentaries*, Rev. and expanded ed., (New York: Oxford University Press, 2004). In this volume, Mary Bucholtz found "radical," "liberal," and "cultural" feminist strands of her scholarship, suggesting that she defied easy classification (ibid., 121–27).

13. Nancy Henley, *Body Politics*, (Englewood Cliffs, NJ: Prentice-Hall, 1977), ix.

14. Nancy Main Henley, "A psychological study of the semantics of animal terms" (PhD diss., Johns Hopkins University, 1968); Nancy M. Henley, "A Psychological Study of the Semantics of Animal Terms," *Journal of Verbal Learning and Verbal Behavior* 8 (1969): 176–84.

15. Marianne LaFrance, "Nancy M. Henley (1934–2016)," *Psychology of Women Quarterly* 41, no. 1 (2017): 7. The original paper abstract submitted to the American Psychological Association was entitled "Touch Hierarchy" but was changed by the time Henley presented it in September.

16. Roger Brown and Albert Gilman, "The Pronouns of Power and Solidarity," in *Language and Social Context*, ed. Pier Paolo Giglioli (Baltimore: Penguin Books, 1976 [1960], 252–82).

17. See Marcyliena Morgan's remarks on Labov's early anti-racist interventions. Although Labov effectively refuted racist deficit models of Black Americans, Morgan argued that he also unwittingly reproduced a divide between authentic and inauthentic Black English speakers through his notion of a Black "vernacular" that contrasted ideologically with a presumptively white "standard English" (Morgan, "Theories and Politics in African American English," *Annual Review of Anthropology* 23 [1994]: 328–29.) On the related issue of disagreements between Black communities and linguists of Black English, see Morgan, 336–39.

18. Heller and McElhinny, *Language, Capitalism, Colonialism*, 195, chap. 7. On investigations and accusations leveled at social scientists, see David H. Price, *Anthropological Intelligence: The Deployment and Neglect of American Anthropology in the Second World War* (Durham, NC: Duke University Press, 2008); David H. Price, *Cold War Anthropology: The CIA, the Pentagon, and the Growth of Dual Use Anthropology* (Durham, NC: Duke University Press, 2016).

19. Henley, "The Politics of Touch," 421, 431; Henley, *Body Politics*, 3.

20. On plausible deniability, including its use for resistance, see Henley, *Body Politics*, 191. On covert control, ibid., 3. On the reproduction of macropolitical structure, 179.

21. "Finally, I would like to point out vehemently that all the correctives I have just listed are mere stopgaps which cannot begin to alter the male chauvinist nature of male–female interactions; I doubt, in fact, that they can be applied in the present nature of things. Only when these power relations themselves are destroyed, not just their indicators, will we strip the indicators of their power symbolism." Henley, "The Politics of Touch," 433.

22. In scholarship on linguistic performativity, we may recall Michael Silverstein's distinction between "presupposing" and "entailing" indexicality. Presupposing indexicals point to a context that exists independently of the indexical sign itself, while entailing indexicals create

the context to which they point (Silverstein, "Shifters, Linguistic Categories, and Cultural Description"). Compare with Judith Butler's later arguments about the politics of performativity in *Excitable Speech: A Politics of the Performative* (New York: Routledge, 1997). Although Henley recognized that the nonverbal techniques she documented were used to control all kinds of minoritized others, not just women, she argued that "nonverbal control is of particular importance to women, who are more sensitive to its cues and probably more the targets of such control" (Henley, *Body Politics*, 180).

23. Henley, *Body Politics*, 13.

24. Henley, "The Politics of Touch," 426.

25. Experiments in Hostility. *Off Our Backs*, February/March 1973 3(6): 12. Also, January 1973 3(5): 16.

26. Nancy Main Henley, "Oral History with Nancy Main Henley," interview by Jane Collings, 2001.

27. On interactional activism for women, Henley, *Body Politics*, 123; on what men can do, ibid., 203.

28. Gal and Irvine, *Signs of Difference*, 168 et passim.

29. O'Connor, "How to Think Like a Clinician: Evolution of a Theory," 8. See Todd Gitlin's *The Sixties* for a vivid account of the mounting frustrations and alienation women experienced in New Left organizations like SDS. (Gitlin, *The Sixties: Years of Hope, Days of Rage* [Toronto: Bantam Books, 1987].)

30. See Webb Keane's *Ethical Life* (pp. 187–98) for a semiotic account of the way CR ritual involved ethical perspective shifting that transformed individual into collective plight, unreflective habit into heightened reflexivity.

31. Camila Domonoske, *Disrespect To Miss-Respect*, Code Switch, podcast audio, November 29, 2017, https://www.npr.org/transcripts/567085033.

32. On CR's ambivalent but generative relation to therapy, see a classic argument by Ellen Herman, *The Romance of American Psychology: Political Culture in the Age of Experts, 1940–1970* (Berkeley: University of California Press, 1995). For a recent issue on the interplay between psychology and feminist activism, see Alexandra Rutherford and Michael Pettit, eds., "Feminism and/in/as Psychology," vol. 18(3), Special Issue of *History of Psychology* (American Psychological Association, 2015), 223–323. On CR's roots in the New Left, see Sara M. Evans, *Personal Politics: The Roots of Women's Liberation in the Civil Rights Movement and the New Left*, (New York: Knopf: distributed by Random House, 1979), 134–35; see also Gitlin, *The Sixties*, 357. On ties to pedagogical experimentation, see Christopher P. Loss, " 'Women's Studies Is in a Lot of Ways— Consciousness Raising': The Educational Origins of Identity Politics," *History of Psychology* 4, no. 3 (2011): 292ff.

33. Robert Freed Bales, *Personality and Interpersonal Behavior* (New York: Holt, Rinehart, and Winston, 1969), 512.

34. Bales, *Personality and Interpersonal Behavior*, vii, 512.

35. Bales, "Cooley-Mead Award 1983: Robert F. Bales," 101. Late in his career, upon accepting the Cooley-Mead award for scholarship in social psychology, Bales came around to praise Lewinian action research. If you "persist in participant observation," you will eventually "stumble on what the people themselves think is important." And as you "begin to study their attitudes and values" your methods will become "more participative and more democratic."

36. See, for example, Eva S. Moskowitz, *In Therapy We Trust: America's Obsession with Self-Fulfillment* (Baltimore: Johns Hopkins University Press, 2001).

37. Herman, *The Romance of American Psychology*, chap. 10.

38. "How to Start Your Own Consciousness-Raising Group," *Ladies' Home Journal*, August 1970, 71.

39. Lynn O'Connor, "Our Politics Begin with our Feelings," manuscript in possession of Lynn O'Connor, 1970, Redstockings West, San Francisco Meeting of Women's Liberation, March 21, 1970, 2.

40. On these points I rely especially on a thoughtful study by Voichita Nachescu ("Becoming the Feminist Subject: Consciousness-Raising Groups in Second Wave Feminism" [PhD diss., State University of New York at Buffalo, 2006]), which discusses the racial and class-based exclusions of CR while recovering Black and Chicana CR groups. See also Natalie Thomlinson, "The Colour of Feminism: White Feminists and Race in the Women's Liberation Movement," *History: The Journal of the Historical Association* 97, no. 327 (2012): 453–75. For early reflections on CR's exclusions, see Black feminist Celestine Ware *Woman Power: The Movement for Women's Liberation*, (New York: Tower Publications, 1970), 35, 108–18, discussed in Nachescu, 58–62, 143–47.

41. "How to Start Your Own Consciousness-Raising Group"; Claudia Dreifus, *Woman's Fate: Raps from a Feminist Consciousness-Raising Group* (New York: Bantam Books, 1973), 5; "A Guide to Consciousness-Raising," *Ms.*, 1972, 18.

42. On CR's movement from radical to liberal circles and its increased resemblance to therapeutic genres, see Naomi Bruan Rosenthal, "Consciousness Raising: From Revolution to Re-Evaluation," *Psychology of Women Quarterly* 8, no. 4 (1984): 309–26. Nachescu suggests that white feminists were more troubled by the likeness between CR and therapy, because Black feminists had not had the same history of access to therapy ("Becoming the Feminist Subject," 15).

43. Anne Enke, *Finding the Movement: Sexuality, Contested Space, and Feminist Activism*, (Durham, NC: Duke University Press, 2007).

44. Maren Lockwood Carden, *The New Feminist Movement* (New York: Russell Sage Foundation, 1974), 34. Lynn O'Connor, "Defining Reality," *Tooth and Nail* October, no. 2 (1969): 5, 15; "A Guide to Consciousness-Raising"; Lee Jenkins and Cheris Kramer, "Small-Group Process: Learning from Women," *Women's Studies International Quarterly* 1 (1978): 70.

45. Georg Simmel and Kurt H. Wolff, *The Sociology of Georg Simmel* (Glencoe, IL: Free Press, 1950), 87.

46. Kathie Sarachild, "A Program for Feminist 'Consciousness Raising,'" in *Notes from the Second Year: Women's Liberation, Major Writings of the Radical Feminists*, ed. Shulamith Firestone and Anne Koedt (New York: 1970), 78–80. On CR groups that did experiment at including men, see Nachescu "Becoming the Feminist Subject."

47. Dreifus, *Woman's Fate*, 16; "internal democracy" in radical feminism, Shulamith Firestone, *The Dialectic of Sex: The Case for Feminist Revolution* (New York: Morrow, 1970), 39.

48. "A Guide to Consciousness-Raising," 22.

49. See a notable firsthand ethnographic study of CR group communication by Susan Kalčik: "'. . . Like Ann's Gynecologist or the Time I Was Almost Raped': Personal Narratives in Women's Rap Groups," *Journal of American Folklore* 88, no. 347 (1975): 3–11.

50. Kathie Sarachild, "Consciousness-Raising: A Radical Weapon," in *Feminist Revolution: An Abridged Edition with Additional Writings, Redstockings of the Women's Liberation Movement* (New York: Random House, 1978 [1973]); soft and hard CR, Dreifus, *Woman's Fate*, 13–14; on Sarachild's confrontational style, see Alice Echols and Ellen Willis, *Daring to Be Bad: Radical Feminism in America, 1967–1975*, American culture, (Minneapolis: University of Minnesota Press, 1989), 88.

51. Dreifus, *Woman's Fate*, 21.

52. O'Connor, "Our Politics Begin with our Feelings," 1; Echols and Willis, *Daring to be Bad*, 186.

53. Pamela Allen, "Free Space," in *Radical Feminism*, ed. Anne Koedt, Ellen Levine, and Anita Rapone (New York: Quadrangle Books, 1973 [1970]), 272.

54. Betty Friedan, *It Changed My Life: Writings on the Women's Movement*, (New York: Random House, 1976), 193.

55. Dreifus, *Woman's Fate*, 6.

56. Sarachild, "Consciousness-Raising," 146.

57. Henley, *Body Politics*, 198.

58. Firestone, *The Dialectic of Sex*, 90.

59. Erving Goffman, *Gender Advertisements*, (New York: Harper & Row, 1976), vii. Compare with Elise Kramer's reassessment of the language and gender literature, which argues that the "linkages between feminism and the study of language are not merely historical happenstance; rather, the two share key methodological and theoretical underpinnings, and each enriches the other in different and productive ways." Kramer, "Feminist Linguistics and Linguistic Feminisms," 66.

Chapter Nine

1. Nancy Henley, *Facing Down the Man*, (Pittsburgh, PA: Undated), 1–2.

2. Henley, *Body Politics*, 52.

3. Henley was either unaware of earlier efforts to study interruption by interaction scientists like Eliot Chapple, detailed in part 2, or else found these irrelevant.

4. The study of Zimmerman and West was included in a volume that Henley coedited with Barrie Thorne, *Language and Sex*.

5. Don H. Zimmerman and Candace West, "Sex Roles, Interruptions and Silences in Conversation," in *Language and Sex*, 111.

6. Charles Goodwin and René Salomon, "Not Being Bound by What You Can See Now: Charles Goodwin in Conversation with René Salomon," *Forum: Qualitative Social Research (Sozialforschung)* 20, no. 2 (2019): 1–32.

7. For a detailed introduction, see Schegloff, *Sequence Organization in Interaction: A Primer in Conversation Analysis* (Cambridge, UK: Cambridge University Press, 2007); Jack Sidnell, *Conversation Analysis: An Introduction*, Language in Society, (Chichester, UK: Wiley-Blackwell, 2010).

8. Zimmerman and West, "Sex Roles, Interruptions and Silences in Conversation," 115. The work of Zimmerman and West sparked debate over how best to distinguish overlaps from interruptions and how to think about what these behaviors "did" pragmatically. For important early, critical reviews, see Susan Gal, "Between Speech and Silence: The Problematics of Research on Language and Gender," in *Gender at the Crossroads of Knowledge: Feminist Anthropology in the Postmodern Era*, ed. Micaela Di Leonardo (Berkeley: University of California Press, 1991), 175–203; Susan Gal, "Language, Gender, and Power: An Anthropological Review," in *Gender Articulated*, 169–82; Deborah James and Sandra Clarke, "Women, Men, and Interruptions: A Critical Review," in *Gender and Conversational Interaction*, ed. Deborah Tannen (New York: Oxford University Press, 1993), 231–80; Deborah Tannen, *Gender and Discourse* (New York: Oxford University Press, 1994), 53–83.

9. Zimmerman and West, "Sex Roles, Interruptions and Silences in Conversation," 124; Firestone, *The Dialectic of Sex*, chap. 4.

10. Candace West and Don H. Zimmerman, "Women's Place in Everyday Talk: Reflections on Parent-Child Interaction," *Social Problems* 24, no. 5 (1977).

11. Zimmerman and West, "Sex Roles, Interruptions and Silences in Conversation," 114; Candace West, "Against Our Will: Male Interruptions of Females in Cross-Sex Conversation,"

Annals of the New York Academy of Sciences 327, no. 1 (1979): 81. "Against Our Will" was presented in 1977 at the New York Academy of Science meeting of Anthropology, Psychology and Linguistics Sections, October 22, New York, NY.

12. West, "Against Our Will," 83.

13. Erving Goffman, *Interaction Ritual: Essays on Face-To-Face Behavior* (New York: Anchor Books, 1967), 40.

14. West, "Against Our Will," 83. On supportive speech overlaps, she credits Gail Jefferson "A Case of Precision Timing in Ordinary Conversation Overlapped Tag-Positioned Address Terms in Closing Sequences," *Semiotica* IX (1973): 47–96. On deep interruptions, 82, 86.

15. Zimmerman and West, "Sex Roles, Interruptions and Silences in Conversation," 106.

16. As the subtitle of Thorne and Henley's 1975 volume—*Language and Sex: Dominance and Difference*—suggested, dominance versus difference was a fault line in early studies of gender and language; that is, whether tensions between men and women were a matter of a clash of different cultures or of power. West placed herself in the domination camp. Although West's empirical studies relied on the gender binary, she did not want to invite readings of her argument that fell back on "difference" as an explanation for the behavior she witnessed. In fact, so concerned was West not to reify gender differences as an explanation that she ended her dissertation by trying to keep the gender binary under erasure. "I have attempted to employ . . . preliminary observations in the analysis of same-sex and cross-sex conversational interactions to show how 'gender' is a social construction, that a world of two 'sexes' is a result of the socially shared, taken-for-granted methods which members use to construct reality." Suzanne S. Kesseler and Wendy McKenna, *Gender: An Ethnomethodological Approach* (Chicago: University of Chicago Press, 1978), cited in West, "Communicating Gender: A Study in Dominance and Control in Conversation" (PhD diss., University of California Santa Barbara, 1978), 199.

17. Goffman, *Gender Advertisements*, 74, 194.

18. Adeline Marie Masquelier, *Prayer Has Spoiled Everything: Possession, Power, and Identity in an Islamic Town of Niger*, (Durham, NC: Duke University Press, 2001), 21. In the language and gender literature, see Kira Hall et al., *Locating Power: Proceedings of the Second Berkeley Women and Language Conference, April 4 and 5, 1992*, 2 vols. (Berkeley: Berkeley Women and Language Group, University of California, Berkeley, 1992).

19. Sherry B. Ortner, "Theory in Anthropology since the Sixties," *Comparative Studies in Society and History* 26, no. 1 (1984): 146.

20. Compare with Gal and Irvine, *Signs of Difference*, 120ff.

21. Nancy Fraser and Linda Nicholson, "Social Criticism without Philosophy: An Encounter between Feminism and Postmodernism," *Theory, Culture & Society* 5 (1988): 378–79, 390.

22. For a discussion of Chomsky's politics in relation to his view of language, and in relation to forms of sociolinguistics that came to oppose Chomsky, see Heller and McElhinny, *Language, Capitalism, Colonialism*. As should be clear, I do not argue that autonomizing an object necessarily "depoliticizes" it, as many assume, as that fails to recognize the diverse forms that scholarly politicization has taken. Heller and McElhinny, for instance, underscore how Chomsky "sought to harness the tools of universal grammar to unmasking the effects of state and corporate propaganda" (ibid., 182) even as they also note the way his emancipatory mobilization of expertise was informed by liberal and Cold War commitments. Compare, too, with Love's *Underdogs: Social Deviance and Queer Theory* (Chicago: Chicago University Press, 2021). This alternative genealogy of queer theory shows how midcentury sociological studies of "deviance" used modes of description that were pragmatically political within the scholarly field in ways that are now difficult to recognize.

23. Zimmerman and West, "Sex Roles, Interruptions and Silences in Conversation," 107.

24. Candace West, "Communicating Gender," 54 (Emphasis mine). Marjorie Harness Goodwin, *The Hidden Life of Girls: Games of Stance, Status, and Exclusion* (Malden, MA: Blackwell Publishing, 2006), 9.

25. Ray L. Birdwhistell, from a double conference session on "Film Analysis of Culture and Communication" held at the 1970 meetings of the American Anthropological Association, San Diego, California, December 20–21. HSFA at the Smithsonian, Washington, DC. Recordings SR 002, SR 003.

26. Goffman's work tended to be received sympathetically by second-wave feminist sociologists (e.g., at Berkeley where Goffman had taught in the '60s [personal communication, Arlie Hochschild]). As for sociologists of communication, Candace West credited Goffman frequently and later wrote an essay assessing—positively—his relevance for feminism (Candace West, "Goffman in Feminist Perspective," *Sociological Perspectives* 39, no. 3 [1996]: 353–69.) For over fifty years various scholars have attempted to identify Goffman's "politics." A notable early example is Gouldner's sustained critique, which charged that Goffman's dramaturgical subject was none other than the late capitalist bourgeois subject who experienced a "transition from an older economy centered on production to a new one centered on mass-marketing and promotion, including the marketing of the self." (*The Coming Crisis of Western Sociology* [New York: Avon, 1970], 381.) As for the 1960s and the question of Goffman's positioning, see Richard Handler's way of reading his works that yields an image of Goffman as "critic of the 1950s, stranded on the farther shore of the 1960s" (Handler, "What I'm Reading," 188); see also Richard Handler, "Erving Goffman and the Gestural Dynamics of Modern Selfhood" in *The Politics of Gesture: Historical Perspectives*, ed. M. J. Braddick (Oxford: Oxford University Press, 2009), 280–300.

The most sustained investigation to date on the question of Goffman's politics is offered by Heather Love in *Underdogs*. Love reclaims Goffman for queer studies, noting how indebted this literature has been not just to Goffman's work but also to earlier sociological "deviance" studies. In terms of politics of the period, Love does occasionally assimilate Goffman perhaps too quickly to a generalized view of Cold War social science, characterized by rampant surveillance and technocratic social science scholarship. However, if we compare Goffman's work to the then dominant "small-group" forms of interaction research, we can appreciate how dramatically Goffman differed. The small-group researchers tended to be passionately technocratic and technophilic, whereas Goffman seemed antagonistic to both. As Love notes, he was notorious for saying that he did not want to claim that his scholarship could be "useful"—and usefulness was precisely a liberal promise made by the technocratically motivated small-group researchers (who tended to be uncritical of the ends to which their science was put). He was also notorious for eschewing mechanical recording technologies and would occasionally poke at scholars who fetishized equipment. What is more, it was never the steely laboratory that represented the paradigmatic site for studying interaction, as it was for small-group researchers, but rather naturally occurring situations. In these and other ways, Goffman distanced himself—dramatically, it would seem—from forms of interaction science that did enact Cold War social science virtues.

Chapter Ten

1. Pamela M. Fishman, "Interactional Shitwork," *Heresies* 2 (1980): 100–101.

2. Pamela M. Fishman, "Interaction: The Work Women Do," *Social Problems* 25, no. 4 (1978): 397; Hugh Mehan and Houston Wood, "The Morality of Ethnomethodology," *Theory and Society* 2, no. 4 (1975): 519. For Mehan's own reflections on his career and trajectory, see Hugh Mehan,

"The Serendipity of Connections and Their Consequences," *Education Review* 27 (2020): 1–20; Hugh Mehan, "Engaging the Sociological Imagination: My Journey into Design Research and Public Sociology," *Anthropology & Education Quarterly* 39, no. 1 (2008): 77–91.

3. Aaron Victor Cicourel and John I. Kitsuse, *The Educational Decision-Makers*, (Indianapolis: Bobbs-Merrill, 1963). For an early, classic review essay of the then "new sociology of education," see Jerome Karabel and A. H. Halsey, "The New Sociology of Education," *Theory and Society* 3, no. 4 (1976): 529–52.

4. See, for example, Hugh Mehan, "Assessing Children's Language Using Abilities," in *Comparative Sociological Research*, ed. Michael J. Armer and Alan S. Grimshaw (New York: Wiley-Interscience, 1973), 309–43; and Hugh Mehan, *Learning Lessons* (Cambridge, UK: Cambridge University Press, 1979).

5. The word surfaced with a different sense in Louis Smith "The Microethnography of the Classroom," *Psychology in the Classroom* 4, no. 3 (1967): 216–21. For Smith, microethnography did not imply mediatic recording and playback and transcription methods, as it did for Erickson. For a brief history of microethnography, see Jürgen Streeck and Siri Mehus, "Microethnography: The Study of Practices," in *Handbook of Language and Social Interaction*, ed. Kristine L. Fitch and Robert E. Sanders (Mahwah, New Jersey: Lawrence Erlbaum Associates, Publishers, 2005), 381–404.

6. Frederick David Erickson, "The Cycle of Situational Frames: A Model for Microethnography in Urban Anthropology" (Midwest Anthropology Meeting, Detroit, Michigan, April 30, 1971; unpublished manuscript), 2. For a sweeping cultural history of the videorecorder, see Peter Sachs Collopy, "The Revolution Will be Videotaped: Making a Technology of Consciousness in the Long 1960s" (PhD diss., University of Pennsylvania, 2015). For a history of film and videography in interactional microanalysis, see Frederick Erickson, "Uses of Video in Social Research: A Brief History," *International Journal of Social Research Methodology* 14, no. 3 (2011): 179–89. Frederick Erickson, "Origins: A Brief Intellectual and Technological History of the Emergence of Multimodal Discourse Analysis," in *Discourse and Technology: Multimodal Discourse Analysis*, ed. Philip LeVine and Ron Scollon (Washington, DC: Georgetown University Press, 2004), 196–207.

7. Edward T. Hall, *Beyond Culture*. (Garden City, NY: Anchor Press, 1976), 129.

8. Personal communication, Frederick Erickson, 2020.

9. Roger Garlock Barker and Herbert Fletcher Wright, *One Boy's Day: A Specimen Record of Behavior* (New York: Harper, 1951); Frederick Erickson, "The 'Daily Round' as a Unit of Analysis in Urban Ethnography" (American Sociological Association, Anaheim, CA, 2001). Unpublished manuscript.

10. Personal communication, Frederick Erickson (2020). Erickson's early talks addressed such issues, such as "The Cycle of Situational Frames" and "The Chicano in a Black Mask: A Microethnography of Communication Behavior" [Society for Applied Anthropology, Miami, Florida, April 15, 1971].

11. Frederick David Erickson, "Discussion Behavior in the Black Ghetto and in White Suburbia: Comparison of Language Style and Inquiry Style" (PhD diss., Northwestern University, 1969), 73.

12. On Black English, Erickson, "Discussion Behavior in the Black Ghetto and in White Suburbia: Comparison of Language Style and Inquiry Style," 17, 16.

13. Frederick Erickson, "Gatekeeping and the Melting Pot: Interaction in Counseling Encounters," *Harvard Educational Review* 45, no. 1 (1975): 45.

14. Erickson, "Gatekeeping and the Melting Pot"; on appearances mattering, ibid., 67, on ethnicity and race as background variables, 50.

15. Karabel and Halsey, "The New Sociology of Education," 531.

16. Erickson, "Uses of Video in Social Research," 181.

17. As described in Erickson ("Uses of Video in Social Research," 181), the apparatus combined videography with simultaneous 16mm film recording, and for pickup it relied on a directional microphone.

18. Erickson, "Gatekeeping and the Melting Pot," 58. On rhythmic integration in social interaction, Erickson drew from William Condon, whom E. T. Hall had invited to Northwestern while Erickson was a graduate student. See, especially, Condon and Ogston, "A Segmentation of Behavior"; William S. Condon and Louis W. Sander, "Neonate Movement is Synchronized with Adult Speech: Interactional Participation and Language Acquisition," *Science* 183, no. 4120 (1974): 99–101.

19. Transcript from Erickson, "Gatekeeping and the Melting Pot," 54.

20. Erickson, "Gatekeeping and the Melting Pot: Interaction in Counseling Encounters," 55.

21. Erickson, "Gatekeeping and the Melting Pot," 54. Erickson's viewing sessions at first had only epistemological importance. Playback and elicitation ensured you paid attention to junctures that participants themselves found meaningful. His next major study was on a kindergarten classroom and here, like the Lewinians and their "action research," he and his collaborators began to envision teachers as researchers in their own right. Viewing sessions evolved from epistemological methods to transformative exercises that could help effect change.

22. Burton R. Clark, "The Cooling-Out Function in Higher Education," *American Journal of Sociology* 65, no. 6 (1960): 569–76. See also Burton R. Clark, *The Open Door College: A Case Study*, Carnegie ser. in American Education, (New York: McGraw-Hill, 1960), 160–61. Erving Goffman, "On Cooling the Mark Out: Some Aspects of Adaptation to Failure," *Psychiatry* 15 (1952): 451–63. Erickson, "Gatekeeping and the Melting Pot," 66.

23. John J. Gumperz, T. C. Jupp, and Celia Roberts, "Crosstalk: A Study of Cross-Cultural Communication," (London: National Centre for Industrial Language Training in association with the BBC, 1979), Television broadcast.

24. Gumperz visited Erickson's lab at Harvard for two days in the winter of 1975, after which Gumperz invited Erickson to Berkeley in 1976. It was shortly after Erickson's visit that Gumperz joined Roberts on the *Crosstalk* project. Personal communication, Frederick Erickson, 2022; confirming correspondence from Celia Roberts.

25. Erving Goffman, "The Interaction Order American Sociological Association, 1982 Presidential Address," *American Sociological Review* 48, no. 1 (1983): 1–17, https://doi.org/10.2307 /2095141. At the close of this discussion, Goffman extended the trope of people-processing encounters, suggesting that "in a less candid form, this processing is ubiquitous; everyone is a gatekeeper in regard to something" (ibid.). Goffman noted his appreciation of Erickson's gatekeeping work in a person letter to Erickson, circa 1977. I thank Frederick Erickson for sharing this correspondence.

26. C. Wright Mills, *The Sociological Imagination* (New York: Oxford University Press, 1959), 85–86.

27. On "liberal practicality," Mills, *The Sociological Imagination*, 23. Erickson, "Gatekeeping and the Melting Pot," 68–69.

28. Frederick Erickson, "Some Lessons Learned about Teaching, Research, and Academic Disputation," *Education Review / Reseñas Educativas* 24 (2017): 12.

29. Harold Garfinkel, *Studies in Ethnomethodology* (Englewood Cliffs, NJ: Prentice-Hall, 1967); Norman K. Denzin, "Symbolic Interactionism and Ethnomethodology: A Proposed Synthesis," *American Sociological Review* 34, no. 6 (1969): 922.

30. Dennis H. Wrong, "The Oversocialized Conception of Man in Modern Sociology," *American Sociological Review* 26, no. 2 (1961): 193; Harold Garfinkel, "Studies of the Routine Grounds of Everyday Activities," 11, no. 3 (1964): 225–50.

31. For early scrutiny of Garfinkel's adoption of "indexicality" from the philosophy of language, see, for example, Barry Barnes and John Law, "Whatever should be done with indexical expressions?" *Theory and Society* 3, no. 2 (1976): 223–37; James Heap, "Non-Indexical Action," *Phil. Soc. Sci.* 5 (1975): 393–409; Paul Attewell, "Ethnomethodology since Garfinkel," *Theory and Society* 1 (1974): 179–210.

32. On Gouldner's book and its legacy in sociology, see especially George Steinmetz and Ou-Byung Chae, "Sociology in an Era of Fragmentation: From the Sociology of Knowledge to the Philosophy of Science, and Back Again," *Sociological Quarterly* 43, no. 1 (2002): 111–37; James J. Chriss, *Alvin W. Gouldner: Sociologist and Outlaw Marxist* (Aldershot, UK: Ashgate, 1999).

33. Mills, *The Sociological Imagination*, 42.

34. Jack D. Douglas, *Understanding Everyday Life: Toward the Reconstruction of Sociological Knowledge* (Chicago: Aldine Pub. Co., 1970), 8.

35. Douglas, *Understanding Everyday Life*, 5, 25, x.

36. Lewis A. Coser, "Presidential Address: Two Methods in Search of a Substance," *American Sociological Review* 40, no. 6 (1975): 696; David Sudnow, "Temporal Parameters of Interpersonal Observation," in *Studies in Social Interaction*, ed. David Sudnow (New York: Free Press, 1971), 229–58.

37. For Goffman's own avowed positioning toward "symbolic interactionism" and "ethnomethodology," see especially a 1980 interview (Verhoeven, "An Interview With Erving Goffman, 1980"). From the start of the 1970s, Goffman did occasionally adopt the prefix "micro" as a caption for his scholarship. "Microstudies" appeared in the subtitle of *Relations in Public* (Goffman, *Relations in Public: Microstudies of the Public Order* [New York: Harper and Row, 1971]), though tellingly the term received no real attention in the text itself, and, in a note, he instead expressed unease with all the terms, including "face-to-face interaction" and "microsociology" (ix). Goffman used "microanalysis" frequently and unapologetically (e.g., *Frame Analysis: An Essay on the Organization of Experience* [New York: Harper Colophon Books, 1974], 495; *Forms of Talk*, [Philadelphia: University of Pennsylvania Press, 1981], 2, 197; "The Interaction Order," 2, 9). Only in his last book, *Forms of Talk*, did "microsociology" make a single cameo appearance in the body of his text (197), just as it sprung up once again in a posthumous 1983 essay ("Felicity's Condition," *American Journal of Sociology* 89 [1983]: 1–53). In print, Goffman first entertained the word "microsociology" with scare quotes—reflective of the word's then novelty—back in 1957, but he did not propose it then, or after, as a branding for his approach. "On Some Convergences of Sociology and Psychiatry: A Sociologist's View," *Psychiatry: Journal of Interpersonal Relations* 20, no. 3 (1957): 201–3.

38. Fishman, "Interactional Shitwork," 99.

39. Roslyn Wallach Bologh, "The Promise and Failure of Ethnomethodology from a Feminist Perspective: Comment on Rogers," *Gender and Society* 6, no. 2 (1992): 200–201. Compare with the late Dorothy Smith's influential feminist adaptation and synthesis of ethnomethodology, phenomenology, and Marxism in *The Everyday World as Problematic: A Feminist Sociology* (Boston: Northeastern University Press, 1987).

40. For an astute analysis and critique of Gouldner's gendered self-presentational style in calling out scholars as more and less political, see Heather Love's *Underdogs*.

41. Karabel and Halsey, "The New Sociology of Education," 535.

42. John Heritage, *Garfinkel and Ethnomethodology* (Cambridge, UK: Polity Press, 1984), 311.

43. For Pollner, the trope illustrated how CA had neglected ethnomethodology's commitment to "radical reflexivity." As "ethnomethodology is codified into an empirical program concerned with interactional, conversational, or scientific practices per se, radical referential reflexivity is muted, discounted, or disowned" (Melvin Pollner, "Left of Ethnomethodology: The Rise and Decline of Radical Reflexivity," *American Sociological Review* 56, no. 3 [1991]: 374.) See also Paul Atkinson, "Ethnomethodology: A Critical Review," *Annual Review of Sociology* 14 (1988): 441–65.

44. On linguistic influences, see, for example, Don H. Zimmerman, "Ethnomethodology," *American Sociologist* 13, no. 1 (1978): 8; see also Murray, *American Sociolinguistics: Theorists and Theory Groups*, 157. On less familiar influences, see Wilf's recent discussion of Garfinkel's indebtedness to cybernetics. Eitan Wilf, "Separating Noise from Signal: The Ethnomethodological Uncanny as Aesthetic Pleasure in Human–Machine Interaction in the United States," *American Ethnologist* 46, no. 2 (2019): 202–13.

45. Richard A. Hilbert, "Ethnomethodology and the Micro–Macro Order," *American Sociological Review* 55, no. 6 (1990): 798.

46. Hilbert, "Ethnomethodology and the Micro–Macro Order," 794, 800.

47. Harvey Sacks and Gail Jefferson, *Lectures on Conversation* (Oxford: Blackwell, 1995), 65. In his dissertation, Schegloff also did not seem particularly hostile to the discourse of micro, as evidenced indirectly, for instance, by the way he wrote sympathetically of what he termed "microecological" approaches to the study of human social interaction (Emanuel A. Schegloff, "The First Five Seconds: The Order of Conversational Opening," [PhD diss., University of California, Berkeley, 1967], 10–11), as in work by E. T. Hall on proxemics.

48. Anthony Giddens, *The Constitution of Society: Outline of the Theory of Structuration* (Berkeley: University of California Press, 1984), 139.

49. Giddens, *The Constitution of Society*, 139.

50. Pierre Bourdieu, *Outline of a Theory of Practice*, trans. Richard Nice (New York: Cambridge University Press, 1977), 81–82. Bourdieu spared Goffman a similar charge. See, for example, a memorial he wrote for Goffman, which, in effect, assimilated Goffman's scholarship to his and cast Goffman as someone who was observationally microscopic but who never made the mistake of autonomizing interaction as a paracosmic level of social reality or embracing the unchecked situationalism of conversation analysis and ethnomethodology (Bourdieu, "Erving Goffman: Discoverer of the Infinitely Small").

51. On constitutive ethnography, Hugh Mehan, "Structuring School Structure," *Harvard Educational Review* 48, no. 1 (1978). 36; on compatibility with Marx, Mehan and Wood, "The Morality of Ethnomethodology," 519, 521.

52. McDermott and Roth, "The Social Organization of Behavior: Interactional Approaches," 323, 322. Sapir "Communication," in *Encyclopaedia of the Social Sciences* (New York: Macmillan, 1935) cited in McDermott, 323. On McDermott's use of recording technologies, see Erickson, "Uses of Video in Social Research."

53. Gary Alan Fine, "Small Groups and Culture Creation: The Idioculture of Little League Baseball Teams," *American Sociological Review* 44, no. 5 (1979): 733–45; Randall Collins, "On the Microfoundations of Macrosociology," *American Journal of Sociology* 86, no. 5 (1981): 984–1014.

54. See an influential critique of CA by Michael Billig "Whose terms? Whose ordinariness? Rhetoric and Ideology in Conversation Analysis," *Discourse and Society* 10, no. 4 (1999): 543–58. Representing Critical Discourse Analysis (CDA), Billig argued that CA rests on ideological assumptions that it fails to recognize. CA's object "conversation," Billig wrote, is an ideologically laden category with a genealogy stemming from early modern Europe, as traced by Burke ("The Art of

Conversation"). In this genealogy "conversation" emerged as a category of communication that normatively promoted equality of participation. Billig charged that CA remains uncritically committed to this conception. This is evident in its transcription practices, as suggested by the use of first names for interlocutors, for instance; it is also evident in the way CA came to define "conversation" against "institutional discourse," where norms of equal participation do not apply.

55. Emanuel A. Schegloff, "Between Micro and Macro: Contexts and Other Connections," in *The Micro-Macro Link*, ed. J. C. Alexander et al. (Berkeley: University of California Press, 1987), 208.

56. Gail Jefferson, "A Note on Laughter in 'Male–Female' Interaction," *Discourse Studies* 6, no. 1 (2004): 117–33.

57. Schegloff, "Between Micro and Macro," 208, 216.

58. Prevignano and Thibault, *Discussing Conversation Analysis: The Work of Emanuel A. Schegloff*, 33.

59. Schegloff, "Between Micro and Macro," 221.

60. Compare with Latour's pedagogy of "clamps" in *Reassembling the Social*.

61. For critiques of CA's approach to transcription, see Billig, "Whose terms? Whose ordinariness? Rhetoric and ideology in Conversation Analysis," 553–54; see also Bucholtz, "The Politics of Transcription." The contrast between Schegloff and Gumperz is stark. Both men were committed to recording and careful transcription. Whereas Schegloff was at pains to prevent an intrusive macrosocial "context" from contaminating the empirical truths of transcripts, Gumperz was at pains to understand how this context, which was independent of the immediate interaction and didn't show up directly in the transcript, nevertheless got activated—"cued"—and ferried in by communicative practices of participants themselves.

62. Schegloff, "Between Micro and Macro," 229.

63. Goffman, "The Interaction Order," 3, 11.

Chapter Eleven

1. Fred Erickson. *Talk and Social Theory: Ecologies of Speaking and Listening in Everyday Life* (Cambridge, UK: Polity Press, 2004), 16.

2. Compare with Abbott's recent argument for processualism in sociology, which centers on an appreciation of constant change and the primacy of events, yet without maintaining a micro–macro antinomy (*Processual Sociology* [Chicago: University of Chicago Press, 2016], 108 et passim).

3. Charles H. P. Zuckerman, "Video Footage and the Grain of Practice," *HAU: Journal of Ethnographic Theory* 13, no. 1 (2023): 128–45. By "bundling," I allude to Webb Keane's notion from his reflections on semiotics and materiality (in "Semiotics and the Social Analysis of Material Things"). "Qualisigns must be embodied in something in particular," such that "redness," for instance, "cannot be manifest without some embodiment that inescapably binds it to some other qualities as well . . ." (414). Though I cannot develop this argument here, an analogous bundling in source media has been both opportunity and problem for the mediatic sciences I discuss in this book. It has been a problem, because, to simplify brutally, when you return to video, as Zuckerman ("Video Footage") describes, you typically find more than what you were looking for. It has also been an opportunity, because it is this excess that also makes mediatic returns a condition of possibility for epistemological "discovery."

4. On not treating interaction as a domain, see, for example, Michael Lempert "No Ordinary Ethics." *Anthropological Theory* 13, no. 4 (2013): 370–93.

5. For contemporary reflections on holism in anthropology, see Otto and Bubandt, *Experiments in Holism Theory and Practice in Contemporary Anthropology*.

6. R. M. Williams, "Sociology in America: The Experience of Two Centuries," in *Social Science in America*, ed. C. M. Bonjean, L. Schneider, and R. L. Lineberry (Austin: University of Texas Press, 1976), 87.

7. See Irvine, "Going Upscale: Scales and Scale-Climbing as Ideological Projects" in *Scale*, Carr and Lempert.

8. Marilyn Strathern, *Partial Connections*, (Savage, MD: Rowman & Littlefield Publishers, 1991), xv.

9. Heather Love, "Close but Not Deep: Literary Ethics and the Descriptive Turn," *New Literary History* 41, no. 2 (2010): 371–91; "Close Reading and Thin Description"; "Small Change: Realism, Immanence, and the Politics of the Micro," *Modern Language Quarterly* 77, no. 3 (2016): 419–45. Love herself draws inspiration from midcentury fine-grained observers of face-to-face interaction, notably Erving Goffman, whom she uses to avoid these scalar extremes in favor of "close but not deep reading." In "Close but Not Deep," she illustrates the utility of this in a reading of Toni Morrison's 1987 *Beloved*, and in *Underdogs* she offers a genealogy of queer studies that highlights inputs from Goffman.

10. For a historical essay on early troubles with studying the economy as a "whole," see Mary S. Morgan, "Seeking Parts, Looking for Wholes," in *Histories of Scientific Observation*, 303–25.

11. Robert E. Lucas, *Models of Business Cycles*, Yrjö Jahnsson lectures, (Oxford: B. Blackwell, 1987), 107–8.

12. Recent volumes have been reassessing the status of microfoundations. As Kevin Hoover reflects, the idea of microfoundations is older than the 1970s. Hoover, "Microfoundational Programs," in *Microfoundations Reconsidered: The Relationship of Micro and Macroeconomics in Historical Perspective*, ed. Pedro Garcia Duarte and Gilberto Tadeu Lima (Cheltenham, UK: Edward Elgar, 2012), 19–61.

13. On "microfoundation" as a way to frame the "microsociological" contributions of interaction research, see Collins, "On the Microfoundations of Macrosociology."

14. Goffman, "The Interaction Order."

15. Keith M. Murphy, "Transcription Aesthetics," *Semiotic Review* 9 (April 2021), 1–32.

16. A classic essay that argued this is Ochs, "Transcription as Theory." On prioritizing source video, see Charles Goodwin's comments about his craft in Frederick Erickson, Sherman Dorn, and Alfredo Artiles, "Charles Goodwin: Participant Presentation for "Learning How to Look and Listen" (Session 1, Part A)," (2016), Video.

17. Clifford Geertz, "Being There: Anthropology and the Scene of Writing," in *Works and Lives: The Anthropologist as Author*, ed. Clifford Geertz (Stanford, CA: Stanford University Press, 1988).

18. On the way certain sociolinguistic styles have come to be seen as more or less "immediate," and the way realist transcript conventions and genres emerge, see Inoue "Word for Word"; see also Bucholtz, "The Politics of Transcription"; Bucholtz, "Captured on Tape: Professional Hearing and Competing Entextualizations in the Criminal Justice System"; Mark Sussman, "Charles W. Chesnutt's Stenographic Realism," *MELUS: Multi-Ethnic Literature of the United States* 40, no. 4 (2015): 48–68.

19. Michael Silverstein wrote extensively about this trajectory, which became well-known in linguistic anthropology and important to its self-understanding. For a thorough introduction, see Michael Silverstein, *Language in Culture: Lectures on the Social Semiotics of Language* (Cambridge, UK: Cambridge University Press, 2023); see also William F. Hanks, *Language and*

Communicative Practices (Boulder: Westview Press, 1996). On this history in relation to closely related fields, such as sociolinguistics, see, for example, Michael Silverstein, "Forty Years of Speaking (of) the Same (Object) Language—Sans le Savoir," *Langage et Société* 160–61, no. 2 (2017): 160–61; Michael Silverstein, "How We Look from Where We Stand," *Journal of Linguistic Anthropology* 16, no. 2 (2006): 269–78. See also Dell Hymes "The Pre-War Prague School and Post-War American Anthropological Linguistics," in *The Transformational-Generative Paradigm and Modern Linguistic Theory*, ed. E. F. K. Koerner (Amsterdam: John Benjamins Publishing Company, 1975), 359–80, cited in Duranti "Language as Culture in US Anthropology: Three Paradigms," *Current Anthropology* 44, 3 (2003):note 4, 325.

20. On this issue, see an introduction by Elizabeth Keating, "The Ethnography of Communication," in *Handbook of Ethnography* (2001), ed. Paul Atkinson, Amanda Coffey, Sara Delamont, John Lofland, and Lyn Lofland (New York: Sage Publications Ltd.), 2. As Keating and others have frequently observed, this new appreciation for language-as-action and speaking as an activity embedded in context resonated with Malinowski's arguments in Malinowski, B. "The Problem of Meaning in Primitive Languages," in *The Meaning of Meaning*, ed. C. K. Ogden and I. A. Richards (New York: Harcourt, Brace & World, Inc., 1923), 451–510; and Malinowski, B. *Coral Gardens and Their Magic, Vol II: The Language of Magic and Gardening*, ed. Thomas A. Sebeok, et al., Indiana University Studies in the History and Theory of Linguistics, (Bloomington: Indiana University Press, 1965 [1935]).

21. Constantine V. Nakassis, "Deixis and the Linguistic Anthropology of Cinema," *Semiotic Review*, November 9, 2020, 65:1–2, https://www.semioticreview.com/ojs/index.php/sr/article/view/65; see also Nakassis, "Linguistic Anthropology in 2015." Nakassis's argument is not limited to the ethnography of communication, but it should be noted that Hymes denied that this nascent field's relationship to cultural anthropology was unclear or complicated. In response to a similar argument by Alessandro Duranti, who wrote that Hymes's ethnography of communication had an "ambiguous relationship to cultural anthropology," Hymes countered, "As for the ethnography of speaking's 'ambiguous relationship with cultural anthropology,' I never thought of it as separate" (Duranti, "Language as Culture in US Anthropology: Three Paradigms," 328, 338.)

22. As Duranti and other linguistic anthropologists have observed, and often lamented, this reflected a subordinate "service" orientation toward other fields, as if linguistic anthropology existed only to teach methods for studying language and thereby help other subfields, principally sociocultural anthropology. (Duranti, "Language as Culture in US Anthropology," 324.)

23. Michael Silverstein, "Commentary," *Pragmatics. Quarterly Publication of the International Pragmatics Association (IPrA)* 7, no. 4 (1997): 626. Silverstein developed a multifaceted critique of CA over the years. (See, for instance, Michael Silverstein, "The Improvisational Performance of "Culture" in Real-Time Discursive Practice," in *Creativity in Performance*, ed. Robert Keith Sawyer [Greenwich, CT: Ablex, 1997], 265–312; and Silverstein, " 'Cultural' Concepts and the Language-Culture Nexus.")

24. Goffman, "The Interaction Order," 2. Goffman's thinly veiled critiques of CA appeared in Goffman, "Replies and Responses" and "Felicity's Condition"; for a response and a critical assessment of Goffman's own scholarship, see Emanuel A. Schegloff, "Goffman and the Analysis of Conversation," in *Erving Goffman: Exploring the Interaction Order*, ed. P. Drew and A. Wootton (Cambridge, UK: Polity Press, 1988), 89–135.

25. See, for example, Kathryn Graber's analysis of interactions that occur at critical points in the global commodity chains involved in making and moving Mongolian cashmere. (Kathryn E. Graber, "Textures of Value: Tactility, Experience, and Exclusion in the Cashmere Commodity

Chain," *Economic Anthropology* 10, no. 2 [2023], 186–96). On global hip hop, see, for example, Samy H Alim, Awad Ibrahim, and Alastair Pennycook, eds., *Global Linguistic Flows: Hip Hop Cultures, Youth Identities, and the Politics of Language* (New York: Routledge, 2009).

26. Stanton Wortham, *Learning Identity: The Joint Emergence of Social Identification and Academic Learning* (Cambridge, UK: Cambridge University Press, 2005). By comparison, see Asif Agha's conception of a "speech chain," detailed in *Language and Social Relations*, which he used to conceptualize and track histories of register formation. Compare, too, with the sociologist Randall Collins's very different notion of "interaction ritual chains" (*Interaction Ritual Chains*, [Princeton: Princeton University Press, 2004].)

27. Agha "Introduction: Semiosis across Encounters," *Journal of Linguistic Anthropology* 15, no. 1 (2005): 1. For an early, influential, and illustrative example of this kind questioning in sociocultural anthropology, see Akhil Gupta and James Ferguson, "Beyond 'Culture': Space, Identity, and the Politics of Difference," *Cultural Anthropology* 7, no. 1 (1992): 6–23.

28. On studying scalar experience through discourse, see especially Jan Blommaert, "Sociolinguistic Scales," *Intercultural Pragmatics* 4-1 (2007): 1–19; Jan Blommaert, Elina Westinen, and Sirpa Leppänen, "Further Notes on Sociolinguistic Scales," *Intercultural Pragmatics* 12, no. 1 (2015): 119–27. For other experiments at this, see especially chapters in *Scale* (Carr and Lempert) and Gal and Irvine, *Signs of Difference*.

29. Agha, *Language and Social Relations*, 3.

30. For a classic essay on language and political economy, see Judith T. Irvine, "When Talk Isn't Cheap: Language and Political Economy," in *The Matrix of Language: Contemporary Linguistic Anthropology*, ed. Donald Brenneis and Ronald H. S. Macaulay (Boulder: Westview Press, 1996), 248–67. For an influential demolition and reworking of micro and macro in the study of discursive interaction, see Agha, *Language and Social Relations*. For a recent volume representing the culmination of some two decades of collaborative reflection on "language ideology," see Gal and Irvine, *Signs of Difference*. On raciolinguistics, see Jonathan Rosa, *Looking Like a Language, Sounding Like a Race: Raciolinguistic Ideologies and the Learning of Latinidad* (New York: Oxford University Press, 2019). See also Samy H. Alim, John R. Rickford, and Arnetha F. Ball, *Raciolinguistics: How Language Shapes Our Ideas About Race* (New York: Oxford University Press, 2016).

31. For early, influential literature on this theme, see, for example, Dennis Tedlock and Bruce Mannheim, eds., *The Dialogic Emergence of Culture* (Urbana: University of Illinois Press, 1995); Jane Hill, "The Voices of Don Gabriel: Responsibility and Self in a Modern Mexicano Narrative," in *The Dialogic Emergence of Culture*, ed. Dennis Tedlock and Bruce Mannheim (University of Illinois Press, 1997), 97–147; Richard Bauman, *A World of Others' Words: Cross-Cultural Perspectives on Intertextuality* (Malden, MA: Blackwell Publishing, 2004). Asif Agha and Stanton Wortham, eds., "Discourse across Speech Events: Intertextuality and Interdiscursivity in Social Life," special issue, *Journal of Linguistic Anthropology* 15, no. 1 [2005]: 1–150. More recent examples abound.

32. Krystal A. Smalls, Arthur K. Spears, and Jonathan Rosa, "Introduction: Language and White Supremacy," *Journal of Linguistic Anthropology* 31, no. 2 (2021): 154.

33. Not everyone has acceded to the demand to demonstrate interscalar connection as a condition for scholarly relevance. The best example is an extraordinary book by Jürgen Streeck, *Self-Making Man: A Day of Action, Life, and Language*, (Cambridge, UK: Cambridge University Press. 2017), where he focuses on a single individual—an auto mechanic—for a single day. Streeck followed him around on a workday for eleven straight hours, camera in tow, yielding a trove of data. This is the apotheosis of a certain vision of microethnography. The book required,

by his estimate, some 7,000–8,000 hours of his research time. It is a book that succeeds where projects like the Natural History of an Interview arguably failed. Streeck made good on a promise made by most microanalysts, that if you just attend carefully enough and stay with the data long enough, you will eventually find the fullness of your object. Unlike his other work, which often ranges across events, this text revels in the micro and does not purport to offer anything interscalar. Interpersonal life in the shop is not interesting because it reflects and refracts truths that play out elsewhere. His book instead makes the exquisite choreography of verbal and kinetic activity engaging and illuminating *without* suggesting that it all amounts to some kind of "sociological miniaturism" (John F. Stolte, Gary Alan Fine, and Karen S. Cook, "Sociological Miniaturism: Seeing the Big through the Small in Social Psychology," *Annual Review of Sociology* 27 [2001]: 387–413.)

34. Stephan Fuchs, "The Constitution of Emergent Interaction Orders: A Comment on Rawls," *Sociological Theory* 6, no. 1 (1988) 122–24.

35. Goffman, "The Interaction Order," 9.

36. Here and below I draw directly on Michael Lempert, "Interaction Rescaled," in *Scale*, ed. E. Summerson Carr and Michael Lempert, 53–54; see Latour, *Reassembling the Social*, 200–202.

37. See Lempert, *Discipline and Debate: The Language of Violence in a Tibetan Buddhist Monastery* (Berkeley: University of California Press, 2012) and Lempert, "Interaction Rescaled."

38. In cultural anthropology, a notable experiment in both collaboration and scalar reimagination has been the "Matsutake World Research Group" Anna Lowenhaupt Tsing, as discussed, for example, in "Worlding the Matsutake Diaspora: Or, Can Actor-Network Theory Experiment With Holism?" in *Experiments in Holism Theory and Practice in Contemporary Anthropology*, 47–66.

Index

Page numbers in italics refer to figures.

www.ingramcontent.com/pod-product-compliance
Lightning Source LLC
Chambersburg PA
CBHW022139020426
42334CB00015B/970